Peter William Clayden

Rogers and His Contemporaries

Vol. 1

Peter William Clayden

Rogers and His Contemporaries
Vol. 1

ISBN/EAN: 9783337802127

Printed in Europe, USA, Canada, Australia, Japan

Cover: Foto ©Thomas Meinert / pixelio.de

More available books at **www.hansebooks.com**

ROGERS

AND HIS CONTEMPORARIES

VOL. I.

ROGERS

AND

HIS CONTEMPORARIES

BY

P. W. CLAYDEN

AUTHOR OF 'SAMUEL SHARPE, EGYPTOLOGIST' ETC.
'THE EARLY LIFE OF SAMUEL ROGERS'
ETC.

IN TWO VOLUMES

VOL. I.

LONDON
SMITH, ELDER, & CO., 15 WATERLOO PLACE
1889

PREFACE.

I CANNOT send out to the world the volumes which complete my Life of Samuel Rogers without offering my very cordial thanks for the high appreciation expressed by so many organs of literary opinion of the first part. 'The Early Life of Samuel Rogers' necessarily dealt with that portion of his unexampled career in which he was establishing his position as a popular poet, a patron of literature and art, and a man of taste. I had to show from what origin he sprang, and to trace the two characteristic lines of English middle-class life—the Tory churchmen, manufacturers and squires, with a dash of French blood, from whom he inherited his family name; and the Whig Nonconformists, proud of their descent from the Rev. Philip Henry, yet themselves diverging from the orthodoxy of their parents, who, through his mother, gave him his chief intellectual characteristics, and his political and religious opinions. I had to show him leaving the business career in which he had been brought up, turning his back with hesitation on his quiet suburban life, and plunging into the

great stream of London Society. These new volumes
begin just at the point at which he took the step which
led him from literary to social distinction. I have shown
in 'The Early Life' the remarkable and growing popularity his poem, 'The Pleasures of Memory,' was enjoying at the time when he settled in St. James's Place,
and made his small and unostentatious house the most
tastefully furnished dwelling in London. It was the
eve of a great literary development; and Rogers's love
of cultivated society soon made his home a favourite
meeting-place of the chief poets, writers, and artists
of his time. The social success followed, and for fifty
years Rogers was a prominent—for a long time the
most prominent—figure in London life. He was the
one man, and his house was the one house, that every
stranger from the Continent, or from the United States,
or from the English shires, desired to see. He was surrounded, too, by such a group of poets and wits and
artists and literary men and men of great conversational
powers, as the world had never seen before and has not
witnessed since. As the 'Oracle of Holland House,' to
use Macaulay's words, he became the intimate associate
of most of the great statesmen of his time. His time,
moreover, was two whole generations. It included the
Gordon riots and the repeal of the Corn Laws, the
French Revolution and the Great Exhibition. It linked
together Fox and Sheridan and Windham and Lord
Grenville with Sir Robert Peel and Earl Russell and
Mr. Gladstone. Among his poetical contemporaries

were Cowper and Tennyson, with the Byron episode and the whole Lake School coming between them; and among his friends were the authors of 'Zeluco' and 'The Man of Feeling,' and the writers of 'Vanity Fair' and 'Master Humphrey's Clock.'

The story of fifty years passed in such society as Rogers lived in may be told in two ways. It may be worked up into a brilliant narrative, or it may be left for the actors in it to describe in their own diaries and letters. I have chosen the latter course. I have tried to show what was the kind of society of which Rogers was the centre, and what was the impression he made on his friends and acquaintances. He has been so slightingly spoken of since his death, that it will surprise many of my readers to find how highly he was esteemed —indeed, with what remarkable admiration he was regarded—during his life by many of the best, the truest, and the greatest of his contemporaries. Meanwhile many appreciative notices of him have been published, such as Mr. Hayward's article in 'The Edinburgh Review,' that of Dr. Carruthers in the eighth edition of 'The Encyclopædia Britannica'; and in later years the excellent account of him in the ninth edition of that Encyclopædia by my friend Professor Minto, and the 'Reminiscences' in 'The Quarterly Review' for last October, which, I regret, must remain anonymous. Mr. Hayward, however, included in his article some rather scornful references to him by two ladies who, as will be seen in the second volume of this work, were among his most devoted friends when he was alive. These, with Lady Morgan's fables, and Mr. Dyce's Table Talk, did lasting injury to his memory. Now, at length, the world will see, from the remarkable series of letters in these volumes, what Rogers really was, and the impression he made on the men whose friendship and esteem form one of the foundations of his enduring fame.

The dislike which Coleridge felt for Rogers on first meeting him at Wordsworth's house (p. 9, vol. i.), contrasts in a very striking way not only with Coleridge's own subsequent regard for him, but also with the affection which Wordsworth entertained towards him. The world now learns for the first time how much Rogers and Wordsworth were to one another. It learns something too of the great Lake poet himself. The letters from Wordsworth which are spread all through these volumes give a closer view of him as a man, and in his domestic relations, than is to be found in any book I know. It is not the Wordsworth of his nephew's stilted biography, but the Wordsworth of every-day life. The bishop tried to show only the great man—his sublime head, like Horace's, striking the stars—in these letters he is a man among men, with the wants and the weaknesses, the small interests and the fretting cares of common life. I have seen no such picture of Wordsworth as these letters and other references to him in these volumes give. Next to Wordsworth, Tom Moore is the most prominent of Rogers's contemporaries in my pages. He is here, however, rather as a diarist than as a correspondent. I have had to point out some defects in his biographies. His Life of Byron contained a good many letters from Byron to Rogers. He had the originals in his hands, and I find on them the pencil marks which directed the copyist what to omit. He printed the letters without any sign of these omissions, and in reproducing them I have restored most of the missing passages. I have also pointed out, in correction of Medwin's vulgar misrepresentations, how Byron's rhymed attack on Rogers is really to be taken.

In writing his 'Life of Sheridan' Moore had all Rogers's papers before him; but overlooked one, which he probably thought was nothing but the inventory of a sale. I have shown, however, that it solves a mystery as to Sheridan's income which has puzzled all who have written about him.

The letters which passed between Rogers and Richard Sharp during the great political crisis in 1834 present a most lively picture of the personal movements and views of the chief actors in the drama. The message from Lord Grenville conveyed by Rogers's letter to Lord Lansdowne seven years before this, his correspondence with Lord Grey, and the remarkable series of letters on public affairs addressed to him by Lord Brougham after Rogers was laid aside, are striking evidences of his interest in political affairs. His own letters to his sister give glimpses of English country life in two generations.

I have to acknowledge my indebtedness to Lord John Russell's 'Memoirs, Journal, and Correspondence of Thomas Moore'; to Dr. Sadler's admirably edited 'Diary, Reminiscences, and Correspondence of Henry Crabb Robinson'; and to Mrs. Kemble's 'Records of Later Years.'

The materials for Rogers's biography were placed in my hands by the relatives to whom he left them. His executors were his nephews, the late Mr. Samuel Sharpe and the late Mr. William Sharpe, and most of the letters from various eminent persons, and the diaries, in these volumes and in the earlier volume, were entrusted to me by Miss Sharpe and Miss Matilda Sharpe, of 32 Highbury Place, and Mrs. Sharpe, of 1 Highbury Terrace. Miss Blanche Rogers and Miss Meta Rogers, great-granddaughters of Rogers's oldest brother, Daniel Rogers, have supplied me with much additional material, chiefly with Rogers's own letters to his brother Henry and his sister Sarah, and have given me valuable assistance in other ways. Mrs. Sharpe, of the Grove, Hampstead, gave me the recollections of his uncle's conversation put down by her husband, the late Mr. Henry Sharpe. To Mrs. Drummond, of Fredley and Hyde Park Gardens, I am indebted for the use of the important and valuable letters of Richard Sharp. My authority for the statement that Rogers once made an offer of marriage to Lavinia Banks, afterwards Mrs. Forster, is her granddaughter Miss Poynter.

My grateful thanks are also due to those who have so readily responded to my request for permission to print letters. First of all to her most gracious Majesty the Queen, for leave to publish the letter in which Prince

Albert, in her name, offered Rogers the Laureateship on the death of Wordsworth; and next to the Duke of Wellington and the Duke of Sutherland, the Marquis of Dufferin and Ava, the Earl of Lytton, Lord Grantley, Lord Monteagle, Lord Knutsford, Sir Robert Peel, Captain Sir George Beaumont, Mr. S. E. Bouverie-Pusey, Mr. Ernest Coleridge, and Dr. Charles Mackay, for similar permission, cordially given. To the late Lord Brougham I am indebted, not only for granting leave to print his brother's letters, but for reading them all before they were sent to the press. At the request of the Dowager Lady Lilford, Sir Charles Newton kindly gave me similar help with the letters of Lord and Lady Holland. With respect to the letter on page 309, vol. i., Sir Charles Newton tells me that in the Gem room of the British Museum is to be seen the snuff-box given by Napoleon to Lady Holland, his writing which accompanied the gift, and General Fox's memorandum written on a separate card. I am indebted to Earl Grey, not only for permission to publish the letters of his illustrious father, his mother, and his brother, but for the explanation I have been able to give of his own letter on page 284, vol. ii., and to Lord Ashburnham who kindly read his grandfather's letters and supplied me with one or two annotations on them.

I have further to acknowledge my indebtedness to the Countess Russell for leave to publish her own and Lord John Russell's letters, and to Lady Agatha Russell for kind assistance in editing them; to the Dowager

Marchioness of Ely, the Baroness Burdett-Coutts, and Mrs. Gladstone; to the Honourable Justice Denman for Rogers's lines addressed to him; to Mrs. Maxwell Scott for leave to print the letters of Sir Walter Scott; to Miss Mackenzie of Edinburgh for copies of Rogers's letters to her grandfather, 'The Man of Feeling,' and permission to use his letters both in these volumes and in 'The Early Life'; to Mr. T. Price, executor of Lady Price, for sanctioning the use of the valuable and interesting letters of his uncle Sir Uvedale Price; to Sir John Farnaby Lennard, of Wickham Court, for leave to include those of Henry Hallam; to Lady Eastlake for similar leave and some valuable hints; to Mrs. Arthur Severn for looking over Mr. Ruskin's letters during his illness, and to Mr. Ruskin himself for letting them appear. For the inclusion in the volumes of Dickens's most characteristic and amusing letters I am indebted to Miss Georgina Hogarth; while Mrs. Forster and Mrs. Kemble, with the greatest readiness, responded to my request. Mr. George Ticknor Curtis, of New York, and Messrs. G. Putnam's Sons, of the same city, cordially sanctioned the printing of letters by Washington Irving and Daniel Webster.

In giving me leave to use the letters of his grandfather, Mr. William Wordsworth writes: 'I had the pleasure in my schoolboy days of breakfasting on two or three occasions with Mr. Rogers in the last years of his life, and I have a lively and grateful recollection of the great amiability and courtesy which he extended to all the members of my family whenever we visited him';

and the Rev. Charles Cuthbert Southey, in sanctioning the use of his father's letters, says, 'I have a vivid recollection of Mr. Rogers, though very young when I had opportunities of being in his society. I well remember being at a remarkable breakfast at his house when Sydney Smith, Tom Moore, my father and, I think, Wordsworth, were among the guests. There were giants in those days.'

There are a few letters from people eminent in their time who left no near relatives behind them and whose heirs I have failed to trace. In such cases I have thought it better to print the letters than to omit them; but I have only done so where the interest was entirely of a public character and no private matters were involved.

P. W. CLAYDEN.

13 TAVISTOCK SQUARE, LONDON :
March 1889.

Lord Byron to Samuel Rogers.

Absent or present, still to thee,
  My friend, what magic spells belong!
As all can tell who share like me
  In turn thy converse and thy song.

But when the dreaded hour shall come,
  By Friendship ever deem'd too nigh--
And ' Memory ' o'er her Druid's tomb
  Shall weep that aught of thee can die—

How fondly will she then repay
  Thy homage offer'd at her shrine,
And blend, while ages roll away,
  Her name immortally with *thine*.

April 19, 181 .

CONTENTS

OF

THE FIRST VOLUME.

CHAPTER I.

1803-1805.

Rogers at St. James's Place—His Poetical Contemporaries—His Social Position—His Friends—Reasons for his choice of a Bachelor Life—Gilpin's Last Letter—R. Bloomfield—Walter Scott—Journey to Scotland—Visit to Wordsworth—Coleridge's First Impressions of Rogers—Burns's Grave—Glasgow in 1803 —'Man of Feeling' Mackenzie—Francis Horner—Mackintosh —Sydney Smith—'To a Girl Asleep'—Southey's 'Madoc'— Scott's 'Lay'—The Young Roscius—Rogers and Dr. Burney— Windham—Rogers and T. Moore's 'ever-memorable party' . . 1

CHAPTER II.

1805-1809.

Rogers and Fox—Visits to Fox—Fox's Last Illness—Death of Fox —Holland House—Rogers and Lord and Lady Holland— Death of Maria and Sutton Sharpe—Their Children—Catharine Sharpe—Rogers and Thomas Moore—Moore's Duel with Jeffrey —Richard Sharp in Parliament—Windham—Mrs. Inchbald— Uvedale Price—Rogers and Wordsworth—Brighton in 1808— Rogers and Lord Erskine—Rogers and Walter Scott—Hoppner —*The Quarterly Review*—Lines on Mrs. Duff—Scott on Mrs. Duff's Death—Letter from Luttrell—Rogers and the Princess of Wales 27

CHAPTER III.

1810-1812.

Columbus—Letters to Richard Sharp—T. Moore—An Idyll at Hagley—Recollections of Porson, Windham, Cumberland, Horne Tooke—Tooke's Adventures—His Funeral—Rogers and Byron—Meeting of Moore, Campbell, and Byron at Rogers's House—Coleridge's Lecture—'Childe Harold'—Tom Grenville's Criticism on the Poem—Byron and Lord Holland—Rogers at the Lakes—The Mackintoshes and Sharp—Dr. Bell—Wordsworth's Lost Child—Rogers at Ormithwaite, Keswick, Lowther—Lord Lonsdale—Brougham—Rogers at Glenfinnart—Lord Dunmore—Letters to R. Sharp, to H. Rogers, to Sarah Rogers—Letter of Lord Holland—Rogers at Crewe 65

CHAPTER IV.

1813-1814.

'Columbus'—Ward's Review in *The Quarterly*—Rogers's Epigram on Ward—Mackintosh's Review in *The Edinburgh*—Wordsworth on Scott—Byron's Letters—His Verses on Rogers—Rogers at Bowood; at Woolbeding—Byron's Estimate of Rogers—Rogers and Sheridan—An unsuspected Source of Sheridan's Income—Byron's Letters to Rogers - Jacqueline—Luttrell's Criticism—Lady Jersey—Letter from Wordsworth—Jekyll—Rogers's Love for Children—Epigram on the White Cockade—Sir George Beaumont's Epitaph on Johnson—Uvedale Price 119

CHAPTER V.

The Peace of 1814—Rogers goes to France, Switzerland, and Italy—Diary of the Journey—The English in Paris—Napoleon Legends at St. Cloud—Fontainebleau—The Journey South—Bossuet's House—Coppet—Geneva—News from Richard Sharp of Friends at Home—Rogers in Venice—Petrarch's House at Arqua—Florence—A Winter in Rome—Visit to the Pope—Naples and Murat—The Hollands—The Princess of Wales—Bonaparte's Return from Elba—War Preparations—Homewards through War Alarms—Paestum—The Diary the Germ of 'Italy' 157

CONTENTS OF THE FIRST VOLUME   xvii

CHAPTER VI.
1815-1816.

Rogers on Poetical Composition—Lines at Meillerie—Letters from Mackintosh, Coleridge, Uvedale Price, and William Lisle Bowles—At Lady Hardwicke's—The Authorship of 'Auld Robin Gray'—Rogers at Lord Spencer's—Captain Usher—Paris under the Allies—Letters from Richard Sharp—Rogers to his Sister—Rogers's Twelfth-night Parties—His Love of Children—Letters to Richard Sharp   185

CHAPTER VII.
1816-1818.

Rogers and Lord Byron—Letter from Mackintosh—Rogers, Byron, and Godwin—Byron's Appeal to Rogers—Letter from Walter Scott—Rogers and Sheridan—Sheridan's Deathbed—Rogers's Recollections of Sheridan—Lord John Townshend's Letter—Grattan—Lord Erskine—Ugo Foscolo—Benjamin Constant at Breakfast—Byron, Rogers, and Lady Caroline Lamb—'Glenarvon'—Rogers at Sydney Smith's, at Tom Moore's, at Wordsworth's, at Southey's, at the Lakes—Letter from Southey—'An unfledged Eagle'—Wordsworth on Bernard Barton—Rogers and Crabbe—Crabbe's Visit to London—Breakfasts at Rogers's—Crabbe, Moore, Rogers, and Campbell at Sydenham—The Rev. W. Lisle Bowles—'The Abbot of Fonthill'—The Death of the Princess Charlotte—Lord Bathurst and the Regent—Story of the Father of George III.—Letter from Byron—Letter from Ugo Foscolo on his Literary Plans . . .   209

CHAPTER VIII.
1818-1819.

Lines on the Temple at Woburn—Luttrell's Lines on Rogers's Seat—Lord Holland's Pamphlet—His 'Dream' of University Extension—Sketch of a Poem—Moore and Rogers at Bowood—Stories of Sheridan—Rogers to Mrs. Greg—Sonnet by Lord Holland—Moore and Rogers—Crabbe and his Publisher—Rogers's 'Human Life'—Don Juan on Rogers—Offers of Help to Moore—Letter from Crabbe—Rogers out of Politics—Two Generations of Literary Talk   263

CHAPTER IX.
1820-1821.

Rogers's House—His Love of Harmony—His Literary Position—
Campbell and Schlegel—Parr and Mackintosh reconciled—
Letters from Walter Scott—Lady Holland and Napoleon—
Rogers and Moore in Paris—Rogers and his Sister and Niece
in Switzerland—With Kemble and Mrs. Siddons at Lausanne
—Rogers's Letters from Italy—His Meeting with Byron—
Rogers's Letters from Rome—With Byron at Pisa—Byron,
Shelley, and Rogers—Medwin's Misrepresentations—Rogers
on Byron 297

CHAPTER X.
1822-1824.

The First Part of 'Italy'—Moore and Rogers in Paris—Wordsworth
on his Sister's Diary—Dorothy Wordsworth to Rogers—Wordsworth at Rogers's—J. P. Kemble's Death—Mrs. Siddons's Letter
—Rogers and the Duke of Wellington—Uvedale Price—An
English 'Ginevra'—Walter Scott's Remuneration—Southey's
Letter—Rogers and Lord Grenville—Lord Grenville on Dante
—Lord Ashburnham's Letter—Moore, Wordsworth, and Rogers
—Letter of Miss H. M. Williams—R. Sharp to Rogers—Lord
Byron's Death—Rogers and Byron's Memoir—The Funeral—
Rogers's Commonplace Book—Uvedale Price on Dropmore;
on Queen Caroline's Oysters—Luttrell on a Greek Epigram—
Letters of Sir J. Mackintosh and Uvedale Price . . . 341

CHAPTER XI.
1825-1827.

Rogers's Bank—Retirement of Henry Rogers—Samuel Sharpe a
Partner—Letters from Wordsworth—Rogers's Advice to Wordsworth—Wordsworth and his Publishers—Moore at Rogers's—
Uvedale Price—The University of London—Brougham—
Rogers's Parties—Sir Thomas Lawrence and Lord Dudley—
Sydney Smith at Rogers's—Lord Grenville's Inkstand—Letter
from Lord Holland—Rogers with Wordsworth and Sir George
Beaumont—Sir G. Beaumont's Last Letter—Moore and Rogers
—Wordsworth and Rogers—Rogers in two New Characters—
Appeal to Lord Lansdowne to join the Junction Ministry—
Tom Grenville—Mackenzie's Appeal for R. Pollok—Rogers at
Bowood—Letter from Wordsworth—Rogers at Strathfieldsaye 401

ROGERS

AND HIS CONTEMPORARIES.

CHAPTER I.

.1803-1805.

Rogers at St. James's Place—His Poetical Contemporaries—His Social Position—His Friends—Reasons for his choice of a Bachelor Life—Gilpin's Last Letter—R. Bloomfield—Walter Scott—Journey to Scotland—Visit to Wordsworth—Coleridge's first Impressions of Rogers—Burns's Grave—Glasgow in 1803—'Man of Feeling' Mackenzie—Francis Horner—Mackintosh—Sydney Smith—'To a Girl Asleep '—Southey's 'Madoc'—Scott's 'Lay'—The Young Roscius—Rogers and Dr. Burney—Windham—Rogers and T. Moore's 'ever-memorable party.'

SAMUEL ROGERS was just forty years old when he finally settled down to bachelor life in his beautiful house in St. James's Place. He had been born at Stoke Newington in 1763, the third son of his father. His eldest brother, Daniel Rogers, had incurred his father's severe displeasure by marrying his cousin, and had settled down as a country gentleman. His next elder brother, Thomas Rogers, had died in his twenty-seventh year, and in 1793 his father had followed to the grave. At thirty, therefore, Samuel Rogers had found himself the head of the firm, into which, only nine years before, he had been introduced as the youngest of five partners. He had an ample income from a well-established business, which every year needed less and less of his attention, and which was now almost entirely left under the able and conscientious management of his partners, especially of his youngest brother, Henry Rogers. He had been as fortunate in his literary ambition as in his business arrangements. His chief work, 'The Pleasures of Memory,' published early in 1792, had been one of the most popular poems of the time. In eleven years the sale had not slackened, and a new edition, of two thousand—the fourteenth—had just been called for. He had obtained universal recognition as a popular poet, and none of his contemporaries, illustrious as some of them afterwards became, had as yet overshadowed his fame. Campbell had published 'The Pleasures of Hope,' written in emulation of the success of 'The Pleasures of Memory,' had just composed 'Lochiel's Warning' and 'Hohenlinden,' and was on his way to London to devote himself to literature as a profession. Southey had written 'Thalaba,' but it had been coolly received; Wordsworth, married in the year before, was writing 'The Prelude,' but had only actually published the enlarged edition of 'Lyrical Ballads;' Coleridge had composed some of his best poems, but was little known; and was earning his living by writing for the *Morning Post*. Walter Scott had translated 'Goetz von Berlichingen,' and issued 'Minstrelsy of the Scottish Border,' but was not yet known to fame. Tom Moore, then called 'Anacreon Moore,' because he had translated Anacreon, was travelling in America, and Byron was a boy at school. Cowper, who had been three years in his grave, was regarded as the great poet of the evangelical school, while Rogers was the favourite with society.

It is important to understand Rogers's literary position at this period if we are in the least to comprehend his social success. The mere possession of a beautiful house in St. James's Place, even the reputation of having made it the most artistically furnished house in London, would not have enabled him to launch on the remarkable career which was now opening before him. There were many richer men than he who entertained everybody and whose splendid parties were the talk of the town. One of these was Miles Peter Andrews, gunpowder manufacturer, popular dramatist, and Conservative member of Parliament, whose confidence Rogers had shared in the Margate season of 1795, who had bought Lord Grenville's house and filled his rooms with all the fashion of the time. But Andrews was dead and forgotten when Rogers was, as it were, only on the threshold of his fame. His social success was one of quantity—Rogers's was of quality. You met at Andrews's receptions everybody who could pretend to be anybody; you met at Rogers's table the few whose intellectual distinction made them worth meeting. Dr. Burney, writing of Rogers in May, 1804, says, ' He gives the best dinners to the best company of men of talents and genius I know;' and Henry Mackenzie, author of ' The Man of Feeling,' writing to Rogers after a visit he had paid him in March of the same year, says, in his self-depreciatory way, that though he can ill participate in, he can fully enjoy, 'the pleasures of that Society, the Literature, the Science, the Taste which it affords,' when he is ' allowed to be of that community.'

I find in one of his early diaries a list of friends and acquaintance, made out apparently at the close of the last century or the beginning of this. It contains nearly a hundred names, and among them are the most representative men and women of the time. Statesmen, men of letters, artists, antiquaries and actors, soldiers, sailors and divines, with literary women and women of fashion, make up the catalogue. Some of them were already eminent, others were then unknown, though they are illustrious now, and some then of the first consideration are now almost forgotten. Fox, Fitzpatrick, Erskine, Windham and Sheridan, Horne Tooke, Mackintosh (not yet Sir James), Lord John Townshend, Courtenay, Lord Northwick, William Lamb (afterwards Lord Melbourne) and Lord Henry Petty (afterwards Lord Lansdowne), Lord Cowper, Lord Richard Spencer, Lord Clifden, Lady Cork, the Grevilles, and Sir F. Burdett were among the friends of these early days. One might have met at his house Mrs. Barbauld and Mrs. Inchbald, Mrs. Siddons and Mrs. Piozzi, Mrs. Damer and Mrs. Crewe (afterwards Lady Crewe). Dr. Moore's celebrated sons, General (not yet Sir) John Moore and Graham Moore, then only a captain waiting the further opportunity of distinguished service, which came in the summer of 1803, were both friends of their father's friend. Among other names are those of Gifford, Sotheby, Henry Mackenzie, Dr. Aikin, Richard Cumberland, Payne Knight, Porson and Parr, Mitford the historian, Sir Richard Worsley the historian and antiquary, Joseph Windham the antiquary and artist, Sir William Scott (afterwards Lord Stowell); Francis,

Jekyll the wit, Sargent, Sir George Beaumont, Uvedale
Price (afterwards Sir Uvedale), George Ellis, whom Scott
praises in 'Marmion;' Dr. French Lawrence the friend
of Burke, Planta the librarian of the British Museum,
Ward (afterwards Lord Dudley), Luttrell, Spencer, Lord
Boringdon, Tuffin, Weddell, John Allen, and, at the
top of all, Richard Sharp. Tierney, William Smith the
member for Norwich, Sir Francis Baring, Grattan,
Scarlett, Sydney Smith and Robert Smith (Bobus), are
not in the list, though at this period they were among
his friends. His brother-in-law Sutton Sharpe, with
Maltby, T. Campbell, Hoppner, Carr, Combe, Stothard,
Flaxman, Faringdon, W. Lisle Bowles, Bloomfield the
poet, Lock the owner of Norbury, Opie, Fuseli, Cosway,
with many others, are in a list headed 'Breakfast.' He
seems to have begun his breakfast parties—to which in
later days all the world wished to crowd, and even
princes asked for invitations—by gathering together a
few of his most intimate friends.

Rogers never deliberately planned the kind of life he
lived for so many years in St. James's Place. I have
shown, in telling the story of his early life, that it was
after a mental struggle he gave up his suburban home
and plunged into the life of London. His ideal was a
home where he could lead the life of satisfied desires,
surrounding himself with some of the choice spirits of
his time. He by no means contemplated final settlement as a bachelor, though he had given up the idea of
marriage before he finally determined on the house in
St. James's Place. The letters to his friend Richard
Sharp show not only that he was susceptible to the

charms of domestic life, but that on more than one
occasion he contemplated marriage. Since the 'Early
Life' was published, I have learned that he actually
made an offer of marriage to Lavinia Banks, the
daughter of his old friend Thomas Banks, the eminent
sculptor. Miss Banks married the Rev. Edward Forster
in 1798 or 1799; and Mrs. Forster lived on some years
longer than Rogers himself. An intimate and affectionate friendship was maintained between them to the
close of Rogers's life; and Mrs. Forster made no secret
of the fact that she had refused his offer of marriage
when they both were young. The date of her union
with Mr. Forster harmonises with that of Rogers's
'Lines to a Friend on his Marriage,' and with 'The
Farewell,' as well as with hints as to mental suffering
in some of the family letters. His precarious health,
which had driven him to lodgings at Exmouth in the
winter of 1799-1800, probably combined with this disappointment in determining him not to marry; and
he seems to have come back with the resolve to accept
the lot of loneliness. Some of the letters to his sister
Sarah in these volumes show a sort of longing for the
companionship of a woman, which her close and constant sisterly affection partially satisfied.

There is a glimpse of an earlier friendship, which
may have been something more, in one of the last letters
Rogers received from his old and venerable friend and
correspondent, the Rev. William Gilpin. 'The Bishop
of Lincoln,' says Gilpin, writing at the end of 1802,
' has lodgings in Lymington, and has paid me two or
three visits. I showed him your account of France, with

which he was much pleased. . . . Mrs. Pretyman, who was with him, went upstairs to see Mrs. Gilpin, and after she was gone the Bishop told me his wife had been once acquainted with you; but lately you had not seen each other. He said it, however, in a manner which seemed to me to have some mysterious meaning, and I could not help suspecting she was one of those ladies whom you had sprinkled with the dews of Helicon. . . . She is a very pleasing woman, and was once, I dare say, what in my eye would have been handsome. They were both very well acquainted with your poetry; and the Bishop spoke with much animation of your " Memory." ' Rogers did not reply; and another letter from Gilpin, early in 1803, brought their long and, to Rogers, useful and interesting correspondence to an end. Gilpin closed his long, busy, energetic, and in many senses heroic life in the succeeding spring.

A letter from the poet of 'The Farmer's Boy'—the chief poem Robert Bloomfield had then published—shows that he had long known Rogers and received many benefits from him. Bloomfield had just given up his situation in the Seal Office and gone to the neighbourhood of Shooter's Hill to recover his health and peace of mind. His family, he says, had been dreadful sufferers from small-pox; and he had in consequence felt most forcibly the importance of the Vaccine discovery, and had written a poem of about four hundred lines on the subject, which had pleased Mr. Capel Lofft, and which Dr. Drake had approved. The poem was now to be sent to Rogers and to Dr. Jenner for their judgment on it. Bloomfield adds, 'I hear that you inquired after me at Mr. Stothard's. Thank you, sir, for this, and every kind remembrance; this sweet kind of friendship springs up like a fountain in a desert; it is inexpressibly gratifying. By the bye, I have [in] a small piece called "Barnham Water," something on the subject which I should like you to see.' Bloomfield never fully recovered his health, and some years after this letter was written, Rogers exerted himself to procure a pension for him. He was three years younger than Rogers, and died in 1823.

Two of the most illustrious names in English literature were added to Rogers's list of personal friends in the year in which he took up his abode in St. James's Place. In the spring Walter Scott had paid a visit to London, and had been introduced to Rogers, probably by Mackintosh. In the summer Rogers and his sister Sarah set out on a tour to Scotland, his first journey thither since the memorable time when he had made the acquaintance of Adam Smith, Robertson, Blair, Henry Mackenzie, and the Piozzis, in one week in July, 1789.[1] A brief diary of this journey shows that they set off by the north road through St. Albans on the 24th of July, and slept the first night at Newport Pagnell. On the way to Northampton they 'met Dr. Parr riding to a christening,' and at night 'slept at Loughborough with the Bishop of Durham.' Then on through Derby, Ashbourne, Ilam '(the meadows the most beautiful,' he says, 'I ever remember to have seen'), Dovedale (where were a file of ladies and the Oakover servants junketing), Matlock, Chatsworth ('more elegant than

[1] *Early Life*, pp. 89-95.

beautiful'), Sheffield, Barnsley, and through 'pleasant country disfigured by commerce and commercial opulence' to Wakefield and Leeds. Leaving Leeds, they sheltered at Kirkstall Abbey during a storm, and got on in the evening to the Green Dragon at Harrogate. At Harrogate, 'saw Bannister in the theatre in "Peeping Tom." The Green Room was a kitchen.' In the drawing-room of the Granby at night, 'heard the Silver Miners' and met Professor Young of Glasgow, with his wife and daughter, Mr. Milnes Rich, Sir John Nesbit, and Miss Dick. The weather was wet, but there were sunny intervals, and they went up Wensleydale and by Sedbergh to Rydal, and stayed at Ambleside. On the next day, the 8th of August, Rogers writes : 'Rode to Grasmere Church and returned by Wordsworth's Cottage; Rydal and Grasmere waters unruffled and bright as silver.' On the 9th of August 'drank tea with Wordsworth and Coleridge.'

There is every reason to believe that this was the first time Rogers and his sister had met the Wordsworths and Coleridge, and to one of the party at Grasmere the meeting seems not to have been pleasant. In a letter to Sir George Beaumont, written three days after Rogers's visit, Coleridge says : 'On Tuesday evening, Mr. Rogers, the author of "The Pleasures of Memory," drank tea and spent the evening with us at Grasmere—and this had produced a very unpleasant effect on my spirits.'[1] He then makes some very

[1] *Memorials of Coleorton*, edited by W. Knight, vol. i. p. 2. Professor Knight omits the name and makes it read 'Mr. R——, author of The —— of ——,' but there is no doubt to whom the reference points, and no reason why it should not be stated.

depreciatory remarks on Rogers, and, with a very near approach to a breach of confidence, proceeds : 'Forgive me, dear Sir George, but I could not help being pleased that the man disliked you and your Lady, and he lost no time in letting us know it. If I believed it possible that the man liked me, upon my soul I should feel exactly as if I were tarred and feathered.' This was a hasty judgment, probably due to his being at the time, as he tells Sir George Beaumont, 'unwell and sadly nervous.' Coleridge himself revised his early impression, and a few years later we find him expressing his 'unfeigned regard' for Rogers. Sir George Beaumont soon after became one of Rogers's fast friends, while the acquaintance with the Wordsworths, begun on this Tuesday evening at Grasmere, ripened into a close and affectionate intimacy which only death dissolved.

Coleridge's dislike of Rogers on this first acquaintance probably accounts for the very slight mention of him in Miss Wordsworth's interesting 'Journal of a Tour in Scotland.' Rogers records that on the 13th of August he 'walked into a grove by the lake side with Wordsworth;' and on the 14th Wordsworth, leaving his young wife and baby at home, set off with his sister and Coleridge for this Scottish journey. Rogers and his sister went a day or two later and overtook the Wordsworth party at Dumfries. They had been to see Burns's grave, new only six years before, and with no stone as yet to mark it. They then went to Burns's house, where the Rogerses met them. They were making the journey in what Dorothy Wordsworth calls a car, though Rogers described it as very much like a cart. Wordsworth and

Coleridge occupied the time in poetical reverie and transcendental talk while Dorothy acted as their manager and guide. All the practical details of the journey fell upon her. She selected the cottages where they could get meals by day and lodging at night, looked after the stabling of the horse, and was responsible for the comfort and welfare of the whole party. Coleridge, as Wordsworth records, was in low spirits and too much in love with his own dejection. Afraid to face the wet weather, Coleridge turned back at the end of August, while Wordsworth and his sister continued their journey. On their way back they met Scott at Melrose and travelled with him to Jedburgh, where he recited part of 'The Lay of the Last Minstrel,' then unpublished. Wordsworth in after years confessed to Rogers that he was not greatly struck with the poem, and there are other proofs in these volumes that he was no great admirer of Scott's poetry. After leaving Dumfries, Rogers and his sister went on to the Clyde. On the 19th they were at Hamilton House, and Rogers notes, not only the Rubens, but a Vandyke of the Earl of Digby, and portraits of the Duke of Hamilton, of his old friend Dr. Moore and of General Moore, painted in Italy. They were at Glasgow on the 20th. Rogers's account of Glasgow in the summer of 1803 is worth quoting :—

'Glasgow, a good object, with its cathedral of white stone. The streets very wide and handsome, particularly Argyll street; multitudes walking along the flagged footway, and coming and standing fearlessly in the midway, not a carriage appearing once in an hour. [Argyll Street] as wide as Cornhill, if not wider, the houses rather low than high, carts very scarce, and barrows not seen at all. Most of the women and girls waiting for their turn at the pumps, which are handsome, and stand beyond the footways. Women also surrounding the milk carts, their earthen and tin vessels supplied from a barrel by means of a plug. Naked feet innumerable among the women and boys. Many barbers' shops, and at each of their doors suspended a basin of burnished brass; many fruit shops, ice, grapes (hothouse) two shillings a pound; hackney coaches but no stand for them; a recruiting party parading with the bagpipe. Saw no coffee houses except the Tontine. Houses of white stone, and in general very neatly built. The streets opening into Argyll Street short and straight, generally consisting of very handsome private houses, and terminating with a bridge on one hand or a church or a hospital on the other; but these, probably on account of the time of year, had a neglected air. Girls with earrings and gilt combs in their hair, without shoes and stockings. Singular cries, not resembling those of London. Walked through the College and round its garden or meadow. At least equal to second-rate college of our universities. Shops small and poorly furnished. Roofs slated generally.'

The journey was cut short by an accident to Miss Rogers, and they came back through Edinburgh, calling on Henry Mackenzie and visiting Holyrood and Melrose. This renewal of his acquaintance with 'The Man of

Feeling' was the beginning of a long correspondence, and led to visits from Mackenzie to Rogers in London.

It seems to have been Rogers's habit, when meeting men of genius in the country, to offer them hospitality when they visited London. It is scarcely too much to say that he kept open house for men of letters, and many distinguished writers of the time owed to him their introduction to London society. A large part of the correspondence which has been preserved arose out of such visits, and much of the very high distinction which Rogers's house attained is due to the kindly mention made of it by men who had themselves helped to render it attractive. It differed in many respects from the houses of mere rich men or men of title who played the patron of poor authors. Rogers entertained them as one of themselves. He was not the patron but the poet. Literary men and artists even at this day feel the difference between visiting one another and visiting people who only want to parade them before their friends. How much greater was the distinction when this century was young!

At this period we begin frequently to meet with Rogers's name in contemporary memoirs. Francis Horner writes in his diary:—

'*January* 22*nd*, 1804.—At Sydney Smith's, the happiest day I remember to have ever spent. Mackintosh, Whishaw, Sharp, Rogers, and three interesting women of unlike character and manners.'

'*January* 25*th*.—At Rogers's: Mackintosh, Sharp, Sydney Smith, Wilkins, &c. Somewhat a melancholy evening, for it was the last Mackintosh is to spend in London.'

The departure of Mackintosh from London just at this moment, though regarded by Rogers and his friends as a serious blow, probably gave Rogers larger opportunities of entertaining them under his own roof. Mackintosh, as a correspondent of his biographer tells us, had established a kind of society which met once or twice every week at his own house, and once a week at the house of Sydney Smith. The regular members of these small evening parties were Rogers, Horner, Sir James Scarlett, Sir Thomas Lawrence, Colonel Sloper and his daughter (afterwards Mrs. Charles Warren), Richard Sharp, Hoppner, and the two hosts, Mackintosh and Sydney Smith. To these, others were joined as occasional visitors, and on everybody the same happy impression which Horner records, was left.

One of Rogers's earliest visitors from a distance was Henry Mackenzie, who was in London with an invalid son early in 1804, and who renewed his acquaintance with literary men in London at Rogers's table. A long correspondence followed, but Mackenzie's letters, as Rogers used to say, had none of the brilliancy of his published works, but were entirely commonplace.[1] Mackenzie's first letter is one of thanks. He sends a brilliant forgery on Burns, and a fancy drama by a girl of eleven, asks Rogers to correspond with him, and urges him soon to give the world the poem on which he had been some

[1] Rogers's recollection was at fault in saying to Mr. Dyce that the correspondence began after his first visit to Edinburgh. It was, as the letters show, after Mackenzie's visit to London in 1804.

time employed. This was 'Columbus' which was talked of, and partly shown at Rogers's parties, for years before it was published. Rogers replied:—

'In return I have nothing to send you but a stanza or two upon a girl asleep. Do you think they would be of any use to Mr. Thomson? They are quite at his service. *Eccole!*

> Sleep on and dream of Heaven awhile,
> Though shut so close thy laughing eyes,
> Thy rosy lips still wear a smile,
> And move, and breathe delicious sighs.
>
> Ah, now soft blushes tinge her cheeks,
> And mantle to her neck of snow;
> Ah, now she murmurs, now she speaks,
> What most I wish yet fear to know.
>
> Sleep on secure. Above control
> Thy thoughts belong to heaven and thee,
> And may the secret of thy soul
> Still rest within its sanctuary
> For ever undisturbed by me.

Columbus returns his best acknowledgments for your obliging inquiries. He has crossed the Atlantic, and will be glad to make the voyage with you whenever you are at leisure. How are your nerves? for the new world is full of "black spirits and white, blue spirits and grey." I rejoice to hear your son bore the journey so well. The bitter East has at last retired into his cave, and the air here to-day is as mild as in summer. Let us hope he will revive with all nature in that delightful season

> When May flowers blow and green is every grove,
> And the young linnet sings "I love, I love."

How charming are those lines of Tasso,[1] here so faintly imitated :—

> Odi quello usignuolo,
> Che va di ramo in ramo
> Cantando *Io amo, Io amo.*

I wish I had any news to send you. In what a pleasant confusion we are at present! How will it end? The new coalition is now closely cementing and hostilities will recommence immediately if no surrender takes place. Adieu, my dear Sir; I accept very thankfully your friendly offer, though I fear you will find in me an unworthy correspondent. You are now, I picture to myself, revisiting the mild scenes of Roslin and Hawthornden. If you can command there at will such society as you have peopled my dreams with, you are wise indeed in shunning the bustle and impertinence of what is vulgarly called good company.'

Rogers appears to have been in feeble health this summer. Writing to Mackenzie in November, he says :—

'When yours arrived here I was from home. I returned full of cold and fever, and a thousand fancies which have clung to me ever since, and have rendered me absolutely fit for nothing. But I am now beginning to breathe again, and hope by means of two great doctors, not Galen and Hippocrates, but a horse and a cow, to become a miracle of health and strength. . . . So the star which first discovered itself in your sky is soon to be visible in ours? Mrs. Siddons, from a discreet regard to her amplitude of person, begs leave to

---

[1] Tasso, *Aminta*, act i. sc. 1.

decline comparison with this actor from Liliput, but we are all on tiptoe and prepared to die in the crowd. . . . There is a printer, I understand, in our town who is perfectly intoxicated with happiness, and who stops his friends to inquire whether any man was ever so distinguished before. He is at once employed on "Madoc" and on "The Lay of the Last Minstrel," so we may expect great amusement this winter. . . . S. Smith is now very happy and very busy preparing, as he says, his moral philosophy for the ladies. I met him not long ago in the fields, lost in thought and full of his subject. Roscoe's "Leo X." is nearly printed, which reminds me of a book I have just read with great delight. Alas! there are not above six copies of it existing, but I will not rest till it is reprinted, I mean Tenhove's "Memoirs of the House of Medici." It is, if I may say so, all kernel and no shell, and as interesting as a French Memoir. If histories were written as histories should be, boys and girls would cry to read them.'

Mackenzie replies in the middle of December, and asks for four more lines for the ode on the Sleeping Girl, which Mr. Thomson means to marry to a Welsh air, but wants some other turn of expression than the *casse-dent* 'sanctuary.' He adds:—

'"Madoc"[1] is printing here, and so is "The Lay of the Last Minstrel,"[2] the author of which is very proud of your attention. . . . Our friend Sydney Smith came

[1] *Madoc* was published in 1805.
[2] 'In the first week in January, 1805, the *Lay* was published,' says Lockhart, 'and its success at once decided that literature should be the main business of Scott's life.'

off, I understand, with great *éclat* in his introductory lecture. I think him extremely well qualified to teach the ladies moral philosophy, as he has a very happy knack at delineating the *petites morales* particularly incumbent on the sex.' He then asks Rogers for his opinion of 'The Young Roscius,' and says, 'You see my judgment of him is more than confirmed by your nfallible London tribunal.' Rogers's reply is full of interest:—

Samuel Rogers to Henry Mackenzie.

'My dear Sir,—I have at last seen the boy who has enchanted old and young, and till then I had resolved to deny myself the pleasure of writing to you. I will not say I was surprised, for I went with great expectation, but he certainly came up to the idea you had led me so long ago to form of him. Thro' many passages he hurried without feeling, and his countenance wanted the changes which time only can give it; but he is a prodigy, and, with careful culture, will delight, if he lives, the rising generation. His acting may now be compared to painting in water-colours,—by-and-by it will acquire more force and body. Mrs. Siddons has retired to Hampstead for her health, and, what is odd enough, tho' she has seen a play, she has not seen him, nor does she disguise her scepticism on the subject. 'I heard her read the trial scene in "The Merchant of Venice" the other night with great effect.

Our public speakers are divided. Mr. Grey can see no merit in him, and Mr. Windham sees but little—while Mr. Pitt has become a playgoer, and Mr. Fox, with whom

I saw him in "Hamlet," thought his acting during the *play* better than Garrick's. I ought to make many apologies to Mr. Thomson for my unpardonable delay. He wants another stanza. *Eccola!*

> She starts, she trembles, and she weeps!
> Her fair hands folded on her breast—
> And now, how like a saint she sleeps,
> A seraph in the realms of rest!
>
> Sleep on secure! Above controul,
> Thy thoughts belong to Heaven and thee,
> And may the secret of thy soul
> Be held in reverence by me!

'I will not say I am satisfied, and Mr. T. I am sure will not. However, he will take it, I hope, as a proof of good intention. I have done what I could. I have lately visited other times with Mr. Scott, and have returned with great regret to the present. Mr. Fox expressed a wish to make the same enterprise, and I found him busily engaged yesterday in reading my copy.

'We have received, as you may have heard, some very interesting letters from Mackintosh. He thirsts for European society like an Arab in the desert, and looks forwards with impatience to the distant day of his return. He gives audiences every day to grotesque figures from strange countries, but such novelties have already ceased to amuse him. Don't you rejoice in our friend Smith's success? His lecture on wit yesterday deserved the praise it met with. Let me hope you have weathered the winter well, with all its changes. What a restless life does the quicksilver lead in such a climate as ours! Since you wrote I have suffered a great loss in Mr. Townley. You may remember to have seen him lying on a couch among his marbles last spring. A kinder heart and a more elegant mind were never found together. I don't know how it is, but there is something so soothing and delightful in such a character, when the hey-day and bustle of life is over, that I have almost always, even when a young man, been led to cultivate the friendship of people much older than myself. Pray follow a better example than I have set you, and write soon to say that you intend us a visit this spring. Be assured, my dear sir, that it cannot give greater pleasure to anybody.

'Yours with very great sincerity,

'SAML. ROGERS.

'St. James's Place, London:
'March 24th, 1805.'

The only points of interest in Mackenzie's reply are a short criticism on Betty and a reference to Walter Scott. Of the former he says, 'One half of his Hamlet was, I think, a wonderful performance, the other half he did not seem quite to understand; the playfulness of melancholy is, indeed, one of those shades of mind which it requires very nice colouring to hit off.' Of the latter he remarks, 'Yours and Mr. Fox's approbation will make one author of my acquaintance, Mr. Walter Scott, very happy. I really think the "Lay" a work of very great genius. Some things discretion might have shortened, and some things good taste might have left out; but there is always an impression and an interest which lays hold on the mind.'

There is a contemporary account of Rogers at this

period which, being written from the point of view of a political opponent, gives striking proof of his personal popularity. He had been for several years a Fellow of the Royal Society—a distinction then more often given that it is now for other than scientific eminence. Soon after he had settled in St. James's Place he put down his name for admission to the Literary Club, which then met at the Thatched House in St. James's Street. This club had been founded by Sir Joshua Reynolds with the help of Johnson, Burke, and Goldsmith, in the year in which Rogers was born (1763). Boswell, who was one of its members, tells us that they met for supper once a week at seven o'clock, but that, after about ten years, instead of supping weekly they dined together once a fortnight during the meeting of Parliament. Malone, writing in October, 1810, said that from its foundation to that time it had had seventy-six members, of whom fifty-five had been authors. Rogers was proposed by Courtenay and seconded by Dr. Burney, but was blackballed. This rebuff to so popular and successful a person was a nine-days' wonder of literary society at the time. Dr. Burney says that Rogers was rejected on account of his politics, and Rogers himself always believed that he owed his exclusion to Malone. Rogers was little of a politician, though he made no secret of his sympathy with the Whigs. Dr. Burney describes him as not fond of talking politics—meaning, of course, in mixed company—and says patronisingly, 'He is no *Jacobin enragé*, though I believe him to be a principled Republican, and therefore in high favour with Mr. Fox and his adherents.' He adds that Rogers 'is never intrusive, and neither shuns nor dislikes a man for being of a different political creed to himself; it is therefore that he and I, however we may dissent upon that point, concur so completely upon almost every other, that we always meet with pleasure. And, in fact, he is much esteemed by many persons belonging to the Government and about the Court.'

There are glimpses of Rogers and his friends in Windham's Diary. He meets him at Boddington's on the 31st of May, 1805, together with R. Sharp, Lord H. Petty, Ward, Lady Cockburn, Mrs. Hibbert, and Mrs. Opie. On the 5th of June he meets him with Littleton, W. Spencer, Luttrell, and H. Greville at Hampstead, and he records on the 2nd of August a 'long talk with Rogers while sheltering ourselves from a shower.' Joanna Baillie writes about this time, asking Rogers to meet Mrs. Siddons and her daughter, Mr. Sotheby, and Mr. Harness at dinner at six o'clock exactly; ' the ladies are to come in morning gowns and early, to walk on the heath, perhaps to look after houses; so if you are inclined to walk, come early too, and in your boots or anyhow.'

The first appearance of Rogers's name in Lord John Russell's 'Life of Moore' is in 1805; and about the same date Moore is mentioned in a letter from Rogers to his sister. Their friendship had been prepared for by Moore's early admiration for 'The Pleasures of Memory.' Moore came to London in 1799, but probably did not meet Rogers till 1805, after returning from his journey to America. Writing to Lady Donegal in that year, Moore tells her he is a little terrified at Rogers's account of her multitudinous company-keeping at Tunbridge Wells, and adds, 'I like Rogers better every time I see him.' Writing to his mother in November, Moore says, 'I am just going to dine third to Rogers and Cumberland. A good poetical step-ladder we make. The former is past forty, and the latter past seventy.' Moore was then six and twenty, but Rogers survived him. The two poets had probably had a good deal of intercourse during a visit to Tunbridge Wells, which Moore, writing of it thirty years afterwards, describes as having taken place in 1805-6.[1] In a letter to his sister Sarah, describing this visit, Rogers speaks of 'your friend Moore.' Moore himself records that he talked over the visit thirty years later with Miss Berry, who reminded him of several incidents of the period. The 'ever memorable party,' as Moore calls it, consisted, he tells us, of the Dunmores, Lady Donegal and her sisters, the Duchess of St. Albans, Lady Heathcote, Lady Anne Hamilton, with the beautiful Susan Beckford (afterwards Duchess of Hamilton) under her care, Thomas Hope, making assiduous love to Miss Beckford, William Spencer, Rogers, Sir Henry Englefield, &c. The following is Rogers's contemporary account of this 'ever memorable party':—

Samuel Rogers to Sarah Rogers.

'Tunbridge: 13th Octr. 1805.

'My dear Sarah,—You will no doubt be surprised to receive another letter from this Castle of Indolence; but

---

[1] It was, in fact, in the early autumn of 1805.

here I have remained (with only two short flights to town) partly from my own dilatory nature, but still more from my companion's, till I begin to despair of ever moving till Mount Zion and Mount Ephraim are loosened from their foundations. A set of people so warm-hearted, so distinguished for talent and temper, were perhaps never assembled before. Our happiness was the subject of hourly congratulation from each to each, and the unfeigned regret with which we have parted is the best proof of it. This morning, after breakfasting together, we lost the Beckfords, who are gone to Eastbourne, and to-morrow we set off for Lord Robert Spencer's. On the way we shall pass a day or two at Brighton, where I hope to see Patty and her nursery, and also the Chinnerys, and we shall at Worthing just look in upon the Jerseys. Perhaps you know that the late Lord J. died here, when we were in the very act of setting off on a party of pleasure. We have had music every evening; your friend Moore and Miss Susan Beckford have charmed us out of ourselves, and our mornings have passed away in curricles and sociables and four. Our morning excursions have generally mustered twenty, and you will smile to hear that I have exhibited daily as a curricle driver. Mr. Jodrell's barouche was an addition to us for a week, and he seemed a very good-humoured man. Your time has passed much more quietly, and I dare say much more profitably. Pray write to me in St. James's Place and tell me, my dear Sarah, what you mean to do. It was my intention to visit Wassall,[1] and I sent a message by

---

[1] The residence of his brother Daniel.

Tom to know when [it would suit best; but I suppose, on account of the Durys, I heard nothing on the subject till long nights and cold weather came to cool my spirit of enterprise; and now, I must own, I could look with more pleasure to it as a dream of the next summer. I have, moreover, a foolish cold which has for some days kept me to a barley-water diet. I rejoice to think that Mr. H. is better. Pray give my best remembrances to one and all, and believe me to be, ever yours,

'SAML. ROGERS.

'I hope to be in town by the end of this month at farthest. I have heard nothing for the last three weeks, tho' I have written to Maria. Poor Lady Buggin[1] died here last week, and Mr. Cumberland, at the head of his Corps, escorted her body out of the town. He was here for a week and was very much affected by her death. Miss S. Beckford is a daughter of Fonthill, very beautiful, and a prodigy in every respect. She was surprised to hear that I knew Miss Brettell, whom she knew in Wiltshire. To-morrow the only relic of our party will be T. Hope. We have had a most delightful autumn, and I have spent it very differently from the last—but every dog has his day. Remember, Sarah, I do not allude to that pleasant time we spent together at the first coming of winter. At Woolbeding (Lord Robert Spencer's) I expect to see Mr. and Mrs. Fox; but I begin amazingly to long for winter quarters. I wish you had

---

[1] Wife of Sir George Buggin, of Cumberland Place. She died on the 29th September, and was buried at St. Dunstan's-in-the-East by torchlight.

partaken a little of my gaiety here, my dearest Sarah, for I have had more than enough to spare, and none would have contributed or received her share with greater success than yourself. Many, many thanks for your kind letter, which I found lying on my table when I went last to town.'

CHAPTER II.

1805-1809

Rogers and Fox—Visits to Fox—Fox's Last Illness—Death of Fox—Holland House—Rogers and Lord and Lady Holland—Death of Maria and Sutton Sharpe—Their Children—Catharine Sharpe—Rogers and Thomas Moore—Duel with Jeffrey—Richard Sharp in Parliament—Windham—Mrs. Inchbald—Uvedale Price—Rogers and Wordsworth—Brighton in 1808—Rogers and Lord Erskine—Rogers and Walter Scott—Hoppner—*The Quarterly Review*—Lines on Mrs. Duff—Scott on Mrs. Duff's Death—Letter from Luttrell—Rogers and the Princess of Wales.

THE intercourse which Rogers had with Mr. Fox in the last years of that great statesman's life always remained among his most cherished recollections. More than a third of his volume of 'Recollections'[1] is devoted to Fox, and Rogers records that these scraps of conversation —which year after year he repeated to new friends at his celebrated breakfast parties—were read by Lord Holland with tears in his eyes. They give us the home view of a great political leader—what he was in free talk with a friend. 'I am well aware,' says Rogers in a brief prefatory note, 'that these scraps of conversation have little to recommend them, but as serving to show his playfulness, his love of letters, and his good nature in

[1] *Recollections*, by Samuel Rogers, edited by his nephew, William Sharpe, and published in 1859.

unbending himself to a young man.' The first meeting
with Fox he has put on record was at Mr. Stone's in
1792,[1] but the first conversation recorded in the 'Recollections' took place at William Smith's house in 1796.
At the earlier meeting, Talleyrand, then only known as
the Bishop of Autun, was present, with Sheridan,
Madame de Genlis (then Madame de Sillery), and Pamela.
Sheridan was, or pretended to be, desperately smitten
with Pamela, and Madame de Genlis tells us he made
her an offer of marriage. On this particular evening
Sheridan was busy writing verses to her in very imperfect French. Shortly afterwards she married the
unfortunate Lord Edward Fitzgerald. During the
evening, Fox's natural son, a deaf and dumb boy, came
in, and Fox flew to receive him with the most lively
pleasure. He conversed with the boy by signs, and
Talleyrand remarked to Rogers how strange it was to
meet the first orator in Europe, and see him talking only
with his fingers. The chief political remark of Fox's,
which Rogers records in his diary, is that ' all titles are
equally ridiculous.' The next record of Fox's conversation is that with which the ' Recollections' open. It was
at a dinner at William Smith's, and Rogers puts on
record that he was delighted with Fox's 'fine tact, his
feeling, open and gentlemanlike manner, so full of
candour and diffidence, and entering with great ardour
and interest into the conversation.' The next meeting
recorded was at Sergeant Heywood's, when Lord Derby,
Lord Stanley, and Lord Lauderdale were present, and Fox
pooh-poohed political economy, and spoke lightly of Adam

[1] *The Early Life of Samuel Rogers*, pp. 244-45.

Smith. From this time Fox seems to have numbered Rogers among his friends. They had much intercourse at Paris in 1802, and Rogers visited him in January, 1803, at St. Anne's Hill. The last visit to Fox's country house was in July, 1805. Rogers records that he 'went down with Courtenay and a brace of Weymouth trout.' Leaving London at eleven, they reached St. Anne's Hill at three, and found Fox in his garden, dressed in a light-coloured coat and nankeen gaiters, and wearing a white hat. He complained of the coldness of the summer, and of the gnats, and said he had not seen the Chertsey hills for a fortnight. 'How d'ye do?' he exclaimed, when it cleared in the evening, and the hills became visible. The talk during this visit fills nearly thirty pages of the 'Recollections.' Fox was very cordial. They arrived on the Wednesday, and proposed to return home on Saturday, but Fox insisted on making them stay till Monday, that they might have a quiet day on Sunday. Such a visit to the great Whig orator, when his life was fast drawing to its premature close, was likely to remain, as it did, among the proudest and most cherished of Rogers's recollections. In his poem of 'Human Life' there is an apostrophe to Fox, in which this and other visits are described:—

> Thee at St. Anne's so soon of care beguiled,
> Playful, sincere, and artless as a child;
> Thee who would'st watch a bird's-nest on a spray,
> Through the green lanes exploring day by day,
> How oft from grove to grove, from seat to seat,
> With thee conversing in thy lov'd retreat,
> I saw the sun go down. Ah! then 'twas thine
> Ne'er to forget some volume half divine;

> Shakespeare's or Dryden's, through the chequered shade,
> Borne in thy hand behind thee as we strayed,
> And where we sat (and many a halt we made)
> To read there in a fervour all thine own,
> And in thy grand and melancholy tone,
> Some splendid passage, not to thee unknown,
> Fit theme for long discourse.

In the succeeding February, after Fox had been appointed Secretary of State for Foreign Affairs in Lord Grenville's 'Ministry of All the Talents,' Fox removed to a house in Stable Yard, Westminster, and there Rogers saw him. At one of these visits Fox was talking earnestly about Dryden, of whom he was so fond that he once thought of editing his works. In the warmth of conversation with a sympathising listener, he forgot that a levee was being held, which, as a Minister of State, it was his duty to attend. When he suddenly recollected it, there was no time to dress, and he set off in his ordinary attire. Reminded that he was not in a Court suit, 'Never mind,' he replied; 'he is so blind, he will never know what I have got on.'

On the 23rd of March Rogers called on him, and found him reading Scott's 'Lay of the Last Minstrel,' which Rogers had lent him. They had been together to see 'the Young Roscius' a short time before. Fox's health was already failing, and, early in April, Rogers was summoned to visit him by a pathetic letter from Mrs. Fox. This letter shows the esteem in which Rogers was held by Fox and his wife, and proves that Mrs. Fox had been very anxious about her husband's health a month before she communicated her anxiety to Captain

Trotter, who says that she first spoke to him on the subject early in May.

Mrs. Fox to Samuel Rogers.

'My dear Sir,—If you can find time any evening before half-past ten to call here, I am sure Mr. Fox will be very happy to see you, as he has very often wished to do, particularly since he has been ill. He is now, thank God, better, but indeed, my dear Mr. Rogers, I have been very wretched for some days. Pray come soon, as I know he will enjoy seeing you.

'Yours very truly,
'Elizth. Fox.

'Stable Yard, Saturday.'

This Saturday was either the 5th or 12th of April. Rogers went at once and found Fox lying with Hippocrates open before him. The remark recorded in the 'Recollections' was made in an interval of his fits of stupor. He recovered for a time, and on Sunday, the 20th, Rogers dined at his house by formal invitation to a six-o'clock dinner. This was probably the last time Rogers saw him. In May, Mrs. Fox mentioned to Trotter the anxiety her husband's illness caused her; in June he became worse; and in July, longing to be back at St. Anne's Hill, set out for home, intending to take Chiswick House on the way. He never got beyond this first stage of the journey, but died at Chiswick on the 13th of September.

The death of Fox gave Rogers occasion for one of the best of his smaller poems. He had for him an unfeigned admiration and affection, and was in complete sympathy

with the feeling of numb despair with which the Whig
party saw the disappearance of their illustrious leader
just as the way seemed opening before him and them
into a better time. In one of his most prosaic pieces
Wordsworth, writing when Fox's death was hourly expected, spoke of a power passing from the earth. Rogers
wrote his 'Lines in Westminster Abbey,' when the power
had passed:—

> In him, resentful of another's wrong,
> The dumb were eloquent, the feeble strong;
> Truth from his lips a charm celestial drew,
> Ah! who so mighty and so gentle too?
> What though with war the madding nations rung,
> Peace, when he spake, was ever on his tongue,
> Amid the frowns of Power, the cares of State,
> Fearless, resolved, and negligently great
> . . . .
>
> Friend of all human kind! not here alone
> (The voice that speaks was not to thee unknown)
> Wilt Thou be missed. O'er every land and sea,
> Long, long, shall England be revered in Thee;
> And when the storm is hushed, in distant years,
> Foes on thy grave shall meet and mingle tears.

The distant years have come and the poet's prophecy
is fulfilled. Fox's fame is part of the proud inheritance
of Englishmen, to whatever party they belong. After
more than eighty years, in which we have had statesmen
as fearless, leaders as 'resolved and negligently great,'
and orators as powerful, it is not possible to realise the
disappointment, the distress, and the anxiety for the
future, which the passing away of this power from the
earth caused to the friends of freedom and progress

everywhere, as well as to his own immediate circle. It was a time when death seemed busy with the great. Nelson had died on the 21st of the previous October; Pitt had gone on the 23rd of January; and now Fox had followed within eight months. To the Whig party the loss seemed almost fatal. There was no one to take his place. How poignant the personal sorrow and the public and party disappointment were, is illustrated by one of Rogers's recollections. Many years after Fox's death he was at a party at Chiswick, and roamed with Sir Robert Adair over the house. They talked of the lost leader, and Sir Robert Adair asked in which room he died. 'In this very room,' replied Rogers, and Sir Robert Adair burst into a flood of tears.

In his later years Rogers often told and retold the story of his early intercourse with the greatest of the Whigs. He had introduced Wordsworth to Fox at a ball given by Mrs. Fox. Wordsworth was then little known, but he had already sent Fox a copy of the 'Lyrical Ballads,' with a letter in which he had drawn special attention to 'The Brothers' and 'Michael' as containing pictures of the domestic affections as they exist among the small cultivating proprietors called in the north country 'statesmen.' Fox had replied pointing out that 'Harry Gill,' 'We are Seven,' 'The Mad Mother,' and 'The Idiot Boy' were his favourites, and expressing his dislike of blank verse for subjects which are to be treated of with simplicity. This correspondence was probably in the minds of both when Fox and Wordsworth met, and accounts for Fox's greeting, 'I am glad to see you, Mr. Wordsworth, though I am not of your faction.'

It is easy to understand how Rogers's 'Recollections' of Fox, which every student of English history reads with satisfaction and interest, even in these distant days, told as they were in a manner which all contemporary accounts agree in describing as singularly effective and attractive, endeared him to the Whig circles in which he moved. It is in those 'Recollections,' embracing as they did Fox, Burke (through Mrs. Crewe and Dr. Lawrence), Grattan, Porson, Tooke, Talleyrand, Erskine, Scott, Lord Grenville, and the Duke of Wellington, that we have the real Table Talk of Samuel Rogers. The qualities which recommended him to these men, all of whom except Burke he knew personally, and with all of whom except Burke and Talleyrand, and perhaps Wellington, he lived on terms of intimate friendship, must of course be taken into account in any estimate of the causes which made him not only the oracle of the Holland House circle, but of London society generally for so many years. Fox, in illness, often wishing to see him, bears testimony to the pleasure his society gave to men who found a refuge in it from the tedium of weakness, from the anxieties of business, and from the cares of State.

Rogers's acquaintance with Lord and Lady Holland sprang in all probability out of his intimacy with Fox. He had become a familiar visitor at Holland House before the death of the great Whig orator and statesman, and their common reverence for his memory formed a strong tie between Rogers and Lord Holland, though no two men could more widely differ from each other. They were united by literary sympathies, by political opinions, and by social likes and dislikes; but still more by that complete dissimilarity which made the one, in many respects, the complement to the other. Writing of Holland House in 1831, after he had received his first invitation to it, Macaulay calls it 'the favourite resort of wits and beauties, of painters and poets, of scholars, philosophers, and statesmen,' and he tells his sister that 'Rogers is the oracle of that circle.' Rogers had got very early into high favour with the stern and eccentric guardian of its portals, without whose approval few could enter them and none remain. Lord Holland could not ask a friend to dinner without consulting his wife. One day, shortly before his death, Lord Holland met Rogers at the door. He had been calling on Lady Holland, and Lord Holland asked him if he returned to dinner. 'I have not been invited,' answered Rogers, and went away. Macaulay describes her, in 1831, as 'a large, bold-looking woman, with the remains of a fine person and the air of Queen Elizabeth.' In three brief sentences he sums up the characters of both host and hostess : ' Lord Holland is extremely kind. But that is of course, for he is kindness itself. Her ladyship too, which is by no means of course, is all graciousness and civility.' Rogers told Mr. Dyce that, when she wanted to get rid of a fop, she would beg his pardon and ask him to sit a little further off, adding, 'There is something on your handkerchief I do not quite like.' When men were standing with their backs close to the chimney-piece, she would call out to them to stir the fire. In 1843, when Brougham and Lady Holland were abroad with Rogers, Brougham writing to Rogers to propose an excursion remarked, 'Among other inducements don't forget how very angry it will make Lady H. She hates anybody doing anything.' It is a striking proof of the essential gentleness of Rogers's character that he kept the fast friendship, and, as her letters show, the affectionate regard of this imperious person for over forty years.

Lord Holland had a sincere admiration for Rogers's poetry; and Rogers had a hearty affection for Lord Holland as a man. Macaulay expresses his wonder 'that such men as Lord Granville, Lord Holland, Hobhouse, Lord Byron, and others of high rank in intellect, should place Rogers, as they do, above Southey, Moore, and even Scott himself.' His explanation is that 'this comes of being in the highest society of London.' But Macaulay here confuses between *post hoc* and *propter hoc*. Rogers was in the highest society of London in 1831 because his poems had been so heartily admired for nearly forty years. 'The Pleasures of Memory' had made him the fashion before Macaulay was born. There is no doubt that Lord Holland did much to confirm and sustain the fame of his friend. The lines he inscribed on the summer-house in the garden of Holland House are reproduced in the memoirs or the letters of scores of distinguished visitors. It was no ordinary homage from such a man that the summer-house should be called Rogers's seat, and that he should have inscribed upon it—

> Here Rogers sate, and here for ever dwell
> For me those pleasures which he sang so well.

The lines were put into Latin by Luttrell—

> Rogeri solitas sedes hic aspicis—hic mi
> Usque voluptates habitant quas tam bene cantat.

Rogers repaid the compliment paid him by Lord Holland. In the 'Lines written in Westminster Abbey,' after Fox's funeral, he had spoken of Fox—

> When in retreat he laid his thunder by
> For lettered ease and calm philosophy.
>
> . . . .
>
> There, listening sate the hero and the sage,
> And they, by virtue and by blood allied,
> Whom most he loved, and in whose arms he died.

His intimacy with the Hollands had not then begun; but when, some years later, he wrote 'Human Life,' it had become very constant and close. At the end of the apostrophe to Fox in that poem he refers to Lord Holland—

> Thy bell has tolled!
> —But in thy place among us we behold
> One who resembles thee.

The gloom which settled down over the prospects of the nation in this disastrous year was reflected in some of Rogers's domestic relations. Rogers himself has given the world, in a passage in his poem on 'Human Life,' a glimpse of what may fitly be described as a domestic tragedy. It is, perhaps, the most pathetic part of his writings; and Macaulay, in his review of Moore's Life of Byron, describes the last dozen lines as most sweet and graceful. In a letter to his sister, Macaulay tells her why he thus dragged in a compliment to Rogers, but he assures her that it is 'not undeserved.' The whole passage, however, is, as I have already shown other parts of this poem to be, taken from his own personal experience, and is full of testimony to the strength and purity of his domestic affections—

> But man is born to suffer. On the door
> Sickness has set her mark; and now no more
> Laughter within we hear, or woodnotes wild
> As of a mother singing to her child.
> All now in anguish from that room retire,
> Where a young cheek glows with consuming fire,
> And Innocence breathes contagion—all but one,
> But she who gave it birth—from her alone
> The medicine-cup is taken. Through the night,
> And through the day, that with its dreary light
> Comes unregarded, she sits silent by,
> Watching the changes with her anxious eye:
> While they without, listening below, above,
> (Who but in sorrow know how much they love?)
> From every little noise catch hope and fear,
> Exchanging still, still as they turn to hear,
> Whispers and sighs, and smiles all tenderness
> That would in vain the starting tear repress.
> Such grief was ours,—it seems but yesterday—
> When in thy prime, wishing so much to stay,
> 'Twas thine, Maria, thine without a sigh,
> At midnight in a Sister's arms to die!
> Oh, thou wert lovely—lovely was thy frame,
> And pure thy spirit as from Heaven it came;
> And, when recall'd to join the blest above,
> Thou died'st a victim to exceeding love,
> Nursing the young to health. In happier hours,
> When idle Fancy wove luxuriant flowers,
> Once in thy mirth thou bad'st me write on thee;
> And now I write—what thou shalt never see!

The door on which sickness had set her mark was that of his brother-in-law, Sutton Sharpe, where, in these latter years, Rogers had often heard the laughter of his little niece and nephews, the children of his sister Maria. She was Sutton Sharpe's second wife, and at their wedding, in 1795, Samuel Rogers had given her away. Her husband, as has been previously said, had taught Rogers all he knew of art, and Rogers owed to him his introduction to and acquaintance with the chief artists of the time. Their married life of nine years and a half had been a very happy one. Mrs. Sharpe had won the affection of her husband's only child by his first marriage, and this stepdaughter—a girl of thirteen when the marriage took place—had shared with her the family and household cares. In the beginning of the year 1806 the stepdaughter was away from home, and the little girl, Mary Sharpe, then five years old, was attacked by fever. Before she had recovered, a little boy of three, Henry Sharpe, was also attacked; and his mother, reluctant to break her stepdaughter's holiday, kept the illness from her and undertook the nursing herself. The anxiety proved too much for her. While the children were still only convalescent, another was born, and a fortnight later the mother caught the fever and died, 'a victim to exceeding love,' as her brother says. Sutton Sharpe never recovered from the blow, and in five months' time it was followed by another. His brothers-in-law, Samuel and Henry Rogers, as his bankers, had to tell him that he was ruined, and the next day he was found dead in his brewery.

Both the children recovered, and, with their four brothers, grew up under the constant motherly care of their elder half-sister, to form a family of every one of whom their poet uncle had reason to be proud. Their half-sister—and from this period their second mother—Catharine Sharpe was twenty-four. The story of this group of the children of one father covers a period of almost a hundred years. Catharine Sharpe was born on the 2nd of May, 1782; and Samuel Sharpe, the survivor of the group, died on the 28th of July, 1881. There was a story worth telling in every one of their lives. Sutton Sharpe became an eminent Queen's Counsel, a leader of the Chancery Bar, a Commissioner on Chancery Reform, and when he was struck down by paralysis in 1843, in his forty-sixth year, had before him, as the *Examiner* said, the most brilliant professional prospects. Of Samuel Sharpe, the eminent Egyptologist, the translator of the Bible, the benefactor of University College and School, and the Unitarian philanthropist, it is needless to speak. Mary married Mr. Edwin Wilkins Field, whose statue in the Law Courts is the testimony of the legal profession to the services he rendered it. Henry, a successful merchant, spent his leisure in various forms of philanthropic work, one of which is recorded in Hampstead Parish Church in a medallion monument raised, as the inscription says, ' by those who derived benefit in their youth from his disinterested efforts for their instruction and improvement, and who, though scattered through the world, gratefully unite to perpetuate the memory of a life devoted to the good of others.' William Sharpe, who ably edited Rogers's 'Recollections,' and with Samuel was left by Rogers as his literary executor, was, at one time, President of the Incorporated Law Society, and was consulted by successive Lord Chancellors on important Bills. There is a story of a Lord Chancellor who one day sent him a Bankruptcy Bill which was to be introduced in the House of Lords on the next day. William Sharpe studied it carefully for a good part of the night, and early the next morning hurried off to report that the scheme would not work. 'You are quite right,' said the Chancellor, 'the Bill won't work; but it must pass, for we have promised the places.' The Bill did pass, and did not work. The places were given, and soon after the placemen were displaced and compensated. Daniel Sharpe, the youngest brother, was a partner with his brother Henry. He was as eminent in geology as his elder brother Samuel was in Egyptology. He was killed by a fall from his horse in 1856, and at the time of his death was President of the Geological Society,[1] Fellow of the Royal Society, as well as of the Linnean and Zoological Societies. It is very rarely indeed that all the sons of a family attain distinction or success; and that this group of children, left orphans in their infancy, lived such useful and honourable lives is due, in the first place, to the qualities they inherited, and, in the second, to the careful nurture and the considerate training they received in the home of which their elder half-sister, Catharine Sharpe, was the self-sacrificing guardian and head.

Tragedy and comedy, like laughter and tears, lie so close together in life that the tale of Tom Moore's duel with Jeffrey wove itself in naturally enough among the

[1] I am told by an accomplished geologist that Daniel Sharpe's views on cleavage and other disputed points are now generally accepted, and that the value of his work is obtaining general recognition.

painful experiences of this fatal year. Moore has devoted a special monograph to this episode in his life, into which he seems to have gone, as he did into most things, by mere impulse. Jeffrey had written a slashing review of Moore's 'Epistles, Odes, and other Poems,' in the *Edinburgh Review* for July, 1806, and was apparently conscious that he had done Moore injustice. Rogers met him at Lord Fincastle's at dinner in the early summer, and the conversation turned on Moore. Lord Fincastle described the new poet as having great amenity of manner, and Jeffrey laughingly replied, 'I am afraid he would not show much amenity to me.' The insult and challenge followed soon after this conversation, and a meeting was arranged at Chalk Farm. William Spencer had heard of it, and had told the police, and, when the combatants were about to fire, the police appeared and took them all off to the station. Moore sent for Spencer to bail him, but Rogers had heard of the arrest and was on the spot in time to give the necessary security. This quarrel of two friends gave Rogers an opportunity of playing his favourite part of peacemaker. He carried messages between the combatants, containing, as Moore says, those formalities of explanation which the world requires, and arranged that they should meet at his house. The meeting took place on one of the Mondays in August, and resulted in a warm and lasting friendship between Moore and Jeffrey. In the autumn, Rogers was at Tunbridge Wells, and Miss Godfrey, writing to Moore, tells him that they have had from Rogers the whole history of the affair, even to the slightest particulars. 'If I had never known you,' she says, 'the story would have interested me, the way he tells it. He makes you out a perfect hero of romance. But what pleased me most was to hear that Jeffrey took a great fancy to you from the first moment he saw you in the field of battle, pistol in hand to kill him. I believe Rogers to be truly your friend on this occasion.' The romance of which Moore was the hero was not the duel in which Rogers had no share, but the reconciliation of which he was the agent.

Little more than a month after the death of Fox, there was a dissolution of Parliament, and at the general election which followed, many of Rogers's personal friends found seats in the House of Commons. The Grenville Ministry was so successful at the polls that Horner declared it to be a misfortune for the country that it was deprived of any opposition. The ministry, however, was not strong in itself, and Lord Eldon, anticipating by fifty years a remark attributed to Mr. Disraeli, had declared that Englishmen do not love coalitions. Among Rogers's friends in the new Parliament were Richard Sharp, who had been returned for Castle Rising, J. W. Ward (afterwards Earl of Dudley), William Lamb, the Lord Melbourne of the Reform era, and Lord Henry Petty (afterwards the Marquis of Lansdowne). The name of Lord Palmerston, then returned for the first time, and spoken of by his contemporaries as a mere lad, seems to link this Parliament of 1806-7, and the transitory gleam of hope it brought to the long-suffering Whigs, with our own times. On the 23rd of March, Sharp, as Mackintosh tells us, greatly distinguished himself by an excellent speech against the

Copenhagen expedition. Ward speaks of it in a letter to Rogers.

J. W. Ward to Samuel Rogers.

'Thursday Morning.

'My dear Rogers,—I cannot refuse myself the pleasure of being one of the first to communicate to you the news of our friend Sharp's success. He made his *début* last night in reply to Sturges Bourne. Nothing could be more happy. He was of course a good deal alarmed, but luckily his alarm by no means suspended the exercise of his powers, and the speech was received, as it well deserved, with the utmost applause and favour by the House. His voice and manner both excellent. Take notice, I am not merely telling you my own opinion, but that of far more competent judges.

'Pray don't desert my dinner on Saturday in order to behold him in glory at the K. of Clubs.

'I am far from well, and go not out except in a carriage.

'Yours always most truly,
'J. W. WARD.

'Don't forget the present you have promised to make me.'

There were great hopes at this time among Richard Sharp's friends that he would take a distinguished position in Parliament. Mackintosh, writing to Whishaw in February, 1808, expressed his delight at Sharp's rejection from the Committee of Finance in the new Parliament, which he hoped would rouse his strength.

Hence the delight expressed by his friends at the success of his speech on the Copenhagen expedition. It was not followed up. Sharp was more fitted to be, as he was for a generation, the private counsellor of statesmen than a prominent politician in that stormy time. His parliamentary career was abruptly closed. This Parliament, short and evil as its days were, stands distinguished in history for performing what Lord Grenville, without any exaggeration, described as one of the most glorious acts which had ever been done by any assembly of any nation in the world. It abolished the Slave Trade. An attempt to make one further step in emancipation was stopped by the king, the ministry resigned, the Parliament was dissolved, the brief gleam of political spring passed away, and the winter of exclusion and depression closed over the Whigs for more than twenty years.

A personal interest in the political fortunes of his friends constituted in these days the whole of Rogers's political activity. Fully as he always sympathised with the Whig leaders, he took no part in political life. He had gone to see Gilbert Wakefield in prison in 1800, and he paid a similar visit to Sir Francis Burdett in 1811; he was often at Wimbledon on a visit to Horne Tooke, and nobody sat at Rogers's table without being conscious that Fox's memory pervaded the house. But though Rogers had voted for Horne Tooke in the Westminster election of 1796, when his own brother-in-law, Sutton Sharpe, had taken part in his nomination, he never again exercised the franchise till Sir Samuel Romilly stood for the same constituency in 1818. His name is found in all the Whig memoirs of these times;[1] but it is as a figure in society. He was enjoying life, reaping the full satisfaction of his uneclipsed poetic fame, making a young man's use—for at forty-five he was still young —of his wealth and his opportunities, with only the occasional drawback of imperfect health. Writing to Miss Godfrey in March, 1807, Moore asks her, 'How go on Spencer and Rogers and the rest of those agreeable rattles who seem to think life such a treat that they can never get enough of it?' This seems to show that Rogers at this period gave his friends the impression that he enjoyed life. Yet there is ample evidence that he did not live for mere enjoyment, and that the pleasure he chiefly sought was that of intercourse with the most eminent people of his time.

There are letters of this date from Miss Joanna Baillie and Mrs. Barbauld, which show that he was on close terms of friendship with those eminent women. A call on Mrs. Inchbald,[2] then in the height of her fame, brought from her a curious and characteristic apology.

Mrs. Inchbald to Samuel Rogers.

'My dear Sir,—I consider myself so much obliged to you for the attention you paid me in calling yesterday

---

[1] For example :—'*July* 16, 1808.—Went to dinner at Ward's. Rogers, Lord Ponsonby, Lord Cowper, Lord Morpeth.' '*June* 16, 1809.—Dined at Rogers's. Lord and Lady Charlemont, Elliot, Horner.'—*Diary of the Right Hon. W. Windham*, pp. 477, 492.

[2] Rogers quotes 'an excellent writer' in one of his notes to the poem of 'Human Life.' The quotation is from Mrs. Inchbald's *Nature and Art.* He met her one day in London, and was told that she had been calling on her friends, but none of them would see her. 'I knew Mrs. Siddons

that I cannot resist my desire to apologise for your reception.

'For the sake of a romantic view of the Thames, I have shut myself in an apartment which will not admit of a second person. It is therefore my wish to be thought never at home. But when the scruples of the persons who answer for me baffle this design, and I have received a token of regard which flatters me, I take the liberty thus to explain my situation. Dear sir, with much esteem, your most humble servant,

'E. INCHBALD.

'16th March, 1808.'

Among the acquaintances made at this time was Uvedale Price, one of the quaintest figures, the best letter writers, and the most eccentric people of his time. He was celebrated as an improver of landscapes, and had published, in 1794, an 'Essay on the Picturesque as compared with the Sublime and Beautiful, and on the Use of Studying Pictures for the purpose of Improving real Landscapes.' He became a warm friend of Rogers, and found the comfortable house in St. James's Place a most convenient lodging in many of his visits to London. Rogers occasionally visited him at his house at Foxley, in Herefordshire, and it was there, in August, 1808, that General Fitzpatrick gave Rogers some of the stories of Fox which are recorded in the 'Recollections.' One of the most characteristic of these was told of Uvedale Price himself, who thought himself the most accomplished

was at home,' she complained, 'yet I was not admitted.' She shed tears. Rogers tried to comfort her, and asked her to go home with him and dine; she refused. She died in 1821.

of critics. Fox allowed him to see the MS. of his
'History of the Reign of James the Second.' He made
a multitude of verbal criticisms upon it and sent them
to Fox, who threw them into the fire. Fitzpatrick told
Rogers that Mackintosh had offered, and Fox had accepted, his assistance in that History.

Rogers was already in correspondence with Wordsworth and Walter Scott. The earliest letter of Wordsworth's which has been preserved, arose out of the
collection made for a family in Easdale whose parents
had perished in a storm.

Wordsworth to Samuel Rogers.

'Grasmere: Sept. 29, 1808.

'My dear Sir,—I am greatly obliged to you for your
kind exertions in favour of our Grasmere Orphans, and
for your own contribution. It will give you pleasure to
hear that there is the best prospect of the children being
greatly benefited in every respect by the sum which has
been raised, amounting to nearly 500*l.* They are placed
in three different houses in the Vale of Grasmere, and
are treated with great tenderness. They will be carefully taught to read and write, and, when they are of a
proper age, care will be taken to put them forward in life
in the most advisable manner.

'The bill you sent me—31*l.* 8*s.*—I have already paid
into the hands of the Secretary.

'I was glad to hear that our friend Sharp was so
much benefited in his health by his late visit to our
beautiful country. We passed one pleasant day together,
but we were unlucky, upon the whole, in not seeing

much of each other, as a more than usual part of his time was spent about Keswick and Ulswater. I am happy to find that we coincide in opinion about Crabbe's verses, for poetry in no sense can they be called. Sharp is also of the same opinion. I remember that I mentioned in my last that there was nothing in the last publication so good as the description of the parish workhouse, apothecary, &c. This is true, and it is no less true that the passage which I commended is of no great merit, because the description, at the best of no high order, is, in the instance of the apothecary, inconsistent —that is, false. It no doubt sometimes happens, but, as far as my experience goes, very rarely, that country practitioners neglect and brutally treat their patients; but what kind of men are they who do so?—not apothecaries like Crabbe's professional, pragmatical coxcombs, "all pride, generally neat, business, bustle, and conceit" —no, but drunken reprobates, frequenters of boxing-matches, cock-fightings, and horse-races. These are the men who are hard-hearted with their patients, but any man who attaches so much importance to his profession as to have strongly caught, in his dress and manner, the outward formalities of it may easily indeed be much occupied with himself, but he will not behave towards his "victims," as Mr. Crabbe calls them, in the manner he has chosen to describe. After all, if the picture were true to nature, what claim would it have to be called poetry? At the best, it is the meanest kind of satire, except the merely personal. The sum of all is, that nineteen out of twenty of Crabbe's pictures are mere matters of fact, with which the Muses have just about as much to do as they have with a collection of medical reports or of law cases.

'How comes it that you never favour these mountains with a visit? You ask how I have been employed. You do me too much honour, and I wish I could reply to the question with any satisfaction. I have written since I saw you about 500 lines of my long Poem, which is all I have done. What are you doing? My wife and sister desire to be remembered by you, and believe me, my dear sir,

'With great truth, yours,
'WM. WORDSWORTH.

'We are here all in a rage about the Convention in Portugal. If Sir Hew were to show his face among us, or that other doughty knight, Sir Arthur, the very boys would hiss them out of the Vale.'

The long poem Wordsworth had then in hand was 'The Excursion,' from which he seems, after writing to Rogers, to have turned aside to give vent to his rage in a pamphlet on 'The Convention of Cintra,' and to express other feelings in two noble sonnets on the same subject.

A short note from Rogers to Richard Sharp curiously illustrates one of the differences between those days and our own. Sharp writes to ask Rogers to go down to Mickleham that they might go together to Leatherhead fair. Rogers replies on the 6th of October, 1808—

'I shall have great pleasure in accepting your kind invitation. Who can resist round-abouts and see-saws, and gilt gingerbread and King Holofernes? I cannot for one. Do you go on horseback? If you do, perhaps we can meet on the road. I hope the sun will shine upon us.

'If I don't enlist at the fair, it is my intention to go on to Brighton on Wednesday.'

He seems to have gone on to Brighton as he intended, and a letter to his sister Sarah contains glimpses of some interesting people—

Samuel Rogers to Sarah Rogers.

'Brighton: 26 Oct. 1808.

'When I received your kind letter, my dear Sarah, I felt a strong wish to answer it directly, but at that time Mrs. M. was writing, and I have since put it off from time to time—I am sure I don't know why—for I never feel more pleasure than when I sit down to write to you. I did indeed fear you would be cruelly disappointed. [He then refers at some length to a picture about which this cruel disappointment had been experienced, and continues.] But the pen-drawing done in the Temple, slight as it is, is however something to remember by. It was done as you sat, and it tells you how you used to sit together, and there are some circumstances about it, my dear, dear Sarah, that would make me value it more than any picture. I rejoice to hear you are passing your time comfortably—pleasantly, I hope. Perhaps you have left Quarry Bank and are now at Cheadle. But I think it best to direct to Mrs. Greg's, to whom pray remember me very affectionately. Henry, I thought, seemed to like his journey pretty well, though he made it very short, and caught cold at Brighton, as I have done.

I left town to go again to Leatherhead fair, which was very pretty, though the day was not so fine as last year. I dined afterwards at Norbury, and there met a Miss Barton, a cousin of Mrs. Wm. Lock, who inquired very particularly after you. She had seen you, I believe, at Cheadle. Mrs. Lock's booth cleared 50*l.* the first day. Mrs. Fox was there; she had come over from St. Anne's. Miss Willoughby, she says, is very poorly. She says we must go to her fair next year—and, indeed, I wish now we had paid her a visit. The next night I dined and slept at Chart, Sir Charles Talbot's, and the day afterwards came here, riding all the way (except one stage in a returned chaise). Alas! I met with a sad misfortune the other day. I was walking the poor old mare very near my lodgings, when down she came and cut her knees to the bone; but she kept her head erect, poor thing! so I felt little or no shock, and I am happy to think she has never thrown me in the fifteen years we have spent together. They say she will never do again, so I must look out for some place of rest for her, if she is not shot, like Golumpus and the other old worthies of the family. I have been here a fortnight to-morrow, and have a very small house in a street leading from the Marine Parade, which last is now very expensive, and which is very gay on a fine day.

'Before our old house there now stands a group of asses and ponies for the idle and luxurious. My great resource is Lady Donegal and Miss Godfrey, with whom I pass most of my time, though I have twice dined with Lady Jersey, whose daughter is still lingering, very cheerful, but with no chance of recovery. Every evening she flatters herself that her feverish fit will not come on, and then it comes. She does not leave her room. The weather has been sunshiny but very cold, but now it is very forlorn indeed, and nothing stirring but the winds and waves—a circumstance I am not sorry for, as I seldom stir out but to catch cold. I am now reading the Italian again, and am in the horrors of the Inquisition. I wish you were with me, but wishing does no good. I sometimes go to the music on the Parade, but, as you remember, it is a very cold place. Brighton at present is very full. The warmest place is the front of the Marine Library, and a never-failing scene of entertainment. The scarlet cloaks are innumerable. The Grattans are at Worthing, where they went the week after they dined with us. Mr. G. is now with them. They come here as soon as lodgings are cheaper. S. Boddington has been there for six weeks with Grace, and has just taken a house here in the New Steyne. He is now in town, but she is here with her *gouvernante*, and I have just been paying her a visit. She is really growing, I think, a fineish girl, but she has a bad cold just now, and is almost as deaf as her mother used to be. I have just received a letter from Wm. Maltby. He stands for Porson's place at the Institution, "by the deliberate advice," he says, "of those who are most likely to know the disposition of the electors." He says he has daily communication with Henry on this subject. John Mallet was here last week, but is now gone.

'Westall has been sketching boats and fishermen for a few days here; he went to-day. Lady Donegal goes on Friday, and I go on Monday to Glynde, a seat of Lord Hampden's near Lewes, for three or four days, and then return home. I once thought of Crewe and of

Cheadle, my dear Sarah, but at present I feel chilly and frightened at the thoughts of such an expedition. When do you mean to come back to us? I hope the time won't be long, but of the time exactly you are not unfortunately complete mistress. Pray remember me very particularly to all at Cheadle, about whom I feel just as warmly as I ever did, notwithstanding the letter which I thought it my duty to write when acting in my commercial character for others, as well as myself. The Prince is not here this season, but his stables are nearly finished, and are exactly like one of those Indian mausoleums in Daniel's views. They are really very pretty, and are done by Porden, who is building Lord Grosvenor's near you. Here is hunting, but I am now too old for even such a part as I used to take in it. We have had a most miserable supply of fish, but this place is now a town, shooting out in all directions but one, where the sea presents a small obstacle. The George Edisons are here. Farewell, my dear Sarah! Pray write to me in town, and believe me to be,

'Ever yours,
'SAML. ROGERS.

'Henry wants me to write to Parsons on his marriage: what am I to say?'

A great part of the correspondence with Richard Sharp during this part of Rogers's life was devoted to the poem of Columbus. Rogers records in his Commonplace Book that he was fourteen years at work upon this poem. This means that he began it as soon as his 'Epistle to a Friend' had been published in 1798, but did not finally issue it till 1812, and that during the whole of that time he was more or less occupied with it. It was his custom in these days to read parts of it to his friends, among whom it became a familiar topic of conversation. It is mentioned in their letters to Rogers, who is constantly urged to publish it. A characteristic letter from Erskine shows not only the curiosity Columbus had excited, but the estimation in which Rogers's poetry was held by the most acute minds when this century was young.

Lord Erskine to Samuel Rogers.

'Dear Rogers,—As I have always great pleasure in visiting you, I should have been sorry to be engaged (as I am) at York Place on Saturday if I had not resolved not to come to St. James's Place *any more till I see Columbus*, as you promised long ago.

'I had not read the Pleasures of Memory from the time of its first publication till last week, and I cannot find words to tell you how delighted I was with the reconsideration of its beauties. I admit that its author ought to pause before he publishes, as it is not easy not to disappoint those who, in the double sense of the expression, have *the Pleasures of Memory*; but let me see Columbus, and I will give you my opinion.

'Yours ever,
'ERSKINE.'

There is a further testimony to the literary position Rogers occupied in the desire of Gifford to secure his assistance in the newly-established *Quarterly Review*, Gifford asked Hoppner to conduct the negotiation which he opened in the following letter :—

John Hoppner to Samuel Rogers.

'Dear Rogers,—You are too much a man of the world to embark in any undertaking that has not received the sanction of public approbation. I can, with a little more confidence, endeavour now to press you into the service of the *Quarterly Review*, since the work increases in circulation to an extent that much exceeds the expectation of the most sanguine of the undertakers. It is the wish of the leaders of this *Review* that you would assist in supporting it with your talents occasionally, leaving it to your own choice to remain concealed, or to claim the honours of your pen. The work they wish you to take in hand, at present, is Shee's last publication, the notes to which I propose to examine in conjunction with you. I am at present employed in dissecting Hayley's Life of Romney, which is immediately wanted, and I have neither health nor leisure enough to undertake both for the next number. Have the goodness to inform me, in the course of a day or two, whether you are inclined, or not, to accede to this proposal. It is at the express desire of G. Ellis and Gifford that I press you upon this subject.

'The last week was an eventful one to me and my family. I arrived on Saturday se'ennight at Ryde, after rather a fatiguing journey on horseback. On Sunday I was with difficulty kept awake the whole day, and went in consequence early to bed. About ten o'clock the same evening Mrs. Hoppner found me on the floor, and I lay from that time in a state of total insensibility for two nights and two days. From this stupefaction I was with difficulty roused, having cataplasm to my feet, a blister on my head, and one on my back so large as to flay it from the shoulder to the loins. To speak a truth, they used me like a horse, and I believe a less degree of irritation would have [sufficed]. . . The blisters, however, did their business so well that I was enabled to get downstairs on Thursday. On Friday I walked down the town, that people might see I was not dead, as was reported. On Saturday I rode on horseback, and to-day I feel better than I have done for years. You may imagine all this appears to me like a dream. I have no recollection of being taken ill, and can scarce credit my own feelings sufficiently to persuade myself I am well.

'I have more letters to write, and must therefore take a hasty leave, requesting you to believe me,

'Yours very faithfully,

'J. HOPPNER.

'Ryde, Isle of Wight: Monday.'

Rogers had met Hoppner at the house of his late brother-in-law, Sutton Sharpe. Hoppner, as his letter indicates, was a very choleric person. He and Rogers were members of a club called 'The Council of Trent,' because it consisted of thirty persons; and on Rogers once proposing an artist whom Hoppner disliked, he wrote him a letter of violent reproach and abuse. Hoppner was the son of a German attendant at Windsor Castle, and in his boyhood had been a chorister at the Royal Chapel. He and Gifford were closely-attached friends, but their quarrels were the amusement of their acquaintances. He was popular in society and was to be met everywhere, though, like Moore, he accepted invitations to great houses and left his wife to mope in solitude at home. He suffered from chronic disease of the liver, and died a few months after the letter to Rogers was written. Rogers declined to write for the *Quarterly* or to be associated with the men who had founded it. He was opposed, moreover, to anonymous writing, and regarded anonymous criticism as a kind of fighting in a mask. His only contribution to this kind of literature was a part of a review of Cary's Dante in the *Edinburgh Review*.

A further testimony to Rogers's literary position is contained in the following letter.

Walter Scott to Samuel Rogers.

' My dear Rogers,—I am about to ask a great boon of you, which I shall hold an especial courtesy if you can find in your heart to comply with. I have hampered myself by a promise to a young bookseller, whom I am for various reasons desirous to befriend, that I would look over and make additions to a little miscellany of poetry which he has entitled " English Minstrelsy," and on which his brother, James Ballantyne, the Scottish Bodoni, intends to exert the utmost extent of his typographical skill. The selection is chiefly from the smaller pieces of dead authors, but it would be very imperfect without a few specimens from the present Masters of the Lyre. I have never told you how high my opinion, so far as it is worth anything, ranks you in that honoured class. But I am now called on to say, in my own personal vindication, that no collection of the kind can be completed without a specimen from the author of the Pleasures of

——,¹ and therefore to transfer all responsibility from myself to you, I make the present application. Beggars should not be choosers; therefore I most generously abandon to you the choice of what you will give my begging-box, and am only importunate that you will not turn me empty from your door. I would not willingly exert my influence with you in vain, nor have my Miscellany so imperfect as it will be without something of yours.

'Why won't you think of coming to see our lands of mist and snow? Not that I have the hardness of heart to wish you and George Ellis here at this moment, for it would be truly the meeting of the weird sisters in thunder, lightning, and in rain. The lightning splintered an oak here before my door last week with such a concussion that I thought all was gone to wrack. I have pretty good nerves for one of the irritable and sensitive race we belong to, but I question whether even the poet laureate would have confided composedly in the *sic evitabile fulmen* annexed to his wreath of bays.

'Believe me, dear Rogers,

'Ever yours most sincerely,

'WALTER SCOTT.

'Ashestiel by Selkirk: 18 August [1809].'

In answer to this letter Rogers seems to have sent a copy of the small poem, addressed to the Duchess of St. Albans,² on the death of her sister, the wife of James,

---

¹ The word 'Hope' is crossed out in the MS., but no other word is substituted for it. It should be 'Pleasures of Memory.'

² In the Poems the stanzas have only the heading 'To . . .,' with a note at the bottom of the page, 'on the death of her sister.'

afterwards Viscount Macduff, who died at Edinburgh—of a fever it was said at the time—in December, 1805. The lines 'On a Voice that had been Lost' belong to the same period. They were addressed to Miss Crewe, who, as we learn from Scott's letter, lost two notes of her voice in a visit to Scotland in the winter of the same year. The following is Scott's letter of acknowledgment for the poem on Mrs. Duff—

Walter Scott to Samuel Rogers.

'Accept my best thanks, my dear Rogers, for your letter with the beautiful enclosure, a delightful though a melancholy tribute to the fate of poor Mrs. Duff, with whom I had the pleasure to be acquainted. I dined in company with her during the time that the hidden infection was in her veins, and have often since reflected upon her manner and conversation during the course of that day. She mentioned the story of the dog repeatedly (indeed, it seemed to hang upon her spirits), but never dropt the slightest hint of his having bitten, or rather grazed, the skin of her face. It is a melancholy recollection, and your pathetic verses have awakened it very strongly. Many thanks to you, however, for the gratification they have afforded me, though chastened by these sad reflections.

'I rejoice to hear that you are coming forth soon. I hope your little jewel, the Columbiad, is at length to be drawn out of the portfolio and given to the press. I also hope to meet with another old and admired acquaintance, the copy of verses addressed to Miss Crewe when she lost two notes of her voice in our rude climate. Pray do not linger too long over your proof-sheets, but let us soon see what we have long longed to see.

'I have been deeply concerned for Mr. Canning's wound;[1] he is one of the few, very few, statesmen who unite an ardent spirit of patriotism to the talents necessary to render that living spirit efficient, and I don't see how the present ministry can stand without him. That, however, would be the least of my regrets were I certain that his health was restored.

'The weather here has been dreary indeed, seldom two good days in continuance, and though not much afraid of rain in any moderate quantity, I have been almost obliged, like Hamlet, to forego a custom of my exercise, and amuse myself within doors the best way I can, in the course of which seclusion I have, of course, blotted much paper.

'Believe me, dear Rogers, ever your truly obliged,
'W. SCOTT.

'Ashestiel: 4th October, 1809.'

This letter, written nearly three years after the event, gives the only indication of the circumstances which made Mrs. Duff's death peculiarly painful, and explains the line—
That in her veins a secret horror slept.

One of the few letters from Luttrell which have been preserved illustrates the sort of life Rogers and his friends were living. It is a fit introduction of his name

[1] Canning's duel with Lord Castlereagh took place on the 21st of September. Canning was wounded in the thigh, but on the 11th of October he had so far recovered as to be able to attend the levée held on that day and to give up the seals of office.

into Rogers's biography, though it suggests the association of Rogers with Luttrell's schemes of amusement. Rogers had a high opinion of Luttrell's talent, spoke of him as a pleasant companion and brilliant talker, and expressed regret that he gave up nearly all his time to people of fashion.

Henry Luttrell to Samuel Rogers.

'Brocket Hall: Wednesday, Sept. 20 [1809].

'My dear Rogers,—It is singular enough that just as your letter was put into my hands, I had determined to write to you by this day's post. Now, and at all times, I feel flattered and happy to be associated in any scheme of amusement or any arrangement of society with you, and I was, with this object in view, preparing to communicate my autumnal movements and to inquire into yours. I am desired, on the part of Lord and Lady Cowper, to say that they will be most happy to receive you at Panshanger as soon as they remove there, which will be very early in the next month. Our intended progress in the meantime is as follows. From hence to town on Friday, on Monday next to Woolbeding for four or five days, and thence to Petworth for two or three, after which the Cowpers certainly return to Panshanger, where they will remain for the rest of October. Now what I should like, if it suits you, would be to meet you at the Deepdene on my return from Petworth, and, having paid our visit there, return with you to London for a couple of days. We might then start together for Panshanger. I hold myself in a manner pledged to Hope, deeming it as ungracious not to *accept* as not to *give* a second invitation, as the natural conclusion to be drawn from both is the same, that, on trial, the parties have not been pleased with each other. Yet I should not choose to encounter him alone, as the apprehension of his embarrassment would embarrass me. As it is possible I may be in town even to-morrow, pray let a few lines be deposited in my letter-box at Albany to say how far the arrangement I here propose can be made to square with your convenience. If it should not suit, I am, after the Woolbeding and Petworth visits are spun off my reel, quite at your disposal for any other that may be more agreeable to you.

'I hope you have not quite abandoned your intention of a trip to Tunbridge, before the possibility of fine weather is extinct, as I have a most longing desire to see the lions of the Pantiles under your auspices. This I would do either after or before Panshanger at your option. God bless you, and believe me, my dear Rogers,

'Ever most truly yours,

'H. LUTTRELL.

'Am I justified or no in considering the occasional address attempted to be spoken at the opening of C. G. Theatre [1] as the very worst copy of verses in any language, and the following line—

Solid our building, heavy our expense—

---

[1] The new theatre was opened on Monday the 17th of September. The address was spoken by John Kemble in the midst of an uproar which made it entirely inaudible. It contained fifty lines. The last four were:

'Solid our building, heavy our expense,
We rest our claim on your munificence—
What ardour plans a nation's taste to raise,
A nation's iberality repays.'

as the worst in it, and consequently the worst in the world, as I am inclined to do, *nisi quid tu docte Trebati dissentis* ' ?

This literary and other correspondence completely exhibits the position of consideration and esteem which Rogers had attained at the close of the first decade of the nineteenth century. His social position may be illustrated by a brief letter addressed to him in the summer of 1810.

'Kensington: Sunday, 19 August [1810].

'Dear Mr. Rogers,—I am commanded by H.R.H. the Princess of Wales to say she will call for you in St. James's Place to-morrow evening at eight o'clock to take you to the play.

'Pray believe me happy to give you these gracious commands, and allow me to say that I am very sincerely yours,

'Charlotte Maria.'

CHAPTER III.

1810–1812.

Columbus—Letters to Richard Sharp—T. Moore—An Idyll at Hagley—Recollections of Porson, Windham, Cumberland, Horne Tooke—Tooke's Adventures—His Funeral—Rogers and Byron—Meeting of Moore, Campbell, and Byron at Rogers's House—Coleridge's Lecture—' Childe Harold '—Tom Grenville's Criticism on the Poem—Byron and Lord Holland—Rogers at the Lakes—The Mackintoshes and Sharp—Dr. Bell—Wordsworth's Lost Child—Rogers at Ormithwaite, Keswick, Lowther—Lord Lonsdale—Brougham—Rogers at Glenfinnart—Lord Dunmore—Letters to R. Sharp, to H. Rogers, to Sarah Rogers—Letter of Lord Holland—Rogers at Crewe.

THE chief literary occupation of Rogers's life in these years was the poem entitled ' The Voyage of Columbus.' The theme is a great one, and it fully possessed his imagination. His object was to call up the great navigator ' in his habit as he lived,' and at the same time to give lyrical expression to the feelings which inspired and sustained him. He desired to transfuse into a modern poem the spirit of the old Spanish chroniclers of the sixteenth century, with their full belief in the supernatural, their strong religious feeling, and their wonder at an achievement which seemed almost too great for unaided man. He points out in his preface that 'no National Poem appeared on the subject,' and that 'no Camoens did honour to the genius and the virtues' of Columbus, though the materials were surely not unpoetical. Rogers's design was to reproduce the warmth of colour and the wildness of imagery which the old writers employed, and this design led him to conceive the idea of a poem written not long after the death of Columbus, 'when the consequences of the Discovery were beginning to unfold themselves, but while the minds of men were still clinging to the superstitions of their fathers.' The idea was never fully worked out, and the poem was published under the title of 'Fragments of the Voyage of Columbus.' He had been at work on it for a dozen years, when in 1810 he was induced to put it into type. It had been brought out in many a talk with his friends after breakfast or after dinner, when parts of it had been read and discussed, and he had conveyed to them his own enthusiasm for the subject. When it was at length in type it was sent to some of his friends for criticism, and many of his letters to Richard Sharp, and some of those to Moore, at this period are full of alternative lines, arguments, suggestions, replies to criticisms, and pleas for a decisive judgment. He never seems to have been satisfied with the poem. He had found, twenty years before, that his chief faculty lay not in lyrical passion, but in quiet, gentle description and meditation, and he hesitated long in giving a second lyrical poem to the world. Line after line, stanza after stanza, were discussed in letters to Richard Sharp. One of the earliest and one of the latest of these numerous letters will sufficiently show the nature of this correspondence. Soon after the first proof had been sent out, Rogers wrote to Richard Sharp—

'My dear Friend,—*Eccolo*. Pray tell me frankly. I have not yet quite learnt to like the expression, though I think it a very important addition. If you see anything to wish altered, in language or punctuation, in the lines or the note, now is, alas! the time. "Tho' come it will" sounds ill in my ear—what do you think?

'"Cazziva, gifted by the Gods to know"—would perhaps throw more light on the new passage, but the line would suffer on the whole.

'If you can call, I shall be at home every evening this week; if not, pray write me a line of advice or encouragement; for I want them.

'"Shall" in the third line is scriptural, but I fear not grammatical.

'Ever yours,
'S. R.

'Thursday night (15 Feb., 1810).

'How do you like the black line in "Signs like the ethereal bow"?[1] I have some thoughts of altering the stops.

> Unseen, unheard! Hence, Minister of Ill!
> Hence, 'tis not yet the hour—tho' come it will!
> They that foretold, too soon shall they fulfil;

But I believe it is best [as] printed.'

In a postscript to a letter from Keswick, two years and a half later, he writes—

> Say who first pass'd the portals of the West,
> And the great secret of the Deep possess'd,

---

[1] Canto xii., line 13. 'Signs like the ethereal bow—that shall endure.'

> Who first the standard of his Faith unfurl'd
> On the dread confines of an unknown world;
> Sung ere his coming, and by Heaven design'd
> To lift the veil that covered half mankind.
> Oh, I would tell of Him! My hour draws near,
> And He will prompt me when I faint with fear.
> . . . Alas, He hears me not! He cannot hear!
>
> Him would I now invoke! My hour draws near;
> And He can prompt me when I faint with fear.
> . . . Alas, He hears me not! He cannot hear.

The first of these stanzas is an alternative beginning of the first canto. The present beginning is—

> Say who, when age on age had rolled away,
> And still, as sunk the golden Orb of day,
> The seamen watched him, while he lingered here,
> With many a wish to follow, many a fear,
> And gazed and gazed and wondered where he went,
> So bright his path, so glorious his descent,
> Who first adventured—In his birth obscure
> Yet born to build a Fame that should endure,
> Who the great secret of the Deep possessed,
> And, issuing through the portals of the West,
> Fearless, resolved, with every sail unfurled,
> Planted his standard on the Unknown World?
> Him by the Paynim bard descried of yore,
> And, ere his coming, sung on either shore,
> Him, ere the birth of Time by Heaven designed
> To lift the veil that covered half mankind;
> None can exalt . . .

The last three lines of the suggested opening appear in the published poem at the beginning of the twelfth canto, which opens thus—

Still would I speak of Him before I went,
Who among us a life of sorrow spent,
And, dying, left a world his monument;
Still, if the time allowed! My Hour draws near,
But He will prompt me when I faint with fear.
. . . Alas! He hears me not! He cannot hear.

This correspondence, with its minute discussion of alternative lines and phrases, was not wholly one-sided. Richard Sharp, too, consulted Rogers about lines and phrases in his own poems. The following letter bears on Richard Sharp's 'Epistle to a Friend on his Marriage.'

Samuel Rogers to Richard Sharp.

'My dear Friend,—The alterations are all good, but I confess there is a strength of expression in the line—

And weeds soon hide his unfrequented tomb,

which I should be sorry to part with.

'I may be wrong, but I think Pope or Dryden might have written the following—

He dies—no traces from oblivion save,
And weeds soon hide his unfrequented grave.

But they are all good, and you cannot choose amiss. Your last reading is certainly most artist-like; but there is more feeling, I think, more forlornness, in the last line as it stood at first.

'Ever yours,
'S. R.

'I am rather for "mourn his doom," I don't know why, than "weep his doom." Perhaps after all I like this best—

> He dies and is forgot—none mourn his doom,
> And weeds soon hide his unfrequented tomb.' [1]

In his 'Commonplace Book' Rogers makes the following remarks on his own poem:—'It was, indeed, a singular story to choose, in which almost the only passion called forth into exercise from the beginning to the end of it is Fear, the most selfish and least dignified of all the passions; and Fear in its least dignified character—a fear arising from ignorance, such as children feel in the dark. The only exception, if there is one, is the hero, but, like most other heroes, he exhibits none of the passions in any pathetic degree.' The poem bears evidence of Rogers's admiration for America—a feeling which lasted all his life.

> Assembling here all nations shall be blest,
> The sad be comforted, the weary rest;
> Untouched shall drop the fetters from the slave.

The last line was prophetic; but he did not live to see its fulfilment. His Whig principles came out in the opening to the sixth canto—written, it should be remembered, in the very height of the struggle against Napoleon—

> War and the Great in War let others sing,
> Havoc and spoil, and tears and triumphing;
> The morning-march that flashes to the sun,
> The feast of vultures when the day is done;
> And the strange tale of many slain for one!

[1] The lines as they stand in the poem as it was published in Sharp's *Letters and Essays* read—

> 'He dies and is forgot! Scarce known his doom,
> And weeds soon hide his unfrequented tomb.'

> I sing a Man, amidst his sufferings here,
> Who watched and served in humbleness and fear;
> Gentle to others, to himself severe.

This was written and published before Byron's 'Childe Harold;' and Mr. Samuel Sharpe reminds us that it was many years after peace had been established, and after he had become acquainted with the Duke of Wellington, that he added the note to these lines beginning with the words, 'Not but that in the profession of arms there are, at all times, many noble natures.'

Next to Richard Sharp, one of Rogers's most constant companions at this time was Tom Moore. His life, for some years, might almost be written out of Moore's letters and diaries. The diary shows that when Moore gets back to his London lodgings in 1810, after two years' absence, almost his first thought is of Rogers, who is away from home. In May, 1811, Moore meets Jeffrey at Rogers's at a Sunday-morning breakfast, and on the following Tuesday takes his new wife to dine at Rogers's to meet Lady Donegal. In the summer 'Rogers is at his brother's in Shropshire.' In January, 1812, he tells Lady Donegal that 'Rogers has been at Lord Robert Spencer's this fortnight past, but I have this instant got a note from him asking me to a *tête-à-tête* dinner.' A little later he tells his mother that Rogers has sent him a most beautiful reading-desk, which puts the rest of his furniture to the blush. 'I took Bessy to Lord Moira's,' he writes to Miss Godfrey, 'and she was not half so much struck with its grandeur as I expected. She said, in coming out, "I like Mr. Rogers's house ten times better;"' but she loves everything by association, and she was very happy in Rogers's house.' Rogers, in a letter to Moore, gives quite an idyllic account of his visit to the house his eldest brother Daniel, at Wassall, near Stourbridge.

Samuel Rogers to Thomas Moore.[1]

'Aberystwith: Sept. 20th, 1811

'My dear Moore,—You know me and my faults too well to be much surprised at my long silence, and now (forgive me for my selfishness) I am not sure I should have written at all but to make you write, and tell me something about yourself, &c. What have you done? Is the dramatic concluded and the epic begun? Are you now in a pavilion on the banks of the Tigris; or in the shape of a nightingale singing love-songs to a rose in the gardens of Cashmere? As for me, I have been visiting an elder brother, who, many years ago, retired from the world to cultivate his own patrimonial fields and read his Homer under the shade of his own beech-trees near Hagley. His farm is beautiful, very woody and uneven, and full of little dingles, and copses, and running waters. A green lane a mile long leads to the house, which overlooks the fields. The prospect, enlivened with a few cottages, is bound by a chain of hills, which affect almost to be mountains, and beyond these appear, every now and then, over their heads, such as are fully entitled to the name, and as blue as a blue atmosphere can make them. From one circumstance or another, it is now some years since I came here; his girls, now being lovely, are nearly grown-up, and I am half tempted to get up every time they come into the room. It makes

[1] Printed in Moore's *Life and Letters*, vol. viii. pp. 94-96.

me feel very old, and very melancholy too sometimes. I think of the time when they used to sit on my knee and tease me to tell them stories of the world they were about to enter into. The other day it was proposed to dine in a wood, and I was surprised when I came to find everything set out there in a Hermitage. The tables, the chairs, napkins, knives, and eatables—all carried on their heads and under their arms; not a servant assisted. How little, said I to myself, when I saw them smiling over their work, would the fine ladies in town be inclined to think of such a thing! But we are all transported to a very different scene—a bleak mountain on a seashore in Wales. How long I shall remain here I cannot say —probably a month. So pray write me a line in the course of a fortnight at least. Rebuke me by setting me a better example. I have received a letter from Mrs. Grattan, and as I am writing a line to her and Lady D., shall inclose both under cover to G. My book, I fear, is at a standstill. I have written but a very few lines, and those of no moment. Some time or other you shall see them. I hope to be in town in about five weeks.

'Ever yours,
'SAML. ROGERS.

'I am very anxious about your proceedings with Arnold, and am continually looking out for an opera. Have you given it a name? My sister desires to be kindly remembered to you.'

Rogers's visit to his brother revived many old associations. They were on the most affectionate terms, and Rogers always felt that his father's strong resentment at Dan's marriage with his cousin was unjust. He was forty-eight and unmarried, and could not help feeling how much he had missed, whenever he saw the domestic happiness in which his brother lived. Friends of his early days were dropping off. Porson, of whom he had good stories to tell to the end of his life, had died in 1808. Rogers had been one of his fast friends, and some notes of his conversation are preserved in the 'Recollections.' He prefaces the few pages thus devoted to the great Grecian by assuring his readers that Porson was not more remarkable for his learning than for his acuteness and correctness of thought. 'Through his whole life,' says Rogers, 'whether in his morning or his evening hours—(there is a world of significance in the fact that Rogers makes the distinction)—he was never heard to utter a mean or licentious sentiment.' This testimony is unusually valuable, for Rogers was in a position to know. Porson often dined with him, and his influence kept him sober; but such was his desire to drink that he would slip back into the dining-room, pour together the drops of wine left by the guests in their glasses, and drink the mixture. Rogers took him one evening to a party at William Spencer's to meet some women of fashion who were curious to see him. He was but half sober, and he entertained them by reciting a number of old Vauxhall songs. He talked wildly and they all withdrew but Lady Crewe, who humorously accused him of borrowing a joke from Joe Miller, and got an angry reply. Porson once dined at Hoppner's, but there was no wine, as Mrs. Hoppner was out and had taken the key of the wine cupboard. After dinner Porson insisted that she probably kept a bottle of spirits for her private use in the bedroom, and induced Hoppner to search for it. A bottle was found, and was put before Porson, who pronounced it excellent gin, and finished it. When his wife came home Hoppner taunted her with the concealed dram, and triumphantly assured her that every drop had been drunk. 'Drunk it!' exclaimed Mrs. Hoppner. 'Good God! it was spirits of wine for the lamp.' It was before the days of methylated spirit. Horne Tooke used to say that Porson would drink ink rather than nothing. Rogers always maintained that all this was only the weak and distressing side of a truly great and noble character.

Another friend, whose memory lingered long in Rogers's talk, was William Windham, who died, after an operation by Cline, on the 4th of June, 1810. He had hurt his hip in assisting to save from fire the library of Mr. F. North in Conduit Street; a tumour formed, and he died after its removal. Rogers compared him to the Eddystone lighthouse, dashed at by the waves, but continuing to give its steady light unaffected by the storm. Yet another and still older friend, a frequent visitor at Rogers's house, sometimes a recipient of Rogers's bounty, was Richard Cumberland, the dramatist, who died in 1811. He was the Sir Fretful Plagiary of Sheridan's 'Critic.' In his earlier days Rogers had seen much of Cumberland, and learned much from him, and in later years had abundantly repaid any obligations thus contracted. At Rogers's table recollections of Sir Fretful long lingered in the talk. The next year, 1812, saw the removal of a friend who had exerted far more influence on Rogers, and whose memory he has himself ensured against oblivion. One of the remaining links between Rogers and the political friends of his earlier time was the man for whom as well as for Sheridan he had voted at the Westminster election of 1796. Horne Tooke and he continued close friends to the last. Rogers was a considerable subscriber to the second part of 'The Diversions of Purley,' published in 1805, and was a great admirer of Tooke and of his writings. It was as a talker Horne Tooke was known in this closing period of his life, and twenty-two pages of Rogers's 'Recollections' are occupied with his conversation. 'His present manners and conversation,' says Rogers in a brief prefatory note, 'remind me of a calm sunset in October.'[1] It was the quiet evening of a stormy life. Horne Tooke was living at Wimbledon, cultivating his garden, and delighting his friends with his talk. He had a group of them to dinner every Sunday, and Rogers was often among them. He has put on record in his 'Commonplace Book' some further recollections of Tooke. Among these is the story of Horne Tooke's adventure at Genoa, one of Rogers's stories which I can give in his own words—

'At Genoa, Tooke went to a ball of nobles not less than two hundred years old, and was introduced by the Marquis F——, who asked his opinion of each lady as she entered. He professed to admire all, but one appeared whom he thought truly beautiful. The Marquis

[1] The 'Recollections' were strictly contemporary. They were pu down day by day.

informed her how warmly the Englishman had expressed himself concerning her. She immediately appointed him her *cavaliere servente* to attend her in her coach to mass, conversazione, opera, corso, &c. Her family inquired who he was. Some English had never seen him, others had in France, but none knew him. At last it was found out that he was a heretic priest and not a noble, and to wipe off the indignity it was resolved to place a public stigma upon him. One evening when he called to attend her to a party, she was already gone without him; he looked at his watch, but was in time; he followed her and found her already at cards; she answered his compliments coolly; he ascribed it to his seeming want of punctuality, but knew he could justify himself. He walked from table to table, but was received coolly, though respectfully, by the rest. He walked about, took snuff, and, not conceiving any indignity, felt none. Near two hundred persons there, all at cards. After two hours the mistress of the house joined him, expressed her great concern at what had happened (he could not guess what), and her admiration of his cheerful and pleasant behaviour. Presently the rest followed, and were as officious as they had been distant, and were so charmed with his manners that the young men resolved to make a merry night of it, and, taking him through the streets with them, broke windows, attacked watchmen, &c. The next morning he received a letter from the lady, desiring he would come to her and enter by the *lesser* gate; he did, and found her in tears, when she explained the mystery, and said her family would allow her no longer to be attended by him, but that if he would change places with the *cicisbeo* of M. de Felice (Mallet's daughter), her intimate friend, a heretic and no noble, they should then have the same opportunities of being together. This he joyfully accepted, M. de F. was satisfied with less slavery of attendance, and he stayed nine months at Genoa. When leaving Genoa he was cautioned by her brother to stop short at a *villetta* the first day, as his family had resolved to wipe off the disgrace with his blood. On the road he heard pistols, and found an Englishman slightly wounded in his chaise. "Mr. Horne," says he, "this was intended for you." The lady's name was Signora Durazzo, aunt of the Marquis Brignoli.'[1]

There are other stories of Tooke in the 'Commonplace Book.' One of these relates to his school-days. He ran away three times. At one school in the country he was placed with a Methodist clergyman whose house was frequented by Whitefield and other preachers. At fifteen he ran away from a school at Sevenoaks on account of some indignity, without his hat, on a rainy night. Several boys were despatched to pursue him; he concealed himself in the chimney of an old summer-house. He then ran through several lanes till he met a farmer, of whom he asked the way, and who lifted up his lantern, saying, 'Who's there?' and telling him he would soon have been among the gravel pits.

[1] This story is differently told by Mr. Dyce in his *Table Talk of Samuel Rogers*. Tooke is there said to have heard of the assassination of an Englishman who had been taken for him. This is another proof that Mr. Dyce took down Rogers's stories in the days when Rogers's memory was failing.

He took him home, wet to the skin. His wife dressed him in her husband's clothes, dried his, and the next morning sent him off, at his request, to town in the waggon, lending him a flapped hat. His father received him kindly, and sent him to another school. When he was confined in the King's Bench, an old woman desired to see him. It was the farmer's wife or housekeeper. He gave her five guineas and asked her to call often—'which she has done,' said Tooke.

Tooke won 3,500*l.* in one night, at a party at Aix in the South of France, thought it not reputable to decamp immediately for Italy, whither he was going, played on, and lost all but 500*l.* He wore Sir John Dick's embroidered coat in a sedan chair for a week to save it from being seized under Mr. Grenville's Bill. He was invited to a *tête-à-tête* dinner with Lord Lansdowne. Thirty servants waited at table. 'They are only servants,' said Lord Lansdowne. 'I could have been more open among thirty of your friends,' answered Tooke.

Not only was Rogers fond of telling these stories of Tooke, which I have given in his own words, but Tooke's own stories were current at his table as long as Tooke's memory remained. Here are some in Rogers's words:—

The Prince of Zell was in love with a girl he met in Poitiers, and sent to her to come and marry him. She sent word back that she was not the same woman—that she had suffered from small-pox. He persisted in his addresses. She came and was unaltered. Their only child married George the First.

A French Marquis had been divorced from his wife, and was engaged in a lawsuit with her for the only estate left. Both parties were in Paris to solicit a verdict and make favour with the judges. At length the decision came, and the Marquis flew down to the district in which the estate lay, knocked at the gate, threw open the manor house, announced his success, and gave a fête on the occasion to the congratulating neighbourhood. The next morning, with his hat and stick, he walked off on foot, without paying a livre of the expenses. He had lost the verdict. The scene lay at Blois.

Old Hinchliffe drove a hackney coach, and at last, by his industry, became possessor of a stable yard in Westminster. He gave his son a college education, and he became Bishop of Peterborough.[1] The Bishop one day came to him. 'Father,' says he, 'you must be tired of business, and must wish to retire into the country and live in your own way. Four or five hundred a year is at your service.' 'No, Jack,' he replied, 'I will stay where I am. I am proud of you, and I should hope you are not ashamed of me. All I have I have earned, nor shall it be said that old Ben Hinchliffe was indebted to his son or to any man living for his livelihood.'

When Sir Robert Walpole took the Dutch ambassador to his villa, he was delighted. 'The trees are so beautiful, the views are so beautiful, and then there is no water.'

Rogers records these and other stories of Tooke's, and adds: 'When employed in his great work, Horne Tooke amuses himself with thinking how posterity will feel when they read it, and reflect on the persecutions he has suffered.' Posterity unfortunately reads the great work but little, and has formed a less exalted estimate of its

[1] John Hinchliffe, Bishop of Peterborough from 1769 to 1794.

writer than that which was current among his contemporaries and his immediate successors. Tooke is remembered rather for his political associations than for his literary achievements. His best sayings have been immortalised by Rogers in his incomparable volume of 'Recollections.' Some of these sayings have become current coin. For example, 'There are men who pretend that they come into the world booted and spurred to ride you.' 'Pieces of money are so many tickets for sheep, oxen, &c.' 'When a pension is given, or a salary, a draft is issued on the tiller of the soil.' 'So I understand, Mr. Tooke, that you have all the blackguards in London with you?' said O'Brien to him on the hustings at Westminster. 'I am happy to have it, sir, on such good authority,' replied Tooke. When Judge Ashurst said in one of his charges, 'The law is open to all men, to the poor as well as the rich,' Tooke remarked, 'And so is the London Tavern.' Lord Grey said to him, 'If I was compelled to make a choice, I should prefer despotism to anarchy.' 'Then you would do,' replied Tooke, 'as your ancestors did at the Reformation; they rejected Purgatory and kept Hell.' Tooke's political notoriety as an opponent of the Government brought him much annoyance. Rogers went with him one night to Brandenburgh House to private theatricals, and somebody behind them said, loud enough for Tooke to hear, 'There's that rascal, Horne Tooke.' Tooke showed his annoyance and went home, Rogers going with him, and sitting up very late to listen to his talk. He met with similar insults in coffee-houses. One of his sayings was that, when bad times came, he should go to his garret

VOL. I.   G window and take no part in them but that of a looker on. 'When the surgeons are called in, the physician retires.' He retired to his house on Wimbledon Common, and died there, in the seventy-seventh year of his age, on 18th of March, 1812. Rogers received a characteristic invitation to his funeral from Sir Francis Burdett.

Sir Francis Burdett to Samuel Rogers.

'Piccadilly: March 24, 1812.

'My dear Mr. Rogers,—Our friend Horne Tooke used to express his desire that his few real friends should accompany him to that "everlasting mansion" which, like Timon, he had prepared for himself. As I know he counted you one of that number, and as I believe you would like to pay this last sad tribute to his memory, I take the liberty of acquainting you that his remains will be deposited in his garden at Wimbledon on Friday next, the 27th.[1]

'Yours very sincerely,
'F. BURDETT.

'N.B.—We propose meeting at twelve o'clock precisely at Mr. Tooke's house.'

In the early editions of his 'Epistle to a Friend,' Rogers had paid a compliment to Horne Tooke—

When He who best interprets to mankind
The winged messengers[2] from mind to mind

---

[1] This arrangement was not carried out. After the grave in the garden had been opened, and all the preparations made, it was determined that the body should be interred in the tomb of his sister at Ealing, where the funeral took place on Monday the 30th of March.

[2] The title of Tooke's great work is ΕΠΕΑ ΠΤΕΡΟΕΝΤΑ.

> Leans on his spade and, playful as profound,
> His genius sheds its evening sunshine round,
> Be mine to listen.

These lines were written in 1796, and Rogers acted on them. The evening sunshine of Tooke's genius dwelt long on Rogers's mind, and some years after Tooke's death he made references to him in the poem 'Human Life,' which, though indirect, are clear and unmistakable. No reader can fail to see that he had his old friend in mind when he wrote—

> Thus while the world but claims its proper part
> Oft in the head, but never in the heart,
> His life steals on ; within his quiet dwelling
> That home-felt joy, all other joys excelling,
> Sick of the crowd when enters he—nor then
> Forgets the cold indifference of men.

The trial, too, though placed in an earlier age, was Horne Tooke's, at which Rogers had been present, and the reference to him is clear—

> On through that gate misnamed thro' which before
> Went Sidney, Russell, Raleigh, Cranmer, More,
> Or into twilight within walls of stone,
> Then to the place of trial—

And after his acquittal—

> And now once more where most he loved to be
> In his own fields, breathing tranquillity,
> We hail him—not less happy Fox than thee.

Rogers's acquaintance with Byron, which began within a few months of the death of Horne Tooke, arose out of the quarrel between Byron and Moore. 'English Bards and Scotch Reviewers' was published anonymously in the spring of 1809, and contained a reference to Moore's duel with Jeffrey which Moore thought gave the lie to his own account of that farcical event.[1] When Byron put his name to the poem, Moore sent him a hostile letter, which was delayed by Byron's absence from England. In the autumn of 1811 he returned, and Moore wrote again, proposing that Rogers should see Byron on his behalf in the hope that by a satisfactory explanation Byron would enable Moore ' to seek the honour of being henceforth ranked among his acquaintance.' Rogers at once proposed to play his favourite part of peace-maker by inviting both to meet at his table. Byron was asked to fix a day, and in doing so said in a letter to Moore, whom he had not yet seen, ' Should my approaching interview with him and his friend lead to any degree of intimacy with both or either, I shall regard our past correspondence as one of the happiest events of my life.' The dinner took place in the second week of November. Only Moore and Byron were to be present with Rogers, but Campbell—whose acquaintance Rogers had made on Lord Holland's introduction at a dinner at the King of Clubs in 1801—happened to call in the morning, and Rogers persuaded him to join them. The three friends were together in

---

[1] ' Can none remember that eventful day,
　That ever-glorious, almost fatal fray,
　When Little's leadless pistol met his eye,
　And Bow-street myrmidons stood laughing by ? '

A note to these lines stated that, ' on examination, the balls of the pistols were found to have evaporated.'

the drawing-room when Byron knocked, but Rogers thought it better to receive him alone, and Moore and Campbell withdrew. After Byron and Rogers had introduced themselves to one another, Moore and Campbell made their appearance and were formally introduced by Rogers to his new friend. Literary history has few parallels to such a scene. Rogers was the oldest and Byron the youngest of the group, and all four were famous. The host was already regarded by the others as a veteran, while Byron was naturally an object of the greatest curiosity to him and to his other guests. Byron was then at his best. He was three-and-twenty, and his pale handsome face, his 'glossy, curling, and picturesque hair,' as Moore calls it, and his subdued and gentle manners, as though feeling that he was in presence of men to whom he had been accustomed to look up, favourably impressed the older poets. Moore tells us that what principally impressed him was the nobleness of his air, his beauty, and the gentleness of his voice and manners. Rogers, who was eight-and-forty, and looked older than he was, was already distinguished for that perfect courtesy which is now called old-fashioned, but was then diligently cultivated. Moore, who was two-and-thirty and was the smallest man of the group, was as good-looking as Byron and full of the liveliness which made him the idol of society, while Campbell, two years older and a little taller than Moore, was the least distinguished-looking of the four.

No record remains of the talk at this memorable interview. It was the beginning of a friendship between Rogers and Byron and between Moore and Byron, which immediately became intimate, and which lasted till Byron's death. When they sat down to dinner there was nothing Byron would eat. Would he take soup? asked the host, but he said he never took soup: fish? but he never ate fish: mutton? he did not eat mutton. Would he take wine? 'Thank you, I never taste wine.' What would he eat? inquired the discomfited host. 'I eat nothing but biscuits and soda-water,' was the discouraging reply. There was no soda-water to be had and there were no biscuits in the house, so Byron took a plateful of potatoes, mashed them with his fork and drenched them with vinegar, and 'of these meagre materials,' Moore tells us, 'he contrived to make rather a hearty dinner.' Rogers afterwards learned that, on leaving his house—where they all stayed till a very late hour—Byron went to his club and had a hearty meat supper. The conversation after dinner was of Walter Scott, who was then at the height of his fame as a poet, having published 'The Lady of the Lake' in 1810 and 'The Vision of Don Roderick' in 1811; and of Joanna Baillie, whose then latest tragedy of 'The Family Legend' was being played at Edinburgh.

The host and his chief guest on this occasion were prepared to be well pleased with one another. Byron shared the admiration for Rogers's poetry which was universal in those days, except among the little-known but fast rising school of the Lake poets. In 'English Bards and Scotch Reviewers' he had penned a striking eulogy on Rogers—

> And thou, melodious Rogers, rise at last,
> Recall the pleasing memory of the past.

> Arise! let blest remembrance still inspire,
> And strike to wonted tones thy hallowed lyre;
> Restore Apollo to his vacant throne,
> Assert the country's honour and thine own.

In a note to the second of these lines Byron says: 'It would be superfluous to recall to the mind of the reader "The Pleasures of Memory" and "The Pleasures of Hope," the most beautiful didactic poems in our language, if we except Pope's "Essay on Man;" but so many poetasters have started up that even the names of Campbell and Rogers are become strange.' Moore assures us that this eulogy was the disinterested and deliberate result of the young poet's judgment. It was published two years before this first meeting with Rogers and Campbell. The acquaintance between Rogers and Byron soon ripened into friendship. In his letters to Mr. Harness and Mr. Hodgson, Byron expresses a high opinion of his taste, and within a month of their first meeting they make up a party to go to hear Coleridge—'this Manichean of poesy,' Byron calls him—lecture on poetry. He had already attacked Campbell's 'Pleasures of Hope,' and Rogers had been present at a lecture at which Byron says he had 'heard himself indirectly *rowed* by the lecturer.' A month later, in January, 1812, Rogers and Byron were present together at another of Coleridge's lectures, 'not one of the happiest of Coleridge's efforts,' says Crabb Robinson.'[1] In the same month the two first cantos of 'Childe

[1] Crabb Robinson's remark in his diary is: 'In the evening at Coleridge's lecture. Conclusion of Milton. Not one of the happiest of Coleridge's efforts. Rogers was there, and with him was Lord Byron. He was wrapped up, but I recognised his club foot, and, indeed, his countenance and general appearance.' As Rogers and Byron were going

Harold' were in type, and Byron sent them to Rogers in proof. Moore tells us that he first saw the sheets of the poem in Rogers's hands, 'and glanced hastily over a few of the stanzas which he pointed out to me as beautiful.' Rogers, however, did not appreciate the poem as a whole. The two stanzas he most admired then and always were the twenty-fifth and twenty-sixth of the second canto beginning—

To sit on rocks, to muse o'er flood and fell.

He read the two cantos to his sister Sarah, and formed a wrong estimate of them. 'It will never please the public,' he said, ' in spite of its beauty ; they will dislike its querulous repining tone, and the dissolute character of the hero.' Rogers soon found, and cordially admitted, that he was mistaken. The popular taste was changing, and the mellifluous beauty of his own poems soon seemed tame side by side with the movement, the passion, the criticism of life, to use Mr. Matthew Arnold's phrase, of which the new poetry was full.

Rogers's criticism of ' Childe Harold ' was that of many of his contemporaries. He sent a copy of the book, when it appeared, to Thomas Grenville, one of the elder brothers of Lord Grenville, and a life-long friend of Rogers's. Tom Grenville, who was eight years older than Rogers, was one of the best-read men of his time, and his judgment was not likely to be warped by prejudice. Hence his letter is peculiarly valuable as an example of contemporary opinion of Byron and his works.

home together, a crossing-sweeper addressed Byron as 'my Lord.' 'He knows you,' remarked Rogers. 'Everybody knows me,' answered Byron, 'I am deformed.'

Thomas Grenville to Samuel Rogers.

'Many thanks, my dear Rogers, though I must own myself unworthy of 'Childe Harold.' It is written in a deadly spirit of scorn and hate which curdles the blood, and chills every kindly feeling, instead of cheering and promoting them. Two striking stanzas on solitude, marked by your discriminating pencil, and some vigorous poetry on Wellington's battle, though with a cautious avoidance of his name or fame, and a wild and rich imagination nourishing a powerful and vigorous pen, do not compensate in my mind for the impression of disgust which I derive from the odious spirit of his writings.

'Yours ever,
'T. GRENVILLE.'

Just at the time when 'Childe Harold' was published, Rogers introduced Byron to Lord and Lady Holland. The immediate occasion of the introduction was the debate on the Nottingham Frame-breaking Bill, on which Byron wished to speak. Lord Holland was Lord Lieutenant of Nottinghamshire, and Byron and he agreed as to the absolute necessity of conciliatory measures towards the wretched people whom misery and oppression had goaded into riot and outrage. The intercourse with Lord Holland soon became constant, but meanwhile Rogers had suggested to Byron that it would be grateful to the feelings of Lord and Lady Holland if 'English Bards and Scotch Reviewers' was suppressed. He was then preparing a fifth edition, but on Rogers's hint he resolved on withdrawing it. He told Leigh Hunt that he did

so with great pleasure because he had attacked them
and many others upon fancied and false provocation.
'Rogers told me,' Byron says, 'he thought I ought
to suppress it; I thought so too, and did, as far as I
could.'[1]

In the summer of this year Rogers made a northern
tour, in the remaining records of which there are many
glimpses of interesting places and people. Tom Moore
was living in his cottage at Kegworth, and Rogers paid
him a visit by the way. Moore's letter to Miss Godfrey,
telling her of the visit, is only one more proof of the
high esteem in which Rogers was held by his friends.
'I forget,' says Moore, 'who the man was who set
fire to his house after the Constable Bourbon had been
in it; but I believe I shall do the same by mine (though
for a different reason) after this memorable visit. I shall
be so happy to have had a right good, excellent friend
under my own roof.' In a letter to his mother, Moore
tells her of a delightful little tour with Rogers to Matlock,
'where I was much charmed with the scenery,' and thence
to Dove Dale, 'which delighted me still more. It is the
very abode of genii.' They parted at Ashbourne, Rogers
going on to the lakes. Francis Horner, writing to his
sister describing a journey he had made with Sergeant
Lens, says, 'At Keswick we found Rogers the poet staying at the inn; he was good enough to take an evening
walk with us, and led us to a favourite station of his
which gives the most striking prospect of the lake.'[2] On
the way thither Rogers writes to his sister.

---

[1] Letter to Leigh Hunt in October, 1815.
[2] *Memoirs and Correspondence of Francis Horner, M.P.*, vol. ii. p. 122.

Samuel Rogers to Sarah Rogers.

'[Keswick] Thursday, August 13, 1812.

' My dear Sarah,—Many thanks for your kind letter and Henry's, inclosing four five-pound notes, which last I shall answer in a very few days. I was indeed very much surprised and shocked to hear of J. R.'s death. Coming so soon after another, you and H. must indeed begin to think that all are going. He was a very excellent man and much attached to you, and I know of no other qualities in this world worth a thought. Sharp and I came over from Ulleswater to this place on Sunday. On Monday we saw a wrestling match for a prize in a field near Ambleside. It had been long announced and it drew together all the fine young men of the peasantry from far and near. It was indeed more interesting than I expected it to be, and lasted above an hour, there being many contests. By a foolish custom here, no women were present, though many looked on from the neighbouring hills. Ulleswater looked very beautiful, though we had little or no sun. Everybody was haymaking. The king, without coat or waistcoat, attended by his daughters on the margin of the lake; and the clergyman in the same costume, unattended, tossing his hay about in solitary dignity in the churchyard. The Mackintoshes came here on Monday. Yesterday they went over to Ulleswater for a night, and, Sharp going with them, I walked to drink tea at Grasmere. It was about six miles and the sun burning hot. I set out a little before twelve, meaning to rest myself a little at the inn at Grasmere, before I made my appearance at W.'s. But I did not arrive there (what with sitting wherever I could find shade or seat) till half-past four. They were going to drink tea with Dr. Bell (Lancaster's antagonist), who lodges in a farm-house next door. I went with W. and we drank tea in the garden, and a pretty sight it was, children and all. I found Dr. Bell in manner not very unlike Dr. Babington, but older and as simple as a child, and with a very warm heart. His eyes streamed with good-nature, and, prejudiced as I went, I came away liking him much better than his antagonist. I was glad to hear you prolonged your stay at Brighton, and found it comfortable. Poor Mary! it is a long while in *her* life; but I am glad Cline thinks well of her, and will hope he is right. With regard to the book you and Henry spoke so kindly of, I have had a great vexation. An alteration came into my mind, which, though slight, I thought of some importance; but the booksellers, I hear, have not waited, and 500 are gone forth, with all their imperfections on their head.[1] In a fortnight or three weeks I hope you will receive it and think it rather improved. Pray write to me at Keswick, whither I mean to go on Saturday.

'The Mackintoshes stay there a day only, and then go on for Scotland. If you write after Monday, pray direct to me under cover to the Earl of Lonsdale, Lowther, near Penrith.

'Pray give my love to all, and believe me to be,

'Ever yours,

'S. R.'

---

[1] This was a mistake, as will be seen from the letter to R. Sharp on p. 101.

A letter to his brother Henry is equally interesting.

Samuel Rogers to Henry Rogers.

'Aug. 20, 1812.

'My dear Henry,—I wrote to Sarah on Thursday the 13th, since which I have not heard; but as Lord Lonsdale writes that some letters are lying at Lowther, I hope to find one from home there. I meant to have left this place to-day, but am kept for want of horses. To-morrow I go to Lowther, where I mean to stay about ten days. I will write before I leave it. On Thursday the 13th, Sharp and the Mackintoshes returned to Lowwood from Patterdale. It was a delicious day, and after an early dinner, in M.'s landaulet and dicky, we went through Langdale to Grasmere, where we drank tea with the Wordsworths. Their little girl lies buried in one corner of the churchyard out of sight of their windows. There is a black stone (the stone of the country) at her head, and another at her feet, and the inscription is on the side from the path, so that nobody can read it unless they go on purpose. It was done by the sister unknown to them, and bears this text : " Suffer the little children to come unto Me." The child was three years old. Mrs. W. cries still every day, as I learn from W. Johnny goes every day to school at Ambleside, carrying his dinner in a satchel on his back.

'At Ulleswater I met with Macreary the printer. He was one of a walking party which it would have given you pleasure to see. There were two very nice girls among them, each carrying her sketch-book and all her own baggage in her hand. He spoke with great enthusiasm and regret of P. Mallet. I met them as I was returning from a walk by the lake-side one morning; they were then on their way to Keswick. On Friday the M.'s left us for Keswick; it was a summer day, and S. and I went on the lake to Ray-rig, a favourite station of his, where it is his custom to lie all the morning, looking up and down the lake. In the afternoon Mr. and Mrs. Wordsworth came unexpectedly and drank tea with us in the summer-house on the bowling green. It was a heavenly evening. The Langdale Pikes looked beautiful, and Mrs. W. was enchanted with the scene. She is a very nice woman indeed, very natural, very humble, and seemingly with a very elegant mind. After tea we walked up the Troutbeck Road about a quarter of a mile and saw the sun set on the lake in all its glory. The W.'s were as much affected by it as if they had never seen such a thing before. Indeed, in their little valley, they never can see a sunset. It was the pleasantest evening I have spent since I left home. On Saturday I set off at six o'clock. At Grasmere I dropped Sharp, who went to breakfast with Wordsworth, and I went on to Keswick, where I found the Mackintoshes at breakfast. We then set out together on horseback to Lodore (it was our scheme to have gone so far by water, but, after going out a little way, we disembarked and took to our horses, the lake being rough), then through Borrowdale and over Borrowdale Horse, as it is called, to Buttermere, where we dined. Mary is married to a plain farmer, who keeps the public-house. She has four little children, and is still very handsome, though not in good health. Indeed, the servant girl was something extraordinary, being very handsome, very sweet, and with a certain dignity. At least we were all imposed upon by everything we saw, and Lady M. thought I had done Mary great injustice in my description.

"On Sunday the M.'s left me on their way to Edinburgh, and it rained till five o'clock. I then took a sweet walk by the lake, which was very gay, all the townspeople being out, and many parties on the water. The Keswick women are very dexterous at rowing. On Monday, the 17th, it was very sultry, and I rowed, or rather was rowed, about the lake, visiting Lodore and the islands. In the evening I walked to Ormithwaite, an old house under Skiddaw, commanding a noble view of the lake and vale of Keswick. Its fields are full of old oaks; a path runs through them to the little village of Applethwaite, a few scattered cottages, so called, in a crevice of Skiddaw (I dare say Sarah remembers it), and there I wandered till dusk. On Tuesday I spent the whole morning there, returning at four to dinner, when Mrs. Wood regaled me with a grouse, and in the evening walked by the lake to Friar's Crag. Stephen went with us to Buttermere. He remembers well the chase Parsons gave him up Skiddaw. At Ulleswater I looked up the mountain Parsons descended so expertly. On Monday Cole went up Skiddaw with a party of servants, but he had not been five minutes on the top when a cloud enveloped them. He seemed sadly disappointed, but, however, enjoys himself very much. I shall not be sorry to leave Keswick, not having enjoyed it much. Indeed, I am no longer fit to be alone. Yesterday

I was again at Ormithwaite, and shall go and mope there again to-day for the last time. The two last days have been very wet and stormy. My love to all. Adieu, my dear Henry!

'S. R.'

He was all this time occupied with amending and polishing 'Columbus,' and letters to Richard Sharp are still full of alternative stanzas for his friend's approval. The following letters to him are only parts of a series.

'Keswick, Tuesday night. Rainy.
[18 August, 1812.]

'My dear Friend,—As I am à l'agonie you must not complain of my cries. It has struck me since that something more is absolutely necessary to the beginning, and I here enclose a triplet, the fruit of my visits to the Ormithwaite, which has become my dear delight. Between the village and "the fine house," as the children call it thereabouts—under the old oaks, in that lofty path at the foot of Skiddaw—tracking your footsteps, I threw together the lines in question, and, if your cool and better judgment approves of them, which I much doubt, pray send them to the printer's to be prefixed in the octavo edition, and sent down in a revise at night to me at the Earl of Lonsdale's, Lowther, near Penrith. Perhaps in that case you had better furnish them with a frank; but pray don't stir unless you give your full approbation.

'I found the Marks here on Saturday not quite ready. They had visited Ormithwaite in the morning under escort of Stephen, and we proceeded by Borrowdale to

Buttermere, but returned by Newlands, not having time (in consequence of her ladyship's scheme of a voyage to Lodore) for Lorton. On Sunday they left me, and here I have remained a wanderer ever since.

'The weather on the whole has been very favourable, having never prevented my tiring myself any day. I think the people of Keswick the pleasantest-looking people I ever saw; and the children are beautiful.

'I shall spend a week or ten days at Lowther, where I mean to sleep on Friday. Lord L. writes me word that letters are waiting there for me, and they will regulate my motions northward.

'When I walk at Ormithwaite, particularly in the field nearest Applethwaite, I think Keswick the finest lake of the three. But each vanquishes me in its turn.

'Yours ever,
'SAML. ROGERS.

'To-morrow I mean to ride for variety and to dine at Lodore. To-day Mrs. Wood regaled me with grouse. She is an excellent lady! but I sleep in Gray's blankets notwithstanding.

'Wednesday morning.

'Upon reading the whole again, it strikes me that the pronouns *we* and *our* clash with the lyrical abruptnesses, and give an air of inflation and pomp to them. I therefore incline to give them up for the present, as Xenophon does in a great part of "The Retreat."

'If you call at Cadell's, you will oblige me by asking for a copy of the octavo, on my account, and keeping it till you can get a better.

'I have been again to Ormithwaite, having kept back the letter in hope of getting from myself a better judgment.

'Five o'clock.

'I have but this moment discovered the Rev. Mr. Pitt's inscription on the window. How I should like to see Miss Susan Hatton as she then was!

'After all I am not sure that the Introduction will not be best as it was before.

'I have directed two copies of the quarto to be sent to you, but, on second thoughts, I will not trouble you to send either of them to me, if you have not already. Pray keep them for me.

'Stephen, who desires to be remembered by you, tells me that the churl, who won the belt, works with Nicholson, and has learnt his art from him, and that they divided the money between them.'

There is another letter posted on Saturday the 22nd, with further suggestions of variations, and the lament—
'I have used up all my writing paper and can get no more, the stationer at Keswick having gone to the sea for a little bathing, and shut up shop for the time.' Another, posted on the 23rd, suggests 'another reading, which I rather like, as it is the last.' Sharp evidently exercised his prerogative of deciding between these various changes, and on the 25th of August Rogers writes—

'Lowther: Tuesday [25 August, 1812].

'My dear Friend,—Many thanks! Your arrogance, a you call it, has saved me! I did not forget your gate, I assure you. It was my morning and evening place of assignation with myself.

'On Thursday, the evening before I left [Keswick], Horner and Sergeant Lens arrived—and I took them there [1]—and Horner went there again by himself, while I was making the circuit of the lake on a white pony. Lens was unwell and unable to walk, and their late dinner prevented Horner from visiting the parsonage and Ormithwaite. He described himself as recovered, and appeared to be so. They went off towards Edinburgh early next morning.

'This castle is magnificent, and a fit residence for the proudest baron that broke the neck of King John. The situation, though commanding, rather disappointed me. But the river (out of sight, though within a five minutes' walk) is exquisite. It runs for many miles (quite to Penrith) along a narrow wooded valley (I may call it a glen) with great noise and rapidity, a path follows it, on one side hanging woods feathering into it or retiring to make way for gigantic docks and other water-plants, and on the other side noble beech woods, now open, now shut, and now discovering a lawn or two, which are here (and very deservedly) called the Elysian fields. The path is generally near the water, but is sometimes at a very great height above it, which glimmers through the enormous branches of old oaks and beeches. The rock is very scanty, but very good of the kind; for sweetness it appears to me to exceed anything I can conceive on the Esk, which it most resembles. It is more unspoilt by the hand of man than

---

[1] See Horner's account, p. 90.

anything I ever saw. Description is nothing, but it should certainly not be neglected if you pass through Penrith.

'Here I found Lord Morpeth. He is gone, and also Milnes [and] the Speaker, who came afterwards. Bolton of Windermere slept here the first night, and you were more than once mentioned at dinner; and Lord Lonsdale told me, in a voice which expressed some concern, that he had not heard of your being here this summer Here is now only Lord Westmoreland.

'I find it was Sir James Graham who led on the assault that was made upon your viands. They carried me on the first day to Hawes Water. It exceeded my expectations. Its seclusion is very striking, the hills on one side rise abruptly from it, and I am indeed inclined to class it as the fourth lake; but I saw it in rain, and under umbrellas, and with three talking, laughing girls. At the upper end of it—for they took me to the end, three miles—is Mardale chapel in severe solitude. More of it when we meet.

'To show you I have not been idle, I recommend the inclosed to your arrogance, or, properly speaking, your generosity. It is intended to close the tenth canto, but perhaps, if tolerable, had better be reserved for the next edition. You will, however, perhaps drop me a line by return of post to the post office, Hamilton. If a day later, to Glasgow. It will just catch me.

'I inclose a line from Moore.

'The more I reflect, the more I think your criticism just on my triplet, and now find I can trust you. I had better make a vow to make no additions now; but I send this to show you that turtle and venison, and pines and grapes, and lords and ladies every day, cannot quite besot me.

'Ever yours,

'SAML. ROGERS.

'I mistook Knight. The copies were only subscribed for—not parted with—and not a copy will stir without my directions. I take it for granted you have the quarto, and can judge of these lines with the context. Though they are, I know, very feeble, the thought perhaps may some time or other be wrought into something.

'Brougham is unfortunately at the Carlisle Assizes. I shall try for the Nunnery. Lord Morpeth is gone to Castle Howard. Lord Alvanley comes to-morrow, and on Friday I depart.

'Wednesday morning.

'I shall write to Knight, my corrector, to proceed. But if anything suggests itself, pray interfere. R. P. Knight, I fear, will be gone from Scotland.

'*To close the Tenth Canto.*[1]

That night, transported, with a sigh I said,
" 'Tis all a dream!" Now, like a dream, 'tis fled;
And many and many a year has pass'd away,
And I alone remain to watch and pray!
Yet oft in darkness, on my bed of straw,
Oft I awake and think on what I saw;
The groves, the birds, the youths, the nymphs recall,
And Cora, loveliest, sweetest of them all!'

It would be insufferably tedious to multiply these extracts sufficiently to give any adequate impression of the

[1] These lines are now at the close of the eleventh can

amount of consideration which was given to this single poem, which must have occupied Rogers occasionally for a considerable part of his life. Similar discussions of lines and passages occur in letters to Moore which are given in Lord John Russell's eighth volume. The reference to triplets, and to Richard Sharp's approval of them, indicates another question of purely literary interest which was much debated by Rogers and his friends. Rogers fell more and more into the use of triplets as he grew older. In ' The Pleasures of Memory' there is only one in the first part, and there are four in the second part. In the ' Epistle to a Friend,' perhaps the most finished of his poems, there is not one. ' Columbus' contains twenty-three triplets; and in ' Human Life' the number mounts up to thirty-nine. He seems to have thought it needful to append to this latter poem a note in defence of this very constant use of what he calls ' the old-fashioned triplet.' He bases the defence on its frequent occurrence in Dryden who, in ' The Hind and the Panther '—which Pope regarded as the most correct specimen of Dryden's versification—has triplets in every page, though, as Rogers does not seem to have noticed, they are very often used to mark a climax or to close a section. In ' Theodore and Honoria,' however, Dryden, as Rogers points out, introduces triplets, three, four and even five times in succession. Rogers speaks of having followed ' yet earlier and higher examples' and claims the approval, or, at least, the forgiveness ' of those in whose ear the music of our old versification is still sounding.' The plea has not availed to make triplets acceptable to modern ears.

In a conversation which took place during this visit to Lowther, Rogers was able to do Wordsworth an important service. As they were one day walking on the terrace, Lord Lonsdale said to Rogers, 'I wish I could do something for poor Campbell.' Rogers, who had just come from a visit to Wordsworth, replied, 'I wish you would do something for Wordsworth. He is in such straitened circumstances that he and his family deny themselves animal food several times a week.' Wordsworth had left Allan Bank in the year before, and was living at Grasmere Parsonage, where one of his children had died in the June before Rogers's visit. Wordsworth had an hereditary claim on Lord Lonsdale, who was not unwilling to recognise it; and his attention having been called to the poet's necessities, he not only gave him aid, but got him appointed, in March, 1813, Distributor of Stamps for Westmoreland. This appointment put him in a position of easy competence for the rest of his life. For Campbell, as we shall see hereafter, Rogers himself did much in after years.

The tour was continued to Scotland, and in course of it he wrote the poem on Loch Long, entitled, 'Written in the Highlands of Scotland,' and dated September 2, 1812.

There is a reference in the poem to the visit paid to the same spot with his sister Sarah in 1803, and the lines which describe Glenfinnart—

> For now we hail
> Thy flowers, Glenfinnart, in the gale;
> And bright indeed the path should be
> That leads to Friendship and to Thee.
> Oh, blest retreat, and sacred too!

> Sacred as when the bell of prayer
> Tolled duly on the desert air,
> And crosses decked thy summits blue.
> Oft shall my weary mind recall,
> Amid the hum and stir of men,
> Thy beechen grove and waterfall,
> Thy ferry with its gliding sail,
> And Her—the Lady of the Glen.

These lines derive additional interest from the following letter written during his stay in this 'blest retreat.'

Samuel Rogers to Sarah Rogers.

'Glenfinnart: 16 Sept. 1812.

'No, my dear Sarah, I can truly say I do not enjoy it so much as I did and (I may say I think) as you did, when we were together, but I have no right to complain. I am now with friends who do everything they can do to prevent my most secret wishes. I am glad to think that you are so comfortable. Nothing seems to be wanting but our Fanny to make Cheadle what it once was. It is indeed very unlucky that Quarry Bank should be left the moment you came. You are right as to your conjecture of Moore's house. The two windows belong to the kitchen, the bay window to the dining-room. Two small parlours (one of them his book-room) look into the garden behind. Their bedroom is over the dining-room, the nursery over the kitchen, and there she was sitting and peeping when I came. At Arrochar I dined between my two voyages, and I saw the landlady, now a matronly but a very nice-looking woman, in her garden. Alas! I had neither grapes nor grouse, and grouse I have only seen twice since I left Lowther, though a man goes out every day among the hills to shoot some for me. This is a very pretty place; and to give you a notion of where I am, I subjoin an attempt at a map. The house is very small and neat, in a narrow, rocky glen running up among steep mountains, with its small river, and a beautiful beech grove between it and the lake. A ferry is within sight of the windows; and while we sit at dinner, we see the little boat passing and repassing continually. At the ferry-house is kept also a packet-boat, which twice a week sails to Greenock with passengers, and takes and brings back our letters, and brings grapes and peaches from the gardens at Dunmore, so that I can even read of your luxuries without a sigh. Indeed, we are so supplied that we are obliged to consume the peaches and apricots in tarts and puddings. What would Fingal and his family have thought of this? An old laird, who lives on a lake immediately behind these mountains, dines with them once a year generally, and always eats with great relish what he calls their "apples with stones." Our family consists of my host and hostess, and two little boys—one five years old, one two—and no human being have I seen besides, except the schoolmaster and the ferryman and the passengers on the sea-shore. We breakfast at nine, and dine at half-past three, and go to bed at ten. All the mountains far and wide on our side Loch Long belong to Lord Dunmore, who is planting everywhere. From the windows you see the lake and the opposite shore a mile off, and also the shore on the other side of the Clyde towards Greenock, and from the ferry-house half a mile from us (my favourite sauntering place) the look up the lake to Arrochar, nine miles, is, as you may conceive, sublime, mountain behind mountain receding one behind another, on each side of the lake, till the vista terminates in a point, and these clad in the softest and richest colours that mist and sunshine can give them. Indeed, I think in its way it surpasses everything of the kind we ever saw together. Poor Mary! an accident has happened here which has made me often think of her and you. Poor Lady Dunmore, returning home from a walk in a shower after dusk the other night, and crossing a little stream, one of the stepping-stones slipped from under her, and terribly sprained her foot. I came forwards, as you may suppose, with the vinegar and oatmeal, which worked wonders, and the next day she put her foot to the ground—a fatal measure that has thrown her back again, and she is now on the sofa. This has deprived me of the harp in the evening and has produced still greater consequences. At the end of a fortnight they were to have made a little tour with me to Loch Katherine and Dunkeld, and we were to have concluded with a little visit at Hamilton, from which I meant to have gone to Edinburgh, and so on to Wassall, where I hoped to have met you and Henry; but now my schemes are defeated, and they beg so earnestly that I will wait a week or ten days, when she expects to be able to set out, that I am at a loss how to refuse. Indeed, to make the journey by myself would be very uncomfortable as well as expensive. I am indeed so quiet and happy here, that I ought not to repine, though, as you say, I never think myself quite well. This place is the wettest in Scotland, though the summer has been better than they have long known it (it was remarkably rainy last year, only think it!), we have seldom two fine days together, and sometimes it rains and shines alternately every five minutes; but I pop in and out continually, and generally tire myself in the course of the day. I have also a charming white pony at my command all day, though I seldom use it. I have made but two excursions since I came, with Lord Dunmore. Once our horses were ferried across, and we rode over to see Roseneath, a beautiful place of the Duke of Argyll's, returning round the shore along the Clyde opposite to Greenock till we came back to the ferry again—a beautiful day and a glorious ride—and once we rode along our own shore to the Clyde, and round up Holy Loch, on the banks of which we saw the burial-place of the Argyll family (in our way we saw Dumbarton Castle in a view up the Clyde), and along Loch Eck till we came down our own glen again.

'I had a very kind letter from Henry the other day, and was sorry to hear such an account of poor Mary. What my plans are now I cannot say, but I fear I shall not leave Scotland before the latter end of October. Adieu, my dear Sarah! Pray give my kind remembrances to one and all who inquire after me, not forgetting Mary and Mrs. H., and believe me to be,

'Ever yours,
'SAML. ROGERS.

'I expect my book now every day.'

Samuel Rogers to Richard Sharp.

'Glenfinnart: Sept. 28, 1812.

'My dear Friend,—I must again try your patience by throwing my burden upon you. The following, though very far from pleasing me, seems to bring it out more fully—though I know something is lost by it—

> Know I went forth, one of that gallant crew,
> And saw, and wonder'd whence his Power He drew;
> Yet how much more had wonder'd had I there
> Known all that pass'd in earth, and sea, and air;
> Then uninstructed.[1]

'Now I will confess to you that I shall be better pleased if you continue firm for the first reading, as I hope you will do, and in that case pray send the inclosed to Knight in Bolt Court; but if the new lines (and all things are possible) strike you (bad though they are) as decidedly the best, pray let them be inserted in p. 204. But, remember, *no further reference* is to be made to me. I would rather that it should continue as it is, whatever may be your opinion, than that any further delay should arise. I think, the moment you read these new lines, you will wonder at my hesitation and continue firm to the old. In that case, pray send the inclosed to Knight, without a comment; and if the least preference in your mind remains for the old reading, pray send the inclosed to Knight in like manner; but if otherwise, and you should incline in the least to the new, it will only increase the page by an additional line, and I know you

---

[1] The lines are in the third canto. They now read—

> 'Oh, I was there, one of that gallant crew,
> And saw—and wondered whence his Power he drew,
> Yet little thought, tho' by his side I stood,
> Of his great Foes in earth and air and flood,
> Then uninstructed.'

will run your eye over the revise to see that it agrees with my copy here given. I have now spent a month in a little glen half-way down Loch Long from Arrochar, and when I shall stir I know not. Many, many thanks for your kind letter. I hope the negotiation at Lewes has concluded to your complete satisfaction. There is said to be a great stir in the North, but not a murmur of it invades me in this retirement. I wish you could but look up Loch Long from hence.

> Great Ocean's self! 'Tis He who fills
> That dark and awful depth of hills!

'In a week or ten days I hope to visit Loch Katherine. In the meantime, should you be commissioned to offer me the Archbishopric of York or the Chancellorship, my direction is at the Earl of Dunmore's, Glenfinnart, by Greenock, N.B.

'We receive our letters twice a week by his packet (only think of it—a packet!) and in the intervals I wander and look up a mountain vista eighteen miles in length! But pray don't write on the subject of the poem, as I shall be well satisfied, whatever way you decide. Pray could you convey a copy to Mackintosh, paying the carriage?

'From Lowther I flew to Luss—then rowed to Tarbet—then crossed the isthmus on foot to Arrochar, where I met with the Mackintoshes, and then by water came down Loch Long to Glenfinnart, a singular voyage, as I met with a grampus, a shoal of herrings, and (after dark) a luminous sea, no unusual phenomenon on this lake. But these and many other wonders I shall reserve for my quarto book of travels.

'Ever yours,

'S. R.

'After all I have written I think I see a great objection to the new lines. If he saw *all* that passed, he would see the interposition of the good Angel in favour of Columbus, and no longer wonder. I will, however, send you the letter. I cannot close the letter without adverting to our sad loss in Mrs. Pigou. The few lines she wrote to me at parting—for I did not see her—were (now I am convinced) written under the impression that she should never see me again. How our friends (the friends of our earlier days) drop off, one by one—and how much it should teach us to value the remainder! The friends of our youth (like the wife of our youth, as Solomon expresses it) are indeed to be prized—for what can supply the place of them?'

Samuel Rogers to Henry Rogers.

'Glenfinnart: Sept. 30, 1812.

'My dear Henry,—Many thanks for your kind letter, which I received at Glenfinnart, where I have remained ever since. It was my intention to spend only a fortnight here, and then proceed with the Dunmores on my journey through some part of the Highlands, but, my hostess having sprained her foot, I have been led on from day to day and from week to week in the expectation of her being able to set out. We shall now leave this place on Saturday the 3rd, and, after visiting Loch Katrine and Dunkeld, proceed on to Hamilton, where perhaps I may rest a week, and then pass through Edinburgh on my way to England. At Edinburgh I don't mean to spend above a day or two, and then go to Howick, Lord Grey's, for a day or two. I received a letter from Sarah about a fortnight ago, and was happy to hear her give so good an account of herself. It is indeed a sad thing the Gregs should be all away just now. I hope Lucy and George have long been quite well. Poor Mary! If she is gone to the sea, I hope she bore her journey well. I hope your sufferings are over in some degree from the paint, and that you are now preparing for your long-talked-of journey into Worcestershire. I have indeed passed my time very tolerably here, as everything has been done that could be to make me happy, and I have felt very grateful if not very happy. We breakfast every morning at nine, and dine at half-past three, and retire to bed at half-past ten, and by no accident can any visitor break in upon our trio. A solitary walk on the Loch side or up the glen is my morning task; so we are not very gay, and should perhaps be dull but for two little boys, the eldest five years old. The packet sails twice a week with letters to and from Greenock, the only event in our lives. Two rides of some length I have taken over the mountains, and one voyage to an old castle in a neighbouring loch. We have no neighbours, and those who come must come by water; and the only people in the glen who wear shoes and stockings are ourselves, except the ferryman and the schoolmaster. It is a very pretty sight—it occurs many times a day—to see the ferry-boat with its sail among the trees, crossing the loch, which is two miles broad, with highlanders in it, this being the highland road from Glasgow to Inverary. I hope you have had better weather in the South than we have had, for this is the wettest part of all Scotland; and though this season is thought much dryer than any they have had for some years, it generally rains two entire days in a week, with many showers besides. Farewell, my dear Henry; pray give my love to Patty and Maria and Lucy, and all the great and small, not forgetting Mr. T., and believe me to be,

'Yours affectionately,
'SAML. ROGERS.

'My next direction will be under cover to The Lord Archibald Hamilton, The Palace, Hamilton, N.B.'

Samuel Rogers to Henry Rogers.

'Palace, Hamilton: 25 Oct. 1812.

'My dear Henry,—Your letter overtook me last week at this place, on my arrival after a little journey of eight days through the Highlands, three of which were fine—a large allowance, I believe, in the North. Menteith lake, Loch Katrine, Loch Erne, Dunira, Dunkeld, Killiekrankie and Loch Leven were the principal sights, and amply rewarded us. I say us, for the Dunmores were with me. Loch Katrine surpassed my expectations, and is indeed the most beautiful thing of the kind I ever saw. I am here within a mile of Chatelherault, which Sarah remembers, and within two miles of Bothwell Castle, which unluckily we did not see; but I hope to see all with her before I die. I wrote her a long letter into

Cheshire a month ago, and begin to fear she never received it, as I have not heard from her. This I address to you at Wassall, flattering myself that you are now there, and happy should I be to meet you there; but one thing after another has delayed me. I am now waiting to see Jeffrey, who is coming here in a day or two, as he says, very kindly, to see me. He is to bring Dugald Stewart with him, and when they go, I shall proceed instantly to Edinburgh, and, after staying there two or three days, to Howick, if the Greys are at home to receive me. I shall not, therefore, reach Wassall before the latter end of next month, I fear; but I have set my heart upon being there, sooner or later. I rejoice to hear that all the invalids are better, and hope they will soon be well.

'So Scarlett has lost, and Brougham. Creevey, I was very sure, would hang as a dead weight round his neck. Sharp wrote me word that he was setting off to Honiton, but I have heard nothing since. It must have been a joyful meeting at Wassall and worth going far to see. If you write a line on receiving this, pray direct to me at the post office, Edinburgh; if within a week, to Alnwick, Northumberland, through which I must pass, whether I stop at Howick or not. It was part of my scheme to spend two or three days at Castle Howard, but it will not now, I fear, be in my power. This is a very large old house, and so cold that I can hardly keep body and soul together. In my room is a whole-length of the beautiful Duchess of Hamilton by Sir Joshua Reynolds. On the table in the gallery lies the book in which visitors enter their names, and it moved me a little to see Sarah's and mine there written nine years

VOL. I.   I

ago. How many things have happened since! With respect to Scotland, it certainly strikes me as much as ever, and I am sure I have every reason to be pleased. I was glad to hear Mrs. R. was better, and hope you have found her well. Pray give my love to Dan and Mrs. R. and all the family of girls and boys, and to Sarah if with you, and believe me to be ever, my dear Henry, yours affectionately, 'SAML. ROGERS.

'I am much obliged to you for your kindness to Milly, and fear James has fallen a victim to his idleness. I am very sorry indeed for Maltby.'

During Rogers's absence on this northern tour the general election took place. Parliament was dissolved on the 24th of September and the new Parliament met on the 24th of November. Sharp lost his seat, and Sheridan was defeated at Stafford, his defeat, as Moore tells us, completing his ruin. Meanwhile Byron was at Cheltenham, and as the addresses advertised for had all been rejected, Lord Holland had persuaded him to write a prologue to be spoken on the opening of the new Drury Lane Theatre.[1] The writers of some of the rejected addresses were angry at the choice of the Committee, and Dr. Busby, who had sent in a monologue which Byron satirised,[2] published a pamphlet on the subject. These are the matters alluded to in the following letter.

[1] The Address was spoken on Saturday the 10th of October.

[2] The Satire is entitled 'Parenthetical Address by Dr. Plagiary.' Busby's lines are quoted and laughed at thus—

'"A modest monologue you here survey"
Hissed from the theatre "the other day,"
As if Sir Fretful wrote "the slumberous verse,"
And gave his son "the rubbish" to rehearse.'

Lord Holland to Samuel Rogers.

'Holland House: Oct. 22, 1812.

'Dear Rogers,—Where are you during this pleasant autumnal weather? Not on the warm sunny bend close to the old colonnades, as I wish you were, and hope you will be before Parliament meets. We then go to St. James's Square. You cannot conceive how much I have missed you, both at your "accustomed bench" and elsewhere, and how sincerely I hope you will repay us for the time we have lost.

'I am almost ashamed of having induced Lord Byron to write on so ungrateful a theme (ungrateful in all senses) as the opening of a theatre; he was so good-humoured, took so much pains, corrected so good-humouredly, and produced, as I thought and think, a prologue so very much superior to the common run of that sort of trumpery, that it is quite vexatious to see him attacked for it. Some part of it is a little too much laboured, and the whole too long, but surely it is good and poetical. What do you think of Busby? Does not his conduct exceed all that satirists have ever described of the extravagance of men smit with the love of their own verses? You cannot imagine how I grew to like Lord Byron in my critical intercourse with him, and how much I am convinced that your friendship and judgment have contributed to improve both his understanding and his happiness.

'Lady H. has been very ill, but is better. She begs her best love, and I am, my dear Rogers,

'Ever truly yours, VLL. HOLLAND.

'P.S. We shan't lose much, and the Ministers will gain still less, by the dissolution. What a horrible campaign in Russia! and what a wretch that Rostopschin is!'[1]

Rogers did not return as Lord Holland hoped. He finished the year away from London. He writes to his sister.

Samuel Rogers to Sarah Rogers.

'Crewe: 8th Dec. 1812.

'My dear Sarah,—I received your kind letter here, soon after my arrival. This is an old house, not unlike Holland House. The staircase is unique and very striking, and under the windows is a large lake of above a hundred acres, now frozen over and covered with wild fowl. Mr. Luttrell and Mr. Lyttelton are here, and the company, which has been very numerous and changeable, have every day overflowed to a side-table at dinner. I was not, I will confess, much surprised that you were gone from Wassall, much as I wished to find you there. It is high time, I think, that I should follow your example, as I have wandered about long enough, and begin to wish for my home, though I have no "wife and children dear" expecting me. I slept one night at Syd. Smith's and then came on to this place, where a stage-coach set me down at the gate, and where I have met with such a scene of old English hospitality as I never saw before. The dinner-bells are ringing every hour of the day. Mr. Lyttelton is shooting and hunting all day long, and indeed most of the rest, so that there are many quiet hours

---

[1] This is evidently a reference to his determination to burn Moscow.

in their absence. To-morrow morning I shall get to Birmingham as I can, and I hope to dine with Dan at Wassall on Thursday. I shall be very happy to do all I can for Felix, though I think there is another person who ought to stir first in his favour, and who can place him above all dependence. It is too provoking that it should be necessary to supplicate for the only child of a man who is worth more than all of us put together. Castle Howard is indeed a magnificent place, and I now wish I had stayed another day or two there to see more of it; but I was impatient to get on, as I knew I must spend a little time here, having been so very long in coming. I received a letter from Dan as you predicted. You speak so very lightly of the sick at Newington, that I hope by this time they are all as well as ever, though I fear it will be long before poor Mary can jump about, and it will be a sad thing to miss her on Twelfth-day. . . Have you seen the new theatre, and what do you think of Betty? But I hope you will wait for these things till I come. I thought it possible you might have brought another girl from Wassall, but I dare say you have determined for the best. As for Moore, I have heard nothing of him, though I dare say there is a letter from him among the heap of things lying for me in town. Milly's loss has vexed me not a little, and I wish it was the only vexation of the kind in my household. I fear I must make a great change. The book, as you say, what with vignettes innumerable, and wide printing, is a good thick book. I much doubt whether the additions are for the better—but others had no doubt, so I ventured. At least it seemed to make it more dramatic—but those parts I know are too few. Sharp must find a great change in his life, and many must miss him in the House, as his was a very active part in the background. He must be a great loss to Grattan, with whom he always sat. I expect a very just encomium on Mrs. Barbauld in *The Edinburgh Review*, from a conversation I had in Scotland. Farewell, my dear Sarah; pray give my love to Henry and Patty and Mr. T. and all at Highbury and Newington, and believe me to be,

'Ever yours,
'SAML. ROGERS.

'Your journey across must be very practicable just now. I hope to be in town in a fortnight.'

CHAPTER IV.

1813-1814.

'Columbus'—Ward's Review in *The Quarterly*—Rogers's Epigram on Ward—Mackintosh's Review in *The Edinburgh*—Wordsworth on Scott—Byron's Letters—His Verses on Rogers—Rogers at Bowood; at Woolbeding—Byron's Estimate of Rogers—Rogers and Sheridan—An unsuspected Source of Sheridan's Income—Byron's Letters to Rogers—Jacqueline—Luttrell's Criticism—Lady Jersey—Letter from Wordsworth—Jekyll—Rogers's Love for Children—Epigram on the White Cockade—Sir George Beaumont's Epitaph on Johnson—Uvedale Price.

'COLUMBUS' had been printed in 1810 in the old-fashioned thin quarto in which it was still the lingering custom to print original poems. In this form it made a book of thirty-four pages. The poem was divided into six parts; there was no introduction, nothing about an original in the Castilian language, and no intimation that it was to be regarded as 'Fragments.' The copy before me now has no date or title, it never had a title-page, and there is written outside and inside in pencil, 'Pray don't show it.—S.R.' A comparison of the opening lines of this edition with those of the published poem shows the change of plan it underwent. In the first it is the Muse who is to sing of the deeds of the hero; in the second it is one of his companions who celebrates his triumph after his death. The original opening was—

> Say who first pass'd the portals of the West,
> And the great secret of the deep possess'd—
> Who first the standard of his faith unfurl'd
> On the dread confines of an unknown world?
> Him would the Muse exalt—by Heav'n design'd
> To lift the veil that cover'd half mankind!

In its published form in 1812, and again in the edition of 1816, the poem began—

> Who passed at length the portals of the West,
> And the great Secret of the Deep possessed?
> Say, who the standard of his Faith unfurled
> On the dread confines of an Unknown World?
> Him, by the Paynim bard descried of yore,
> And ere his coming sung on either shore.
> Him could not I exalt—by Heaven designed
> To lift the veil that covered half mankind![1]

The poem as first printed contained three hundred and seventy-seven lines; as published, it had six hundred and forty-eight lines; in its final shape it has six hundred and seventy-two lines, besides the Introduction and the stanzas in the romance or ballad measure of the Spaniards at the end. It was not published separately, but in a volume containing his other poems, and entitled 'Poems, by Samuel Rogers, including Fragments of a Poem called The Voyage of Columbus.' The volume contained 'The Pleasures of Memory,' 'An Epistle to a Friend,' with his other earlier poems, and in addition to these the lines 'To the Torso,' the verses 'Written in Westminster Abbey,' those 'Written in the Highlands of Scotland,' 'Written in a Sick Chamber,' and 'The Butterfly.' In the number of *The Quarterly Review* for March, 1813, the volume was the subject of one of the articles, and the opportunity was

---

[1] The present beginning is given on p. 68.

taken for a cold, critical, and somewhat severe review of all Rogers's poems, and an estimate of his position as a poet. The article began with an admission of the popularity of 'The Pleasures of Memory,' which it described as 'that sort of popularity which is perhaps more decisive than any other *single* test of merit. The circulation of it has not been confined to the highly-educated and critical part of the public, but it has received the applause which, to works of the imagination, is quite as flattering— of that far more numerous class who, without attempting to judge by accurate and philosophical rules, read poetry only for the pleasure it affords them, and praise because they are delighted. It is to be found in all libraries and in most parlour windows.' Of 'Columbus' the article was more critical, and, as Byron said in a letter to Murray, 'not *too* fair.' Its sting, however, lay in its charging the author with haste. Fixing on the one inharmonious line in the poem—then in Canto X., now in Canto XI.—

There silent sat many an unbidden guest,

the writer asked, 'What, for instance, but extreme haste and carelessness could have occasioned the author of "The Pleasures of Memory" to mistake for verse such a line?' and proceeded to blame him for impatience to publish. The writer of the review was J. W. Ward, who knew, as all Rogers's friends did,[1] the long preparation he had given to the poem, the hesitation he had shown in publishing it, and the pressure to produce it which had been put upon him by many admirers of his works. The

---

[1] Moore says in a letter to Miss Godfrey: 'The accusing him of haste is really too impudent a humbug, when they and all the world know so entirely to the contrary.'

publication of this review produced a coolness between Rogers and Ward which ended in Ward expressing his regret for an attack which he admitted to be indefensible. Rogers, however, had meanwhile taken his revenge in an epigram which is never likely to be forgotten—

> Ward has no heart they say, but I deny it;
> He has a heart, and gets his speeches by it.

Asked by a lady one day during the period of estrangement, 'Have you seen Ward lately?' Rogers asked, 'What Ward?' 'Why, our Ward to be sure!' was the reply. '*Our* Ward!' sneered Rogers, 'you may keep him all to yourself.' Mr. Dyce tells us that, just after the review was out, Rogers called on Lord Grosvenor and found Gifford, the editor, sitting with him. They were not friends, but Rogers was more cordial than usual, and chatted with Gifford in a most friendly manner. 'Do you think he has seen the last *Quarterly*?' asked Gifford of his host when Rogers had left. Mr. Dyce thinks Rogers had not seen it; to me his extra cordiality is a proof that he had seen it, and would not show that he was hurt.

In the succeeding October the poem was reviewed by Mackintosh in *The Edinburgh Review*, in an article which he says was regarded as 'too panegyrical.' It discussed the causes of the popularity of 'The Pleasures of Memory,' of which it was remarked that 'it was patronised by no sect or faction. It was neither imposed on the public by any literary cabal, nor forced into notice by the noisy anger of conspicuous enemies. Yet, destitute as it was of every foreign help, it acquired a popularity, originally very great, and which has not only continued amid extraordinary fluctuation of general taste, but increased amidst a succession of formidable competitors.' This was the exact truth at the time, and it remained true for many years after it was written. The article concluded with the sentence, ' Whatever be the rank assigned hereafter to his writings, when compared to each other, the writer has most certainly taken his place among the classical poets of his country.' Byron agreed with this estimate. He wrote in his journal, ' Redde *The Edinburgh Review* of Rogers; he is ranked highly, but where he should be. There is a summary view of us all,[1] Moore and me among the rest; and both (the first justly) praised, though by implication (justly again) placed beneath our memorable friend.' The review gave Rogers great satisfaction. It confirmed the voices of the earlier critics and gave the highest literary recognition of the age to his established position and fame.

Wordsworth was at this time preparing to publish ' The Excursion,' and he appears to have consulted Rogers about it. It is one remarkable feature of Rogers's life that he was constantly asked, and almost as constantly undertook, to manage business matters for his literary friends. They thought nothing of asking him to see a publisher for them, to arrange the details, and to take general charge of their interests. His business experience fitted him to do this; his ample leisure enabled

---

[1] Byron's memory misled him. There is no such comparison in the article, only an indirect reference to the partial failure of an attempt ' by a writer of undisputed poetical genius to enlarge the territories of art by unfolding the poetical interest which lies latent in the common acts of the humblest men, as well as in the most familiar scenes of Nature.'— *Edin. Review*, vol. xxii. p. 38.

him thus to oblige his friends, and his generous willingness to help them could always be reckoned upon. Wordsworth, as I shall have occasion to show, was greatly indebted to Rogers for help of this kind, and even Byron availed himself of similar friendly services.

William Wordsworth to Samuel Rogers.

'My dear Sir,—I am gratified by your readiness to serve me in the affair of my intended publication, but I am obliged to defer it, and by a cause which you will be most sorry to hear, viz., the recent death of my dear and amiable son, Thomas. He died this day six weeks past of the measles; he was seen by the medical attendant about twelve at noon, pronounced to be as favourably held as child could be, and his dissolution took place in less than five hours from that time. An inflammation in the lungs carried him off thus suddenly. You must remember him well; he was our second son (six years and a half old), and, I recollect well, made one of the party that fine afternoon when we all drank tea together with Dr. Bell in his garden. This sudden blow, coming when we were just beginning to recover from one equally sudden, has overwhelmed us. Last summer we lost a sweet little girl, four years old, and brother and sister now rest side [by side] in Grasmere churchyard, where we hope that our dust will one day mingle with theirs. If at some future time I can force my mind to the occupation which was thus lamentably interrupted, as I trust I shall be able to do, then I will again have recourse to your kindness in this concern. We find it absolutely necessary to quit a residence which forces upon us at every moment so many memorials of the happy but short lives of our departed innocents, and we have taken the house called Rydal Mount, lately the property of Mr. North and occupied [by] him, but now belonging to Lady Le Fleury. We shall be pleased to see you there; you know that the house is favourably situated.

'It gives me much satisfaction to learn that your time has passed so agreeably in Scotland. May sorrow that is perpetually travelling about the world be long in finding you! I am glad that Sharp is in expectation of returning to Parliament; if you see him, remember me affectionately to him, and be so good as to communicate to him our loss. I am obliged to Miss Rogers for her remembrance of me; pray present my regards to her in return. Mrs. W., my sister, and Miss Hutchinson join in kind remembrances to you,

'And believe me, my dear sir, faithfully yours,

'W. WORDSWORTH.

'Grasmere: January 12th, 1813.

'P.S. You make no mention of the volume of your poems which you promised. I am disappointed at this. What you say of W. Scott[1] reminds me of an epigram something like the following—

> Tom writes his verses with huge speed,
>   Faster than printer's boy can set 'en,
> Faster far than we can read,
>   And only not so fast as we forget 'en.

---

[1] 'Did you ever see much worse songs than those in *Rokeby*?' asks Moore of Mr. Power. There was a growing impression that Scott's poetry was falling off.

'Mrs. W., poor woman! who sits by me, says, with a kind of sorrowful smile, "This is spite, for you know that Mr. Scott's verses are the delight of the times, and that thousands can repeat scores of pages."'

Thomas Campbell to Samuel Rogers.

'Sydenham: 10th February, 1813.

'My dear Sir,—It is long since I have seen you, but since the period when I had that pleasure, I have had a winter of repeated sicknesses, and have been but seldom in town. Now that some of the last of my poor little critical vignettes are printing off, I often wish I had your friendly eye to look on them; but since I am denied that happiness, I dare say you will not refuse me a little assistance of a different kind. You once showed me a volume of modern poems (one of them was on an infant which struck us both as having merit), out of which I think I could find something worth extracting. If you still have the volume, and could favour me with a short loan of it, I should send a careful person for it, and return it very soon. I should be exceedingly thankful to you to drop me a line on this subject. The poems which I mean were of a date somewhat about 1780 or 90.

'Believe me, with much regard,
   'Yours faithfully,
      'THOS. CAMPBELL.'

A letter from Lord Byron, on his private affairs, shows how close the intimacy between him and Rogers had already become, though they had only known each other a year and a half.

Lord Byron to Samuel Rogers.

'March 25, 1813.

'I enclose you a draft for usurious interest due to Lord B.'s *protégé*. I also could wish you would state thus much for me to his Lordship. Though the transaction speaks plainly in itself for the borrower's folly and the lender's usury, it never was my intention to *quash* the demand, as I legally might, nor to withhold payment of principal, or perhaps even *unlawful* interest. You know what my situation has been, and what it is. I have parted[1] with an estate (which has been in my family for nearly three hundred years, and was never disgraced by being in possession of a *lawyer*, a *churchman*, or a *woman*, during that period) to liquidate this and similar demands; and the payment of the purchase is still withheld, and may be, perhaps, for years. If, therefore, I am under the necessity of making those persons *wait* for their money (which, considering the terms, they can afford to suffer), it is my misfortune.

'When I arrived at majority in 1809, I offered my own security on *legal* interest, and it was refused. *Now*, I will not accede to this. This man I may have seen, but I have no recollection of the names of any of the parties but the *agents* and the securities. The moment I can, it is assuredly my intention to pay my debts. This person's case may be a hard one, but, under all circumstances, what is mine? I could not foresee that the purchaser of my estate was to demur in paying for it.

---

[1] Byron then believed that he had sold Newstead for 140,000*l.*, but the sale on this occasion was not completed.

'I am glad it happens to be in my power so far to accommodate my Israelite, and only wish I could do as much for the rest of the Twelve Tribes.

'Ever yours, dear R.,

'BN.'

In the spring Byron published his fragment, 'The Giaour,' and Moore tells us what remarkable developments it underwent in subsequent editions. The idea of writing a poem in fragments had been suggested to him by Rogers's 'Columbus,' and to Rogers Byron dedicated it 'as a slight but most sincere token of admiration for his genius, respect for his character, and gratitude for his friendship.' The time was a merry one for the group of which Rogers was the centre. Byron lived in London for six months, and Moore speaks of the wild flow of his spirits and the many gay hours they passed together. Byron and Moore were dining with Sheridan one night at Rogers's, when the conversation turned on the addresses which had been sent in to the Committee of Management of Drury Lane Theatre. Sheridan seemed on that evening to renew his youth. He told stories of his early life, some of which Rogers treasured up in his retentive memory and brought out in after years. Among the rejected addresses was one of Whitbread's, who, like most of the others, dragged in the Phœnix, but, as Sheridan said, 'made more of the bird than any of them. He entered into particulars, described its wings, beak, and tail—in short, it was a poulterer's description of a Phœnix.' Shortly after this glorious evening Byron and Moore went home with Rogers from an early party, and Byron, who had gone for two days without his dinner, was hungry and asked for food, but he would have nothing but some bread and cheese. They were in a mood of the wildest merriment. 'Seldom have I partaken,' says Moore, 'of so joyous a supper.' As all three were poets, poetry was uppermost in their minds. Byron made merry over a new volume of poems just published by Lord Thurlow, and Rogers in vain took up its defence. At last they lighted on a poem in praise of Rogers himself. Moore tells us that they both heartily agreed in it; but they were in the mood for laughter, and Byron read it aloud, turning it into mockery, and laughing at every word. Rogers himself caught the contagion of their merriment, though feeling that the mockery was utterly unjust, and all three spent the remainder of the evening in inextinguishable laughter. A few days later Byron sent Moore a poem of half-a-dozen verses, of which only the first two and the last two have been published—

I.

When Thurlow this d——d nonsense sent
(I hope I am not violent)
Nor men nor Gods knew what he meant.

II.

And since not e'en our Rogers' praise
To common sense his thoughts could raise,
Why *would* they let him print his lays?

III.

. . . .

IV.

. . . .

V.

To me, divine Apollo, grant O !
Hermilda's first and second canto,
I'm fitting up a new portmanteau.

VI.

And thus to furnish decent lining,
My own and other's bays I'm twining,
So, gentle Thurlow, throw me thine in.

Another poem on the same subject was sent to Moore on the same day. It was on Lord Thurlow's lines—

I lay my branch of laurel down,
Then thus to form Apollo's crown,
Let every other bring his own.

To Lord Thurlow.

I.

'I lay my branch of laurel down.'

Thou lay thy branch of *laurel* down,
  Why, what thou stolest is not enow;
And were it lawfully thine own,
  Does Rogers want it most or Thou?
Keep to thyself thy withered bough,
  Or send it back to Doctor Donne;
Were justice done to both, I trow
  He'd have but little and thou—none.

II.

'Then thus to form Apollo's crown.'

A crown! why, twist it how you will,
  Thy chaplet must be foolscap still.
When next you visit Delphi's town
  Inquire amongst your fellow-lodgers,
They'll tell you Phœbus gave his crown,
  Some years before your birth, to Rogers.

III.

'Let every other bring his own.'

When coals to Newcastle are carried,
  And owls sent to Athens as wonders,
From his spouse when the Regent's unmarried,
  Or Liverpool weeps o'er his blunders;
When Tories and Whigs cease to quarrel,
  And Castlereagh's wife has an heir,
Then Rogers shall ask us for laurel,
  And thou shalt have plenty to spare.

Another result of the evening's merriment was that Moore borrowed the volumes of Lord Thurlow's poems from Rogers, and wrote what Rogers regarded as a very ill-natured article upon them in *The Edinburgh Review*. Rogers was greatly annoyed, for he had a high opinion of some of Lord Thurlow's poems, and Moore knew it. When Lord Thurlow published one of his volumes, Rogers wrote to him expressing the feeling he really entertained about it. Lord Thurlow was greatly pleased, and in reply returned Rogers's compliments with compound interest. 'It is most flattering to me,' said Lord Thurlow, 'that you should approve them, to whose poetry, at once the most beautiful and most polished, I have always paid the tribute of my admiration, since in my judgment, if I may be permitted to say so, the "Epistle to a Friend" is a poem, which, in its peculiar kind, has no equal in all antiquity; I cannot but be most sensibly flattered that its author should think my early efforts in verse worthy of his approval.' Rogers especially admired Lord Thurlow's verses on Sir Philip Sidney, and charged Moore with attacking him only because it was the fashion to do so.

In June, 1813, Leigh Hunt was in prison, and Moore and Byron visited him. On the day before the visit to Horsemonger Lane gaol, where the courageous editor of the *Examiner* lay, Byron wrote Moore a poetical epistle which contains these lines—

> I suppose that to-night you're engaged with some codgers,
> And for Sotheby's blues have forsaken Sam Rogers;
> And I, though with cold I have nearly my death got,
> Must put on my breeches and wait on the Heathcote.

Among Rogers's papers there is a very curious letter about Lady Heathcote. With the exception of the words 'it is really so' above the other signatures it is in Rogers's writing, and it had been folded up as a small note, sealed with black wax, and addressed outside, 'The Duchess of St. Albans.'

'Lady Heathcote is here *alone*, and in *great danger*. If you have any regard for your Sister, pray come instantly, as she is now sitting on a sofa with the most *innocent* man in England. 'S. R.'
'it is really so.'
'K.S.H.'
'R. B. Sheridan.'

There is no explanation of the note.[1]

Byron writes, early in July, 'Rogers is out of town with Madame de Staël,' but at the end of the month he tells Moore that he is in training to dine with Sheridan and

---

[1] I should think from the appearance of the MS. that the Duchess got the note, opened it, folded it in her hand, went off to obey the summons, and, when she arrived, handed it back to Rogers as a sign that she had come in answer to it. Rogers put it in his pocket, and so it was preserved.

Rogers, and adds, 'I have a little spite against R. and will shed his "Clary wines pottle-deep."' In September he writes to Moore, 'Rogers wants me to go with him on a crusade to the Lakes, and to besiege you on the way. This last is a great temptation.' Rogers persuaded Byron that *The Quarterly* would attack him next—a sure sign that Ward's article gave him serious pain. At the end of September Byron talks, in a letter to Moore, who was then living at Ashbourne in Derbyshire, of the proposed journey north, and says Moore must 'go to Matlock and elsewhere, and take what in flash dialect is poetically termed "a lark" with Rogers and me for accomplices.' The 'lark' never came off. Meanwhile we meet with Rogers in one of Madame D'Arblay's letters to her father. Madame D'Arblay says, 'I dined at Mr. Rogers's, at his beautiful mansion in the Green Park, to meet Lady Crewe, and Mrs. Barbauld was also there, whom I had not seen for many many years, and, alas! should not have known. Mr. Rogers was so considerate to my *sauvagerie* as to have no party, though Mr. Sheridan, he said, had expressed his great desire to meet again his old friend Madame D'Arblay.' Mrs. Barbauld, who was twenty years older than Rogers, was then seventy. Madame D'Arblay was much pleased with her lines, 'Life, we've been long together,' which Rogers taught her. Sitting with her one day just before her death, Rogers asked her if she remembered them. 'Remember them?' she said; 'I repeat them every night before I go to sleep.'

In October Rogers went down to Bowood, from whence he writes to his sister—

Samuel Rogers to Sarah Rogers.

'Bowood: Monday, 25 Oct., 1813.

'My dear Sarah,—As I wish much to hear from you and flatter myself you wish to hear from me, I shall do what I have meant to do for many days, and entitle myself to a letter from you, which I hope will not be very long in coming. I set off in the rain, but the sun soon broke out. At Salthill I breakfasted in the same room but on much better materials than when we were together. I travelled seventy miles alone, with the exception only of a young lady for five miles; but at dusk Mr. Horace Twiss descended from the roof and amused me very much till we parted. I found the Lansdownes, as I expected, at tea. They had nobody with them but the Abercrombies and Jekyll and his eldest boy, as full of Twelfth-night as ever. Jekyll left us in four days, but we have since received great reinforcements—there being at this time in the house the Romillys, Mackintosh, Mme. de Staël and Mlle. Dumont, and several others. M. de Staël and the Portuguese minister arrive to-day, and on Thursday Ward is expected, so that the house is growing into a little city. It is very superbly furnished and is certainly a grand place altogether. A great piece of water is before the windows, and the park is very uneven and woody, though there are no old trees, but Marlborough Downs break in here and there continually through the plantations. They are six or seven miles off, resemble much the Southdowns of Sussex, and, in the hazy air of morning and evening, have a very mountainous effect. Bowles has dined and slept here twice, and I have twice breakfasted with him. He lives about three miles off (the walk is a very pleasant one) in a very pretty vicarage by the side of a very pretty church, and on the brow of a hill. His windows look over a fine valley, and in front appears the *white horse* cut on the downs, which has a very singular and pretty effect, as indeed it has at Bowood, through a vista in the pleasure grounds. Yesterday I went to his church, and he was very anxious to exhibit his choir to advantage. He has a violoncello, a bassoon, and a hautboy. The first is his own, and the transportation of it to and from church across the churchyard and among the congregation (not in its case) makes an odd appearance. He seems amazingly respected there, notwithstanding his odd manners. He came out of church in his surplice, but without his hat, having left it in the reading-desk, and there he stood, till the clerk, who had more of his wits about him, came running after him with it. The band sit in the gallery, and none of the congregation below join, except the parson, who sat singing very loud in his desk, to the trial of my nerves. They sang three very long Psalms and the responses (Mason's) to the Commandments. I have promised to go next Sunday, if I am still here, as he did not preach yesterday, though he read prayers—Douglas, the Chancellor of Salisbury (the late Bishop's son, and as odd a fellow as his friend Bowles), having preached for him. We set out together after church on horseback to visit a Moravian establishment, but could not make much progress—Douglas, a very tall and pompous-looking man on a tall horse, stopping his horse all the way to gather blackberries. Mme. de Staël makes a bustle here, but, having arrived only yesterday, we have as yet had no shawl dance, and no recitations. How long I shall stay, I cannot say exactly, but hope to be in town some time in next week. I have sometimes thought of going on to Mamhead, but cannot bring my mind to it, though my journey here was delightful, and so little fatigued was I, I was almost sorry it was over. Farewell! Pray give my love to Henry and Patty and all, and believe me to be,

'Ever yours most affectionately,

'S. R.'

In November he was in London again, and we meet with him in Byron's diary. The next letter to his sister Sarah is from Woolbeding—

Samuel Rogers to Sarah Rogers.

'Woolbeding: Dec. 1 [1813].

'My dear Sarah,—Lord Folkestone sleeping here last night, I made use of him to write to you, though I have little to say. I hope all the colds are gone, as mine is, and that you persevere, as I have begun, in turning the sunshine to good account. Pray thank Patty for her kind letter, and tell her that, as we have begun again, I hope she will not suffer our correspondence to drop. The fault shall not be mine. I am sorry to hear of the robbery, but hope they will not repeat their visit. I am glad to hear that there is some chance of a good situation for Sutton. May it answer all our wishes! So there is an alarm about Mary! I shall break my heart if she and you don't pay me a visit. If you can contrive it, I will endeavour to make it as comfortable to you as I can, under all the circumstances I am placed in. Pray do it if you can. On Friday I hope to sleep at home, and on Saturday to see you all. I have resumed my walking as usual, but now, alas! my old friend from the east is blowing, and I am half a prisoner. Little change has taken place in this family. C. Moore is gone and Sir H. Englefield come, who is a great acquisition, as we wanted a talker.[1] Pray tell Maria that we have two pheasants in a dish every day. The plea is—and a very good one it is—that, if one turns out ill, the other may prove better. They are seldom lessened by above a single slice, and oft they go to the servants' hall with a hare uncut and a hundred luxuries. The estate abounds in rabbits, and to what purpose do you think they are applied?—for they seldom appear on table. To make the sauces! This place appears more and more beautiful every time I see it, though I never see it to advantage. I have had a very entertaining letter from T. Moore. He seems happy and says he writes fifty lines a week, but who can keep up with Lord Byron? Before I return, he will be again, I see, before the public. What strange turns of fortune in this mortal world! The news from Paris is very curious. Moore has been paying a visit to some of the Strutts at Derby,[2] where the Edgeworths passed some time in the summer, and where he found old E. the favourite! They have a nest of young poetesses in

---

[1] Rogers used to say that Sir Henry Englefield had a notion that he smelt of violets. Lady Grenville, knowing this weakness, one day remarked in his presence, 'Bless me, what a smell of violets!' 'Yes,' said he with great simplicity, 'it comes from me!'—Dyce's *Table Talk* p. 156.

[2] See Lord John Russell's *Memoirs of Moore*, vol. i. p. 365.

the family, that assemble every Sunday night and bring each her copy of verses; and it is quite surprising, he says, how well they write. They made him an honorary member of the Society. His cottage smokes and lets the rain in everywhere, but he looks up, I think, notwithstanding. Good-bye, my dear Sarah; the post is going, and I dare not read what I have written. Pray give my love to all, and believe me to be,

[*Signature cut out.*]

'So Alexander Baring has taken the business of Hope at Amsterdam? The family have made it over to him at a great loss to themselves. What a change is this in his favour if it hold good as it seems to promise!'

The references to Rogers in Byron's diary at this period are of the greatest interest. On the 22nd of November, Byron writes—

'Rogers is silent, and, it is said, severe. When he does talk, he talks well; and on all subjects of taste his delicacy of expression is as pure as his poetry. If you enter his house, his drawing-room, his library, you of yourself say, "This is not the dwelling of a common mind.' There is not a gem, a coin, a book thrown aside on his chimney-piece, his sofa, his table, that does not bespeak an almost fastidious elegance in the possessor. But this very delicacy must be the misery of his existence. Oh the jarrings his disposition must have encountered through life!'

Two days later, Byron puts on record an estimate of Rogers as a poet. He calls Scott 'the Monarch of

Parnassus, and the most English of Bards.' He then says—

'I should place Rogers next in the living list (I value him more as the last of the *best* school), Moore and Campbell both *third*—Southey and Wordsworth and Coleridge—the rest, οἱ πολλοί, thus :'

He then draws a triangle which is divided into four parts. Above the apex is Scott; in the apex is Rogers; in the division below, Moore and Campbell; under them, Southey, Wordsworth, Coleridge; and at the base the many. This estimate belonged to the time. It is now just three-quarters of a century old, and it is interesting to note how completely posterity has reversed it. Distance has revealed the greatness which nearness hid, and Rogers has suffered in consequence. He was the last of a school, and posterity has not agreed with Byron in regarding it as the best school. The account of Rogers as a man of taste and of society, and of his house and surroundings, is confirmed by the testimony of all who knew him for forty years after Byron wrote it.

There are frequent references to Sheridan in Byron's diary and letters during this stay in London. It was the closing period of poor Sheridan's career. I find it stated, in all the accounts of Sheridan that I have seen, that he had never had any considerable source of income but Drury Lane theatre.[1] But I have before me a

---

[1] In Professor Minto's admirable article on Sheridan in the new edition of the *Encyclopædia Britannica*, he tells us that ' his biographers always speak of his means of living as a mystery ;' and he proceeds to say that 'it is possible that the mystery is that he applied much more of his powers to plain matters of business than he affected or got credit

document endorsed outside, 'Sheridan's Trust. Copy. Driver's Valuation between Mr. Sheridan and Mr. Hudson.' The valuation is of 'Land belonging to R. B. Sheridan, Esq., for Sale. Copyhold, Brown's Barn Farm, Leatherhead Parish.' The acreage of seven different pieces of land is then stated, the total being 32 acres and 19 poles, and the valuer adds: 'The above being subject to a heriot and quit rent I estimate to be worth 750*l*., exclusive of the timber &c.' There is added in Sheridan's handwriting, 'This I must keep.' The next table is headed 'Freehold, Mickleham Parish,' and gives the acreage of six pieces of land with a total of 72 acres and 28 poles. The valuer adds: 'The above I estimate to be worth 1,705*l*. exclusive of the timber &c.' The valuation is signed 'A. P. Driver, Kent Road, May 30th, 1812.' On the other side of the sheet of paper is a table headed 'Totals brought forward, R. B. Sheridan, Esq., T. Hudson, Esq.' This includes another freehold estate of 44 acres, besides those already mentioned, and 15 acres of copyhold, part of Yew Tree Farm. The freehold is valued at 2,280*l*., and the total is 4,735*l*. The value of the additional copyhold is put at 425*l*. There is also a memorandum in Sheridan's handwriting—

'There is coming to me for land, &c., I sell him full 3,000*l*. H. rents near 700*l*. per ann. of me.

'Metcalfe dines with me to-day to forward matters. I have only to get down to —— [*the word is illegible*].

'I send Driver's valuation.'

for.' This is no doubt true, but the document I have given is a further contribution to the solution of the mystery—which, indeed, is now a mystery no longer.

In the same envelope with this I find an order on T. Hudson, Jun., Esq., of New Bridge St., to pay Rogers, 'from the money coming to me from Kent Lane,' 150*l.* This order was never presented for payment, nor was a cheque for 100*l.* on Messrs. Biddulph, Cocks's, and Ridge, which Sheridan gave to Rogers for value received in July, 1815. A letter from Mr. Murray to Rogers without date, except the word Sunday, says that he has been in vain in search of his solicitor, that he doubts whether any instrument drawn up on that day could be rendered legal, but adds, 'If you will pledge your word to the creditors for 300*l.*, I will pledge mine to you for 300*l.*, as soon to-morrow as Mr. Sheridan signs a regular instrument of assignment to me of the "Speeches in Westminster Hall," or upon any other convertible security that you can suggest, without which even your long friendship for Mr. Sheridan would not, I think, advise me to proceed.' These documents are proofs of the interest Rogers took in Sheridan's affairs, and of the trouble he gave himself in efforts to help his friend in these dark days of his decline. There is among them one relic of a happier time. It is in a clearer and steadier hand than Sheridan's other writing, and is merely a postscript to a letter: 'When will you come and choose a spot in our Arcadia? I have a commission from T. Moore to find him a cottage.'

Byron writes on the 12th of December, 1813, 'Sheridan was in good talk at Rogers's the other night.' In the early months of the next year he records several visits to Rogers, at most of which Sheridan and Sharp were present. He mentions Rogers, too, among those who had been urging him to 'make it up with Carlisle,' though he had 'as lief "drink up Eisel —eat a crocodile."' On this subject several letters passed between Rogers and Byron. Moore prints Byron's letters with certain needless omissions, and gives no indication whatever that anything has been omitted. In the first of the two following letters I have supplied, from Lord Byron's manuscript, several sentences which Moore has omitted without a sign—

Lord Byron to Samuel Rogers.

'February 16th, 1814.

'My dear Rogers,—I wrote to Lord Holland briefly, but I hope distinctly, on the subject which has lately occupied much of my conversation with him and you. As things now stand, upon that topic my determination must be unalterable.

'I declare to you most sincerely, that there is no human being on whose regard and esteem I set a higher value than on Lord Holland's; and, as far as concerns himself and Lady Holland, I would concede even to humiliation without any view to the future, and solely from my sense of his conduct as to the past. For the rest, I conceive that I have already done all in my power by the suppression. If that is not enough, they must act as they please; but I will not "teach my tongue a most inherent baseness," come what may. I am sorry that I shall not be able to call upon you to-day, and, what disappoints me still more, to dine with you to-morrow. I forwarded a letter from Moore to you; he writes to me in good spirits, which I hope will not be impaired by any attack brought upon him by his friendship for me. You will probably be at the Marquess Lansdowne's to-night. I am asked, but am not sure that I shall be able to go. Hobhouse will be there. I think, if you knew him well, you would like him.

'Believe me always yours very affectionately,

'B.'

Lord Byron to Samuel Rogers.

'February 16th, 1814.

'My dear Rogers,—If Lord Holland is satisfied, as far as regards himself and Lady Holland, and as this letter expresses him to be, it is enough.

'As for any impression the public may receive from the revival of the lines on Lord Carlisle, let them keep it—the more favourable for him, and the worse for me the better for all.

'All the sayings and doings in the world shall not make me utter another word of conciliation to anything that breathes. I shall bear what I can, and what I cannot I shall resist. The worst they could do would be to exclude me from society. I have never courted it, nor, I may add, in the general sense of the word, enjoyed it—and "there is a world elsewhere."

'Anything remarkably injurious I have the same means of repaying as other men, with such interest as circumstances may annex to it.

'Nothing but the necessity of adhering to regimen prevents me from dining with you to-morrow.

'I ever am yours most truly,

'Bn.'

Rogers's intimacy with Byron led to some increase in his own social popularity. He had amusing stories to tell of the efforts of some ladies of title to get Byron to their parties by inviting Rogers, and adding in a postscript to the invitation, 'Pray could you contrive to bring Lord Byron with you?' He told Mr. Dyce that, at a party at Lady Jersey's, Mrs. Sheridan ran up to him and said, 'Do as a favour try if you can place Lord Byron beside me at supper.' Lady Jersey and Rogers had been allies from the old Brighton days in which he had written some lines to her daughter Harriet. The flirtation with the Regent was now over, and Byron wrote some verses on the return of her picture. It must have been about this time that the circumstance happened which Rogers used to tell about her. He was at a party at Henry Hope's in Cavendish Square. Lady Jersey took Rogers aside into the gallery to tell him something of importance. They met the Prince of Wales, who stopped, looked at Lady Jersey, drew himself up and passed on. Lady Jersey returned the stare, and turned to Rogers with a smile and a boast, 'Didn't I do it well?' The particular communication seems, then, not to have needed to be made.

Moore prints several letters from Byron to Rogers, dated in the spring and summer of 1814. Only one of them, which he considerably shortens, need be reproduced here—

Lord Byron to Samuel Rogers.

'Tuesday.

'My dear Rogers,—Sheridan was yesterday at first too sober to remember your invitation, but in the dregs of the third bottle he fished up his memory and found that he had a party at home. I left and leave any other day to him and you, save Monday, and some yet undefined dinner at Burdett's. Do you go to-night to Lord Eardley's, and if you do, shall I call for you (anywhere), it will give me great pleasure?

'Ever yours entire,
'B.

'P.S. The Staël out-talked Whitbread, overwhelmed his spouse, was *ironed* by Sheridan, confounded Sir Humphrey, and utterly perplexed your slave. The rest (great names in the Red-book, nevertheless) were mere segments of the circle. Ma'mselle danced a Russ saraband with great vigour, grace, and expression, though not very pretty. . . .'

The letter ends with praise of her eyes and figure. The next letter, dated 27th of June, is correctly printed by Moore, and it is only necessary to give one extract—

'You could not have made me a more acceptable present than "Jacqueline." She is all grace, and softness, and poetry; there is so much of the last that we do not feel the want of *story*, which is simple, yet enough. I wonder that you do not oftener unbend to more of the same kind. I have some sympathy with the *softer* affections, though very little in *my* way, and no one can depict them so truly and successfully as yourself.'

'Jacqueline' had occupied Rogers's leisure for the past year. He had put it into type and sent it privately to a few of his friends some time before its actual publication.

Byron was at the same time printing 'Lara,' and on the 8th of July wrote to Moore that Rogers and he had almost coalesced into a joint invasion of the public. He adds, 'I am afraid "Jacqueline," which is very beautiful, will be in bad company. But in this case the lady will not be the sufferer.' The coalition was made, and Murray asked to publish the volume. It was the only one of Rogers's poems which was issued at the publisher's risk. Murray, however, paid both Byron and Rogers half-a-guinea a line for the right to publish the first edition. The publication was anonymous, but no secret was made of the authorship, and both poets had the satisfaction of learning from Murray that the sale had been so good as to make the bargain a very profitable one for him. Samuel Sharpe, in his brief account of his uncle, says that 'Jacqueline' 'is an apology for a disobedient daughter; and Mr. Rogers, in his own family, had seen with pain a father claim too great control over his children's wishes in regard to marriage.' The reference is to the displeasure his own father had shown at the marriage, by his eldest brother Daniel, of his cousin Martha Bowles. 'Jacqueline,' however, has some echoes in it of Rogers's earliest poetical composition. The volume was not out till the London season of that year was over. When Luttrell read the lines in the first canto—

> She stops, she pants; with lips apart
> She listens—to her beating heart!

he cried, 'What nonsense!' It was a strong man's criticism. 'It is not nonsense,' said Rogers. 'I remember once when I was in bed at Holland House, I could not fall asleep because of a loud noise, thump, thump, which seemed to be caused by something near me. I discovered that it was the beating of my own heart.'

Three or four letters in the spring and summer of 1814 contain interesting glimpses of men and things in that exciting time.

Samuel Rogers to Richard Sharp.

'Wednesday [17 March, 1814].

' My dear Friend,—If you should happen to be disengaged to-morrow, and to have any evening engagement in this part of the world, you would perhaps oblige me with your company to dinner—or after it—but only on the *last* condition; and it would rejoice the heart of a very old and excellent friend. I expect only Blair and Dr. Holland from Albania. The new dedication to " Childe Harold " is very beautiful in *his* way. It is to a child I have often kissed on my knee—

' Love's image upon earth without his wing.

And, again, which will remind you of Wordsworth, though not as a plagiarism—

' Young Peri of the West, 'tis well for me,
My years already doubly number thine,
. . . . .
Happy I ne'er shall see thee in decline.

After which I fear you will turn away from,

' " Thee hath it pleased. Thy will be done," he said,
Then sought his cabin and the fervour fled;
And round him lay the sleeping as the dead,
When by his lamp to that mysterious guide.

' Ever yours,
' SAMUEL ROGERS.'

In April an event occurred which drew from Rogers a political epigram. Louis the Eighteenth was on his way from his retreat at Hartwell to re-occupy the throne of his ancestors. He was invited by the Prince Regent, in the words of a contemporary chronicler, 'first to display the royal dignity in the capital of England.' On the 20th of April, therefore, he made a triumphal entry into London, a troop of gentlemen on horseback, in white jackets and with white hats, leading the way. The postilions of the Prince Regent were dressed in the same way and bore the white cockades. The soldiers also wore the Bourbon emblem. This element in the public rejoicing at what was then thought to be the final close of the war, excited hostile comment among the circle at Holland House, where great admiration for Napoleon and sympathy with him was felt by the host and hostess and communicated to their intimate friends. Rogers expressed their feeling and his own in lines which have ever since remained in the privacy of his Commonplace Book—

*To the Military
on their wearing the White Cockade on the public entry
of the French King into London.*

Wear it awhile. Against him led
With your own blood you'll dye it red.
—But had your brave forefathers worn it,
Great Nassau from their brows had torn it.

It need not be inferred from these lines that there was any feeling in Rogers's mind but unmingled satisfaction at the new hopes of lasting peace. In the summer the allied sovereigns came to London, and a reference in a letter of Wordsworth's to Rogers seems to show that he, too, was not altogether satisfied with the 'convocation of emperors and other personages.' Rogers naturally stayed in London till the festivities were over, planning, however, a long visit to the reopened Continent. The following are among the letters he received during the summer—

William Wordsworth to Samuel Rogers.

'Rydal Mount: May 5, 1814.

'My dear Sir,—Some little since, in consequence of a distressful representation made to me of the condition of some person connected nearly by marriage with Mrs. Wordsworth, I applied to our common friend, Mr. Sharp, to know if he had any means of procuring an admittance into Christ's Hospital for a child of one of the parties. His reply was such as I feared it would be. . . . He referred me to you. . . . I have to thank you for a present of your volume of poems, received some time since through the hands of Southey. I have read it with great pleasure. The Columbus is what you intended. It has many bright and striking passages, and poems upon this plan please better on a second perusal than the first. The *gaps* at first disappoint and vex you.

'There is a pretty piece [1] in which you have done me the honour of imitating me, towards the conclusion particularly, where you must have remembered the Highland Girl. I like the poem much, but the first paragraph is hurt by two apostrophes to objects of different

---

[1] This piece is the lines 'Written in the Highlands.'

character, one to Luss and one to your sister, and the apostrophe is not a figure that, like Janus, carries two faces with a good grace.

'I am about to print (do not start) eight thousand lines, which is but a small portion of what I shall oppress the world with if strength and life do not fail me. I shall be content if the publication pays the expenses, for Mr. Scott and your friend Lord Byron flourishing at the rate they do, how can an honest poet hope to thrive?

'I expect to hear of your taking flight to Paris, unless the convocation of emperors and other personages by which London is to be honoured detain you to assist at the festivities.

'For me, I would like dearly to see old Blucher, but, as the fates will not allow, I mean to recompense myself by an excursion with Mrs. Wordsworth to Scotland, where I hope to fall in occasionally with a ptarmigan, a roe, or an eagle, and the living bird I certainly should prefer to its image on the panel of a dishonoured emperor's coach.

'Farewell. I shall be happy to see you here at all times, for your company is a treat.

'Most truly yours,
'W. WORDSWORTH.'

Sir George Beaumont to Samuel Rogers.

'Ashburnham: July 12th, 1814.

'My dear Rogers,—I wish I could make you a better return for your friendly patience and attention on Sunday, but as you expressed a wish for the epitaph, I send it to you; if it be not a likeness, it has nothing else to recommend it. You justly observed, every one should correct his own verses, for this reason, among others, that no one else could be so much interested in them; and although I could not perceive through your kindness any confirmation of this observation, yet, as I am sensible it is almost impossible for another to touch upon a picture or poem without making a spot of something better or worse, I have endeavoured to profit by your advice, and to alter the words objected to. What think you of "each virtue fostered," and "primeval" instead of "eternal" night?

'I had a delightful journey to this fine place with Lord Ashburnham. I wish you knew him more. When intimacy has subdued his shyness I assure you he possesses a rich vein of humour, which makes him a delightful companion. He is making great alterations here. Our friend Dance is his architect, and you know his ability. His domain is varied and extensive, and the views are highly interesting.

'The post is going out, and as we shall, I hope, meet soon, I will finish, with my best wishes, ever truly yours,

'G. H. BEAUMONT.'

Epitaph.

Here Johnson reclines in this grave, den, or pit,
The bugbear of folly, the tyrant of wit.
As an ox, overdriven, attacks in the streets,
And gores without mercy each creature he meets,
So this bellowing critic assailed every day
All his friends who had something or nothing to say.
Then he pitched and he rolled with a turbulent motion,
Like a First-rate just after a storm in the ocean

And if modestly silent, his censure to balk,
He exclaimed in a fury—Sir, why don't you talk?
If you said black was black, still his answer was, No, Sir,
And thundering arguments followed the blow, Sir.
For though lies he disdained from the days of his youth,
Still, the Doctor loved victory better than truth.

But, peace to his shade, if his powerful mind
Would sometimes break loose in expressions unkind,
He himself felt the blow when reflection came in,
For the Doctor had naught of the bear but his skin.
And in streams deep, majestic, o'erwhelming, and strong,
Full tides of morality flowed from his tongue.
Religion in him found a zealous defender,
And he never pretended to garble or mend her.
In his presence profaneness presumed not to dwell,
And sedition and treason shrank back to their hell.

Joseph Jekyll to Samuel Rogers.

'Tuesday, July 19th, 1814.

'My dear Rogers,—Kindness to children is a leading feature in you, kindness to me I never forget, and never shall I forget an unhappy night when you meditated so long with me on a subject which soon terminated so fatally.

'To-day I leave town, and have just sent excuses to the Lord Chamberlain's about Thursday night at Carlton House.

'My good old friend Mrs. Bird, who bred their mother up, is a sort of grandmother to my boys. She is in such an antiquated fidget about the fireworks, as to their safety in getting only to your house on the night they are to be played off, that I must ask your leave to let them come at any early hour in the evening. She is alarmed about ———. You will put them where you please in the house, and my servants will attend them home.

Yours, my dear Rogers, most obliged and most affectionately,
'JOSEPH JEKYLL.'

This letter tells its own story. Jekyll's children were to go to Rogers's house, with a host of other boys and girls, to see the fireworks which celebrated the Peace. It exhibits a side of Rogers's character which has not hitherto appeared—his fondness for children and his kindness to them. Of the many recollections of him which are still cherished by friends and relations, I find this feature always the most vivid. There are many hundreds of persons now living who speak of him with the warmest affection from their cherished recollections of his kindness to them in their childhood.

Uvedale Price was in London at the Peace rejoicings and gives an amusing account of his unsuccessful efforts to reach Rogers's house—

Uvedale Price to Samuel Rogers.

'Sunning Hill: Wednesday (August 1814).

' My dear Sir,—I think myself very unlucky during my two excursions to town, short as they were, to have seen you only once, and that in a crowd. It was not my fault. I called upon you several times, and at all hours, but you were not stirring, or just gone out earlier than usual, or not returned; in short, never to be found. On Friday, the day before I left town, I made a last attempt and the most unfortunate of them all. In spite of the rain I set out across the Park, but when I came to the passage the door was locked. I determined to go round by the stable yard, but on coming to the end of your garden I perceived that the path was railed across and a sentinel posted there. As I saw a gentleman walking that way I stopped to see what happened; he got upon a low rail and climbed over the high one close to the sentinel; I thought I might climb too, advanced boldly and had put one foot on the low rail, when the sentinel told me I must not get over; I pleaded the precedent I had just seen, he only said he must stop somewhere, and that I should not pass. Not feeling quite equal to scaling the palisade and knocking down the sentinel, I sorrowfully turned back, cursing these warlike effects of peace.[1] My next recourse was the door by the canal; that too was fast; and after having traced back my steps to Hyde Park Corner, I had not the courage to begin my journey again with the uncertainty of catching you at home. I wish this history were as interesting as it is long and melancholy, but Dogberry could not be more determined to bestow all his tediousness. I wished very much to have found you at home on various accounts. I wanted to thank you for "Jacqueline," which, indeed, George Ellis had already shown me. I have read it more than once, and with great pleasure. There were a few very trifling remarks that occurred to me, not worth putting down, but which, if I had seen you, I should have mentioned. I also wanted to take my revenge, if it can be so called, and, after having received so much pleasure from your poetry, to torment you with some of

[1] A reference to the preparations for the fireworks in the Park.

my prose. You probably shudder at this and think of
the famous lines on the Metromane—

> ' tous mes sens se glacent à l'approche
> Du griffonnage affreux, qu'il a toujours en poche.

' You have not quite escaped, and, seriously, as the
whole of this griffonage does not amount to more than
a dozen pages, I should be very glad if you would take
the trouble of looking it over. The subject, I think, is
curious, and I rather believe it has not been treated; it
is on the application of the terms that answer to beautiful in ancient and modern languages; that is in those
with which I am at all acquainted. I have shewn it to
a few learned and ingenious critics, who have liked it
more than I expected, and have thought the argument
drawn from it very convincing. My knowledge of Greek,
as you know, is very scanty indeed, and my reading as
confined. The examples I have given are chiefly from
Homer, the only book in the language with which I am
even tolerably acquainted; they are, however, the most
material of any. Now, I could wish for some others from
later poets and from the prose writers, or at least to be
assured whether in them there are any applications of
the word that essentially differ from those in Homer. I
believe you are well acquainted with Dr. Burney, with
whom my acquaintance is but slight, and it would be a
great piece of service to me if you could induce him to
look over and consider what I have written; supposing
that after you have read it yourself you should think it
at all worth his notice. I feel that I am imposing a
heavy task on you, and shall not be surprized or in the

least offended if you should beg to decline it altogether. Let me hear from you, however, and if you can make up your mind to receive it, and to read it yourself at least, I will send it you when I have copied it, for at present I have not a very fair copy. We set out for Foxley on Monday. I wish there were any chance of seeing you here or there, and all here most heartily join in the same wish.

'Most truly yours,
'U. PRICE.

'I shall not be in any hurry to have the MS. returned, and it may be sent to Foxley in two or three covers.'

CHAPTER V.

The Peace of 1814—Rogers goes to France, Switzerland and Italy—Diary of the Journey—The English in Paris—Napoleon Legends at St. Cloud—Fontainebleau—The journey South—Bossuet's House—Coppet—Geneva—News from Richard Sharp of Friends at home—Rogers in Venice—Petrarch's House at Arqua—Florence—A Winter in Rome—Visit to the Pope—Naples and Murat—The Hollands—The Princess of Wales—Bonaparte's Return from Elba—War Preparations—Homewards through War Alarms—Paestum—The Diary the Germ of 'Italy.'

I HAVE already said, that as soon as Peace had been concluded, in April 1814, Rogers began to contemplate a continental tour. He had never been in Italy, and, indeed, had not had many opportunities of visiting the Continent at all. Europe had been almost entirely closed to English people for half a generation. Rogers had been to Paris in 1791, and had seen the chiefs of the great revolution which was then in its apparently smooth career, with only the suspicion in the minds of a far-seeing few of the frightful rapids towards which it was bearing them on. His diary in that memorable visit has been given at full in the 'Early Life.' He had visited Paris again, as I have there recorded, with Fox and Mackintosh and his brother-in-law Sutton Sharpe, and a great crowd of artists and statesmen and distinguished people, during the brief gleam of European quiet which the Peace of Amiens brought in 1802. When that short interval had passed, the Continent was closed again for a dozen years. Peace had now once more been made. Napoleon was at Elba, and Europe breathed freely. As in 1802, there was again a great flight of the English to see scenes and places from which they had been so long shut out. Rogers and his sister Sarah started on their tour as soon as the London season was over, and Rogers spent all the remainder of that short respite from war in the most interesting journey of his life. They went first to Paris, then on to Switzerland, crossing the Alps by the Simplon. The winter was spent in visiting Milan, Venice, Florence, Rome, and Naples, and it was the beginning of April before they turned their faces homewards. At Florence they were met by the news of Napoleon's return to France, and when nearing Bologna became aware of the sudden outbreak of the war. They came home in consequence through the Tyrol and Germany, passing through Brussels while the British troops were gathering for the final struggle, meeting at Ghent with the fugitive King, whom they had seen welcomed into London twelve months before. They reached London six weeks before the battle of Waterloo.

This journey of eight months had a lasting effect on Rogers's life. He was busy at home with his poem of 'Human Life,' but he appears to have put that work entirely aside for a careful study of Italy. He went there as the poet and the man of taste, and he made his stay there the opportunity for the completion of his artistic culture. Nothing escaped his notice, and almost everything he observed was elaborately described and criticised in a diary written day by day, in evident and careful preparation for some future work. This diary is far too long to be reproduced here. It would fill a volume, and if published it would constitute a guide book to the natural beauties and the artistic treasures of a great part of Italy. It contains much of the material out of which his poem of 'Italy' was afterwards wrought. It is supplemented by letters to his friends, some of which epitomise the more personal parts of the Diary itself. These letters, with some others from that eminent favourite of London society, 'Conversation' Sharp, which kept him in touch with his friends during his absence, and a few extracts from the Diary, will sufficiently tell the story of this interesting journey.

The Diary begins:—

'*August* 20*th*, 1814.—Set sail at dusk from Brighthelmstone; a thousand sparks of light, like so many little stars, dancing in the dark sea under the boat.'

'*August* 21*st*.—No wind. Hailed by the French pilots.'

'*August* 22*nd*.—Landed at Dieppe as day was breaking, and left it at noon. Harvest people dining in groups by the roadside. A shepherd following his flock and knitting, his staff flung behind him. Descent into Rouen. The cathedral. Over the curtain in the theatre is inscribed Pierre Corneille, and over a small gateway in the rue de la Pie, "Ici est né 9 Juin, 1605, Pierre Corneille."'

'*August* 23*rd*.—Chalk-hills, cornfields, and orchards. Gathered apples and pears from the barouche box as we went along. At Mantes, where we slept, met with thunder and lightning; and Curran returning from Paris.'

'*August* 24*th*.—Terrace of St. Germains. Malmaison. Avenue from Neuilly to Paris.'

'*August* 25*th to* 28*th*.—Paris. The region of the Court a blaze of magnificence. Paris, the city of the great king, as London is the city of a great and enlightened people.'

'*August* 30*th*.—Mass in the Royal Chapel. Questions put to us by the people. Which was the king? Which Monsieur? Who was that lady? "Je l'ai bien vu," said a Frenchman as the King went by afterwards in his carriage. From the church tower of Montmartre saw the field of battle.'

'*August* 31*st*.—St. Cloud. Conducted through it by a servant who used to sleep by the bedside of Bonaparte. "He never changed his servants. A new face was death to him. Seldom slept above four hours. Was never heard to talk in his sleep. A mouse stirring would wake him. Walked fast with his eyes on the ground and his hands joined behind him. Spoke seldom and brusquement (mimicked his talk and his walk). Took coffee when he rose. Was to be seen there, in that alley, before five o'clock in the morning. Ate little at dinner, some bouillon, some poulard, that was all, his snuff-box by his side. Beaucoup de tabac, beaucoup de café." The gardener had been there thirteen years, but said he knew less of him, said he disliked observation and hurried away his servants, " un homme dur." The Empress submitted to him in everything. "They used to breakfast together, *à la fourchette*, in that avenue. She sat with her back to the library window, and he had a screen placed behind him when the wind blew." From the courtyard there is an uninterrupted view of the city, a city without smoke, and here not unlike a rough stone quarry.'

'*September 1st.*—Grand retrospect of Paris. Forest of Fontainebleau. Walked before the Château by moonlight.'

'*September 2nd.*—If walls could speak—those of Fontainebleau—how much would they tell of. The gallery of Francis I., painted in fresco by Primaticcio; the gallery of Diana, the scene of his gallantries; the gallery of the Cerfs, stained with the blood of Mondaleschi; the chambers inhabited successively by the kings of France, their wives, and their mistresses; by Henri IV., by Louis XIV., by Marie Antoinette, by Marie Louise (and all have left their footsteps); the oratory in which for fourteen months the Pope performed his daily devotions; the closet in which Bonaparte signed his abdication; the courtyard in which he took leave of his guards, his carriage at the gate to convey him away to Elba—these now silent and empty serve only to remind us of the fleeting nature of things.

'Long avenues through the forest; a post-house full of bullets. A Cossack horse. Broken bridges. Cathedral at Sens. The Yonne at Joigny; walked on the bridge by moonlight.'

'*September 3rd.*—Auxerre—Avallon. The College. One of the professors saluted me as the first poet of the age, and in return (could I do less?) I sent him back to render homage to our fellow traveller as the most upright

Judge, the most eloquent Senator, and the future Historian of Great Britain.'

'*September 4th.*—A bleak open country. The Bise blew to-day, and we were glad to warm ourselves at the fire in every post-house. Rock and wood as we draw near Dijon.'

'*September 5th.*—Bossuet's house; now a bookseller's. His study and little chapel. Before we descended into Dôle we found ourselves in the midst of a vast plain bounded by blue hills. Left Dôle through a grand avenue; a snow mountain in the S.E. Is it Mont Blanc? A hay harvest. Sunny features under a broad umbrella-like straw hat, which is sometimes slung behind very gracefully.'

'*September 6th.*—A fair at Champagnole. Slept at Morez.'

'*September 7th.*—Walked a post and a-half to the Rousses. A milk girl climbing the meadows and singing short stanzas, ending with "*la guerre.*" . . . The churchyard of the Rousses looks up a rude valley in which a little lake is shining, *le lac des Rousses,* and some heath ground to the right was pointed out to us that belongs to Madame de Staël, and lies in Switzerland. Three or four leagues off in this wild region stands the Château de Joux, in which Toussaint breathed his last. Little did the tyrant believe that he himself should so soon be conveyed in like manner across an ocean, and to a speck of land so small as to have made its existence denied by those who were sent to it. Went on, and at a turn of the road had a full view of the glaciers over a dark wood of firs, the snows of a dazzling brightness, and giving me the exhilaration I have often felt in an English shrubbery at Christmas; but it was mingled with other feelings; we now saw what we had so long wished to see; it was one of the days in our lives which we were sure to remember with pleasure, and all was congratulation. Came to a beautiful village, and, as we left it, the Valais, the Lake of Geneva, and the Alps of Savoy (Mont Blanc above all) burst upon us. Slept at Coppet. Sismondi, Schlegel and Davy there.' From Geneva he writes:—

Samuel Rogers to Richard Sharp.

'Geneva: September 8, 1814.

'My dear Friend,—Here we are in the presence of Mont Blanc; and I cannot tell you what were our feelings yesterday, when, at a turn of the road, as we descended the Jura, the Alps, covered with snow and glistening in a bright sunshine, presented themselves over a fir forest. We declared it to be the most eventful day in our lives; and in less than half an hour we were sitting on a rocky brow, not unlike yours at Ulleswater, and looking down on the Lake of Geneva; Geneva, Ferney, Coppet, Lausanne, Vevay immediately under us, and on the other side Savoy and its mountains in battle array. . . .

'Normandy is a very pretty country, and certainly worth seeing, even at the expense of the voyage. Rouen is in a beautiful valley; and the Seine and its hanging woods and vineyards accompany you most of the way to Paris; and yet I speak by comparison—with Picardy in my mind, indeed, with Burgundy, and all I saw till we reached Dijon; for a duller tract of country, or fitter to be passed in the night, I think I never saw. What we have seen since has amply repaid us; the passage of the Jura and the descent to Nyon are never to be forgotten. Paris, I must confess, fell short of my expectations; the region of the Tuileries is a little increased in splendour, but in every other part I saw no change but for the worse. There, however, it strikes you as the city of a great king; and you forget for a moment London, so infinitely its superior as the city of a great people. But perhaps we have travelled under unfavourable circumstances. Through Burgundy I wore my great-coat constantly, and we were glad to sit over the fire in many a post-house while the horses were changing. Last night and this morning at Coppet we supped and breakfasted by a fire, and the Bise seems to have set in for the winter.

'To-day we went to Ferney, and saw the room as *he* left it. By we, I mean my sister and myself, for M. [Mackintosh] was engaged to a dinner at Lady Davy's, and to-night he returns to Coppet. He has promised, however, to meet us at Lausanne, and make the tour of the little Canton with us, and I hope he will, though Madame de Staël and Sismondi are great attractions, and the Hollands are on the road. We passed them at Dijon in the dark. Adieu, my dear friend. What will become of us and where we shall go I cannot say—perhaps to Rome, perhaps to London. At all events, believe me to be,

'Ever yours,

'S. R.

' If walls could speak—those of Fontainebleau—what would they not tell of!—the gallery of Francis I., the gallery of the Cerfs, stained with blood, and the apartments of the Pope, from which he stirred out but twice for fourteen months; the closet in which Bonaparte signed his abdication, the courtyard in which he took leave of his guards—not to mention Henri IV. and Louis XIV., Marie Antoinette and Marie Louise, whose footsteps are in every room—what house in the world was ever like it! By the way, Marie Louise is now at Secheron, and we met her at the garden gate as she passed through it this morning. She is tall and fair, and not plain, but certainly not handsome, and too erect to be graceful. She was going to angle in the lake.'

There are, in the above letter, several points of close similarity with the Diary. I have left them as illustrating the extent to which the letters summarise the contents of the Diary. Richard Sharp's reply brings us back for a time to what was occurring among Rogers's more immediate friends and contemporaries at home—

Richard Sharp to Samuel Rogers.

'London: 3rd October, 1814.

'My dear Friend,—I cannot tell you how much I am obliged by your letter from Geneva. Were it not in the highest degree interesting in itself, I should value it greatly as a proof that you think of me notwithstanding our distance from each other, and the constant occupations of a journey in such a country as Switzerland. Would that I had been able to accompany you, and by your side had first seen the lake and the glaciers in the descent to Nyon. In your taste, you know, I have an habitual reliance, and I am quite sure that scenes which have made such an impression as you describe on you will produce a similar effect on me, according to the measure of my sensibility. You seem to have been broad awake at Fontainebleau. A common pair of eyes would not have seen a tithe of what you saw there; yet all you mention *was* there.

'I shall follow, I hope, your steps, excepting where you do not encourage me to follow, and at present my notion is that it will be best to go at once to Lyons, omitting Dijon. What struck my brother most was the journey from Geneva to Chamouni, the country about Villeneuve and Vevay, the vales of Lauterbrunnen and Grindelwald, and the upper end of the lake of Lucerne. He also speaks highly of the passage of the Brunig, and the country about Altdorf. I hope you have gone through these mountainous scenes without more fatigue than has been sufficient to give you a sound sleep at night. Some effort is necessary to stimulate one's attention.

'I have but just returned from Cumberland, where I was very lucky in the weather and in my society. I have been travelling with two very excellent persons— Lord Calthorpe and Lady Olivia Sparrow. She is a young and pretty widow, very accomplished and sensible. Both are very intimate with Wilberforce who sits for Lord Calthorpe's borough, and both are of that sort of serious people who are nicknamed "saints." I saw Southey often, but Wordsworth was absent at Lowther.

'From Brougham's most delightful house and grounds,

where I slept two nights, I walked with him through all the river scenery at Lowther, and I have also visited Haweswater. I would not build a castle like Lowther, but if I had a castle I should wish it to have such a neighbour as the river. Haweswater gave me great pleasure, both by its beauty and its quiet seclusion. I went to the Chapel, but without such fair companions as you had there. I spent a day with Canning at Bolton's. He was accompanied by Huskisson and Heber. In returning from Leeds, which you know is in the road from Bolton Abbey, I was overturned near Stilton in a *light* coach, as it is called, solely by its top-heaviness. Nine outside passengers outweighed us four insides, and the road happening to be rather rounder in its form than usual, over we went with a mighty crash in the middle of the night. I received not the least hurt, but one of the inside passengers was stunned, several of the outside were bruised, and one poor woman's ankle, I fear, was broken. A very pretty girl of about fifteen fell on me, and I found her weight much less than I guess you did that of Lady Holland when you were upset at her park gate. I hope she is benefited by her journey, for she is a warm and valuable friend. Long before this time, I take it for granted that you have fallen in with Lord Holland's party, and are probably absorbed by it. I hope, too, that you have seen Boddington. He writes in raptures, and I suppose is now passing the Simplon to Milan.

'I made a strange astronomical discovery this year, that the days are as long in September as in June. I had never travelled so late in the year before, and I had no idea of this undoubted fact before this journey. You cannot have the least suspicion of this important truth unless you go to bed, as I did, about *nine*, and get up at *five*. I am preparing a paper for the "Transactions" of the Royal Society, which will remove all your doubts.

'Southey thinks Wordsworth's last poem his best,[1] but I have not heard what the bookseller reports of the public opinion.

'Lara and his fair companion [2] are in great request, and are much liked in the country, as well as in town. I was more pleased with "Lara" than I expected, although the faults, especially in expression, are innumerable. I suppose your verse is in great vigour? You will go to Italy, of course, and then, " gratulor Œchaliam," you will necessarily write in its praise. A mountain air always did agree well with your muse.

'You will have parted from one of your pleasant companions, whose conversation at Paris, and in Switzerland, must have been invaluable. I have just left your letter under a cover at Clement's Lane, for Mr. Henry Rogers, and I hope to learn how to address this. You will, I trust, not forget me at Florence, Rome, and Naples, for I am very anxious to learn what impression these places make on you. May your journey be as beneficial to your health, and to Miss Rogers's, as it must be delightful to both.

'Yours ever affectionately,

'R. SHARP.'

---

[1] 'The Excursion,' which was published in the summer of 1814.

[2] Rogers's 'Jacqueline,' which was published by Mr. Murray in 1814 in the same volume with Byron's 'Lara.'

Going back to the Diary.

'*September 8th.*—In the garden at Secheron, met the ex-Empress Marie Louise. Geneva. Walked with Dumont and Sismondi. Calvin's pulpit. "Ici est né Jean Jacques Rousseau." "Ici est né Charles Bonnet." No such inscriptions in London : none for Dryden in Gerrard St., Johnson in Bolt Court, Milton in Bread Street and Bunhill Fields. Ferney. 'His chamber just as he left it on the morning he set off for Paris, twelve feet by fifteen. Round his bed hang pictures of himself, Le Kain, Frederick, Catharine and Madame de Chatelet, his little seamstress, and a boy who used to pile fagots on his fire. A delightful situation. Over woods he saw a lake at the foot of the Alps, and many a sunset must he have had, all *couleur de rose.*'

The journey continued, and the Diary tells day by day of scenes which have since become familiar to most English people. Rogers notes the literary and historic associations of the places seen ; spending, for example, at Rousseau's house, 'a five minutes such as I never felt before,' and borrowing Gibbon of a bookseller that he might read on the spot his description of Lausanne. At Zug he parted with Mackintosh, who had proved a very difficult travelling companion. Further portions of the Diary are epitomised in another letter.

Samuel Rogers to Richard Sharp.

'Venice : October 23, 1814.

' My dear Friend,—To-day, in my gondola, I vowed I would write to you to-night, if it was only to tell you to write to me at Rome, where I hope soon to be. You must have received my letter from Geneva long ago.

An excursion to Chamouni, and another to the Lake of Lucerne, two delicious days passed in the Isle of St. Pierre, and two more under the rocks of Meillerie, I should like much to talk to you about, but I don't know where to begin. Everywhere in Switzerland, the Alps, all snow, bounded the horizon. They shone in the sun and seemed impassable; nor was their extent less striking than their height. Indeed, everything perhaps has fallen a little short of my expectations but the Alps alone. They have exceeded them; and whenever they appear they affect me as much as if I was seeing them for the first time—I may almost say, as if I had never heard of them. But the passage over them—of that I don't know what to say. The road itself, smooth as that in Hyde Park, is an object of wonder, winding like a serpent, but in very long lines; and by bridges thrown over precipices and passages cut through the rock, gradually approaching the summit. When you looked back, you saw it running far below you, and in many directions, through those bleak and dreary tracts, like the great wall in Tartary. At last you leave the pine forests beneath you, and the water that falls by your carriage-window and is conveyed in channels under the road freezes into icicles as it falls there. We were ascending for eight hours, drawn by five horses, but the descent into Italy I can do still less justice to. We instantly entered a deep valley, and then opened, or rather shut, upon us one of the most extraordinary scenes in Nature. For twenty miles we went rapidly down through a pass so narrow as to admit only the road and the torrent that fell by our side. Often the road was hewn out of the mountain, and three times it passed *through it*, leaving the torrent to work its way by itself; the passage, or gallery as I believe it is termed by the French engineers, being so long as to require large openings for light. The road was so gradual that our wheel was never locked, the horses were almost always in a gallop, nor turned aside for the mules we met.

'We left Savoy at seven in the morning, and slept in Italy, at Domo d'Ossola, that night. The Lago Maggiore, Milan, the Lago di Garda, Verona, Padua,—what shall I mention next? As for Venice—I seem to wander about in a dream. Am I in St. Mark's Place? I say to myself. Am I on the Rialto? Do I see the Adriatic?—Nor can I tell you what I felt when the postilion, turning gaily round and pointing with his whip, cried out, "Venezia!" And there it was sure enough, with its long line of domes and turrets, white as marble, and glittering in the sun. If Venice is Venice no longer, as everybody tells me, one can, however, see what was never seen before, at least in the way one would like.

'This is the Hall of the Senate—this the chamber of the Council of Ten—into that closet (and it was black as black wood could make it) the state prisoner was brought to receive the sentence from the pozzi or the piombi, after which he was led down that narrow, winding staircase (and I shuddered when I attempted to look down it, for it seemed like a well) and across the Ponte dei Sospiri to be strangled in the first dungeon on the left.

'All this and more I heard with believing ears, such as I wished for at Verona when they showed us Juliet's coffin in a convent garden.

'I think I have made out the best tour in the world for you, I wish I may say for *us*. At all events, I hope you will not start before my return, that I may at least have a chance. I can save many a weary mile and much perplexity which I have experienced.

'Mackintosh left us at Zug, to meet his daughter at Basle; we met him again near Sion in the Haut Valais, on his return to Italy. I hope his health is improved, but it suffers greatly in a city like Paris, and I fear he will leave all he has gained, in the evening conversazioni at Talleyrand's.

'The Hollands we have met with at Paris, at Geneva, and at Milan. They are now, I believe, at Florence. Ward I met in the street at Milan. He is now, I fancy, on the road to Venice with Poodle Byng. The Princess of Wales came up on foot to our chaise window when we were changing horses within a few miles of Milan. She afterwards invited my sister and myself to a party there, which we could not avail ourselves of, and I flatter myself we shall be good friends when we meet at Florence.

'What has become of Boddington? We have followed here and there in his track, but never could overtake him. Has he come into Italy? I hope to meet with him in Tuscany—I say, in Tuscany!

'Oh, if you knew what it was to look upon a lake which Virgil has mentioned, and Catullus has sailed upon, to see a house in which Petrarch has lived, and to stand upon Titian's grave as I have done, you would instantly pack up and join me.

'But to talk seriously, is Fredley yours? I hope it is, and that you by this time possess a fragment of Italian landscape under English laws and with English security. Pray write and tell me all; and believe me to be, with great sincerity,

'Ever yours,
'SAMUEL ROGERS.

'Remember me kindly to Maltby. I read his name in the book at Schwyz. Does he remember the Lake as seen from the landing-place, or, rather, from the inn door at Brunnen? I shall never forget it.

'What a strange thing is fashion! Almost every man in Venice but myself wears boots. The men who wait upon us at dinner are like so many jockeys at Newmarket. How inhuman to rob them of the only four horses they had!'

Richard Sharp to Samuel Rogers.

'London: 2 December, 1814.

'My dear Friend,—I am afraid that my letter to Milan did not reach you, and I therefore in this thank you for yours from Geneva, as well as for that from Venice. You are very good. Nothing can so much lessen my regret for not having been able to accompany you as the pleasure that your letters give me.

'Happening to have nothing of a private nature in them, and being full of pleasant things, I have read them to others frequently, and even lent them occasionally, but with many an injunction and many a denunciation of vengeance against carelessness. It would be mortifying to lose one, and I will not run the risk, as I foresee that at some time or other they may be given to the public.

They would do you great credit. I have sent each to your brother immediately. Charles Ellis has set off for Italy with his sons and daughter, and he will tell you how much the sight of your letters delighted him when he meets you, as he hopes to do. We thought *her* pretty, and I suppose she will be old enough to inspire sonnets in Italy.

'I shall faithfully follow your directions in the journey which I hope to take in the spring; and that I may have a little time to stay in choice places, I think of employing between three and four months in a tour comprehending only Switzerland and the Italian lakes. Mackintosh, Horner, and Bowdler crossed and recrossed the Alps, and I purpose (unless you propose another route) to go by St. Gothard and return by the Simplon. Venice, Florence, Rome, and Naples, must be reserved till I can escape, as I intend, from business altogether. Dumont writes that he expects me to fulfil my engagements with him. From this I learn that he means to go back next year, though he is looked for here in a fortnight. You know that he has been chosen a representative in the council of Geneva, where he sits with Pictet and Sismondi, and with other eminent persons.

'I am not surprised by anything but your candour in owning that Switzerland, excepting when you looked upon the Alps, rather disappointed you. The Alps, however, both on distant and on intimate acquaintance, appear to have greatly transcended your expectations. What would I not have given to descend from the Jura, to cross the Alps, and to enter Venice and Rome with you. Yet, though I cannot have the advantage of being your companion, I shall take care not to lose that of being your follower. Pray do not be sparing of your directions.

'The grand Chartreuse! Did you go there? I have heard that after the Alps it makes but a feeble impression. The Monastery is now, alas, a saltpetre manufactory; but the Album remains, and in it is to be read the Alcaic ode in Gray's own handwriting.

'Boddington tells me that at Florence he got a glimpse of you as you were setting out for Vallombrosa, where, in November, you would find, I guess, the leaves strewn about as in Milton's simile. What present pleasures! What future recollections! Your Muse must have become already a fine Italian lady.

'Johnson says that some men learn more in the Hampstead stage than others from the tour of Europe. With such powers of observation and such an imagination as yours how your mind will be strengthened and animated! You will talk and write better than ever with such an accession of topics and of enthusiasm. Shall we not talk of Vallombrosa and the Apennines in St. James's Street, and in many a town assembly. I have missed you in these places sadly already, and have passed your "shut door with a sigh." Last Sunday I forgot myself, and actually mounted your steps to knock at the door, habit being too strong for memory.

'Since my excursion to the Lakes in September, and my turn-over near Stilton in returning, my occupations have been very dull. Three days at Romilly's on Leith Hill are the only incident of consequence, but I think of overcoming my aversion to great houses and of going to Bowood about Christmas. Lord Byron is the only friend of yours now in town whose society you would care for; for Parliament sat too short a time to bring the women to town, and you properly disdain most of the men.

'The Club met in full strength, where I related your adventures and quoted some of your sayings. I forgot to say that Brougham took me from Ulleswater to his delightful old residence, and showed me his agreeable mother and sister and the river scenery at Lowther. I was very much pleased with Haweswater. Brougham has taken his mother since to Paris and has left her there. She is a niece of your old Edinburgh acquaintance, Dr. Robertson the Historian.

'At Bolton's, on Winandermere, I spent a whole day with Canning, who is now gone to Lisbon. I then fell into a very pleasant party with whom I lived above a week. The attractions were: a sensible, amiable man (Lord Calthorpe), and an extraordinary person, a youngish, handsome, accomplished widow of great possessions, Lady Olivia Sparrow, a daughter of the late Lord Gosforth. You must know her, as you visited her father. They are Wilberforcians, and, like him, she is very lively and very pious. You will soon go on, I suppose, to Naples, which, we hear by the newspapers, is made very gay by our Princess, who is abused in our newspapers for keeping bad company. I can scarcely believe that I am to direct this letter to the author of "The Pleasures of Memory" and "Columbus," at Rome, even Rome itself. If you can spare five minutes from the Vatican and the Coliseum, pray tell me what you felt on entering the sacred city. Pray tell Miss Rogers that I hope she has health and strength to make the most of her opportunities. Farewell.

'Yours ever affectionately,

'R. SHARP.'

From the date of the last letter to R. Sharp the Diary proceeds. On the 24th they were at Arqua visiting Petrarch's house.

'Through a large room, or covered court, we entered a smaller. The ceiling was divided into small squares, each containing a rose, and the beam that crossed it was painted in like manner of a dark colour. The upper part of the walls was painted round, and not ill-painted, in compartments, or rather, a series of pictures in a slight manner, and in light or faded colours, faded from age, but most probably of an after time, representing his interviews with Laura, his grief, and the progress of his passion. In the next room, the ceiling the same, over the door was his cat, dried, in a glass case with some lines written under it in Latin hexameters. A third room, less than the second and much less than the first, contained, behind some old wire trellis, his arm-chair and wardrobe, half perished. Above lay his inkstand, in bronze—the form very elegant. A winged cupid formed the stopper, sitting on the top, and the vessel a circular vase with the heads of four sphinx-like women at the corners, each terminating in a branch or flower; the feet small and scarcely discernible. The chair was an arm-chair. Sitting in it, in a closet, six feet by five, into which another door led, with his head resting upon his hand, he was found dead.[1] The windows mostly down to the floor and opening each into a small iron balcony that looked over the valley. . . . Went again down the hill, and in the churchyard saw his tomb—a large stone sarcophagus on four short columns, resting on a double stone base. On the sarcophagus was sculptured his bust, his head wrapped round in that close head-dress he usually wore, the fashion of the time, and such as he is always represented in. The features, too, the same. A laurel tree, probably often renewed, being of no age, grew at each corner.'

To Rovigo, to Ferrara—where he visits the hospital of St. Anne in which Tasso was confined, the house of Ariosto and the room in which he died, and the University Library, and remarks, 'We tread on classic ground, every hill and valley, every bit of pavement in every town " by sacred poets venerable made." '—to Bologna, then with a muleteer over the mountains to Florence, where they spent 'the Day of the Dead,' and lingered, fascinated, more than half the month. Then on to Rome, which was seen in the morning haze on the 24th of November. The greater part of the Diary is written in Rome, where they stayed till the beginning of February. Interspersed with long accounts of the antiquities and descriptions of things seen with Millingen and bought,

[1] See the lines in 'Italy' on Arqua :—

'This was his chamber—'Tis as when he went,
As if he now were in his orchard grove.
And this his closet. Here he sat and read.
This was his chair, and in it, unobserved,
Reading or thinking of his absent friends,
He passed away as in a quiet slumber.'

are glimpses of the social life of the English in Rome in that winter. 'We dwell among the clouds,' he says, 'and look down on the seven hills of Rome. We are in the Rondinini Palace, distinguished for the possession of the celebrated mask of the Medusa, and, from the windows, command a little world.' The social amusements are innumerable. There are concerts at Lucien Bonaparte's; dinners at Lord Holland's, Lady Westmoreland's, and Lord Cawdor's; visits to Canova and Thorwaldsen; drives with the Torlonias; and a visit to the Pope. He 'was standing in his white cloth habit, buttoned up to the chin, and his shoes of scarlet crimson velvet embroidered with gold flowers. He received us most courteously, and we formed a circle before him; said much of the English, that he was now too old to travel, that he would rather have gone to England than where he did go, that he was going to receive some English ladies in the garden, to each of whom he gives a rosary. When we knelt to kiss his hand he seemed distressed, and affected to shrink back from us, and made many efforts as if to assist us to rise. His manners, however, are very simple, his courtesy equal to the most refined, and the sort of hysteric laugh, half subdued, with which he spoke generally to us as we were named to him, discovered a modesty and an anxiety to please which were very engaging.' This was on Twelfth Day. Twelfth Night was spent at the Hollands', where the Italians were afraid of sitting near the fire. Another day, 'dined at Sir H. Davy's. Canova shewed how he kissed his bed three times when he went into it after dinner. His bed regularly warmed.' On the 17th:

'Early visit from the Cawdors. Dined with the Hollands. Canova sat by at dinner, then came Macpherson, President of the Scotch College here, Lucien Bonaparte, and Rosa introducing a bishop. The Bonapartes and M. came to us in the evening.' 19th: Lord Holland ill ... 24th: 'After dinner at the Duke of Bedford's, the Duchess waltzed and danced with castanets before Canova. Looked in at Lord Holland's, and went to a splendid ball at the Marchioness of Mariscotti's. Silk hangings. Sixty lights in each of the two rooms. Dancing in one, cards in the other.' Many pages are filled with brilliant descriptions of the scenes of the Carnival, as well as with accounts of works of art. On the 8th of February they left Rome for Naples, where they went ' to the locanda del Sole, into a large room with columns and carved ceiling, but without a fireplace, the windows looking directly into a piazza as busy as the Palais Royal, and up to the summit of Vesuvius.' There were English friends everywhere, among them the Princess of Wales, Lady Oxford, Lord Clare, and the Hollands. Murat was king. Rogers was presented to him; he spoke of the weather of Rome as *triste* and of the Pope's enmity. At a ball at the house of the Minister of Finance, 'all the world danced, and the king himself, in a quadrille, with the Princess of Wales. Wonderful play with his limbs, too much so with his head and body. It gave him the balancing air of a rope-dancer, or of a dancing-master teaching ease to his scholars.' Murat was extremely polite to Rogers, whose fame as a poet had reached him. The Queen talked to him about 'The Pleasures of Memory.' Murat himself, as he rode on horseback about Naples, often met Rogers, and always saluted him with the question, 'Eh bien, Monsieur, êtes-vous inspiré aujourd'hui?' Lady Holland would not go to Murat's parties; but he paid great attention to her, and, at a concert given to her, placed her between himself and the Queen.

On the 6th of March, after a visit with Lord Holland to Pompeii, Rogers was at Lord Holland's at night, when the rumour came, 'Bonaparte gone from Elba.' Rogers adds: 'Fainting of his sister the Queen; many conjectures;' 'un peu d'espoir,' says Mosbourg, 'et beaucoup de désespoir.' There was no reason at present for hurrying home. On the 11th 'took leave of the Princess of Wales,' and on Sunday, the 12th, at a magnificent dinner at the Comte de Mosbourg's—'a dinner without end'—and a Ball afterwards; he records, 'Few Neapolitans there. Many rumours and much anxiety.' On the 18th, 'left Naples, a band of music playing God save the King and other tunes at our door. First to Rome, then to Florence, where one day Du Cane, Fazakerley, and Lord John Russell came to dinner, and Rogers writes: 'After all Florence strikes me most. I acknowledge the grandeur of Rome, the beauty of Naples, but Florence has won my heart, and in Florence I should wish to live of all the cities of the world. Rome is sad, Naples is gay, but in Florence there is a cheerfulness, a classic elegance, that at once fills and gladdens the heart.' On Monday, April the 3rd: 'Waked in the night by the baggage and carriages of the old King of Spain passing under the window. A bright moonshine. Overtook them afterwards in a state of hesitation, some returning, those in advance having been seized in Bologna. Men at house doors called to us, saying the Neapolitans were at Bologna and even at Lojano .... Slept at a lone house within twelve miles of Bologna. Next morning rose at half-past three.' Approaching Bologna they found the bridge was shut. 'Sent in a scout, who saw the King get into his carriages and set off with his staff. Went in myself, the gates open, the streets silent, almost empty. Saw the Comte de Mosbourg, "Je m'engage pour vous, Monsieur." Rumours of a battle.' April 5th: 'Troops filing through. A battle last night; a wounded officer leaning on his servant in the street. A General dangerously wounded. Called again on Mosbourg. Said he would write to the King to-night, and asked us to dinner. Lord John Russell and Fazakerley arrived.'

These brief extracts from a voluminous Diary may suffice. All the way home through the Tyrol and down the Rhine through Holland, and over Belgium, there were the signs and sounds of war. Brussels itself was all gaiety and warlike preparation, and Lord Wellington was already there. The road to Ostend was full of English cavalry, and at Ostend itself horses were being slung ashore from English transports, and cannon-balls being landed. As I have given only brief extracts from the more personal references in the Diary, it is only just to add one of the descriptive and reflective passages of which it is full.

'Country open and level; did not see the Paestum Temples till we approached them. The temples in a plain, on three sides shut in by the mountains, on the fourth open to the sea, and the sea itself half shut in by them, by the promontory of Sorrentum, within which are the isles of the sirens. A magnificent theatre, worthy of such objects; the columns almost bare, broken, and of an iron-brown, like iron rust; the floor green with moss and herbage; the columns and cornices of the richest tints and climbed by the green lizards that fly into a thousand chinks and crevices at your approach; the snail adheres to them, the butterfly flutters among them, and the kite is sailing over them; fluted fragments of columns and moulded cornices among briars strew the middle space between the temple and the basilica, and no noise is heard but the rustling of the lizards or the grazing of the silver-grey ox just relieved from the plough. Many twice-blowing roses here, not now in bloom; innumerable violets in bloom among the fragments, the air sweet with them. . . . How many suns have risen from behind the mountains and set in the Tyrrhene sea, throwing these gigantic shadows across the green floor, since in these temples gods were worshipped! Is it true that they remained buried for ages in the night of woods till a young hunter or a shepherd fell in with them? Was it on such an evening as this, the sun's disc just shining through them? Now the sea breeze and the mountain breeze sweep through them. Now the fisherman of Salerno, as he passes, sees them standing on the desert plains, under the mountains, and pilgrims visit them from the corners of the earth. The little towns (Capaccio old and new), that hang upon the mountains like an eagle's eyrie, look down always upon them. Still is the solitude awful from the vastness and grandeur of the theatre.'

These remarks, written in haste in the evening after the visit, compared with the lines headed 'Paestum' in the second part of 'Italy,' sufficiently show how the Diary formed the basis of the poem.

> They stand between the mountains and the sea,
> Awful memorials, but of whom we know not.
> The seaman, passing, gazes from the deck,
> The buffalo-driver, in his shaggy cloak,
> Points to the work of magic and moves on.
>
> . . . .
>
> How many centuries did the sun go round
> From Mount Alburnus to the Tyrrhene sea,
> While, by some spell rendered invisible,
> Or, if approached, approached by him alone
> Who saw as though he saw not, they remained
> As in the darkness of a sepulchre
> Waiting the appointed time! All, all within
> Proclaims that Nature had resumed her right
> And taken to herself what man renounced;
> No cornice, triglyph or worn abacus,
> But with thick ivy hung or branching fern;
> Their iron-brown o'erspread with brightest verdure.
>
> . . . .
>
> How solemn is the stillness! Nothing stirs
> Save the shrill-voiced cicala flitting round
> On the rough pediment to sit and sing;
> Or the green lizard rustling through the grass,
> And up the fluted shaft with short, quick spring,
> To vanish through the chinks that Time has made.
> In such an hour as this, the sun's broad disc
> Seen at his setting, and a flood of light
> Filling the courts of these old sanctuaries
> (Gigantic shadows, broken and confused
> Athwart the innumerable columns flung);
> In such an hour he came, who saw and told,
> Led by the mighty Genius of the Place.

CHAPTER VI.

1815-1816.

Rogers on Poetical Composition—Lines at Meillerie—Letters from Mackintosh, Coleridge, Uvedale Price, and William Lisle Bowles—At Lady Hardwicke's—The Authorship of 'Auld Robin Grey'—Rogers at Lord Spencer's—Captain Usher—Paris under the Allies—Letters from Richard Sharp—Rogers to his Sister—Rogers's Twelfth-night Parties—His Love of Children—Letters to Richard Sharp.

THE Diary, of which I have given a brief account in the preceding chapter, was the prose preparation for the poem by which Rogers is most likely to be remembered by posterity. He had not yet conceived the plan of his 'Italy,' for he was much occupied during the six years from 1813 to 1819 with his poem 'Human Life.' His method of composition involved this long deliberation. He described it himself in a letter, the substance of which was probably sent to more than one budding genius, or, in Southey's words, unfledged eagle, who sent his poems to Rogers with requests for his criticism and help.

Samuel Rogers to ——.

'I need not say how much flattered I am by your request, nor how happy I should be to render any service in my power to any young man of genius, but I would recommend to him a much better scheme, if I may say so, than you propose.

'Let him lay aside his composition for some months and then look at it with fresh eyes, and let him in the interval read attentively some of the great masters (Milton or Dryden for instance) and then read what he has written. His good sense and feeling will then enable him to come to a much better judgment concerning himself than any criticism of mine. I may be wrong, but such was my practice, and I would recommend it to others.'

'S. R.

'P.S. Few, says Sir J. Reynolds, have been taught to any purpose who have not been their own teachers. Some, says Gibbon, praise from politeness, and some criticise from vanity. The author himself is the best judge of his own performance; no one has so deeply meditated on the subject; no one is so interested in the event.'

Rogers was not entirely faithful to the principle contained in these last sentences. He constantly consulted his friends, and his letters to Richard Sharp, and some of those to Moore, are full of lines, and alternative lines, of whatever poem he has in hand at the time. This was in accordance with what seems to have been a custom in his circle. Moore, for example, was fitfully busy at this time with 'Lalla Rookh,' and in one of his letters tells his mother that Rogers's criticisms had twice upset all that he had done, and that he has told Rogers he shall see it no more till it is finished. The immediate poetical result of his continental tour in 1814 and 1815 was the production of a short poem, which was included in the edition of his poems published in 1816, and now, with some changes, forms part of ' Italy.'

Written at Meillerie, September 30, 1814.

These grey majestic cliffs that tower to Heaven,
These glimmering glades and open chestnut groves,
That echo to the heifer's wandering bell,
Or woodman's axe, or steersman's song beneath,
As on he urges his fir-laden bark
Or shout of goatherd boy above them all,
Who loves not ? And who blesses not the light,
When through some loophole he surveys the lake,
Blue as a sapphire stone, and richly set
With chateaux, villages, and village spires,
Orchards and vineyards, alps and alpine snows ?
Here would I dwell ; nor visit but in thought
Ferney, far south, silent and empty now.
As now thy Chartreuse and thy bowers, Ripaille ;
Vevay, so long an exiled Patriot's home ;
Or Chillon's dungeon-floors beneath the wave,
Channelled and worn by pacing to and fro ;
Lausanne, where Gibbon in his favourite walk
Nightly called up the shade of antient Rome ; -
Or Coppet, and that dark untrodden grove [1]
Sacred to Virtue and a daughter's tears !
Here would I dwell, forgetting and forgot ;
And oft, methinks (of such strange potency
The spells that Genius scatters where he will),
Oft should I wander forth like one in search,
And say, half-dreaming, ' Here St. Preux has been
Then turn and gaze on Clarens.

      Yet there is,
Within an eagle's flight, a nobler scene :
Thy lake, Lucerne, shut in among the mountains,
Mountains that flank its waves as with a wall

[1] The burial place of Necker.

Built by the Giant race before the flood;
Where not a cross or chapel but inspires
Holy delight, lifting our thoughts to God
From God-like men—men in a barbarous age
That dared assert their birthright, and displayed
Deeds half-divine, returning Good for Ill;
That in the desert sowed the seeds of life,
Framing a band of small Republics there,
Which still exist, the envy of the World!
Who would not land in each, and tread the ground;
Land where Tell leaped ashore; and climb to drink
Of the three sacred fountains? He that does
Comes back the better; and relates at home
That he was met and greeted by a race
Such as he read of in his boyish days;
Such as Miltiades at Marathon
Led, when he chased the Persians to their ships.
 There, while the well-known boat is heaving in,
Piled with rude merchandise, or launching forth,
Thronged with wild cattle for Italian fairs,
There in the sunshine, mid their native snows,
Children, let loose from school, contend to use
The cross-bow of their fathers; and o'er-run
The rocky field where all, in every age,
Assembling sit, like one great family,
Forming alliances, enacting laws;
No cliff, or headland, or green promontory
But echoing back strains of their fatherland,
Graven to their eyes with records of the past
That prompt to hero-worship, and excite
Even in the least, the lowliest, as he toils,
A reverence nowhere else or felt or feigned;
Their chronicler. great Nature; and the volume
Vast as her works—above, below, around!
The fisher on thy beach, Thermopylæ,
Asks of the lettered stranger why he came,

First from his lips to learn the glorious truth !
And who that whets his scythe in Runnemede,
Tho' but for them a slave, recalls to mind
The barons in array with their great charter ?
Among the everlasting Alps alone,
There to burn on as in a Sanctuary,
Bright and unsullied lives the ethereal flame.
'Twas Freedom kindled it ; Religion guards it.
And mid those scenes unchanged, unchangeable,
Why should it ever die ?

These verses, having been sent to Sir James Mackintosh, called forth from him the following interesting letter.

Sir James Mackintosh to Samuel Rogers.

'Friday, August 18th, 1815.

' Dear Rogers,—A thousand thanks for your beautiful verses, which call before my eyes our agreeable travels. The Lakes of Geneva and Lucerne are strongly and justly contrasted. The first naturally cheerful and surrounded by animated cultivation, or by places distinguished as the residence of men of talent. The second tremendously sublime—a fit scene for heroic virtue. I know not whether the Lake of Lucerne might not be characterised still more clearly, or, to speak more truly, whether its characteristic feature might not be more brought out. What morally distinguishes the Lake of Uri from most, if not all, other spots on the globe, is that it is perhaps the only place where the whole inhabitants, without excepting the most simple and least instructed, contemplate the scenes of the noble acts of their forefathers in far-distant times with a reverence which study, in most places, teaches the best very imperfectly to feel and sometimes to feign. Fields of battle are, indeed, in many countries interesting to the vulgar, but mere acts of patriotic virtue have not rendered any spot in other countries the object of permanent popular veneration. I fear it could scarcely have happened in a Protestant country. A religion which tolerates hero worship was necessary to perpetuate the sanctity of Tell's Chapel. Travellers from the Isles of the Ocean come to announce to the people of Thessaly that the beach of Thermopylæ differs from other portions of their coast. Not many of the neighbouring inhabitants know what was done on Runnymede, and very few indeed pass over it with unaffected feeling. The inhabitants of Altdorf and Gersau look on the Chapel of Tell with probably stronger feelings than their ancestors who saw it rise from the ground.

'In countries of industry and wealth the stream of events sweeps away these old remembrances. The solitude of the Alps is a sanctuary destined for the monuments of ancient virtue. Here all is quiet and unchanged. Six centuries have passed away unmarked by any events but three or four pure victories which guarded from profanation the temples of the patriots, and rooted still more deeply the devotion to their memory.

'Excuse this talk, and believe me, dear Rogers,
'Very truly yours,
'J. MACKINTOSH.'

Immediately on his return from Italy Rogers had been in correspondence with Coleridge, who was then living at Calne. Coleridge had long got over his antipathy to Rogers, if it was ever any more than a passing feeling due to low spirits. He had been at Rogers's house, and one morning, breakfasting there with Hookham Frere, he talked for three hours on poetry, while Rogers and Frere sat spell-bound, and when he had done 'thought him still speaking, still stood fixed to hear.' The correspondence in this spring was about some literary undertaking. Coleridge wrote to Rogers, who replied, and then Coleridge wrote again.

Samuel Taylor Coleridge to Samuel Rogers.

'Calne, Wilts.

'Dear Sir,—I rejoice that you have returned in safety, "lætis quam lætus amicis," and after having seen what no poet or philosopher can have seen in vain—the Benedictine Church of San Paolo fuori del Porto,[1] the Moses of M. Angelo, his prophets, sibyls, and the central picture in the Sistine Chapel, and (I hope that I may add) that rude but marvellous pre-existence of his genius in the Triumph of Death and its brother frescoes in the Cemetery at Pisa. This, and the Moses, were deeply interesting to me, the one as the first and stately upgrowth of painting out of the very heart of Christendom, underived from the ancients, and having a life of its own in the spirit of that revolution of which Christianity was effect, means, and symbol; the other, the same phenomenon in statuary, but unfollowed and unique (for there is no analogy to it in the unhappy attempt at picture petrifactions by Bernini, in whom a great genius was bewildered and lost by excess of fancy over imagination,

[1] This is commonly called 'San Paolo fuori le Mura.'

the aggregative over the unifying faculty). Were I forced into exile, or if, without a perforce, I could take with me those whom I most love and regard, I should wish to pass my summers at Zurich, and the remaining eight months alternately at Rome and in Florence, so to join as much as I could German depth, Swiss ingenuity, and the ideal genius of Italy; that, at least, which we cannot help thinking, almost feeling, to be still there, be it but as the spirit of one departed hovering over his own tomb, the haunting breeze of his own august, desolate mausoleum. For it is scarce possible to live over again in such thoughts and express oneself in the language of one's ordinary feelings.

'I feel, and shall ever retain, a grateful acknowledgment of your great kindness in replying to my letter so quickly after your return, and when both your thoughts and time must be so much occupied. I am still most desirous to undertake the translation either of Cervantes or of Boccaccio's works, the Don Quixote and Decameron excepted, and want no other encouragement than a settled promise from some respectable publisher, such as Mr. Cadell, that he will purchase the manuscript when it is ready for the press. Cervantes will, with the Life and Critical Essay, form three large octavo volumes, each of which will form an entire work. I am about to send a volume of MS. poems in the course of a few weeks to Lord Byron, to whom I was encouraged by Mr. Bowles to write, and from whom I received a no less kind than condescending answer. I trust that they will appear to him not likely to disgrace any recommendation from him.

'Mr. Bowles leaves Bremhill on Monday next for

town. The being so near him has been a source of constant gratification to me. He has an improved edition of his "Missionary" in the press, and a volume of sermons worthy of a calm-minded clergyman, and which will, I trust, contribute to counteract the poison of Fanaticism, by way of preventive antidote; for the already diseased are incurable. We cannot expect that a man should attend to the reason of another, the pride of whose faith is to contradict and abjure his own.

'Should you find an opportunity to speak to Mr. Cadell, I should be only so far solicitous about the terms as that they should not be *humiliatingly* low in proportion to the labour and effort. With unfeigned regard, I remain, dear Sir,

'Your obliged and grateful
'S. T. COLERIDGE.

'May, 1815, Thursday (postmark, 26 May).'

The next letter tells its own story.

Uvedale Price to Samuel Rogers.

'Foxley: June 17th, 1815.

'My dear Sir,—I have often thought of you, often wished to hear of you, and still more to hear from you, but till within these few days (such is the profound ignorance in which we are buried here) I did not know that you were in England. I particularly desired my son to inquire about you, and I was very glad to hear from him that you had escaped all perils and dangers and were returned *sano e salvo*. The last letter I had from you was dated Venice; and in that, which gave me a great desire to receive more of them, you expressed a wish to hear from me again at Florence or Rome. What became of the letter I wrote almost immediately in consequence I know not; but I should be very sorry you should think I had neglected thanking you for the very pleasant one I had received, or giving myself some claim to others of the same kind. I can bring witnesses, if necessary, that I did fill a single letter as full as it could hold, and directed as you desired. I beg, however, to be understood that all this is meant to justify myself from the charge of neglect, not to accuse you. A letter of yours from Rome or Naples would have been highly interesting, and in truth we were all most anxious to receive one. If your conscience tells you that you ought to have written it, there is but one way of making us amends for the disappointment; that is, by coming here, not merely for a day or two, this summer, and telling us *vivâ voce* the whole history of your travels and adventures *dal alto a basso*. If you do this I acknowledge that the amends will be ample, and I beg we may have it soon under your own hand, that nothing shall prevent you coming in the course of the summer or the autumn to this place, where, by the by, I have been doing a good deal in my little way, and flatter myself that I have some interesting things to show you.

'You may, perhaps, remember, though it is a long time ago, that when you set off on your tour you carried a little MS. of mine with you to Paris and then sent it to Dr. Burney. If he received it and did read it he probably thought no more of the paper or its contents, and has now forgot every circumstance about it. It is just possible, however, that he may remember something of it and of what occurred to him at the time. Any remarks of his would be very valuable, and if it would not be giving you too much additional trouble about such a trifle, you will, perhaps, have the kindness to find out whether he ever did receive the paper and whether he recollects anything about it.

'I must now end this letter, *et pour cause*; about two months ago I received a very severe blow on one of my eyes, unfortunately the best and strongest of the two, which has very much impaired the sight of it. On stating my case to Sir William Adams he said that such accidents generally bring on a cataract. *Dii meliora*; as the eye is not only dim but weak, I must leave off. Lady Caroline and my daughter desire to be kindly remembered to you. They depend upon seeing you here.

'Most truly yours,
'U. PRICE.'

There is a letter from another interesting person, who had made a great reputation as a critic and as a pleasing writer of poetry some years before.[1]

Rev. William Lisle Bowles to Samuel Rogers.

'Bremhill: June 21st, 1815.

'My dear Rogers,—Lawyer Williams, the barrister, a friend of Horner's, has been here, since I came home,

---

[1] Bowles published his *Fourteen Sonnets* in 1789. *The Spirit of Discovery* was issued in 1804. His edition of Pope, which created great controversy, appeared in 1807.

and has excited some anxiety in my mind by saying that, according to strict etiquette, I should not have said in my dedication "My dear Lord," but only "My Lord." I am sorry if I have done wrong; you will witness for me it was unintentional, as it was my common mode of address, and I thought to have done otherwise would have appeared affected formality; but he seems to think that, what might be proper in private, might not be so before the public.

'Had I, contrary to my general usage, addressed Lord Lansdowne as "My Lord," it might also appear that I spoke as less independent than I have always been, and always shall be. Dallaway ought to have addressed the Duke of Norfolk, or Crabbe his patron, the Duke of Rutland, so,—but I have no patron, nor want one, though I never forget the most trifling kindness I have ever received in the common intercourse of life; and I do not see, in my situation, why I should use a different language in public, from that which I use in private, to any man living: at the same time there is no one who would less willingly violate the common etiquette of cultivated society.

'Your good-nature will, if I have done wrong, put the thing in such a light that no offence can be taken; indeed, I know it contrary to the nature of so noble a mind to take any.

'I wrote some verses, in the midst of the lame and blind men at Greenwich, which I sent Lady Beaumont, as I thought them something in the way of the Father of the Lake Poets (what blasphemy! her Ladyship will say). I brought you in, I think, happily enough—

'And He, to whom sad Memory gave her shell,
And bade him tones of sweetest music swell,
Was with us.

'As I was *struck* with the circumstance of the *blind man and the bird*, just as it happened, I am pleased with the verses, but shall put them in my little hymn book.

'Remember me to all at Highbury Terrace, and I hope to dine there another Sunday, and I wish I could see the same party to dine some Sunday here.

'So no more from your's ever,
'W. L. B.

'Do write to me and tell me what I am to think of the public news—écrivez. You will seriously oblige me if you will let me know whether all is right about the Dedication, and, if you have had time to look over my corrections and additions, I shall find it an additional favour if you will give me your opinion with respect to the conception and execution of what has been added to the "Missionary" [1]. . .'

Two entries in a diary and a letter to his sister show how Rogers spent a summer holiday this year.

'*July*, 1815.—At Lady Hardwicke's, Tunbridge Wells. "My sister Anne wrote 'Auld Robin Gray' into the album at Dalkeith; and somebody, on a public day there, tearing out several of the leaves, upon one of which it had been written, it became known. She had no idea

---

[1] *The Missionary of the Andes*, published in 1815.

when she wrote it of ever making it public. An old
Laird, a friend of ours, pronounced it instantly modern,
from the use of the words 'a crown' and 'a pound,'
a Scotch pound having been but tenpence of our money.
I wish he had lived to know it was my sister's. It is
always sung incorrectly—'but a kiss' should be 'but
one kiss.'"—*Lady Hardwicke.*

'*August 7*, 1815.—Met Glover, son of the author of
"Leonidas," in St. James's Street. "Did Brydone go
up Etna?" "I saw him at the top." "Did you see
the prospect he describes?" "We could not see an
inch for the mist." "Why was it said he did not go
up?" "The fellow had provoked many by his book.
They said so to vex him."—S. R.'

Samuel Rogers to Sarah Rogers.

'Westfield, Ryde: Friday, six a.m. !! (? 1815).

'My dear Sarah,—I hope you had no cross accidents
in your way to Wassall—that you met with no armies,
no refractory mules or muleteers, no Irish Bishops, and
are now enjoying fine weather in a beautiful country
with everybody well and happy about you. As for me, I
performed my journey almost all the way alone, and,
passing through Portsdown Fair, the gayest scene in the
world, had a beautiful sail to this island in the packet
for one shilling! Lord S[pencer]'s house is deliciously
seated on a green lawn among flowers and flowering
shrubs, and looking over a grove of trees to a sea so blue
and smooth, and so full of sails of all sizes and colours in
perpetual motion, that one does not know which way to

look. I walk to Binstead churchyard in five minutes, and there, in Quarr woods and about Quarr Abbey, I generally pass the best part of the morning, if I don't wander through the grounds of St. John's (Captain Hutt's and Mr. Simeon's), which are still as lovely as ever. The Star Inn is just as we left it; whether our indefatigable attendant is there still, and still talking of Mrs. Clarke, I don't know. Lord Spencer passes most of his mornings in his sailing vessel, but I have hitherto resisted all his kind invitations, though the sea is like glass; but to-day I mean to venture, as it is my last day, and I wish to board a ship of the line once in my life. I found Lyttelton and Lady Sarah here. Lyttelton left us yesterday in the "Northumberland," the Captain, C., being an old friend of his, and having a very natural wish to see, if he can, the man no less attractive, though less accessible, than Gulliver himself. The ship left us last night and dropt down to St. Helen's on her way to Plymouth, having taken in six months' stores and provisions, as Lord Spencer discovered at breakfast the other morning. . . . As we are seldom without an admiral at dinner we learn every way. The other day Captain Usher dined with us who had conveyed Bonaparte to Elba. He is a very interesting man, and was once so bitter against him as to be laughed at by all the Service in the Mediterranean. His cabin was covered with all his caricatures; nor were they removed, as he told me, when B. came into it. U. is now as violent in his favour, and of course has lost his ship. Lyttelton goes directly from Plymouth to his constituents at Worcester, so perhaps you will hear all about his expedition. To-morrow I go with great regret, but, as I shall not stir again for a little while, I mean to console myself now and then with a good sleep at Highbury. . . .

'S. R.

'P.S. I have had a letter from Du Cane. He is delighted with the purchase of the marble, and speaks of you and his journey with you from the Maschero in a way to make me like him. He goes again to Italy in a few weeks, and asks if you have any commissions for Rome or Naples!'

Richard Sharp writes from Paris, whither the English were again flocking when Waterloo had brought lasting peace—

Richard Sharp to Samuel Rogers.

'Paris: Wednesday, 23rd August, 1815.

'My dear Friend,—You said something about visiting Paris in October, and I therefore cannot help informing you that a few days ago I saw sixty pictures of the Dutch School taken away, and a hundred and sixty-five more have since been removed. Yesterday I actually saw two noble statues removed under the direction of a Prussian officer and a superintendent of the gallery. Denon told me yesterday that his heart was broken. It is generally understood that the Emperor of Austria claims all the pictures and statues belonging to his Italian states; and that the Pope has sent a minister to demand his. Ministers are here from all parts of Europe to require restitution. By accident the noble Spanish Raphaels are here. Joseph Bonaparte sent them to be cleaned. The gentleman at whose house we saw them says that the King of Spain has ordered them back, but that they are to be cleaned *first*. Such pictures I never saw. They realise one's notions of the pictures of Apelles. They are called " Lo Spasimo," the " Madonna del pesche," and " The Pearl " and " The Salutation." The tendency of this information and the motive you cannot but see, yet I must fairly add that the diligences to Amiens and to Calais have lately been robbed, and I shall not venture to travel by night.

'It is impossible to give you the faintest conception of the scene now passing before our eyes. Montmartre fortified by the English, who exclude all French from their lines. Three of our regiments encamped in the Champs Elysées. Rufflius, the Prussian Governor of Paris, and Prince Schwartzenberg, live in hotels surrounded by troops. So do the Emperors of Russia and Austria—at Wellington's door are only two sentinels.

' Adieu.
'Ever yours affectionately,
'R. SHARP.

'P.S. I am hourly annoyed by English invitations. You would be covered by cards and notes.'

In the middle of September Rogers followed the universal example and went over to Paris. A letter to his sister is the only record of the journey.

Samuel Rogers to Sarah Rogers.

'Paris: Oct. 14th, 1815.

'My dear Sarah,—I wish you had seen the "Pie Voleuse" with us. It was for the ninetieth time, and, though in a little theatre on the Boulevard, charmingly acted throughout. Palaiseau is a mountain village, and given to the life—the headdresses, I confess, from their extravagance, disturbed me. Little Annette's cap of white crape resembled at a little distance a plume of feathers. I have seen Mlle. Mars many times with great delight, and Talma, though the life is a little laborious, as I am obliged to read Play and Entertainment before I go (a work of three hours at least) or I don't understand a word they say. The best dancer at the opera—the best, they say, they ever had—is a Mlle. Goselin; she is very young and one of a large family. When Talma acts the orchestra is full, and the music sent off. I begin rather to like the French tragedy. Talma plays for his benefit next Thursday "Hamlet" and "Shakespeare Amoureux." The lady, some Warwickshire beauty of course, is to be performed by Mlle. Mars. I was *enrhumé* for many days last week, but the situation of the hotel consoled me a little for the confinement, as from my windows I see the whole of the palace, and the gardens full of orange trees, and statues, and idlers, and newspaper readers. I wish so much that we had lodged there last year. To dine at Very's we only cross the street. The King goes out every day. If you remember, there were two carriages. The last is always empty and follows in case of accident. I suppose some king of France once broke down and had to return on foot. Du Cane had left Paris before I came, I suppose for Italy. When we had been here seven or eight days, who should walk into our room before breakfast but Millingen! He had been detained by illness and had seen B. at a distance in the street. He set off two hours afterwards. I mentioned your regret at missing him. The Conynghams and Lord Ebrington are at Geneva. Stuart is here from Italy; he saw the last of poor Eustace and was at Genoa when Lady Jane died. The Duchess comes home immediately. The Philipses and Dr. H. removed to our hotel and left us ten days ago, returning by Holland. Jeffrey, the Edinburgh Reviewer, succeeded them, and we have generally dined together.[1] As to the English world, I have seen nothing of it. Once I was asked to a ball, but I did not go, and have called on nobody. Lawrence dined with us once at Beauvillier's and walked afterwards in the Palais Royal. Lord Stuart gave him a horse, and he lived upon it. I wonder whether he ever rode before. The Emperor of Russia promised to sit to him, but never did. I think there are more men here without a leg or an arm than I ever saw anywhere. At a dance (*bal paré*) on the boulevard last night (where were more fireworks and a conjuror, and all for two livres) a Frenchman quadrilled and waltzed on a wooden leg with an agility and neatness of execution such as I have not often seen on a natural one. We had a fine day for St. Cloud, but saw only half the house, Blucher having rummaged the

---

[1] Jeffrey says to Moore, 'I was lucky far beyond my deservings in meeting with Sam Rogers at Paris, and we had great comfort in talking of you.'—*Life*, vol. ii., p. 102.

library, and the Duchess of Angoulême, who visits the
château almost every day, being there. I met Lord
Mountmorres and his wife and daughter there. Our old
friends the concierge and the gardener are gone. In our
way we passed, as you know, through the Bois de Boulogne,
full of English tents and just like a fair—many French
with wares and eatables having established their stalls
among them—and I am sorry to say that the axe is very
busy in our hands. Last Sunday we were at Versailles,
the gardens were gay and full of people, the palace still
unfurnished, and I don't think you lost much. With
regard to the gallery, a subject I don't like to begin
upon, it is now only full of picture frames and pedestals,
and the swallows are literally on the wing there. Every
marble of note, except the Borghese Vase and the fighting
gladiator, are gone, and every picture, except a small
Correggio and Titian. Much difficulty and many re-
pulses we found, while they were removing—even from
our own soldiers, to whom our officers often gave in-
structions to admit only officers—but now all is thrown
open and the French have full leave to contemplate the
wreck, a leave none of the better sort avail themselves
of. The French are said to show no feeling; but the
melancholy groups assembled for some days before the
Venetian horses—till our engineers took them down
(for the Austrians did not know how)—and those afterwards round the column with the same sad presentiment,
would have affected you not a little. The English are
very unpopular, a caricature is in circulation of Wellington with large moustaches and a stern countenance,
under-written "M. Blucher," and it is everywhere said

that our officers in the gallery presented their ladies publicly with small Correggios and Raphaels, a tale we contradict to no purpose. Denon has resigned, and, when I called upon him the other day, I found him in a condition that overcame me. I saw Canova out in the open street with the "Transfiguration," the "St. Jerome" of Domenichino, and two other Raphaels, half supported in the dirt, and at a loss how to marshal the Austrian soldiers who were to transport them on their heads, uncovered, to the barrack, where I have been two or three times, and which is a terrible scene of confusion.

'The horses went by our windows, one by one, in as many carts, uncovered, like dead horses, and the people stood at the doors to see them pass by. It is very strange to see an English guard in the Palais Royal and English soldiers strolling in every street. One poor fellow in a jacket accosted me the other day in a Babylonish dialect perfectly unintelligible; at last I said in despair, "Are you an Englishman?" "Thank God, I am, Sir," he answered very briskly. We dine sometimes at Beauvillier's, sometimes at Very's. The first gives far the best dinner and we always see many ladies there—French and English. Why was not it so when we were there? One day when we were there, Lady Caroline Lamb came in alone. I wish Henry had come. We could have lodged him well. It was indeed a cruel thing to come in as Stothard went out. I am glad to hear from Patty (pray thank her for her kind letter—I have just received it) that you have taken possession of your alabasters.

'Our month is out next Tuesday, and I hope to set

out on that day. In that case we shall be in town probably early in the next week, but don't expect me till you see me.

'I have not seen Miss Williams yet. I have called and written and have been asked to a party where I could not go. Mosbourg called and paid me a long visit. My love to Henry and Patty, and all at Highbury and at Newington.

'Ever yours,
'S. R.

'P.S. You remember the avenue by which we entered Paris from Neuilly and St. Germains? The English, men and ladies, and many French ladies, ride up and down there as in Hyde Park every afternoon.

'I have taken our catalogues from the Wagram Hotel, now removed to another street. The moment I mentioned them, our landlord pointed to them on the table tied up as we had left them. The Spanish Raphaels, so celebrated, are now in the picture gallery we saw opposite our hotel.

'One of the Lees from Highbury is here—the only one I know. I spent a beautiful morning at Malmaison yesterday. The Emperor of Russia has bought Canova's marbles, and they are gone with many pictures. The conservatory is the prettiest I ever saw. Mr. Davis from Mark Lane is here. He lost all the gallery. Lord Wellington reviews all the troops to-day under Montmartre—we are going to see them.

'The Chambers are so violent as to alarm even the Court. M. de Richelieu, the Minister, went down, and in the House of Peers remonstrated against their recommendation of further measures of punishment, but without success.'

The following letters to Richard Sharp illustrate the character of Rogers.

Samuel Rogers to Richard Sharp.

'Jan. 11, 1816.

'My dear Friend,—To-morrow I am to exhibit a Twelfth Cake, and an electrical machine, and if you and your little ward are inclined to come and make a little noise with us, I cannot say how happy you will make us. Jekyll and his boys will not fail at half-past five, when our tea-table rites will be beginning. Oh, the evil hour in which you and I removed from Lilliput to Brobdingnag; but we may still visit the first now and then as aliens and foreigners.

'Ever yours,
'S. R.'

This was a yearly custom. An esteemed octogenarian friend, whom I have before mentioned, tells me that one of her most vivid early recollections is of one of these Twelfth Night parties at Rogers's house, some years earlier than the one mentioned in the above letter. The beautiful rooms, she says, were all opened, and on the table in the centre of one of the rooms was a splendid ice-cake, half of which was made of wood. The children drew characters, and this little girl, being the youngest, was made Queen of Twelfth Night. She remembers sitting in State on a sofa of crimson silk, and the King, little Martin Shee, sat by her. Mr. Rogers came up to her and dropped on one knee and kissed her hand, he was followed by Tom Moore, Lord Byron, 'Conversation' Sharp, Boddington, and others. Mr. Rogers then amused the children by conjuring. More than thirty years after this, Crabb Robinson, mentioning Rogers in a letter to a friend, says, 'Rogers loves children, and is fond of the society of young people.' 'When I am old and bedridden,' he says, 'I shall be read to by young people—Walter Scott's novels perhaps.' His living relations bear the same testimony; and there are scores of letters among his papers from ladies of title full of the most affectionate regard arising out of his kindness to them when they were children.

Samuel Rogers to Richard Sharp.

[Jan. 16, 1816.]

'My dear Friend,—Inclosed is the draft. Pray use it as you please.

'Ever yours,
'SAML. ROGERS.

'Ten o'clock.—I am just returned from "Romeo and Juliet." At Verona I could think of nothing else through the night. A strange romantic melancholy hung over me there, such as we remember to have felt at sixteen.

'In a Convent Garden they showed us Juliet's coffin —the spiracle through which she breathed, and the niche in which her lamp stood burning. I looked at it, as you will believe, with the eye of Faith.'

CHAPTER VII.

1816-1818.

Rogers and Lord Byron—Letter from Mackintosh—Rogers, Byron, and Godwin—Byron's Appeal to Rogers—Letter from Walter Scott—Rogers and Sheridan—Sheridan's Deathbed—Rogers's Recollections of Sheridan—Lord John Townshend's Letter—Grattan—Lord Erskine—Ugo Foscolo—Benjamin Constant at Breakfast—Byron, Rogers, and Lady Caroline Lamb—'Glenarvon'—Rogers at Sydney Smith's, at Tom Moore's, at Wordsworth's, at Southey's, at the Lakes—Letter from Southey—'An unfledged Eagle'—Wordsworth on Bernard Barton—Rogers and Crabbe—Crabbe's Visit to London—Breakfasts at Rogers's—Crabbe, Moore, Rogers, and Campbell at Sydenham—The Rev. W. Lisle Bowles—'The Abbot of Fonthill'—The Death of the Princess Charlotte—Lord Bathurst and the Regent—Story of the Father of George III.—Letter from Byron—Letter from Ugo Foscolo on his Literary Plans.

THE great subject of talk in London society in the beginning of 1816 was the separation of Lord Byron and his wife. It was little surprise to Rogers, as Byron had often talked to him of his domestic troubles. He knew more of Byron's peculiarities than most of his friends. He used to say that in the latter days of their brief life together Lord Byron never dined with his wife. He fancied that he could not bear to see a woman eat. When invited to dine with Rogers he would reply with the question, 'Have any women been invited?' and he refused to meet Madame de Staël at Rogers's dinner-table, but came in the drawing-room later in the evening. The first reference to the separation is in a letter written in reply to one in which Rogers had expressed dissatisfaction at Byron's return of a presentation copy of his poems.

Lord Byron to Samuel Rogers.

'F^y 8th, 1816.

'Dear Rogers,—Do not mistake me. I really returned your book for the reason assigned and no other. It is too good for so careless a fellow. I have parted with all my own books, and positively won't deprive you of so valuable "a drop of that immortal man."

'I shall be very glad to see you if you like to call as you intended, though I am at present contending with "the slings and arrows of outrageous Fortune" some of which have struck at me from a quarter whence I did not indeed expect them. But no matter, "there is a world elsewhere," and I will cut my way through this as I can : if you write to Moore, will you tell him that I shall answer his letter the moment I can muster time and spirits.

'Ever yours,
' BYRON.'

Amid all the domestic ruin of this period, Byron was contemplating, at the suggestion of Mackintosh conveyed through Rogers, an act of chivalrous generosity. Desperate as his straits for money were, Byron adhered to the resolution not to use for himself any of the proceeds of his works. He was about to publish 'The Siege of Corinth' and 'Parisina,' and Murray had offered him a thousand guineas for the copyright. Mackintosh thereupon wrote to Rogers with his suggestion.

Sir James Mackintosh to Samuel Rogers.

'Weedon Lodge: Friday.

'Dear Rogers,—It is said that Lord Byron has refused a very large sum from Murray for permission to publish separately two new poems which his lordship wishes only to be added to the collection of his works. Knowing the noble use which he has hitherto made of the produce of his works, I venture to point out to you poor Godwin as a person whom Lord Byron could save from ruin by granting the permission on condition of Murray's giving Godwin such part of the sum spoken of as Lord Byron may be pleased to direct. Godwin is a man of genius, likely, for his independence of thinking, to starve at the age of sixty for want of a few hundred pounds necessary to carry on his laborious occupation.

'If you agree with me I am certain that the benevolence of your heart will need no solicitor. But if you should not make any application to Lord B., I shall conclude that it would be improper. Say yes or no in writing.

'Ever yours,
'J. MACKINTOSH.'

Rogers made the suggestion as Mackintosh's, and Byron at once accepted the proposal.

Lord Byron to Samuel Rogers.

J⁽ʸ⁾¹ 20th, 1816.

'Dear Rogers,—I wrote to you hastily this morning by Murray to say that I was glad to do as Mackintosh and you suggested about Mr. Godwin. It occurs to me now that as I have never seen Mr. G. but once, and consequently have no claim to his acquaintance, that you or Sir J. had better arrange it with him in such a manner as may be least offensive to his feelings, and so as not to have the appearance of officiousness nor obtrusion on my part. I hope you will be able to do this, as I should be very sorry to do anything by him that may be deemed indelicate. The sum Murray offered, and offers, was, and is, one thousand and fifty pounds : this I refused before because I thought it more than the two things were worth to M. and from other objections, which are of no consequence. I have, however, closed with M. in consequence of Sir J.'s and your suggestion, and propose the sum of six hundred pounds to be transferred to Mr. Godwin in such a manner as may seem best to you and his friend. The remainder I think of for other purposes.

'As M. offered the money down for the copyrights it may be done directly, and I am ready to sign and seal immediately, and perhaps it had better not be delayed. I shall feel very glad if it can be of any use to Godwin,

[1] I do not know why Moore dates this letter February. In the MS. the J⁽ᵃʸ⁾ seems clear enough; in the next letter, which Moore does not publish, the J⁽ᵃ⁾ is unmistakable. On the other hand, in the letter on page 210 the F⁽ʸ⁾ is equally clear. I have printed the letters from Byron's manuscript.

only don't let him be plagued, nor think himself obliged, and all that which makes people hate one another, &c.

'Yours ever truly,

'B.'

The generous intention was frustrated, as is explained in the following letter.

Lord Byron to Samuel Rogers.

'Jⁿ 23rd, 1816.

'Dear Rogers,—I am sorry that I cannot dine with you to-day. I have not lately been very well and am under sentence of pill and potion for an attack of liver, &c.

'You may set your heart at rest on poor G.'s business. Murray, when it came to the point, demurred, and though not exactly refusing, gave such sort of answers as determine me to take the MS. away and not publish at all.

'With regard to his offer, I can only say that some weeks ago he even pressed it upon me so far as (after I had returned his draft) to lay the money upon the table if I would consent to a *separate* publication : this I refused, because the pieces were in my opinion better adapted for, and at any rate safer in, the collection he had got together, and for *this purpose* I told him he was welcome to them for nothing. I never said, nor meaned to say, that if he was permitted to publish *separately*, that the purchase of the copyrights would not be accepted. When you sent me Mackintosh's letter, I felt inclined to comply with its suggestion, and went to Murray, at the same time telling him my reason ; in this at the time he acquiesced; but since, on my sending to him that it was thought a smaller sum would do for Mr. G., &c., he returns me an answer which—in short—it is no matter.

'I am sorry for the trouble you have had on this occasion, and still more that I have failed in being of any use to Mr. Gn. Pray explain to Sir J. Mackintosh for me, and believe me,

'Ever yours most truly,
'BYRON.'

A month later Byron writes on the painful subject of which everybody was talking.

Lord Byron to Samuel Rogers.

'March 25th, 1816.

'Dear Rogers,—You are one of the few persons with whom I have lived in what is called intimacy, and have heard me at times conversing on the untoward topic of my recent family disquietudes. Will you have the goodness to say to me at once, whether you ever heard me speak of her with disrespect, with unkindness, or defending myself at *her* expense by any serious imputation of any description against *her?* Did you never hear me say "that when there was a right and a wrong she had the *right*"?

'The reason I put these questions to you or other of my friends is because I am said, by her and hers, to have resorted to such means of exculpation.

'Ever very truly yours,
'B.'

Rogers's answer is not extant. Its tenor may be guessed. He naturally sympathised with his friend. How the literary men of that time viewed the matter may be seen in an incidental reference to it in a letter to Rogers from Sir Walter Scott, written about six weeks after Lord Byron had taken leave of England, as it proved, for ever.

Walter Scott to Samuel Rogers.

'My dear Rogers,—Mr. Skirving of Edinburgh, an unrivalled artist as a painter in crayons, is going to London with the only good portrait of Burns. I think you will like to look at it, and perhaps you may even be disposed to purchase it, provided the artist's intention of selling it holds water till he gets to London. Mr. Skirving is a man of great genius in his art, and is in circumstances of perfect independence, although his dress, unless he should rectify it when he gets to London, would argue something very different. In fact, both his dress and address require all the allowance which genius knows how to make for the caprices and eccentricities of its brethren. Do not give yourself any trouble with him beyond what lies exactly in the way of a lover of art.

'I am sure you will join with me in severely regretting this unlucky business of Lord Byron's. Who would have expected such a consummation last year when I was in town? It is an unlucky business, since it gives stupidity a momentary triumph over genius—and talents. I trust this will find you well in health and enjoying yourself in a milder climate than ours has been this year.

'Believe me, dear Rogers, always most truly and affectionately yours,

'WALTER SCOTT.

'Edin., 30th May (1816).

'I should think Mr. Sharp would like to look at the

Ayrshire Ploughman. If Skirving does sell it, which appears to me very problematical, I wish this unique representation of our great poet to fall into good hands. If I had not been buying a sort of Oxmoor, like Tristram Shandy, and building, hedging, ditching and draining, Rob should not have crossed the Border.'

In the early months of this year Rogers spent a good deal of his time by the sick-bed of Sheridan. Moore speaks of him as one of the very few who watched the going out of this great light with interest. Rogers had preserved his friendship with him through all the reverses of his later years, and, as I have already shown, had given him much assistance in the way of money. In these closing months of his life, when nearly all his friends had forsaken him, Rogers remained steadfast. On one evening early in May he took Lord Holland to see the dying orator, in what Moore calls 'the last corner, where he lay down to die.' Bailiffs were even then in the house, but Rogers and Lord Holland 'comforted him,' Moore tells us, 'with the assurance that some steps should be taken to ward off the immediate evils that he dreaded.' A few.evenings after this Rogers found an almost illegible note lying for him on his table when Moore and he returned home.

'Savile Row.

'I find things settled so that 150*l.* will remove all difficulty. I am absolutely undone and brokenhearted. I shall negotiate for the plays successfully in the course of a week, when all shall be returned. I have desired Farebrother to get back the guarantee for thirty.

'They are going to put the carpets out of window and break into Mrs. S.'s room and *take me*. For God's sake let me see you.

'R. B. S.'

It was after midnight when Rogers opened this pathetic letter, and the two poets at once went up to Savile Row to see what could be done. There was no need to disturb the Sheridans. They spoke through the railings to the servant in the area and learned that all was safe for the night, but that early the next morning the front of the house would be covered with bills announcing the sale. They went back indignant at the dishonour thus threatened to a great orator, dramatist, and statesman, but determined that he should be saved. Early next morning Moore called on Rogers, who gave him a draft for 150*l*., and despatched him with it to Sheridan's house. He found Sheridan full of hope and encouragement, and noted the strength and fulness of his voice and the brightness of his eyes. All would be well if he could but recover and leave his bed. This succour proved a mere temporary relief; and a month later, when he had become seriously worse, a sheriff's officer arrested him in his bed, and was only prevented from carrying him away, bed-ridden and dying as he was, by the threat of Dr. Bain to hold him responsible for the consequences. Dr. Bain, Peter Moore, the member for Coventry, and Samuel Rogers were the only friends that remained to Sheridan, and their fidelity all through this dismal journey to the grave is the one redeeming feature of this melancholy story of fallen greatness. Rogers had much to tell in after years of Sheridan's behaviour on his death-bed. Asked by his doctors if he had ever undergone an operation, he answered, 'Never, except when sitting for my portrait or having my hair cut.' To Rogers he said, 'Tell Lady Bessborough that my eyes will look up to the coffin lid as brightly as ever.' Stories were told of his devout behaviour when the Bishop of London read prayers with him, but the Bishop told Rogers that Sheridan was then totally insensible, his wife raising him up and joining his hands during the service. Sheridan died on Sunday, the 7th of July, and on Saturday the 13th was buried with great pomp in Westminster Abbey, which 'had seldom seen a costlier funeral.'

Rogers had known Sheridan for four or five and twenty years. His recollections of his oratory went back to the trial of Warren Hastings, and his personal acquaintance to the meeting with him in company with Pamela and Fox at William Stone's in 1792.[1] One of his stories of Sheridan was, that seeing Gibbon among the audience in Westminster Hall, Sheridan had spoken of his 'luminous page.' A friend accused him of flattery—you called him 'the luminous author.' 'Luminous,' said Sheridan; 'I meant voluminous.' He pretended never to have read his mother's story, Sidney Biddulph, which Fox, according to Rogers, regarded as the best of modern novels. Stories were told at Rogers's table of the practical jokes played by Sheridan in his younger days. His first wife was a sister of Mrs. Tickell, wife of the poet, and the two men were intimate friends, with almost equal love of

---

[1] *The Early Life of Samuel Rogers*, pp. 244, 245.

frolic. A boyish enjoyment of rollicking fun was a characteristic of Sheridan to the end. In conversation he was not brilliant, Rogers said, till he had been warmed by wine; and he became stupid as soon as he had taken too much.

Rogers's criticism of his life as a whole was summed up in the phrase that he carried the privileges of genius as far as any man ever carried them before. I find in his Commonplace Book: 'In an epilogue written to "The Maid of the Oaks" at Salthill, but which came too late, Sheridan introduced faro—

'Great figure loses—little figure wins.'

'It has been said,' writes Rogers, 'that the "School for Scandal" and the "Duenna" were performed at the London theatres on the night of Sheridan's celebrated speech on the Begums in the House of Commons; a coincidence very delightful to the imagination, but which did not take place. On that night, the 7th of February, 1787, Kemble played Castalio in "The Orphan" for the first time at Drury Lane, and Mrs. Abington played Lady Townley in "The Provoked Husband" at Covent Garden. A discovery made at Burney's at Deptford, 7th June, 1816. Present: Frere, Heber, Burney and R.' Soon after the funeral Rogers had the following letter from one of the old friends of Sheridan and his family.

Lord Frederick Townshend to Samuel Rogers.

'Balls: Aug. 2 (1816).

'My dear Rogers,—Can you tell me anything comfortable about poor Mrs. Sheridan and where she is?

'I had a letter from her soon after the sad event, from which it appeared to me that she was almost heart-broken. You know, perhaps, the unfortunate cause that prevented my attendance with you at the funeral. I was truly sorry not to be there and grieved also that I have not since been able to go and inquire after Mrs. Sheridan and Charles.

'Your most kind, affectionate, and generous attentions to poor Sheridan in his last moments were most sensibly felt by her, and the consolation they gave to our dying friend are not to be described. My son, thank God, is in somewhat a more favourable state.

'Ever truly yours, &c.,
'F. TOWNSHEND.'

This letter may be compared with one from Mrs. Fox in a former chapter. It was no small honour to Rogers to have given comfort to two such men as Fox and Sheridan in the painful closing hours of their lives. A few days after, another of the same family writes.

Lord John Townshend to Samuel Rogers.

'Balls: August 13, 1816.

'My dear Rogers,—I rejoice to hear that Mrs. Sheridan is better. I flattered myself, indeed, this was the case by a few lines I got from her some days ago; but of course there must be recollections yet fresh in her mind that cannot admit of much comfort. The Bishop of London seems to have been very kind indeed to her, and she speaks of him with great affection and gratitude.

'I am glad you like her son Charles so much. My

son Fox is very fond of him, and everybody speaks highly of his goodness and promising talents. But there cannot be *two Sheridans*, as Mrs. S. observed to me in one of her letters.

'I wish it may turn out as you hear. But some parts of "Affectation" have been found amongst poor Sheridan's papers. He was said to have begun it, I think, about the year 1788 or 89, but nobody imagined it was in any degree of forwardness; and I remember some time after saying to Mrs. Sheridan (the first Mrs. Sheridan), when they were assigning this reason and t'other for its not being brought out, that I supposed, in fact, the real reason was its not being quite complete, to which she replied, "the reason it does not come out is not as you suppose, because it is not quite finished, but because it is not even yet begun." But if there should be only one bit of it, and that in a state to see the light, what a *trouvaille* it will be! I had once in my possession several things of his writing, and some of a very early date, which were all exquisite. I had put them up with a number of interesting papers, such as letters from Fitzpatrick, with a number of epigrams, sonnets, &c., that never saw the light, and also various things of Tickell's, which were intended for publication when finished. These became mixed with other papers, and were all unfortunately destroyed when I removed to Balls, as well as some trash of my own, which well deserved to be burnt. One of these *jeux d'esprit*, which Sheridan struck off at a moment one day while we were waiting dinner, was incomparable. The subject would have been thought not very promising—the appraisement of an old, worn-out gig belonging to Fitzpatrick which I was to purchase at Sheridan's valuation. You can have no idea what fun he made of this. Fox used to say it was the most comical thing ever written, and Fitzpatrick, though it was in a good humour and was not a little severe upon him, was delighted with it. But no one, you know, cared so little about a joke against himself as Fitzpatrick, who was as remarkable for his immovable good temper as he was for his excellent understanding and polished wit.

'There was a Westminster song or two, patched up amongst us at one of the elections, but principally Sheridan's doing, which I was sorry to lose. I can only remember one stanza which was Sheridan's. I thought it so good that I used to repeat it over and over again for weeks together, and I remember Wilkes, when he was told of it, was much diverted. The stanza was this (to the tune of "Dr. Arne, Dr. Arne, It gives us concarn ")—

'Johnny Wilkes, Johnny Wilkes,
  Thou boldest of bilks,
How changed is the song you now sing.
  For your dear forty-five
  'Tis Prerogative,
And your blasphemy, God save the King,
  Johnny Wilkes.
And your blasphemy, God save the King.

'This song was printed and may probably be got.

'I am happy to tell you that my son is going on well. Dr. Ainslie's view of his case affords me great comfort. If he continues to improve, I may possibly go to town for a few days. Shall I find you then? I am afraid there

is no inducing you to come and see us at Balls. It would make us very happy if you would. I'll get Malthus to meet you, and Lord Cowper if he should be in the country. Say everything that is most kind from me to Mrs. Sheridan, and believe me, truly and faithfully yours,
'JOHN TOWNSHEND.'

During the spring of this year Grattan was visiting Rogers's friend, Richard Sharp, at Mickleham, and Rogers spent some time with him, treasuring up the talk which forms a pleasant part of his volume of 'Recollections.' 'It was June,' says Rogers, 'and the limes were full of bees.' Standing under the trees, Grattan said, 'Now what are these senators about. A great humble bee is now addressing them—they are now in Committee.' He used to say in the morning, 'Shall we visit those senators?' Rogers put the recollection into his next poem, 'Human Life'—

> A walk in spring—Grattan, like those with thee,
> By the heath side (who had not envied me?)
> When the sweet limes, so full of bees in June,
> Led us to meet beneath their boughs at noon,
> And thou didst say which of the Great and Wise,
> Could they but hear and at thy bidding rise,
> Thou wouldst call up and question.

Sheridan naturally became the subject of some of their talk, and Grattan remarked that his faults were like those of most men of genius—they were of a poetical character, the excesses of the generous virtues. Rogers quoted Sheridan's remark, 'What will they think of the public-speaking of this age in after times when they read

Mr. Burke's speeches, and are told that in his day he was not accounted either the first or second speaker.[1] Grattan replied that Burke's speeches were far better to read than to hear. They were, he said, better suited to a patient reader than to an impatient hearer. The best speaker is to be found among the most enlightened people. Cicero would not have pleased at Athens. He was better to read than to hear.

To this year also some of the recollections of Lord Erskine belong. Rogers had known him intimately from very early days. They had been politically associated before the trial of Horne Tooke. He records that Erskine's recollections were dictated to him as he sat with his pen in his hand after dinner in St. James's Place in 1816.[2]

In the summer Ugo Foscolo came to London. His fame both as a poet and a patriot had come before him, and he was received with favour by men of all parties. Rogers, who was full of recollections of his tour in Italy and of enthusiasm for everything Italian, met Foscolo at Holland House, where he was staying, and where he charmed everybody by his vivacity, his great and various knowledge, his warm sympathy, his lively imagination, and his excellent qualities as a man. 'We are all *engoués* with him,' said Lord Holland, and Rogers was as much *engoué* as any. I find in his Diary, too, a record of the visit of another man of genius.

'*July* 14, 1816.—Benjamin Constant at breakfast. Always kept a diary in a mixed language—German,

---

[1] *Recollections*, p. 89.   [2] *Ibid.*, p. 167.

French and English—unintelligible to others. Now much briefer than formerly, from many motives. "Adolphe," many parts he will confess, from his own experience. He had often in his mind an Englishwoman still living with a Frenchman at Paris—a Mrs. Lindsay. . . . Never corrects his works, though he sometimes adds to them, expecting nobody to read them twice. "Corinne," by far Madame de Staël's best novel. "Delphine" falls off terribly. Her "Allemagne" very fatiguing. She writes her works four or five times over, correcting them only in that way. The end of a chapter always the most obscure, as she ends with an epigram. Rocca,[1] full of simplicity and observation. His work singular and interesting. Marivaux [2] good. His comedies will always be acted, as some actress will always produce them. Mars.[3] Contat.[4] Mackintosh vague in his conversation, particularly when in a *tête-à-tête*. "I always like him best in mixed society." His want of punctuality. Ward very brilliant. Never saw Pitt, Fox, Burke, or Sheridan. Bonaparte lost much of his decision, had a contempt for mankind, having formed his opinion from Voltaire's "Candide," &c.; a good mathematician, a very vague talker, ever restless, because unacknowledged by the kings. No leisure for a man of letters in London. In Paris, no morning visits; if a man calls three times upon a woman he must be in love with her. Racine a

---

[1] M. de Rocca, the young French hussar officer whom Madame de Staël had privately married.

[2] Marivaux, Pierre Carlet de Chamblain de, French dramatist and novelist, author of *Le Jeu de l'Amour et du Hazard*, &c., 1688-1763.

[3] Mlle. Mars, famous actress of the Théâtre Français, 1779-1847.

[4] Mlle. Louise Contat, also of the Théâtre Français, 1760-1813.

better artist than Virgil. Montesquieu a very great man. "Iliad" and "Odyssey" by different men. Has written a tract to prove this, but never published it. The "Odyssey" the best story. The death of Priam very fine.'

One of the literary events of this year was the publication of Lady Càroline Lamb's 'Glenarvon.' It is unreadable trash, and is only of interest as showing how a temporary popularity may be obtained by books which have no literary quality, but which are supposed to bear on the men and the controversies of the time. Lady Caroline Lamb was a kind of Ophelia 'divided from herself and her fair judgment' by her passion for Byron. She wrote to him when his difficulties as to money were reported, assuring him that all her jewels were at his service. Byron, who on this and other matters found a confidential friend in Rogers, showed him this letter. There was no breach of confidence in doing so, for Lady Caroline did not conceal from Rogers her passion for Byron. On returning home at night, Rogers more than once found her pacing his garden waiting for him to implore his good offices with Byron in some passing quarrel. He had seen her waiting in the street to catch Byron on his way home from a party to which she had not been invited. One night, she had waited in this manner outside Devonshire House, and Rogers saw her talking to Byron with such eagerness that half her body was thrust into the window of Byron's carriage. If she met him at a party she nearly always contrived that he should drive her home. They had finally quarrelled before Byron left England, and 'Glenarvon' is an attack upon him, and incidentally upon Rogers as his friend. Rogers, who had the best opportunity of knowing, always asserted that the flirtation, violent as it was, had nothing criminal about it; and in proof of Lady Caroline's state of mind, told the story of a holocaust she made, not of Byron's letters and portrait, but of copies of them. She had retired to the country, and one day made a bonfire in the garden on which these effigies, as it were, were flung, while some girls, dressed in white, danced round, singing a song she had written for the occasion, the burden of which was, 'Burn, fire, burn.'

This is sufficient explanation of a passage in the following letter which Moore omitted, without any indication of the omission, in printing the letter in his 'Life of Byron.'

Lord Byron to Samuel Rogers.

'Diodati, near Geneva: July 29th, 1816.

'Dear Rogers,—Do you recollect a book, Mathisson's "Letters," which you lent me, which I have still, and yet hope to return to your library? Well, I have encountered at Coppet and elsewhere Gray's correspondent (in its appendix), that same Bonstetten to whom I lent the translation of his correspondent's epistles for a few days, but all he could remember of Gray amounts to little, except that he was the most " melancholy and gentlemanlike" of all possible poets. Bonstetten himself is a fine and very lively old man, and much esteemed by his compatriots, he is also a *littérateur* of good repute, and all his friends have a mania of addressing to him volumes of letters, Mathisson, Müller the historian, &c., &c. He is a good deal at Coppet, where I have met him a few times. All there are well, except Rocca, who, I am sorry to say, looks in a very bad state of health; the Duchess seems grown taller, but as yet no rounder since her marriage. Schlegel is in high force, and Madame [1] as brilliant as ever.

'I came here by the Netherlands and the Rhine route, and Basle, Berne, Morat and Lausanne. I have circumnavigated the lake, and shall go to Chamouni with the first fair weather, but really we have had lately such stupid mists, fogs, rains, and perpetual density, that one would think Castlereagh had the Foreign Affairs of the kingdom of Heaven also upon his hands. I need say nothing to you of these parts, you having traversed them already. I do not think of Italy before September. I have read "Glenarvon"—

'" From furious Sappho scarce a milder fate,
——[2] by her love or libelled by her hate "—

and have also seen Ben Constant's "Adolphe" and his preface denying the real people; it is a work which leaves an unpleasant impression, but very consistent with the consequences of not being in love, which is perhaps as disagreeable as anything except being so. I doubt, however, whether all such *liens* (as he calls them) terminate so wretchedly as his hero and heroine's.

'There is a third Canto (a longer than either of the former) of "Childe Harold" finished, and some smaller things—among them a story on the "Château de Chillon"; I only wait a good opportunity to transmit

[1] Madame de Staël.   [2] The dash is Byron's.

them to the grand Murray, who, I hope, flourishes. Where is Moore? Why ain't he out?[1] My love to him, and my perfect consideration and remembrances to all, particularly to Lord and Lady Holland, and to your Duchess of Somerset.

'Ever yours very truly,

'BN.

'P.S. I send you a *fac-simile*, a note of Bonstetten's, thinking you might like to see the hand of Gray's correspondent.'

During the summer Rogers paid a visit to Sydney Smith at Foston, where, we are told, he charmed young and old by his kindness and inexhaustible fund of anecdote. He left London in August, intending to go to Scotland, and to take Tom Moore, Wordsworth and Southey on the way. 'Rogers stayed with us here,' says Moore in a letter to Lady Donegal, ' from Wednesday to Sunday and left " an image of himself " (I mean intellectually speaking) very favourable indeed on the minds both of Bessy and the little ones. He was, indeed, particularly amiable: and took no fright at the superfluity either of melted butter or of maids, and even saw with composure a little boy who comes to clean my shoes, not that I can quite answer for his subsequent reflections on these luxuries.' The subsequent reflections, with pleasant glimpses of many eminent contemporaries, are in the following letters—

[1] The publication of *Lalla Rookh* was postponed because the year 1816 was one of great distress, and consequently unfavourable to publishers. The poem appeared in 1817, dedicated to Rogers, ' by his very grateful and affectionate friend, Thomas Moore.'

Samuel Rogers to Sarah Rogers.

'Low-wood Inn: Friday morning, 28 Aug. 1816.

' My dear Sarah,—I should have written before, but the last post here I missed, and there is one here only every other day. I travelled to Leicester, where I arrived at 11 at night, without an incident, only that in Wells's Row, Islington, we took up an old lady blind and deaf, whose only pleasure seemed to be to shake hands with us all round very often. She spoke, however, of her dinner with great pleasure, and expressed a wish that she might have some fish, an observation to which we could make no reply. Left Leicester next morning at half-past five in an empty coach, and at eleven found myself at Moore's. His cottage is all alone in a pretty little valley with fields and woods about it, and is new and neat. They say, however, it is leaky and smoky. She struck me as much taller and much improved in expression, and still very handsome, tho' a little of her lustre is gone, and she is thinner. But she surprised me agreeably, and would be admired anywhere. The two little girls are not pretty nor otherwise, and quiet and merry and caressing beyond anything. I wished for you with them very often, and they had made arrangements for you. I staid till Sunday—having passed into Dovedale with M. and seen Ilam, and then went off alone (for, after all, he left me in the lurch) to Manchester. Napped there, and at one in the morning came on in the mail to Kendal, arriving here on Monday at three. On Tuesday, after a row on the lake, I walked and drank tea with the Wordsworths, who are all as before. They still talk of their day with you on the Thames, and Miss W. counts the years since she saw you. Their present abode is princely—by the side of Rydal Hall. Their windows command Windermere, and their garden (Miss H. and the clerk keep it full of flowers) looks down upon Rydal water. I was asking my way to them at a cottage door in the road, when the child I spoke to ran in, and a little girl came smiling out and took my hand with a curtsey, It was Miss W., as I guessed, who had called to ask after a child in the measles, and she conducted me to their house. Yesterday I dined there, and to-day he spends the day with me. He is very cheerful and pleasant, and so are they all. I believe they heard of my arrival a few minutes after I came, for they called early the next day while I was on the water. The weather here has been wretched. Now it is mending a little, but still cold and cheerless—the Moores live by a fire, and so do the Ws., and I live in my great-coat. I am now writing in it. What will become of me, I am at a loss to say— but my heart fails me, and I think I shall go on no further. Pray write, my dear Sarah, and tell me your plans, to Lowwood—if you write in four or five days, but afterwards to Keswick. The regatta here is next Wednesday, and W. offers to accompany me to Ulleswater, an offer I am glad to accept, so I think I shall not be at K. before the end of next week. Pray remember me very affectionately to all, and believe me to be,

'Ever yours,

'S. R.

'There is nothing but complaint anywhere. No

posting, nobody travelling—and no wonder—when there is no sun in the sky, and no money in people's pockets.

'The natives here are all astounded at Sharp's absence two years running. Miss W., to whom it was a great event in her retired life, is, I believe, chief mourner, after whom come the innkeepers, &c.'

Samuel Rogers to Sarah Rogers.

'Keswick: Sept. 1, 1816.

'My dear Sarah,—Many thanks for your letter. The mountains and lakes are just as beautiful as ever, and have lost little by the comparison, so you may come and see them without apprehension. After all, I did not see the regatta, as Wordsworth was impatient for Ulleswater. We set off on Monday, and had two beautiful days for it. On Wednesday we dined at a Mr. Marshall's, a Liverpool merchant, whose wife's sister, living in a small house on the lake, said she had seen you at Mr. Lloyd's, and slept at Keswick that night, since which we have had cold, wet and cheerless weather, but on Thursday there were races here on Crow Park on the lake notwithstanding, and on Friday I went up Causay Pike, a huge mountain, with Wordsworth, Southey, and Sir George Beaumont— nor have I ever dined at my inn but once, and then W. dined with me. Mrs. Wood has lost her old mother and her husband; and has married again, and is now Mrs. Jackson. She asked after you the first moment she saw me, and is the same tidy, civil lady as ever, and no older to my eyes. Southey's house is a model of neatness and comfort, the admiration of Wordsworth, and I must say, a contrast to his. We have had two wet days, and

Lady B. lent me Dorothy's "Tour in Scotland," in which we are mentioned.[1] It is full of sweetness, and very interesting from her dialogues with people in the fields and highways. She seems exceedingly affected by the kind or sour looks of her hostess, and many of the last did they meet with on the high roads. A delightful air of *naïveté* and benevolence and enthusiasm runs thro' it, and I know you would enjoy it much. Take the last day's history for a sample—

'"*Sunday, September* 25, 1803.—A beautiful autumnal day. Breakfast at a public-house by the road-side. Dined at Threkeld. Arrived at home between eight and nine o'clock, where we found Mary in perfect health, Mary[2] Hutchinson with her, and little Johnny asleep in the clothes-basket by the fire.

'" Finished copying this journal May 31, 1805, in the moss hut at the top of the orchard. William, Mary, and I finished the moss hut on the afternoon of June 6, 1805. After the work was ended we all sate down in the middle of the seat, looking at the clouds in the west."

'But, after all, it leaves a sadness on the mind from the perpetual difficulties they had to struggle with—rain, fatigue, and bad accommodation. I am very sorry indeed to hear of Sutton. I was in hopes he was better before I left town, and wish with all my heart he was

---

[1] 'Mr. Rogers and his sister, whom we had seen at our own cottage at Grasmere a few days before, had arrived there that same afternoon on their way to the Highlands; but we did not see them till the next morning, and only for about a quarter of an hour' (*Recollections, &c.*, edited by J. C. Shairp, LL.D., p. 5).

[2] It should be Joanna. In the published journal the entry at the close is omitted, but it is surely as characteristic as any the journal contains.

here with me. I have scarcely been warm since I left you, and a vile toothache such as I set out with on our journey abroad began in the night before I set out, and has seldom left me long. I have a glass of brandy now on the table, and dare not be without it night or day, but in other respects have been perfectly well. What will become of me I will not yet say, but I think I shall write in a day or two, and give up Scotland. To-day, snow fell in Borrowdale, and snow is visible from my garret window on several of the mountains. There is ice an inch thick on Skiddaw. No wonder, tho' the sun shone a little to-day, everybody complains of the cold. Southey says the winter is come three weeks earlier than he ever knew it. Farewell, my dearest Sarah, pray direct to me at the Post Office, Penrith, and with my love to all, believe me to be ever yours,

'SAMUEL ROGERS.'

There is a letter without date from Moore to William Gardiner, which Lord John Russell puts too early, in which he says that Rogers 'returning by Kegworth, and not finding me there, has come by the evening coach, and is now sitting by the pianoforte at Mr. Peach's waiting the effect of this note in bringing you back to us. He is a warm admirer of your music, and is anxious to see the author before he leaves Leicester, which must be early in the morning.' In November Sydney Smith writes to Lady Holland: 'I suppose Samuel Rogers is mortgaged to your ladyship for the autumn and early part of the winter. Perhaps you would have the goodness to say that Miss —— thinks him charming. Next to the Congreve rocket, he is the most mischievous and powerful of modern inventions.' He was then in his fifty-fourth year, and at the very height of his social popularity and fame.

The following letters carry on his social history—

Robert Southey to Samuel Rogers.

'Keswick: 13 Dec., 1816.

' My dear Sir,—Without preface or apology, let me tell my story. Some little time ago I received a letter requesting me to peruse a manuscript poem, and allow the writer to dedicate it to me, if I thought it worthy of publication. The writer stated himself to be very young, and that his reason for publishing was necessity. I received the poem, it was brimful of genius, with more of Lord Byron in it than of any other writer; but no more than showed a proper and discriminating sense of Lord Byron's powers. It was crude, exuberant, and ill-planned, had it not been so, I should have thought it far less hopeful. Enquiring into the circumstances of the author, I find that his name is Herbert Knowles, that he is an orphan, taken from a very low situation and placed at an excellent school at Richmond in Yorkshire by the contributions of some persons who had discovered his uncommon talents, the Dean of Canterbury giving ten pounds a year, two other clergymen five pounds each, his relations had promised among them thirty more, and it was intended when he was fit for college to place him upon this allowance as a sizar at St. John's. These times have pressed heavily upon his relations, and they could not fulfil their promise; so that his hopes were struck down at once, and he was advised to go as usher to some school. In abhorrence of such a situation, he thought of authorship. Of course, I pointed out the impracticability of this scheme. I wrote to his master, and obtained the highest possible character of the youth in every respect. My next thought was how to supply the thirty pounds annually for the next four years, it will be one year before he is ready for Cambridge. Ten I will give myself, I think you will not be displeased with me for having thought of you. And if Lord Byron had been in England, I would have asked you to apply to him. Amid all that storm and tumult of unhappy passions, and more unhappy opinions, there must be good and generous feelings, it is wholesome for him that they should be exercised, and proud as he is, it might gratify him to have them acknowledged and appealed to by one who condemns and pities him as I do.

'Sure I am, that Poets can best appreciate each other's merits, and in looking for friends for this unfledged Eagle (indeed I think he is of eagle breed) of whom could I think more properly than you. Among all the Pleasures of Memory there is none so lasting as that of the good which we have done.

'Believe me, my dear Sir, with the highest esteem, very truly and respectfully yours,

'ROBERT SOUTHEY.'

The 'unfledged eagle' never got his wings. His 'Lines written in the Churchyard of Richmond, Yorkshire,' which Southey published, are still to be found in some collections of religious poetry. He died in 1817 at the age of nineteen.

Here is another sign of Rogers's love for children—

Samuel Rogers to Daniel Rogers.

'London: Jan. 21, 1817.

' My dear Dan,—I write just now to say that our grand festival is finally fixed for Monday next, the 27th; the twelfth cake is bespoke and the hurdygurdy; and I hope and trust you will come, one and all—the boys because they are coming at all events, and Lucy to write a full account of it, and Patty to prompt her and console Signor Binda for her long absence, and Mary and Eliza, because I missed them at Derby, and have not seen them for an age, and mamma most of all because she will be most welcome, and you because I lost you the other day when you came. I have no news, and you must have heard all from Highbury. As for me, I have been idling away my time at many castles of Indolence. At Woburn I found Lady M. Palmer, and she talked much of you and Payne. I like her very much indeed. Pray give my love to all, and believe me to be, ever yours,

'Samuel Rogers.

' I am going down to Highbury to-day with Mr. Johnstone, Fanny's husband, and wish you were all of the party. I saw the Lytteltons at Althorp. L. has since been in your country.'

Byron was at this time in Italy, and occasional letters passed between him and Rogers. Moore gives but one—shortened as usual—but I am able to restore it in reproducing it—

Lord Byron to Samuel Rogers.

'Venice: April 4th, 1817.

'My dear Rogers,—It is a considerable time since I wrote to you last, and I hardly know why I should trouble you now, except that I think you will not be sorry to hear from me now and then. You and I were never correspondents, but always something better, which is very good friends.

'I saw your friend Sharp in Switzerland, or rather in the Genevan territory (which is and is not Switzerland), and he gave Hobhouse and me a very good route for the Bernese Alps; however, we took another from a German, and went by Clarens over the Dent de Jaman to Montbovon, and through the Simmenthal to Thun, and so on to Lauterbrunnen; except that from thence to the Grindelwald instead of round about, we went right over the Wengern Alp's very summit, and being close under the Jungfrau, saw it, its glaciers, and heard the avalanches in all their glory, having famous weather therefor. We, of course, went from the Grindelwald over the Scheideck to Brienz, and its lake; past the Reichenbach and all that mountain road, which reminded me of Albania and Ætolia and Greece, except that the people here were more civilised and rascally. I did not think so very much of Chamouni (except the source of the Arveyron, to which we went up to the teeth of the ice, so as to look into and touch the cavity, against the warning of the guides, only one of whom would go with us so close) as of the Jungfrau, and the Pissevache and Simplon, which are quite out of all mortal computation.

'I was at Milan about a moon, and saw Monti and some other living curiosities, and thence on to Verona, where I did not forget your story of the assassination during your sojourn there, and brought away with me some fragments of Juliet's tomb, and a lively recollection of the amphitheatre. The Countess Goetz (the governor's wife here) told me that there is still a ruined castle of the Montecchi between Verona and Vicenza. I have been at Venice since November, but shall proceed to Rome shortly. For my deeds here, are they not written in my letters to the unreplying Thomas Moore? To him I refer you; he has received them all, and not answered one.

'Will you remember me to Lord and Lady Holland? I have to thank the former for a book which I have not yet received, but expect to reperuse with great pleasure on my return, viz., the second edition of "Lope de Vega." I have heard of Moore's forthcoming poem: he cannot wish himself more success than I wish and augur for him. I have also heard great things of "Tales of my Landlord," but I have not yet received them; by all accounts they beat even "Waverley," &c., and are by the same author. Maturin's second tragedy has, it seems, failed, for which I should think anybody would be sorry except perhaps Sotheby, who I must say was capriciously and evilly entreated by the Sub-Committee about poor dear "Ivan," whose lot can only be paralleled by that of his original —I don't mean the *author*, who is anything but original, —but the deposed imperial infant who gave his name and some narrative to the drama thereby entitled. My health was very victorious till within the last month, when I had a fever. There is a typhus in these parts, but

I don't think it was that. However, I got well without a physician or drugs.

'I forgot to tell you that, last autumn, I furnished Lewis with "bread and salt" for some days at Diodati, in reward for which (besides his conversation) he translated Goethe's "Faust" to me by word of mouth, and I set him by the ears with Madame de Staël about the slave-trade. I am indebted for many and kind courtesies to our Lady of Coppet, and I now love her as much as I always did her works, of which I was and am a great admirer. When are you to begin with Sheridan? what are you doing, and how do you do?

'Ever and very truly and affectionately yours,

'B.'

In a letter to Moore, written a week later, Byron speaks of Rogers: 'I hope he flourishes. He is the Tithonus of poetry—immortal already. You and I must wait for it.' Here is a fragment from another of the immortals.

William Wordsworth to Samuel Rogers.

'Rydal Mount: May 13, 1817.

'I presume you are in a state of earthly existence, as I have heard nothing to the contrary since we parted in a shower near the Turnpike Gate of Keswick. Need I add that I hope and wish that you may be well? In the former part of this sentence, you may have divined there lurks a charitable reproach; for you left me with some reason to expect that I should hear of, from, or about you. Though this favour has not been granted, I am not discouraged from asking another, the exact amount of which I am unable to calculate. A friend of mine, a near relation of Mrs. Wordsworth, is smitten with a desire of seeing the pictures brought together by the members of the British Institution, and exhibited in the evening—I feel I have expressed my meaning cumbrously and ill—he wishes to attend the evening greatly, and has applied to me to procure him a ticket, for one night, if I conveniently can. Is it in your power to enable me to gratify this laudable ambition in a worthy person? Having come to the point, I have only to add that his address is, Thomas Monkhouse, Esq., 28, St. Anne's Street; and could you enclose him a ticket, I shall be most thankful.

'Are we to see you among us this summer? I hope so—and also that Sharp will not desert us. How is he in health, and what does he say of Switzerland and Italy, both in themselves and as compared with the scenes in our neighbourhood, which he knows so well? Is George Philips as great an orator as ever, and do you and Dante continue as intimate as heretofore? He used to avenge himself upon his enemies by placing them in H—ll, a thing Bards seem very fond of attempting in this day, witness the Laureate's mode of treating Mr. W. Smith. You keep out of these scrapes, I suppose; why don't you hire somebody to abuse you? and the higher the place selected for the purpose the better. For myself, I begin to fear that I should soon be forgotten if it were not for my enemies. Yet, now and then, a humble admirer presents himself, in some cases following up his introduction with a petition. The other day, I had a letter of this sort from a poetical, not a personal, friend—a Quaker of the name of Barton, living at Woodbridge, in Suffolk. He has beguiled me of a guinea, the promise of one at least, by way of subscription to a quarto volume of poems, which he is anxious to print partly for honour, partly for profit. He solicits my interest to promote his views. I state the fact, I do not beg—I have not sufficient grounds to go upon—I leave the affair to the decision of your own mind, only do not contemn me for abusing—'[1]

In the succeeding month we find Rogers in contact with an older poet, thus linking together in characteristic fashion, two periods of English literary history. Rogers's acquaintance with Crabbe probably began some time between 1810 and 1812. Crabbe's son, in his 'Life' of the poet, published in 1834, speaks of him as having begun at Bowood 'an acquaintance which also soon ripened into a strong friendship with the author of "The Pleasures of Memory."' Rogers probably sought him out at Trowbridge, and not finding him at home, suggested some opportunity of meeting. Crabbe sent thereupon a copy of 'The Borough,' published in 1810, with the following note—

The Rev. George Crabbe to Samuel Rogers.

'Mr. Crabbe feels himself much gratified by the obliging attentions of Mr. Rogers. He has great pleasure in the prospect of meeting a gentleman to whom Mr. Bowles had given him hope that he should be introduced. In the morning, Wednesday, he promises himself this satisfaction, which is abated solely by the fear that (from

[1] This is a fragment which leaves off abruptly.

want of foresight) he has occasioned trouble to Mr. Rogers, when he so obligingly sought to communicate the pleasure he intended that Mr. Crabbe should receive.

'Tuesday morning.'

The acquaintance made, or friendship begun, at Bowood was the immediate cause of the introduction of Crabbe to the literary and social circles to which Rogers belonged. Crabbe's biographer tells us that Mr. Rogers urged him to pay a visit in the summer season to the metropolis, and that he did so, taking lodgings near his new friend's residence in St. James's Place, where he was 'welcomed in the most cordial manner by the whole of that wide circle—including almost every name distinguished in politics, fashion, science, literature, and art—of which Mr. Rogers has been so long considered the brightest ornament.' Crabbe came to London on the 19th of June, 1817, in company with his friend Mr. Waldron. No record has been preserved of the feelings with which he returned to the metropolis, in circumstances which contrasted so happily with those with which he had made the plunge thirty-seven years before. It was not that he showed any reluctance to speak of it. In talking about him, Rogers used to say that Crabbe had spoken of the mixture of feelings with which he stood on London Bridge during his first visit to London. In one of his later visits he was staying at the Old Hummums hotel, where he was only known as an ordinary clergyman, bearing the name of Crabbe. But a friend, calling on him in his absence, told the waiters that their clerical visitor was the celebrated poet, and when he came back Crabbe was astonished at the curiosity he excited, and the attentions paid to him. It was a revelation to him of the extent of his literary fame.

That first visit to London took place in 1780, when Rogers, like Crabbe, was first beginning to dream of literary fame, and thirty years before they were destined to meet. The Suffolk rustic had taken lodgings in the house of Mr. Vickery, a hairdresser near the Exchange, and sometimes had to pawn his watch, and to find how 'it's the vilest thing in the world,' as he says to his sweetheart, 'to have but one coat,' since 'a confounded stove's modish ornament' had caught the elbow of his only one 'and rent it half away.' A generation had passed. He had gone through rural exile, had been, as he described himself, 'a solitary with a social disposition —a hermit without a hermit's resignation'; had been chaplain at Belvoir Castle, and known the intolerable hardships of the cultivated dependant on a great man's patronage; had married, brought up a family, lost the wife of his striving years, and gained competence and fame. He had been presented, three years before, to the living of Trowbridge, and was at work on his last great poem, 'The Tales of the Hall.' He now came back to be an honoured guest in the London where, thirty-seven years before, he had walked twelve miles to seek a job as an amanuensis, and been bitterly disappointed to find that another had been before him. As soon as he arrived, Rogers invited him to meet a few literary friends at breakfast, and he replied in a letter which is an admirable illustration of the tone of this gentle and simple-minded poet in his intercourse with his distinguished contemporaries.

The Rev. George Crabbe to Samuel Rogers.

[June 23rd, 1817.]

'Dear Sir,—I will breakfast with you in the morning, or on Tuesday, or *on both*: one principal purpose of my coming to town again was the pleasure you held up to me when I was so kindly received by you: you told me that I should see Lord Holland, and you made your own house all that was pleasant and engaging. What, dear Sir, can I say? Do not, however, permit me to intrude too much on your time, for I well know how you are consulted and engaged, but, speaking for myself alone, I would say, dear Sir, dispose of me as it seems best to you. I will dine with you when you can take me into your company, and I will wait on Lord Holland when it shall appear to you that his Lordship will be disposed to receive me. In fact, I will commit myself to you in that way which, to a mind like yours, I may do safely and with propriety. You will be a guide to me, and I shall do what is proper and becoming; neither presuming on the kindness which is shown to me, nor coldly withdrawing myself from the honour which I know how to estimate. My few engagements and my small business in town I reckon as nothing—the society to which you introduce me is all! I can put nothing—of my concerns here—in comparison with it. I repeat, therefore, dear Sir, I am at your command, gratefully

'And obediently yours,
'GEO. CRABBE.

'I am ashamed of the trouble your servant has, but I

mean to approach nearer on the morrow or the next day.

'Do not, I entreat, let me, by my desire of being with you, break in upon your better purposes. I am not ignorant of the sacrifices your politeness may make, but I would—if possible—claim the privilege of a friend, and entreat that I may see you only when it is perfectly convenient, and then it will be very pleasant. Will the ladies pardon me if I beg to be respectfully remembered by them.'

Crabbe's Journal records this breakfast in St. James's Place, and many other of his visits to Rogers, and with Rogers, during his stay in London.

'*June* 24.—Mr. Rogers, his brother and family, Mr. and Mrs. Moore, very agreeable and pleasant people. Foscolo, the Italian gentleman, Dante, &c. Play. Kemble in " Coriolanus."

'*June* 26.—Mr. Rogers and the usual company at breakfast. Lady Holland comes and takes me to Holland House. . . . Meet Mr. Campbell. Mr. Moore with us. Mr. Rogers joins us in the course of the day.

'*June* 27.—Mr. Campbell's letter.[1] He invites us to Sydenham. I refer it to Mr. Rogers and Mr. Moore. Return to town. . . . Call on Mr. Rogers. We go to the Freemason's Tavern.[2] The room filled. We find a place about half-way down the common seats, but not

---

[1] Printed in Beattie's *Life of Campbell*, vol. ii. p. 330.

[2] To a festival held to do honour to J. P. Kemble, for which Campbell's valedictory verses, beginning 'Pride of the British stage,' were written.

where the managers dine above the steps. By us, Mr. Smith, one of the authors of the "Rejected Addresses." Known, but no introduction. Mr. Perry, editor of the *Morning Chronicle*, and Mr. Campbell find us, and we are invited into the committee room. Kemble, Perry, Lord Erskine, Mr. Moore, Lord Holland, Lord Ossory, whom I saw at Holland House. Dinner announced. Music. Lord Erskine sits between me and a young man whom I find to be a son of Boswell. Lord Holland's speech after dinner. The Ode recited. Campbell's speech. Kemble's. Talma's. We leave the company and go to Vauxhall to meet Miss Rogers. Stay late.

'*June* 29.—Breakfast at the coffee house in Pall Mall, and go to Mr. Rogers and family. Agree to dine, and then join their party after dinner. Mr. Stothard. Foscolo. Drive to Kensington Gardens in their carriage. . . .

'*July* 1.—Dine with Mr. Rogers. Company: Kemble, Lord Erskine, Lord Ossory, Sir George Beaumont, Mr. Campbell, and Mr. Moore. Miss R. retires early, and is not seen any more at home. Met her at the gallery in Pall Mall with Mr. Westall.

'*July* 2.—Dine at Sydenham with Mr. and Mrs. Campbell, Mr. Moore, and Rogers. Poet's Club.'

Regarding this visit to Sydenham, Campbell writes to Crabbe's son—

'One day—and how can it fail to be memorable to me when Moore has commemorated it?—your father, and Rogers, and Moore, came down to Sydenham pretty early in the forenoon, and stopped to dine with me. We talked of founding a Poet's Club, and even set about electing the members, not by ballot, but *vivâ voce*. The scheme failed, I scarcely know how; but this I know, that a week or so afterwards I met with Perry of *The Morning Chronicle*, who asked me how our Poet's Club was going on. I said, "I don't know—we have some difficulty in giving it a name,—we thought of calling ourselves *The Bees*." "Ah," said Perry, "that's a little different from the common report; for they say you are to be called *The Wasps*." I was so stung with this waspish report, that I thought no more of the Poet's Club.'

The Journal continues—

'*July* 3.—Go with Mr. Rogers in his carriage to Wimbledon. Earl and Countess Spencer. The grounds more beautiful than any I have yet seen; more extensive, various, rich. The profusion of roses extraordinary. Dinner. Mr. Heber, to whom Mr. Scott addresses one canto of "Marmion." Mr. Stanhope. A pleasant day. Sleep at Wimbledon.

'*July* 4.—Morning view, and walk with Mr. Heber and Mr. Stanhope. Afterwards Mr. Rogers, Lady S., Lady H. A good picture if I dare draw it accurately. Return with Mr. Rogers.

'*July* 6.—Call at Mr. Rogers's, and go to Lady Spencer's. Go with Mr. Rogers to dine at Highbury with his brother and family. Miss Rogers the same at Highbury as in town. . . .

'*July* 7.—Dinner at Mr. Rogers's with Mr. Moore and Mr. Campbell, Lord Strangford and Mr. Spencer.

Leave them, and go by engagement to see Miss O'Neil, in Lady Spencer's box.

'*July* 11.—Breakfast with Mr. Rogers; talk of Mr. Frere.

'*July* 14.—Go to Mr. Rogers's, and take a farewell visit to Highbury. Miss Rogers. Promise to go when ——. Return early. Dine there, and purpose to see Mr. Moore and Mr. Rogers in the morning, when they set out for Calais.

'*July* 15.—Was too late this morning. Messrs. Rogers and Moore were gone.'

Extract from a letter, July 25.

'This visit to London has, indeed, been a rich one. I had new things to see, and was perhaps something of a novelty myself. Mr. Rogers introduced me to almost every man he is acquainted with; and in this number were comprehended all I was previously very desirous to obtain a knowledge of.'

During part of Crabbe's visit to London, Tom Moore and his wife and children were staying at Rogers's house, and on the 15th of July, when Crabbe records that he found they were gone, Moore and Rogers had left London on a visit to Paris. In October Rogers was again at Bowood, where Moore found him when he went down to see 'the Cottage, a small thatched cottage, and we get it, furnished, at forty pounds a-year,' near Lord Lansdowne's. While Rogers was at Bowood he saw a family connection and brother poet, from whom he received the following letter.

The Rev. William Lisle Bowles to Samuel Rogers.

'Bremhill: Oct. 1st, 1817.

'My dear Rogers,—I am very anxious that you should inform Lord Lansdowne that, though the house at Heddington is situated very low, yet it is within a quarter of a mile of the most beautiful views in Wiltshire, and has, I believe, every accommodation, and is in complete repair. I should think it would answer his plan very well—but, *verbum sapienti*, he must not go to look at it with Moore, or even send a servant from Bowood, unless he wishes double price to be charged for rent, perhaps treble.

'If he would leave the arrangement to me, in case Moore should like the situation, I am sure I could make a much better bargain, and could either ride over with Moore, or settle with Hughes, in case of approval. I leave that, as I said, to your and Lord Lansdowne's consideration, and have no other object than Moore's interest in the suggestion I have ventured to make.

'A word about Tytherton. I don't know whether you were in earnest about walking there with Mrs. Orde, but, if so, you will come here to-morrow at about a quarter past one o'clock; you could go down with me in the carriage, and my boat, with flag, gardener, and pony, should wait your arrival at Tytherton Bridge, and waft you along the canal to within half a mile of Bowood gate.

'I conclude all this with a song, which I hope you won't mistake for a " vile " Baptist hymn.

'*On hearing a Young Lady sing Haydn's "Benedictus."*

'Oh! in the realms of Light (should I attain
Those seats where saints and angels swell the strain
Before the Throne, 'mid troops of Seraphs bright,
Whose farthest circles fade in distant light),
Even when the high and holy harmony
Went up acclaiming everlastingly,
Should some soft voice more musically clear
Steal with an added sweetness on the ear,
Methinks (for so to my rapt thought it seems
As now I listen, dallying with vain dreams)
I should recall, in Tytherton's still shade,
Thy voice and look, Oh! mild Moravian maid.

'The prose you will submit to Lord Lansdowne; the verse is left to your discretion.

'If you could come to Bremhill, you shall have six white sticks, and stick them in where you like in the garden, and I will plant six trees, or as many or few as you choose, where you mark, for which I have more reasons than one, but which I shall not mention to you. You need not write; come or not, just as you feel inclined, to-morrow. I shall go about two o'clock.

'Yours ever,
'W. L. Bowles.'

Here is an equally characteristic letter from a person living in another moral and intellectual climate.

'If Mr. Rogers continues to feel any inclination to hear the secrets of the prison house of Eblis unfolded, he may perhaps be inspired to appoint a day and a night for the purpose.

'Nothing would afford the Abbot of Fonthill higher gratification.

'Fonthill Abbey,
 'Thursd., Octr. 17, 1817.'

Rogers was at Longleat when this epistle arrived, and he accepted the invitation. He drove to Fonthill, and on arriving at the gates of the Abbey was told that his servant and horses must return, as Beckford's would be at his service. Rogers stayed three days, which were chiefly spent in driving about the grounds in pony carriages. The other visitors were James Smith, the author of a book entitled 'Select Views in Italy,' and a French priest. In the evening, Beckford improvised on the piano or read from one of his unpublished books; two of these were unprinted additions to 'Vathek.' Rogers never told the secrets of the prison house of Eblis, if they were ever unfolded to him. He slept in a bedroom which was approached through a gallery where lights were burned all night, and where there was an illuminated picture of St. Antonio, to which it was reported that Beckford sometimes said his prayers.

In the beginning of November, Rogers was staying with Lord Bathurst, when news came in the evening that the Princess Charlotte had been confined, that the child was dead, but that the Princess was doing well; and this was followed in the early morning by the terrible news that the Princess was dead. Rogers told the story thirty years afterwards to his nephew, Samuel Sharpe, from whose Diary I reproduce it.[1]

---

[1] *Samuel Sharpe, Egyptologist and translator of the Bible*, p. 182.

'At four o'clock in the morning there was a stir in the house; an express had arrived to tell Lord Bathurst that the Princess was dead. He got up immediately to carry the news to the Regent, her father. He went to town, and called up the Duke of York at St. James's Palace, and took him with him. When they got to the Regent's they roused Colonel [Sir Benjamin] Bloomfield, told him their errand, and begged him to inform the Regent of his daughter's death. He positively refused. "Tell it yourselves," he said. "Let him know, then, that we want to speak to him," said the Duke of York and Lord Bathurst. This Bloomfield did, and they were shown up. The Duke of York made Lord Bathurst go into the room first. They found the Regent sitting up in bed, and told him they had sad news for him. He said he had heard it—the child was dead. Then they let him understand that his daughter was dead. He was, of course, much upset, but three hours afterwards he was consulting with those about him as to the ceremony of the funeral.'

Mr. Dyce reports the story, as told by Rogers, somewhat differently. He says, that on hearing of his daughter's death, the Regent struck his forehead violently with both hands and fell forward into the arms of the Duke of York. Among other exclamations the intelligence drew from him was: 'Oh, what will become of that poor man,' referring to Prince Leopold.

At Lord Bathurst's Rogers saw a good many letters of Pope, Bolingbroke, and others, and Lady Bathurst lent him a packet of letters from Queen Mary to King

William (many of which have since been published), of which Rogers recollected one in which she called the king her 'dear husban.' One or two of Lord Bathurst's own recollections are set down in Rogers's Commonplace Book.

'The Prince (father of George III.) was a very weak man. The King, his father, never would be reconciled to him, though the Prince would have done anything for it. The only person of the family he seemed at all to like was the Princess Amelia. He would nod at her sometimes. The day before the Prince died the King was informed of his danger, but took no notice of it. Seven or eight days afterwards he paid a visit to the Princess, and some formal conversation took place, but with little concern expressed, or perhaps felt, on either side, when the Princess Amelia, then a child, seeing them sitting side by side on the sofa, just as her father used to sit with her mother, burst into tears; the King instantly rose, and, taking her up, kissed her, saying, "You are the only person of any feeling in the family," and instantly left the house. The Princess Amelia told me this story.—*Lord Bathurst.*

'The Prince of Wales took delight in giving away, in great form, titles and places beforehand, to be confirmed when he came to the Crown. My grandfather used often to kiss hands.—*Lord Bathurst.*'

The next letter from Byron to Rogers which Moore prints in his 'Life of Byron' is dated Venice, the 3rd of March, 1818. It has no particular bearing on Rogers's story, and it is only needful to mention it here to supply a striking omission which Moore has made without giving any indication of it. This is how the letter really begins—

'I have not, as you say, "taken to wife the Adriatic," but if the Adriatic will take my wife, I shall be very glad to marry her instead. In the meantime, I have had wife enough: as the grammar has it, "tædet vitæ, pertæsum est conjugii." However, the last part of this exquisite quotation only is applicable to my case. I like life very well in my own way.' In the same letter he speaks of his 'mathematical Medea.' He tells Rogers, too, that in his effort to have 'Fazio' brought out at Drury Lane he 'was overruled, as also in an effort I made in favour of Sotheby's trash, which I did to oblige the mountebank, who has since played me a trick or two (I suspect) which, perhaps, he may remember, as well as his airs of patronage which he affects with young writers, and affected both *to* me and *of* me many a good year. He sent me (unless the handwriting be a most extraordinary coincidental mistake) an anonymous note at Rome about the "Poeshie" of Chillon, &c. I can swear also to his phrases, particularly the word "effulgence." Well, I say nothing.'

It will not be inappropriate to close this chapter with a letter from Ugo Foscolo, which is interesting in itself, though chiefly interesting here as a further proof, among many, of the pains which Rogers was always willing to take to do a service to a man of letters. Foscolo, introduced at Holland House, had taken London society by storm. But he was an exile, and must earn an exile's bread. He had been more than half a year in London, and Rogers and Allen had already been in communication with him as to his plans of work, when he wrote the outspoken and pathetic letter which Rogers ever after kept among his literary treasures.

Ugo Foscolo to Samuel Rogers.[1]

'Mon cher Monsieur,—Vendredi, à peine rentré chez moi j'ai été obligé de me faire appliquer un vessicatoire sur la poitrine, ce qui m'a empêché de vous écrire de suite, et je n'avais personne à qui dicter ma lettre. Je commence, monsieur, par vous répéter les sentimens les plus sincères de mon cœur pour les soins que vous prenez avec tant de bonté pour un étranger qui a peu de titres à votre affection, et qui ne vous donne que de nouvelles peines. Veuillez bien dire les mêmes choses à Mr. Allen. Puisque la nécessité me force d'écrire pour vivre (quoique je doute s'il est necessaire que je vive) tous les jours sont précieux pour moi; et tout moment de travail perdu aujourd'hui peut m'être funeste demain, d'autant plus que dans ma manière de travailler il y a deux fatalités inhérentes, et qui sont plus fortes que tous mes raisonnements et mes tentatives pour les éviter. Premièrement, lorsque je pense et écris sur un sujet, je ne puis pas brider mes idées, ma mémoire, ou ma plume. Il m'est dernièrement arrivé d'écrire quinze heures de suite et vingt-sept pages dans un jour. Mais il me faut quinze et quelquefois vingt-sept jours pour arranger le désordre inséparable de l'abondance, pour donner la substance

---

[1] Some obvious slips in grammar and spelling have been corrected, otherwise Foscolo's French has been left untouched.

des idées sans leur indigestion, pour citer les faits avec exactitude et l'érudition sans pédanterie ; enfin pour placer le sujet avec ordre et donner à chaque partie le style convenable—en second lieu (je ne sais si par trop d'égards pour moi ou pour le public), je suis si difficile à me contenter de ce que je fais, qu'avant de donner mon livre à l'imprimeur, il me faut entre la composition et la publication un intervalle de temps convenable pour l'examiner avec l'esprit calme. Il est vrai que l'homme dans le besoin ne doit pas avoir autant d'égards pour sa réputation ni pour les acheteurs de ses livres ; mais je ne suis pas loin de ma quarantième année, j'ai fait bien des sacrifices pour tout ce que je crois honneur et conscience, je ne puis pas me changer, et je répète que ma manière de sentir et d'agir, à ce sujet, l'emporte sur tous mes raisonnemens.

'Mais puisque ces deux difficultés détruisent, pour ainsi dire, une grande partie de mon temps, il faut que je tâche d'en perdre le moins possible, d'autant plus que la grande assiduité et rapidité de travail détruisent aussi ma santé et je suis depuis trois semaines dans un état continuel de fièvre, d'insomnie et de langueur.

'J'ai fait une partie de mes lettres sur le plan dont j'ai souvent parlé à vous et à Mr. Allen et que j'ai envoyé tracé dans une préface à Lord Holland et que vous avez tous approuvé. Mes lettres sont un parallèle des *Usages*, de la *Littérature* et de l'*Histoire politique* d'Angleterre et de l'Italie. Je les ai divisées en *trois séries* selon les *trois sujets* ; je voulais commencer par publier le premier volume qui traite des *Usages*.

'Mais en écrivant et en préparant mes matériaux j'ai

vu s'accroître à chaque instant en nombre et en poids bien de difficultés que j'avais d'ailleurs prévues, mais sans m'apercevoir de toute leur conséquence. D'abord le sujet est très *vaste*, il exige des grandes lectures de toute espèce. Il est *dangereux* pour un homme exilé, et qui doit parler tantôt bien et tantôt mal de la nation où il s'est réfugié ; et provoquer la critique avec des armes inégales : et les voyageurs avant de publier leurs opinions sur les nations étrangères se retirent dans leur propre pays. Enfin ma langue, ma diction trop Italienne combinée avec ma manière particulière d'exprimer mes idées, s'opposent à une bonne *traduction* en Anglais ; surtout les lettres qui traitent des *Usages* exigent que la petitesse de la matière soit relevée par l'imagination et le ridicule. En parlant d'une nation barbare, ou nouvellement découverte, il suffit d'écrire ses usages avec simplicité : la nouveauté et la curiosité font le reste. Mais le *beau monde* en Europe est presque partout le même ; et il est indispensable que l'esprit et le style de l'auteur soient comme une espèce de microscope qui aide les différentes sociétés de l'Europe à distinguer leurs nuances respectives. C'est pour cela que Montesquieu et Goldsmith ont fait écrire leurs lettres par des Persans et des Chinois ; mais malgré que par cette précaution ils ont pu peindre à grands traits, les objets étaient trop menus et trop connus aux yeux de leurs lecteurs ; et par conséquent ils se sont aidés des attractives du style et du ridicule. Mais les *Lettres Persanes* traduites ne font pas la dixième partie de l'effet.

'Comme cette difficulté de la *traduction* est la seule importante au libraire, je me suis livré à la providence—

puisque ma fortune le veut ainsi—relativement aux autres difficultés qui dépendent aussi un peu de moi, et j'ai envoyé à Mr. Murray une longue lettre écrite avec assez d'originalité et de *humour* et de tournure de style, et de verve, afin qu'il la fasse essayer par un traducteur de sa confiance.

'Mr. Murray m'a dit qu'en Angleterre on aime les *quotations* même dans les sujets qui ne sont pas littéraires ; je me crois en état de lui complaire ; mais je n'ai presque d'autres livres que ma mémoire. Il est bien facile de dire que j'aille consulter les bibliothèques de mes amis ; mais il est difficile de sortir chaque jour de chez soi pour courir les maisons des autres chercher des ouvrages que souvent on ne trouve pas, troubler ses amis, prier pour chaque livre qu'on désire et en même temps avoir assez de calme et de loisir pour continuer son ouvrage.

'Mr. Murray a senti ces difficultés et même il les a prévenues, et a eu la bonté de me dire qu'il me fournirait ou me ferait prêter les livres dont j'aurais besoin ; je lui ai envoyé une note de classiques Grecs et Latins et de quelques autres auteurs. En attendant, depuis que je travaille j'ai été souvent forcé de marcher jusqu'à Londres pour consulter un livre, et souvent aussi j'ai dû en acheter, en dépensant les trois choses dont je n'ai pas du reste, le tems, l'argent, et la santé.

'Il est donc de toute nécessité que je sache positivement quelle espèce d'ouvrage Mr. Murray croit plus utile à ses intérêts et aux miens, afin qu'aux autres dommages je ne sois pas obligé d'ajouter la dépense de faire transcrire des manuscrits.

'Vous m'avez dit, Monsieur, que maintenant il désirerait un ouvrage qui traite *principalement de Littérature Italienne*. Je préférerais de mon côté aussi et pour la tranquillité de ma vie et pour mon caractère, de ne m'adonner qu'à *l'histoire critique littéraire*, et je crois d'être pourvu d'assez de moyens pour cette branche de travail. La traduction seroit plus aisée, car le style demanderoit moins d'effusion naturelle d'âme, moins d'art et d'imagination ; et se borneroit à l'élégance et à la clarté nécessaires à la *narration* et au *criticisme*.

'Je donnerais donc pour perdu ou je réserverais pour d'autres occasions le travail que j'ai fait jusqu'ici, et je traiterais uniquement *de littérature* ; mais il faut que je sois positivement assuré de *trois choses*—

'1°. Si Mr. Murray déclare de se servir de mon travail après qu'il sera fait.

'2°. Combien d'argent approximativement il serait disposé à dépenser pour deux volumes, chacun de 400 pages environ in 8° à 30 lignes par page et 40 lettres par ligne.

'3°. Sur quel plan il voudrait que l'ouvrage fût fait—si en forme épistolaire, et par matière, comme par exemple, poésie, histoire, éloquence, et la poésie subdivisée en épique, tragique, satirique, &c., avec des subdivisions pareilles dans les autres branches—ou si par époques d'histoire en commençant depuis le 13ᵉ siècle jusqu'à nos jours. La première manière peut se traiter en *lettres*, en y mêlant aussi des observations comparatives sur la littérature anglaise. La seconde exige d'être traitée dans un cours chronologique.

'Mais quant au plan on peut l'arranger facilement ;

pour le moment ma position me force à exiger une réponse définitive sur les deux premières questions. Il est indispensable que le contrat soit fait d'avance, au moins pour le premier volume ; et d'après le bon ou le mauvais succès, l'on s'arrangera sur le second.

"Si Mr. Murray désire que je continue dans mon projet primitif, l'ouvrage sera en trois volumes et il faudra aussi commencer pour convenir sur le prix ; mais ayez la bonté de le prévenir que la traduction du premier volume qui traite des *Usages* sera tout à fait difficile ; que le second volume traite de la *littérature* plus vaguement que dans le plan proposé au dessus qui n'aura d'autre but que la *Littérature Italienne*, et l'influence que les révolutions politiques, les mœurs, les auteurs de l'antiquité et les livres des nations modernes ont exercés sur elle.

'Dans tous les cas j'ose vous prier d'arranger avec Mr. Allen les choses de manière que je sache positivement ce que je dois faire et sur combien d'argent je pourrai compter à la fin de mon travail. Il faut, mon cher Monsieur, que je me sente le cœur rassuré sans craindre l'avenir ou les dettes, sans éprouver l'humiliation de la honte, sans faire à chaque instant des combats pour relever mon esprit tandis que mon âme par la force de mes circonstances retombe dans la prostration. Dans ces combats toutes mes facultés s'épuisent, et je crains fort qu'elles dépériront bien vite—

'Pectora nostra duas non admittentia curas.

'Vous, Monsieur, et mes amis m'avez fait oublier une grande partie des désagremens de l'exil ; mais l'homme dans mon état de solitude et d'infirmité et sans espérances pour l'avenir, ne peut pas trouver, ni ne doit pas chercher des soulagements que ou dans les personnes qui l'ont connu depuis son enfance, ou dans soi-même. Il est donc extrêmement urgent que je me hâte à prendre un parti définitif. En retardant, il s'agirait de mon honneur, et si je m'enchaîne avec des dettes je perdrai même la liberté de mourir.

'Si Mr. Murray ne peut se décider, il est bien que je le sache tout de suite. En continuant de travailler pour lui, les livres qu'il a promis de me fournir me seront indispensables ; différement (*sic*) ils me sont inutiles ; et je vous prie de le remercier et de lui exprimer ma sincère reconnaissance, d'autant plus qu'à cette promesse il a souvent ajouté des présents de ses publications et toujours avec des manières nobles et obligeantes. Et quant à vous, Monsieur, et à Mr. Allen, je vous donne la plus grande preuve de ma reconnaissance et de ma confiance en vous ouvrant la triste position de mon état. Pour que vous puissiez traiter avec pleine connaissance de cause, j'ai été obligé de vous accabler d'une longue lettre ; mais vous avez le bonheur de savoir en tirer bien vite la substance. Pardonnez aussi à un pauvre malade qui dicte comme il peut de son lit, et qui vraiment n'a presque pas de tête ; mais je ne perdrai pas la mémoire de vos bontés que lorsque je ne pourrai plus me rappeler de moi-même. Mardi matin je serai chez vous, adieu.

'Votre Ami,
'HUGUES FOSCOLO.

'Dimanche matin, 19 février, 1818.'

CHAPTER VIII.

1818-19.

Lines on the Temple at Woburn—Luttrell's lines on Rogers's Seat—Lord Holland's Pamphlet—His ' Dream ' of University Extension—Sketch of a Poem—Moore and Rogers at Bowood—Stories of Sheridan—Rogers to Mrs. Greg—Sonnet by Lord Holland—Moore and Rogers—Crabbe and his Publisher—Rogers's ' Human Life '—Don Juan on Rogers—Offers of Help to Moore—Letter from Crabbe—Rogers out of Politics—Two Generations of Literary Talk.

MOORE's Diary begins in August, 1818, and from that time forward Rogers's life is almost written in it. The first mention of him is in September, 1818, when Moore says that Rogers has made a paraphrase, in blank verse, of two lines from Pindar, for an inscription on the Temple of the Graces which the Duke of Bedford is building at Woburn. These are the lines—

> Approach with reverence. There are those within
> Whose dwelling place is Heaven. Daughters of Jove,
> From them flow all the decencies of life ;
> Without them nothing pleases. Virtue's self
> Admired, not loved; and those on whom they smile,
> Great though they be, and wise and beautiful,
> Shine forth with double lustre.

It was the custom in those days to put up inscriptions of this kind. I have already given the lines placed by Lord Holland on the summer-house in the garden of

Holland House called Rogers's seat. On the same building there were some verses by Luttrell, which, many years later, he showed to Macaulay, adjuring him, with mock pathos, to spare his blushes. Macaulay read the lines and speaks of them as very pretty and polished, but too many to be remembered from one reading. They are preserved in MS. probably as Luttrell sent them to Rogers—

> How charmed is the eye which in summer reposes
> On this haunt of the poet o'ershadowed with roses.
> I'll in and be seated, to try, if thus placed,
> I can catch but one spark of his feeling and taste;
> Can steal a sweet note from his musical strain,
> Or a ray of his genius to kindle my brain.
> Well—now I am fairly installed in the bower,
> How lovely the scene, how propitious the hour.
> The breeze is perfumed from the hawthorn it stirs,
> All is silent around us, but nothing occurs.
> Not a thought, I protest, though I'm here and alone,
> Not a line can I hit on that Rogers would own,
> Though my senses are raptured, my feelings in tune,
> And Holland's my host, and the season is June.
> Enough of my trial; nor garden, nor grove,
> Though poets amidst them may linger or rove;
> Not a seat e'en so hallowed as this can impart
> The fancy and fire that must spring from the heart.
> So I rise, since the Muses continue to frown,
> No more of a poet than when I sat down;
> While Rogers, on whom they look kindly, can strike
> Their lyre at all times and all places alike.[1]
>
> H. L.

June 2, 1818.

---

[1] There are some slight differences between the lines as given in the MS. and the actual inscription at Holland House. The poem begins —as there inscribed—

LORD HOLLAND'S 'DREAM'

Rogers puts on record an inscription written on a pane of glass in a dressing-room at Holland House by J. H. Frere—

> May neither fire destroy nor waste impair,
> Nor time consume thee to the twentieth heir;
> May Taste respect thee, and may Fashion spare.

In the year 1818 Lord Holland printed a small pamphlet, for private circulation, entitled, 'A Dream; addressed to Samuel Rogers.' A copy of this pamphlet was in Rogers's library;[1] and the original manuscript is among the papers he has left. It is a very striking production, and, more than anything of Lord Holland's that has yet been given to the world, shows how far his views on many subjects were in advance of his time. The dream takes him first 'to the spacious apartments of an old castle, and into the presence of a person whose name, since he is still alive, shall be sacred.' He is surprised to find this person's condition infinitely less dismal than waking fancy had often painted it. 'Courtesy and good nature (for I am afraid it was not loyalty, and I am sure it was not hypocrisy) prompted me to inquire, with unusual earnestness, about all that related to his treatment, his welfare, and his feelings in

> 'How happily sheltered is he who reposes
> In this haunt of the poet o'ershadowed with roses,
> While the sun is rejoicing, unclouded, on high,
> And summer's full majesty reigns in the sky.
> Let me in and be seated. I'll try if thus placed,' &c.

In the thirteenth line, 'ravished' is put instead of 'raptured,' and the fifteenth begins, 'The trial is ended.'

[1] In the catalogue of the sale in 1856, is (Lot 313), '*Dream, A*, by Lord Holland, addressed to S. Rogers. Privately printed, morocco, large paper, 1818.' It was bought by the late Lord Holland for 18s.

a situation so different from that in which he has spent the largest part of a very long life. . . . He frankly told me he had never been so happy. . . . He added that, old as he was, and versed as he had been in the great affairs of the world, he had derived more instruction from the short intercourse of a few months with persons now no more than he had collected from the conferences of ministers, the deliberations of councils, the documents of State, or the correspondence with courts for the space of more than fifty years.' To this intercourse with the Immortals the Dreamer was admitted, that he might write down an outline of their talk. The subject for conversation was to be a certain hundred thousand pounds a-year, which his introducer said he desired to bequeath 'in a way creditable to his memory and useful to the world.' Then, adds the Dreamer, 'taking me by the arm, and nodding and whispering to me most significantly, he opened a door into a large apartment, where I perceived several persons sitting in easy and unconstrained postures, and whom I immediately recognised (though I cannot recollect how or why, for I am but an unobservant handler of old prints) to be no less important personages than Sir Thomas More, Cardinal Pole, Lord Burghley, Lord Bacon, Lord Clarendon, Mr. Milton, Mr. Cowley, Sir William Temple, Lord Shaftesbury (author of the "Characteristicks"), Mr. Locke, Lord Somers, Bishop Berkeley, and Mr. Addison.' Sir Isaac Newton had just left the room. The conversation which follows is long and interesting. After a remark from Cowley on the new conditions which make authors no longer dependent upon patrons, Addison points out some of the disadvantages which arise from the new state of things. 'The novelty which diverts for the moment is nobly, we will not say extravagantly, encouraged, while genius, when labouring to improve the taste and morals of mankind, is often neglected, or at least somewhat tardily rewarded. Besides, this new and gigantic Mæcenas, if he has the bulk, has also the stomach of a Leviathan. I will not say his appetite is coarse, but it is exceedingly voracious. There is, therefore, reason to fear that those who study his palate with a view to their own profit rather than to his health will pay more attention to the quantity than to the quality of viands with which they supply his never-ceasing demand.' Hence, without interfering with the consumption of paper or the harvests of Grub Street, he would like ' to place, in point of fortune as well as consideration, the devoted sons of permanent fame (and here he looked at John Milton) more nearly upon a level with those who are so amply remunerated for gratifying contemporary caprice and curiosity. Long and laborious endeavours may be cherished by the judicious encouragement of the State, and the lovers of temporary celebrity, like gaudy insects in the sunshine, be left, nevertheless, to enjoy unmolested the transient but enlivening munificence which has kindled them into existence.' The conversation thus begun leads up to the suggestion for the establishment of a Literary Academy, to which 20,000*l.* a year is to be allotted. Then the voices take a higher range, and the advancement of knowledge, and the improvement and extension of education are discussed, ' and the influence which efforts directed to this end might have in consolidating the strength, concentrating the talent, and uniting the hearts of our countrymen, and thereby exalting the name of Great Britain among the nations of the earth.' In the conversation which follows, the Dreamer is struck with the cordial agreement of the extraordinary personages before him. 'The enthusiasm of Sir Thomas More, of Milton and Bishop Berkeley, was directed to a common object; Cardinal Pole, Mr. Locke, and Lord Shaftesbury concurred in the necessity of rendering education subservient to the ends of religious freedom and national union.' Sir William Temple at length produces a scheme by which England is to establish a great and universal system of education, with the object of preserving, 'by means of colleges, academies, schools, and universities in various parts of her dominions, English habits of thinking, English manners, and English language.' Three great universities, with dependencies of schools, military and naval academies, lecturing and travelling professorships, museums, libraries and observatories, are to be established in three distinct quarters of the globe, within the jurisdiction of the throne of Great Britain. One is to be in Canada or the West Indies, another at Fort William in the East, and the third at Malta, Gibraltar, or some possession in the Mediterranean. They are to be intimately connected with one another as well as with the establishments of Marlow and Hertford, the colleges of Eton, Westminster, Winchester, and Maynooth, and the universities of Dublin, Edinburgh, Oxford, and Cambridge. There is to be absolute religious freedom. In the university at Malta, which is first to be established, there are to be four Christian churches, a mosque, and a synagogue. The scheme of the Maltese University is worked out into minute details; but the Dreamer wakes before the conversation is finished.

This is but a meagre outline of an idea of University Extension sketched by the great Whig potentate for the amusement of his friend. Of course, it was not a serious proposal, and it is only of value as indicating the views and feelings entertained at Holland House before the great war against Napoleon had reached its close. The moral is—'How many Maltese universities would the expenses of a single campaign have endowed? What knowledge might not be purchased, what genius might not have been rewarded with a sum equal to the cost of some senseless and tedious festival, some fantastic and unprofitable building.' The fantastic and unprofitable building was then still growing at Brighton, where the dream was dreamed. At breakfast the Dreamer felt that the unsubstantial pageant belonged only to the world of dreams. The sentiments the talk of the Immortals had raised in his mind seemed 'trite, sickly, and impracticable morality,' and when he took up the newspaper, 'I smiled,' he says, 'though I yawned at reading a long debate on the excesses of expenditure in the Master of the Horse and the Lord Chamberlain's departments.' The manuscript was sent to Rogers, after some delay, with the following letter.

Lord Holland to Samuel Rogers.

'Dear Rogers,—I send you my promised letter under a cover to Colonel Bunbury, who will transmit it to you. It was, indeed, necessary to convey it gratis; at least, it would have been unpardonable to make you pay for such nonsense. As it is, my presumption is not small in submitting so crude a rhapsody to you, who, with a fertile invention, have the good sense of subjecting it always to the control of a severe judgment and a correct taste, but *qu'y faire*, when one is full of a thing, one must write it, and when one has written it, one must show it within twenty-four hours or not at all. I had promised you the dissertation. If I keep it till to-morrow I shall never let you see it, and up to this time I am under the illusion of thinking it all perfection.

'I have no other copy of it, so pray preserve the precious MS., as I should like to shew it to my uncle Ossory and my sister.

'Yours,
'VASSALL HOLLAND.'

Rogers read and approved. It was a prose poem, and he could only suggest that it should be shortened.

Lord Holland replied—

Lord Holland to Samuel Rogers.

'Dear Rogers,—Your long-expected letter arrived this morning and has lost nothing of its sweetness on the road. Praise is delightful, and I hope it is good for me. I like your notion of compression much. The whole thing is too long, and that, if there were not other objections, would form a strong one against any previous description of the individuals. Let me have my MS., for I have no copy and wish much to show it to my uncle Ossory, and if possible, to compress it. Mark the parts you think susceptible of compression with a pencil,

—you shall have it back again, if you wish it, the moment I have taken a copy.

'Yours,
'VASSALL HOLLAND.'

There was much correspondence with Richard Sharp on Rogers's forthcoming poem. As with his earlier writings, so with this, many of the lines were subjected to critical discussion and revision. The idea in the following letter may have been suggested by Wordsworth's most exquisite poem.

Samuel Rogers to Richard Sharp.
[May, 1818.]

'My dear Friend,—What would you say, and what would Wordsworth say, if I throw what follows into verse? Perhaps you would not recommend it. Besides, the thought is yours, and to be twice stolen is a fate reserved only for the bronze horses of Lysippus.

'When first we come, a light divine is on all Nature —on earth, and sea, and sky; but, like the Bologna-stone in the dark, we shed it all ourselves. It came with us; it issues from us; and soon, like that stone of lustre, we shed it no longer. It grows fainter and fainter, and at last it dies. Where we imbibed it, we know not. We did not find it here; and when it goes, nothing, nothing can bring it back again. It goes, leaving us to all the flat realities of this life; and nothing can supply its place but the opening gleams of a better.

'S. R.

'If you don't mean to use it yourself, perhaps you will help me a little.'

A further letter recalls an old matter of anxiety—

Samuel Rogers to Richard Sharp.

'My dear Friend,—It is now twenty years since we discussed together in Norbury Park the subject of "Columbus and the Spirits" and its merits as a poetical subject. Now, may I ask you what you would have said then, and what you have now to say, in answer to an objection which has been triumphantly brought against it, and which Mackintosh seems to admit to be unanswerable—the impropriety of blending truth and fiction together, when the real circumstances are so recent and so well known?

'Perhaps you would rather state your sentiments in conversation than in writing. If so, and you can eat a cutlet with me at six o'clock any day this week, I shall be very happy to see you.

'I have drawn up a short answer, with which I mean to let the subject rest for ever, but I am not quite satisfied with it.

'Yours ever,

'Samuel Rogers.

'St. James's Place: Monday [Aug. 17, 1818].

Moore's Diary continues—

'*October* 18, 1818.—As the morning was fine, set out to Bowood to see Rogers; caught him in the garden on the way to Bowles's; walked with him; talked much about Sheridan. . . Sheridan once told Rogers of a scene that occurred in a French theatre in 1772, where two French officers stared a good deal at his wife, and S., not knowing a word of French, could do nothing but put his arms a-kimbo and look bluff and defying at them, which they, not knowing a word of English, could only reply to by the very same attitude and look. He once mentioned to Rogers that he was aware he ought to have made a love scene between Charles and Maria in the " School for Scandal " and would have done it but that the actors who played the parts were not able to do such a scene justice. Talked of Hastings and the impeachment; asked Rogers whether it was not now looked upon even by the Opposition themselves as a sort of dramatic piece of display, got up by the Whigs of that day from private pique, vanity, &c., &c.,—Francis first urging them on from his hostility to Hastings; Burke running headlong into it from impetuosity of temper; and Sheridan seizing with avidity the first great opportunity that offered of showing off his talent. He said it *was* so considered now, and in addition to all this, Mr. Pitt gave in to the prosecution with much satisfation, because it turned away the embattled talent of the time from himself and his measures, and concentrated it all against one individual whom he was most happy to sacrifice, so he could thereby keep them employed. . . . Sat with Rogers in his room till dinner. Told me that Beckford (*the* Beckford) is delighted with " Lalla Rookh." Heard so from Beckford himself when I met him at Rogers's in the spring. Beckford wishes me to go to Fonthill with R., anxious that I should look over his " Travels " (which were printed some years ago but afterwards suppressed by him) and prepare them for the press. Rogers supposes he would give me something magnificent—a thousand pounds, perhaps; but if he were to give me a hundred times that sum I would not have my name coupled with his. . . . Rogers asked me whether the "Parody on Horace," lately in the "Chronicle," was mine; said how Luttrell was delighted with it at Ampthill and pronounced it to be mine, reading it out to Lords Jersey and Duncannon, who were also much pleased with it. Told me also that he had heard the verses to Sir Hudson Lowe praised at Brookes's.

'19th.—Had promised Rogers, who was coming to me this morning, to meet him half-way. Mrs. Phipps, upon whom I called as I went, came out with me in order to get a glimpse of "*Memory* Rogers." He and I walked to my cottage, much delighted with the scenery around; said he preferred the valley and village before us to the laid-out grounds of Bowood. Shewed him some of my Sheridan papers. He mentioned "Memoirs of Jackson, of Exeter," written by himself, which he saw in MS. some years ago, and in which he remembered there was a most glowing description of his pupil, Miss Linley, standing singing by his side, and so beautiful "you might think you were looking into the face of an angel."

'20th.—. . . Looked over Rogers's poem and marked some lines with pencil. . . . Rogers thinks I must not give extracts from Mr. T. Grenville's letters, he being still living.

'21st.—. . . Walked to meet Rogers, who said he

---

[1] Rogers had recorded in his Commonplace Book, that Jackson 'had known Mrs. Sheridan before her marriage. He spoke of Mrs. Sheridan's countenance when singing as like nothing earthly' (*Early Life*, p. 401).

would call upon me. Talked chiefly of Sheridan. Told me several anecdotes, some of which I have written down in my note-book as fit to use; the rest, practical jokes not easily tellable. His strewing the hall or passage with plates and dishes, and then tempting Tickell (with whom he was always at some frolic or other) to pursue him into the thick of them. Tickell fell among them and was almost cut to pieces, and next day, in vowing vengeance to Lord John Townshend against S. for this trick, he added (with the true spirit of an amateur in practical jokes), "but it was amazingly well done." At another time, when the women (Mrs. Crewe, Mrs. Tickell, &c.) had received the gentlemen after dinner in disguises which puzzled them to make out which was which, the gentlemen one day sent to the ladies to come down to them in the dining-room. The ladies on entering saw them all dressed as Turks, holding bumpers in their hands, and, after looking amongst them and saying, "This is Mr. Crewe"; "No, this is he," &c., &c., they heard a laugh at the door and there saw all the gentlemen *in propriis personis*, for 'twas the maids they had dressed up in Turkish habits. S. was always at these tricks at country houses.

'22nd.—. . . Met R. at the park gate and came on towards the cottage. Told him my delicacy on the subject of the Coalition; unwilling as I should be to offend Lord Holland, yet still feeling it my duty to speak sincerely what I thought of Fox's conduct in that instance. He said there was much to be advanced in palliation, if not in vindication, of that and other coalitions; bid me talk on the subject to Lord Holland and Allen, who had staggered him by their arguments. Lord H.'s idea of three distinct periods in his uncle's life: the first when he was opposed to Lord North and when his eloquence was bold, careless, vehement, vituperative; the second, when Pitt was his antagonist and when he found it necessary to be more cool, cautious and logical; during both these periods ambition of power and distinction was his ruling passion; but in the third and concluding portion of his life all this had passed away, and his sole, steady, *chastened-down* desire was that of doing good. . . . Rogers, Lord St. John (I think), and Lord Lauderdale were in Mr. Fox's room in Stable Yard a short time before his death, when Sheridan called. "I *must* see him, I suppose," said Fox, and when S. came in put out his hand to him. S. has since told Rogers that when Fox called him over and shook him by the hand he said in a low voice, "My dear Sheridan, I love you; you are, indeed, my friend, as for these others I merely," &c., &c. This was an excellent invention of Sheridan, who knew no one would contradict him. Talked of the Scotch novels. . . . Scott gave his honour to the Prince Regent, they were not his; and Rogers heard him do the same to Sheridan. . . . We walked through the Devizes fields to meet Crowe. . . . Talked of Milton; his greater laxity of metre in the "Paradise Regained" than in the "Paradise Lost." R. thought this was from system; but Crowe and I thought it from laziness.'

In November Rogers was at home again, after a summer which had first been broken by a serious illness in June, then by a visit of convalescence to Worthing, and after that to Bowood, where Moore met him. Soon after his return he wrote the following letter.

Samuel Rogers to Mrs. Greg.

'Highbury: Nov. 9, 1818.

'My dear Friend,—Thank you most sincerely for your kind letter. I should, I believe, have answered it that same day—so grateful did I feel for it—but that I waited to make some enquiries respecting Mr. Cogan's school. Mr. Towgood has sent all his sons there but one who was not very strong and has never been to any school but as a day boarder; the youngest is there now, and is just fourteen, so that he can't give a stronger proof of his opinion of it. Only the two eldest of the Sharpes, from some circumstances, have been there, but Miss Sharpe says that she much prefers it to any school she ever heard of, as the boys are not only made to learn while there but are inspired with the love of it, which is certainly of the greatest importance, for what is learnt at school is of trifling consequence provided it is not followed up afterwards. Mrs. Cogan is a very kind and good nurse, but as the house is too much crowded to allow of any rooms being set apart for the sick, it would not be so eligible a situation for a delicate boy whose friends live at a distance, and the majority are certainly under fourteen. Now, if there is anything more you wish to learn about it, do but write and I will send you every particular, which will be no trouble to me to procure. With regard to health, I ought to mention that two physicians whom we know have had all their sons there—Dr. Pett and Dr. Lister—and are, of course, satisfied or they would not have sent one after the other. . . . My spring campaign was cut very short by a short but severe illness which I had in the beginning of June, the effect of which, as far at least as my looks are concerned, my friends tell me I have but just recovered; in other respects, however, I have been quite well some time, but I have spent a very unsettled summer, as I was some time at Worthing for the benefit of the sea air, and then, with that and visits to different friends, I have only been settled at home since last Wednesday, but now I mean to remain stationary for some time. And so this is a long history of myself, which you kindly asked for or I would not have given you so much of. And now I must scold you a little for saying nothing, absolutely nothing, about one in whom I am sure you know I am so much interested,—I need not say I mean you; I trust, however, that you are well. I dined on Friday with Dr. Holland in St. James's Place; as he had so lately returned out of Cheshire I hoped to have heard a great deal about you, and to my disappointment he had not even seen you. He is delighted with his journey to Spa, and well he may. I hear from other quarters that he was so much engaged there professionally that he had scarcely a minute to himself, and could scarcely have cleared less than a thousand pounds,—on Friday he went away to a consultation as soon as we had left the dining-room, and, indeed, almost always is obliged to do so. There can be no doubt of his getting great practice. I am sure your heart must have ached for the Romillys [1] and for poor

---

[1] Sir Samuel Romilly's death, in a moment of aberration caused by the death of his wife three days before, occurred on the 2nd of November.

Dr. Roget. Of those that are left, I think I feel most for him at present; to him I am sure the consequences will be very, very lasting; the young people will sooner recover. No event ever excited a deeper feeling, not only amongst their friends but in every circle. I was very much pleased with the "Life of Mrs. Hamilton." I took it up without the least expectation, as I thought the account of any person living in retirement, however amiable and superior in abilities, could not be very interesting, and, likewise, I was not much prejudiced in favour of the author; she has, however, I think, contrived to make me quite in love with her subject and to be sorry to lay the book down, so, then, for the future, I must, I think, admire the author; and, indeed, I ought to say that I had no reason for my former prejudice, excepting that her appearance and manners were unlike other people. Poor Miss Edgeworth's visits to England must be sadly clouded. I am sorry to hear that she does not mean to publish her father's life; it must have been very entertaining, but, with a daughter's feelings, I almost wonder how it was ever thought of. Lord Byron is soon to appear before the public again. You did not like "Beppo" and won't be glad. Ought I to be ashamed to say how much it entertained me? . . . I am very glad to hear of Sam's having a home, though in the city, as I hope you may be induced to visit him, now that you can do so with so little trouble. It seems to me much longer than usual since I have seen you, and I can scarcely persuade myself it is only two years. This is the first summer I have missed being in Worcestershire for many years. I am sorry to say my sister Towgood has still got a sick house, her second girl has been unwell for some time, though I hope not alarmingly so. The rest of us are well. The two eldest Sharpes have been making tours on the Continent, the third is still in Hamburg and is now in a counting-house there. Accept my brother's and my united kind regards, and believe me, ever very affectionately yours,

'S. ROGERS.'

The following from Lord Holland seems to belong to this period.

Lord Holland to Samuel Rogers.

'You are too indulgent to my verse. I have been altering, I hope correcting, it ever since I sent it you.

'I transcribe the new edition on the other half [sheet], and I had half a mind, so linked is rhyming with vanity, to send a copy of it to Lord Grenville, who used most properly to rebuke me for my heterodoxy about Milton. I have been *compulsus intrare*, and this is my *amende honorable*.

'Excellent as you are both as poet and critic, you don't shine in logic; for your reason for not coming to Brighton is, according to the best forms of syllogism, a reason for coming.

'When a man is cold he should go to the warmest place he can find. Rogers is cold, and Brighton is the warmest place he can find. *Ergo*, Rogers should go to Brighton.

'Yours,
'VASSALL HOLLAND.

'You liked the seventh line with "smoothest *poesy*." I laboured hard to change it, and thought I had improved it, but your approbation shakes me—I had written fouler, and am not sure "grosser" is better—tell me. "Tales" for "toys" is an improvement certainly. I am as full of my own verses as our friend Jack Townshend (who is pretty well) could be.

'Good-bye.

> 'Homer and Dryden, nor unfrequently
>   The playful Ovid, or the Italian's song
>   That held entranced my youthful thoughts so long,
> With dames, and loves, and deeds of chivalry,
> E'en now delight me,—from the noisy throng
>   Thither I fly to sip the sweets that lie
>   Enclosed in tenderest folds of poesy,
> Oft as for ease my weary spirits long.
> But when recoiling from the grosser scene
>   Of sordid vice, or rank, atrocious crime,
>   My sinking soul pants for the pure serene
> Of loftier regions,—quitting tales and rhyme,
> I turn to Milton, and his heights sublime,
> Too long by me unsought, I strive to climb.'

Before the end of November Moore was in London again, and his Diary continues—

'*November 26.*—Went to Holland House. . . . The party at dinner: Lord John, Tierney, Sharp, Whishaw, Roger Wilbraham, Rogers, and Mrs. Sydney Smith.

'*November 27.*—Slept at Holland House. Walked before breakfast with Tierney, Rogers, &c., in the garden, and read Luttrell's very pretty verses[1] written under Lord Holland's in the seat called "Rogers's seat." The breakfast very agreeable. Lord Holland full of sunshine

[1] See p. 264.

as usual. "He always comes down to breakfast," says Rogers very truly, "like a man on whom some sudden good fortune has just fallen." . . . Party at dinner: Rogers, Tierney, Sharp, and Mrs. Smith. . . . Had the pleasure of putting into Rogers's hand a draft for my long-owed debt of five hundred pounds.

'28th.—Rogers wished me to go and dine this day with his brother and sister at Highbury. I assented if he would take upon himself to stand the brunt of Lady Holland's displeasure on the occasion. In for a very amusing scene between them on the subject. She insisting upon keeping me, and he most miraculously courageous and persevering in taking me away. "Why," says she to me, "do you allow him to dispose of you thus like a little bit of literary property?" Dined at Highbury. Miss Rogers very agreeable.

'December 1st.—Had some conversation with Rogers before dinner about his poem which he is daily adding couplets to.

'December 6th.—Breakfasted at Rogers's. Told me of Crabbe's negotiation with Murray for his new volume of tales [1] consisting of near twelve thousand lines.

'7th.—Called upon Rogers at half-past four, when I found that Lord Holland had written to the Longmans to meet him there on Crabbe's business. At five Rees came, and I left them to their deliberations. . . . Went to Rees at nine o'clock. Told me the particulars of the conference at Rogers's; said he had prefaced the offer he had made by telling them they must not expect

[1] The new work was 'The Tales of the Hall," published in 1819. For the copyright of this and of his other poems Murray paid Crabbe 3,000*l.*

anything like what would be given for a work of mine . . . and for the new work and the old had only offered 1000*l*.

'*8th.*—. . . Paddled back through the swimming streets to Rogers, who had fixed, too, for me to call. Found him in consternation about Crabbe, who had written to Murray immediately after the interview with Rees, to say he would accept his offer, but had not heard from him since. Rogers proposed we should go together to Murray, as he wanted to speak to him about his own poem, which he thinks of publishing with him in shares. Went to Murray, and after Rogers had talked to him about his own poem and told Murray that he was printing it himself, to see how it looked; he said, carelessly, "I am glad to find, Mr. Murray, that you have settled with Mr. Crabbe for his new work." This clinched the business. Murray answered very cheerfully that he had, so we set off to poor Crabbe (who was moping dismally at home and had nearly given up all hope of his thousands) to tell him the news which, of course, set his mind perfectly at ease.

'*11th.*—. . . Rogers, on the last morning I was with him in town, took out of a little cabinet the draft I had given him a week before, and said, "What am I to do with this?" I laughed, and said, "Present it for payment, to be sure, my dear Rogers." "Well," he answered, "if it is any convenience to you in your Bermuda business to enable you to allege that you have no means, I will keep it for you."'

The story of the negotiations for Crabbe with Murray had a sequel, set forth in the following letter—

The Rev. George Crabbe to Samuel Rogers.

'Trowbridge, Wilts: January 11, 1819.

'My dear Sir,—Hitherto when I have parted from you in town, I resigned myself to the evil, and knowing that you loved not what is called correspondence—too often, I grant, a very grievous tax on time and patience—I said in my heart, "Farewell till we meet again," but I have not this time the former resignation. I want to know where you dwell, how you are, what you are doing, and sometimes whether you think of me. I want to read your verses as they come and while they are yet in that changeable state between their first birth and their commitment into the furnace of the compositor.

'I miss your morning conversation—your anecdotes—your good humour, and even your tyranny and arbitrary rule over me, for which Heaven forgive you.

'I ordered two clean notes from my brother Timbrell's bank—brother by a kind of civil latitude of speech; our children married—and a clerk has sent me the things I repay you with, indeed, I can command none more unsullied.

'Mr. Murray keeps me employed, but I have a sad affair to communicate. Mr. Colburn, at whose library I was accustomed to meet Miss Carr, and whom I have known and dealt with, by subscription to his collection of novels, &c., and who knew that I was employed in writing a poem (which he calls Recollections, not recollecting the name I gave it), and who always appeared to wish that he might publish for me, though he never in any one speech approximated to the business, nor were any terms offered by him or by me, nor, in short, was there engagement or tendency to engagement, and yet, notwithstanding, has this man not only bitterly complained that I passed him by, and not only affirmed that he would have given me 500*l.* more than any other man, but beside all this, he threatens me with a process of law, on what founded I protest to you I cannot tell: there was a time when I would have listened to him and most certainly should have accepted such proposal as he says he would have made, provided my assurance of his fulfilling his part of the conditions had been well established, but he gave no occasion for my assent to, or rejection of, his terms. Have you any notion, Sir, of what this threatener is to do? I sent his letter to Mr. Murray and told all I knew, for I have nothing to conceal. It appears to me that Mr. Colburn is going to law with me for not getting him that work which he never offered to buy; and I am weak enough to be troubled, though not alarmed. The law, I too well know, is open to all men, and I will not say what a mind of certain stamp, urged by disappointment, may do, and not the less because the disappointment originated in his own folly. Forgive me this —I was vexed, and our friends cannot entirely escape our vexations.

'I hope you are entirely well, and all at Highbury. My son John, who is with me, wants much to know a gentleman who is so kind to his father. My Hampstead friends are detained by the sickness of one in the family and come not yet to Bath. Would that you loved that place of comfort and repose, at least to all who are not members of its peculiar clubs and associations.

'But I will not detain you. I could not keep to myself this attack upon my peace, but I cannot seriously apprehend mischief. Mr. Colburn talks of his damages, they are 3,000*l*., for, he says, a publisher expects to gain as much as he gives. The information is curious, and the note Mr. C. makes of it still more so.

'My best remembrances to Miss Rogers and her brother.

'Will you not tell me how you proceed? I shall be unfeignedly glad to hear.

'I was invited to meet Mr. Moore lately, but the place was too distant and the night too cold, and I did not go. Fortune is against our meeting, but has been very kind in some others, and I ought not to complain.

'If you should see Mr. Murray, would you speak of this man's claim on me?—though I know not what it is,—but he probably considers it as beneath his notice, and that is what I would do, but I am not sure that I can.

'This is very blameably begging your time— pardon me.

'I am, your very obliged, &c.,

'GEO. CRABBE.

'Thanks for the loan of the notes, I had nearly omitted them—grateful people are not the most thankful, are they?'

Rogers, of course, had no difficulty in coming to an arrangement with Mr. Colburn and reassuring Crabbe. Moore writes—

'*Jan. 28th*, 1819.—Went to Breakfast with Rogers,

who is in the very agonies of parturition; shewed me the work ready printed and in boards, but he is still making alterations; told me that Byron's "Don Juan" is pronounced by Hobhouse and others as unfit for publication. . . . Crabbe's delight at having three thousand pounds in his pocket. Rogers offered to take care of them for him, but no, he must take them down to shew them to his son John. "Would not copies do?" "No, must shew John the actual notes." . . . . . . Dined with Rogers. He had cancelled the note about Lord Ossory at Lord Holland's suggestion; it alluded to Lord Ossory's habit of transacting his magisterial business out of doors, which procured for him the name of Lord Chief Justice in Eyre (air). Lord Holland did not wish this joke to remain.'

The poem which Moore saw ready printed and in boards in January, and to which Rogers was still making alterations, came out finally in the spring under the title 'Human Life.' He always regarded it as the best of his poems, perhaps because he felt that he had put into it the best of his life and of himself. No reader of my account of Rogers's early years can fail to see what the inspiration of this poem is. It is full of his early experiences. The boy is himself; the home is the home he had lived in at Newington Green; the mother is the true and tender woman who wrote the letters to her "ever dear T. R."; and the whole philosophy of life which the poem teaches is that which he had learned from Dr. Price. At various stages of this biography I have found it necessary to refer to this poem, and have pointed out how his family affections and his political friendships had got expression in his verse. He was in his fifty-sixth year when it was published. There was a good deal of debate with Sharp as to the reference to—

> Young Byron in the groves of Academe,

and it was finally resolved to print only the initial (B * * * *), as Byron himself had originally printed Rogers's name in 'Beppo.'[1] Rogers was staying at Althorp with Lord Spencer when this point had to be settled. There were with him in the house the Bessboroughs, the Lytteltons, the Duncannons, Vernon, Macdonald and others, when Byron's 'Don Juan' arrived, and Rogers writes to Richard Sharp that its appearance is 'another reason for hastening out my panegyric before the gall and wormwood in the Dedication appear.' So 'Human Life,' after six years of incubation, was hurried out at last.

The gall and wormwood in the dedication were not for Rogers. The references to him, both in the dedication and in the body of the poem, are altogether complimentary, and consistent with Byron's view of Rogers as a poet. Probably most of the guests at Althorp, and the educated public generally, agreed with Byron's estimate of the relative position of the poets he attacks, but Time has reversed it. Seventy years have passed since these lines were addressed to Southey and Wordsworth, the trial has taken place, and so far as

---

[1] 'Men of the world, who know the world like men,
Scott, Rogers, Moore, and all the better brothers,
Who think of something else besides the pen.'
Beppo, stanza 76.

Wordsworth is concerned, the verdict is the very reverse of that which Byron anticipated—

> The field is universal and allows
>   Scope to all such as feel the inherent glow;
> Scott, Rogers, Campbell, Moore and Crabbe will try
> . 'Gainst you the question with posterity.

So Byron wrote, and so many thought. Hence the publication of a new poem by Rogers was regarded all through cultivated society as an important literary event, though there were many who saw that he belonged to the school which must decrease, while Wordsworth and Coleridge belonged to that which must increase. There was nothing remarkable in Rogers being put by Byron on a level with Scott, Crabbe, Campbell and Moore. That was his natural position, and it was equally natural in those days that they should all be put together on a higher level than that of the Lake Poets. In Don Juan's words the orthodox faith still was—

> Thou shalt believe in Milton, Dryden, Pope,
>   Thou shalt not set up Wordsworth, Coleridge, Southey,
> Because the first is crazed beyond all hope,
>   The second drunk, the third so quaint and mouthy;
> With Crabbe it may be difficult to cope,
>   And Campbell's Hippocrene is somewhat drouthy;
> Thou shalt not steal from Samuel Rogers, nor
> Commit — flirtation with the muse of Moore.

Sydney Smith, writing of Rogers's poem before he had seen it, says, ' The Hollands have read Rogers's poem and like it. . . . Luttrell approves.' Writing after he had read it, he says, ' There are some very good descriptions—the mother and the child, Mr. Fox at St. Anne's

Hill, and several more. The beginning of the verses on
Paestum are very good too.' The author of 'The Man
of Feeling' wrote to Rogers a letter of genial criticism,
telling him he had 'pitched "Human Life" too high,' and
incidentally remarking of Crabbe that 'he traces Nature
amid the filth of its mense-lanes and blind alleys in which
the Muse, if she does not forget her proper rank, soils
her petticoats and begrimes her face.' There is a characteristic letter of Erskine's, asking Rogers to send him
a copy of the poem, and adding, 'I am coming to town
next week, but I am invisible to the naked eye, and
therefore, when you ask me to dinner, I shall take up no
room.'

In May, Moore was again in London, and, as usual,
his Diary is full of Rogers. It is 'breakfasted with
Rogers,' 'dined with Rogers,' 'took a bed at Rogers's,'
'went with Rogers making visits,' and so forth, day after
day. Luttrell is constantly at Rogers's, and one day
Grattan is there, and Moore finds him still very delightful. Another day it is Maltby and Crabbe, and still
another it is Mr. Hibbert and his daughters, with Luttrell, Sharp, and Miss Rogers. Luttrell and Rogers are one
morning 'going on the water to follow the Fishmongers'
barge and enjoy the music;' another morning Moore
records that Rogers objects to his making himself a slave
to the booksellers, and thinks he ought to accept the offers
of friends. 'There is my 500*l*.,' he said, 'ready for you.
Your friend Richard Power will, of course, advance
another.' 'I answered,' says Moore, 'No, my dear
Rogers, your 500*l*. has done its duty most amply, and I
am resolved never more, if I can help it, to owe any money

to friends.' Rogers's was not the only offer. At the end of July Rogers received a letter from Francis Jeffrey, which has never been made public, but which is most honourable to Moore's old antagonist, and deserves to be put on lasting record as an example of generous liberality.

Lord Jeffrey to Samuel Rogers.

'Edinburgh : 30 July, 1819.

' My dear Sir,—I have been very much shocked and distressed by observing in the newspaper the great pecuniary calamity which has fallen on our excellent friend Moore, and not being able to get any distinct information either as to its extent, or its probable consequences, from anybody here, I have thought it best to relieve my anxiety by applying to you, whose kind concern in him must both have made you acquainted with all the particulars, and willing, I hope, to satisfy the enquiries of one who sincerely shares in that concern. I do not know, however, that I should have troubled you merely to answer an useless enquiry; but in wishing to know whether any steps have been taken to mitigate this disaster, I am desirous of knowing also whether I can be of any use on the occasion. I have, unfortunately, not a great deal of money to spare. But if it should be found practicable to relieve him from this unmerited distress by any contribution, I beg leave to say that I shall think it an honour to be allowed to take share in it to the extent of 300*l.* or 500*l.*, and that I could *advance* more than double the sum named above upon any reasonable security of ultimate repayment, however long postponed.

' I am quite aware of the difficulty of carrying through

any such arrangement with a man of Moore's high feelings and character, and had he been unmarried and without children he might have been less reluctantly left to the guidance and support of that character. But as it is, I think his friends are bound to make an effort to prevent such lasting and extended misery as, from what I have heard, seems now to be impending, and in hands at once so kind and so delicate as yours I flatter myself that this may be found practicable. I need not add, I am sure, that I am most anxious that, whether ultimately acted upon or not, this communication should never be mentioned to Moore himself. If you please, you may tell him that I have been deeply distressed by his misfortunes, and should be most happy to do him any service. But as I have no right to speak to him of money, I do not think he should know that I have spoken of it to you. If my offer is accepted, I shall consider you and not him as the acceptor, and he ought not to be burdened with the knowledge of any other benefactor.

'Is there no chance of seeing you in Scotland again? We have had a sad loss in Playfair [1]—and one quite irreparable to our society here. It is a comfort to think that we cannot possibly have such another. We had a great fright about Scott too, but fortunately he is quite recovered.

'I have a sort of project of running over to Paris again

---

[1] John Playfair, F.R.S., the eminent mathematician and physicist, died on the 19th of July 1819, in his seventy-second year. He was an Edinburgh Reviewer, and Professor of Mathematics, and afterwards of Natural Philosophy, in the University of Edinburgh. His cousin, the Principal of St. Andrews University, was grandfather of the Right Hon. Sir Lyon Playfair, K.C.B., F.R.S., &c.

this autumn. If I had a chance of finding you in the Rue de Rivoli, I should not hesitate a moment. I am not quite so insensible to the advantages of that encounter as I appeared to be,—and yet I have a thousand times since reproached myself for having made too little use of them. Believe me always,

'Your obliged and very faithful servant, &c.,

'F. JEFFREY.'

Moore's case did not admit of help of this kind, and after a time of great anxiety, of which Rogers had his full share as a sympathising friend, Moore went to Paris, where he arrived on the 8th of October, taking the same rooms Rogers and he had occupied two years before. Meanwhile, Rogers had made his usual round of country visits, and was not able on this occasion to offer Crabbe hospitality during his stay in London. Crabbe writes—

Rev. George Crabbe to Samuel Rogers.

(London: August, 1819.)

'My dear Sir,—My purposed journey into Suffolk has been deferred, and is now fixed for Monday the 23rd inst., when I must immediately return and, if I do any business, it must be done without delay. My people will want me at Trowbridge, and if not I shall want them.

'I have thought of your lines, and will claim your pardon when I suggest another alteration. The boy and the butterfly, though a beautiful, is a common image; and harebells have not only the same objection, but they are so seldom seen in cultivated ground that the name brings the idea of a wood or a wild scene. I therefore prefer the boy's pursuit of insects and flowers in general, to these particular instances. My memory would not permit me to retain a single line of yours, and therefore I was obliged to make the trial in my own way, and I think these general terms may be introduced without taking from the interest of the scene, nor was I willing to give up the reference to Raphael and Correggio. Your child is not a rustic, but an educated boy, and there is no impropriety in the introduction of such names; at least, I see none. And now, having confessed so much, I will forgive you if you tell me I had been better employed about my own business.

'I am not certain when you return to St. James's Place, but I hope to hear, and shall not fail to make enquiry.

'Yours most truly,
'GEO. CRABBE.'

At this period of Rogers's life his divorce from politics seems to have been complete. Closely as he had been associated with Dr. Price and Dr. Priestley in his earlier days, with Horne Tooke as well as with Fox and Sheridan in maturer life, and constantly as he was to be seen in the Whig circle at Holland House, he is never found taking any active part in political life. He voted for Sir Samuel Romilly in the Westminster election in 1818 as he had for Horne Tooke in 1796; but he was still the man of letters rather than the politician. His one desire was to be spoken of and recognised as 'Rogers the poet,' and that desire was fully satisfied. In this dissociation from public affairs he was not alone. How small a part the political history of the time plays in the lives of

Wordsworth, of Campbell, of Crabbe, and of Byron; and in Moore's Diary there is no mention even of the death of George III. and the accession of George IV. They were all intent upon literature, and politics were of small concern to them. The publication of a new poem was an event in their lives, the trial of a Queen, a Manchester massacre, even a new settlement of Europe, were events in the lives of other people. So much larger are things in which we have a share, or of which we are a part, than those which we only look at from a distance. The times were troublesome enough in the year when the Six Acts of an English coercion policy were passed, or when a Bill of Pains and Penalties against the Queen was before the House of Commons. The old King died in January, 1820; and in June, 1820, Grattan was taken away. The summer was a season of extreme heat and drought. Horses dropped dead in the roads, says Miss Martineau, and labourers in the fields; yet, along the line of the mails, crowds stood waiting in the burning sunshine for news of the Queen's trial, and horsemen galloped over hedge and ditch to bear the tidings. 'In London,' she continues, 'the parks and the West-end streets were crowded every evening, and through the bright nights of July neighbours were visiting one another's houses to lend newspapers or compare rumours.' Rogers was, in this matter, on the popular side. But the public quarrel did not disturb his private friendships. Families were divided, coteries were broken up, but in Rogers's circle another interest set these disputes aside. In the beautiful house overlooking the Green Park, small parties of men and women were always gathering to meet great authors or artists, to talk of the last new book, to criticise a poem of Byron's, or Wordsworth's, or Southey's, or Campbell's, or Crabbe's, to roam at will over all literature, sucking the sweets, as bees from flowers, and to enjoy the good stories of one, the epigrams of another, and the cynical wit of a third. It is curious to reflect that in the same house, and under the same host, this intercourse went on for nearly two generations, in spite of wars, and revolutions, and reforms, and the changes made by death. Men came and went, but the stream of happy, brilliant talk flowed on, and the troubles and triumphs of the outer world only cast their shadows or their sunshine on its waves.

CHAPTER IX.

1820-1821.

Rogers's House—His Love of Harmony—His Literary Position—Campbell and Schlegel—Parr and Mackintosh reconciled—Letters from Walter Scott—Lady Holland and Napoleon—Rogers and Moore in Paris—Rogers and his Sister and Niece in Switzerland—With Kemble and Mrs. Siddons at Lausanne—Rogers's Letters from Italy—His Meeting with Byron—Rogers's Letters from Rome—With Byron at Pisa—Byron, Shelley, and Rogers—Medwin's Misrepresentations—Rogers on Byron.

ROGERS had already conceived the idea of his 'Italy.' He had written some of it in the country itself during his visit in 1814-15. During that visit, also, he had sent home some of the works of art which decorated his house. I have not given any account of his various purchases of pictures and other beautiful objects, and it is enough to say that he made each one the subject of careful study and research. In his Commonplace Book are accounts of many of these choice things, but to quote them would be tedious. The two points which he seems to have kept in mind were, first, the value and beauty of objects in themselves, and, secondly, their value and beauty in relation to each other. Some rooms impress the visitor with a sense of general harmony and repose, although nothing in them is costly or rich or rare; others give a feeling of unquiet, of distraction, of ostentation, perhaps, though nearly everything they contain is beautiful in itself. The artistic faculty includes that of co-ordination, and it is only when the perfect taste which has selected all the parts has been able to exercise the same severe supervision over the whole, that the best result is obtained. This co-ordination in Rogers's house was perfect. The general impression was one of complete harmony, and that impression was confirmed by the effect of every detail. As he sat at his writing-table, he looked up at an exquisite picture by an old master;[1] and though Sydney Smith once jocosely said

---

[1] An Article in *The Quarterly Review* for October, 1888, contains the following description of Rogers's Works of Art :—' Mr. Rogers had joined some of the leading noblemen in England in the purchase of the celebrated Orleans Gallery, which reached our shores in 1800, and which more than any other importation has contributed to develop the English taste for the old masters. It had been collected by a not particularly respectable trio—partly by the bad and mad Christina, Queen of Sweden, partly by the notorious Regent Orleans, and partly by Philippe Egalité. No pictures could have told the world more of what was curious, interesting, and scandalous, from their earliest to their latest times. In the atmosphere of St. James's Place they may safely be said to have been worshipped with a purer incense than they ever received before. We may be pardoned for recalling a few of them. Foremost was a Raphael, "Madonna and Child," one of the master's sweetest compositions, the child standing with one foot on his mother's hand. It had been reduced by ruthless rubbings to a mere shadow, but the beauty was ineffaceable: hanging—how well remembered—in the best light on the left-hand wall in the drawing-room. Then two glorious Titians, one of them, "Christ appearing to the Magdalene." The impetuosity with which she has thrown herself on her knees is shown by the fluttering drapery of her sleeve, which is still buoyed up by the air: thus with a true painter's art telling the action of the previous moment. Nor was it the rank of the painters, more than the perfect taste, which had limited the collection to the most trustworthy or most characteristic specimen of each; a genuine work, for example, the little "St. George" by Giorgione, the rarest of all masters; the most *simpatico* ecimen by Bassano, "The Good Samaritan;" a curious cross, unique

that his shaded dinner table, with no blazing chandeliers, and, I may add, no tall plants or huge épergnes to prevent the guests from seeing each other, was all light above, and below all darkness and gnashing of teeth, the ample light there was had shone first on the pictures round the walls. Mrs. Norton said of him after he was dead, 'His god was harmony,' by which she probably only meant to say a sharp thing of one who had said some sharp things to her and done many kind things for her. But such meaning as the phrase contains is only the recognition of a taste which had the power of co-ordination, and could subdue all things to itself. It is the same in his poetry as it was in his home, in his manners as it was in his style of prose composition. 'Of nothing too much' was its motto. There was this artistic finish even in his sneers.

The composition of the first part of 'Italy' was taken up as soon as 'Human Life' was published, and the poem in its two parts may well be considered as the chief work of his ripest years. Rogers was now fifty-seven, and had long held an undisputed position in

in art, between two magnificent masters, as different as Padua is from Antwerp, being a subject from one of Mantegna's "Triumphs" (in Hampton Court Palace) Rubenized by the great Flemish master. This nicety of specimen extended even to the "Strawberry Girl," by our own Sir Joshua. Then there were portfolios of drawings by the old masters, early miniatures, etchings by Marc Antonio, Greek vases, antique gold ornaments, a chimney-piece by Flaxman, a cabinet decorated by Stothard, another carved by Chantrey, an antique female hand as a letter weight on the table, an antique female foot as a weight to the drawing-room door; and lastly, Milton's receipt to the publisher for the five pounds he received for his "Paradise Lost," framed and glazed, and hanging on the door in the next room. Truly was Mr. Rogers known *a sociis*, even in this mute company.'—*The Quarterly Review*, No. 334, pp. 508, 509.

literature and in society. He had around him at this period of his ripe middle age, a group of friends, many of whom have immortalised themselves in literature, many in statesmanship and in arms, and some in science. All the poets of the age were to be met at his house; all its literary society regarded that house as its centre. He was just beginning to be one of the celebrities whom every distinguished visitor to England wished to see. In nearly all the great country houses he was a welcome guest, and an invitation from him was regarded as a kind of social distinction.

Campbell was just started on his German visit, and a letter to Rogers illustrates the relations between the authors of 'The Pleasures of Memory' and 'The Pleasures of Hope.'

Thomas Campbell to Samuel Rogers.

'Address to me—
Poste Restante, Bonn: 10th June, 1820.

' My dear Rogers,—I dare say you thought me a sad fellow for leaving England without seeing you, but I assure you it was from misfortune and not neglect. On the morning of the day which I meant to have devoted to you, I was asked by a friend if I had got a passport. The thought of such a thing being necessary had never occurred to my recollection, but my friend had been just conversing with a Prussian baron, who had mentioned that in the present state of things it was indispensable. I find that he was right. But the time which I had allotted to a conversation with you was spent, in the first place, in a vain application to the Foreign Office, and in the next place, in hunting out the Dutch ambassador, who was more civil to me than the clerks at our own State office.

'I reached Rotterdam after a passage of two days, and being struck with a desire of seeing more of Holland, went out of my direct route as far as Amsterdam and Haarlem. The organ at Haarlem was a reward for a longer journey. We heard it for an hour played by a first-rate performer, and were enchanted. It imitates every sound, from that of thunder and the roar of artillery, to the sweetest tones of the human voice, and makes them harmonise with an effect altogether indescribable. We proceeded thence by Utrecht and Cologne to this place, where I had the happiness to find Schlegel.[1] The great little man is very gracious. His professorship, to be sure, has made him more of a lecturer in conversation than ever, and he is so vain of his English that he will not listen to mine. He speaks many words not quite so well as a cockatoo, but he accounts to me for his fluency and correctness of pronunciation by describing the early pains which he took with our language. Nevertheless, my Schlegel is a good-hearted and enlightened soul, and I am happy to listen to him. The keeper of the library of the University has been so kind as to give me the freest access to it. So I shall sit down to revise my German here for a month or two. The weather here is wretched, so that I can only see the shape of the country without its

[1] August Wilhelm von Schlegel, then Professor of History in the University of Bonn.

beauty. I shall be delighted if you can spare a moment to write to me, and remain,

'Dear Rogers, your affectionate friend,
'T. CAMPBELL.'

It was at this time that Rogers made the attempt, which was only partially successful, to effect a reconciliation between Dr. Parr and Sir James Mackintosh. Parr regarded Mackintosh as a trimmer, and I have already given an account of an ill-mannered rejoinder Parr made to an observation Mackintosh had made about O'Quigley, who was executed as a traitor in 1798.[1] The special cause of their quarrel need not be described here. Parr used to say that Mackintosh had come up from Scotland with a metaphysical head, a cold heart, and open hands. In response to an appeal by Rogers, however, he agreed to meet Mackintosh,—for 'they had been friends in youth,'—at Rogers's dinner table, where, as Mackintosh's biographer tells us, Parr in the most express terms retracted the injurious things he had said of Mackintosh on imperfect information. The following letters passed on the subject.

Dr. Parr to Samuel Rogers.

'Dear Sir,—Permit me to propose Thursday, the third of August, for my having the honour to wait upon you, and this I am the more anxious to do, because in all probability I shall never visit the capital again. I know, from your connections and your taste, that you will bring

[1] *The Early Life of Samuel Rogers*, p. 381.

together a proper party. But you will excuse me for mentioning by name Mr. Whishaw and Richard Sharp. I want to shake hands with Jemmy Mackintosh once before I die. Surely Lord Holland will join our party.

'I am, very truly and respectfully, dear Sir, yours,
'S. PARR.
'July 21 (1820).'

Samuel Rogers to Sir James Mackintosh.

'Dear Mackintosh,—Dr. Parr dines with me on Thursday, 3rd of August, and he wishes to meet some of his old friends under my roof, as it may be for the last time. He has named Whishaw, and Sharp, and Lord Holland, and he says,

'"I want to shake hands with Mackintosh once before I die."

'May I ask you to be of the party? That you can forgive I know full well. That you will forgive in this instance, much as you have to forgive, I hope fervently. Some of the pleasantest moments of my life have been spent in the humble office I am now venturing to take upon myself, and I am sure you will not take it amiss if I wish on this occasion to add to the number.

'Yours very truly,
'S. R.'

Sir James Mackintosh to Samuel Rogers.

'Mardocks: 24th July, 1820.

'Dear Rogers,—I have not the smallest feeling of resentment towards Dr. Parr, and in the present circumstances I wish to accede to his desire if I can do so with propriety. On that question there can be no better opinion than yours, and I beg you to give it frankly.

'My only reason for declining his company was an apprehension that my renewal of intercourse with him, if unaccompanied by some explanation, might seem to be an acquiescence in imputations against me which I had reason to believe were countenanced by him during my absence in India. On my return to England, I declared my readiness to forget what had passed, if he would intimate his belief that I was incapable of improper conduct. Do you think that the time and nature of his present request relieve me from the necessity of again proposing the same condition? If you do, I will indulge my inclination, which strongly leads me to accede to his desire. You, I know, will not advise me to gratify my feelings at any risk of my good name.

'If you have any doubt on the subject, I can have no objection to your asking the opinion of Sharp or Whishaw, or Lord Holland.

'I am, dear Rogers, yours very faithfully,
'J. MACKINTOSH.'

The reconciliation was effected, but the old intimacy was not restored. Dr. Parr died on the 6th of March, 1825.

Rogers had had much ill-health this year. He was very far from well when Walter Scott, made a baronet in April, was in town in the London season. This accounts for a reference in the following letter.

Sir Walter Scott to Samuel Rogers.

'My dear Rogers,—The son of an old friend, a man of much taste and science, Dr. James Russell of Edinburgh, is going to your metropolis on scientific and medical pursuits, and his father asks me for a line of introduction to some of my friends in the literary world. Alas! I have very few left. Our dear George Ellis is gone, and so are many others with whom I used to claim some interest. My tediousness must be the more liberally bestowed on those who remain, and as few have a greater share of my regard than yourself, you must look for a good portion of it. Luckily it never, or very seldom, breaks out into correspondence, but, like the philosophical parrot, pays it off by thinking.

'Why will you never come down and see us? I have had Rose here for several weeks, and he, a greater invalid than you, finds himself comfortable in Conundrum Castle, for so this romance of a house should be called. As you have made the most classical museum I can conceive, I have been attempting a Gothic—no, not a Gothic by any means, but an old-fashioned Scotch museum, full of

'Rusty iron coats and jingling jackets,

rare commodities for a country smith to make hobnails of.

'Rose has been much indisposed, nevertheless killed a salmon of eighteen pounds weight after an hour and a half close struggle; this, as Robinson Crusoe says when he drinks his glass of rum, "to his exceeding refreshment."

'We have had horrid wet weather, and as rough as

ever blew out of our angry heavens, but come next year and we will make it better for you. At any rate, the wind that makes my turrets topple on the warders' heads will have rough work to do, for mine are not the sort of battlements a man outlives, as befell Horace Walpole— our fine stone gives us leave to build with a view to posterity.

'I do not much know the *young bairn*, but have seen him at his father's scientific parties; a clever lad, I think. If you can, without inconvenience to yourself, shew him any notice, his respectable family here will be much gratified as well as, dear Rogers,

'Your truly faithful and affectionate,

'WALTER SCOTT.

'Abbotsford: 26 October (1820).'

During the autumn Wordsworth was abroad, and returned, full of his tour, in the first week of December, when he puts on record his having met Rogers on his way through London.

Scott writes again—

Sir Walter Scott to Samuel Rogers.

'My dear Rogers,—You recollect the apology of the sapient parrot, who, when he was upbraided with not talking, replied, 'I think not the less'; now, if I seldom write to my friends I pay it off, like pretty Poll, by thinking much of them, and of all their kindness. I break my silence just now to remind you that you gave us some hope you would visit Scotland this season, and Abbotsford in particular. We have had such an ungenial spring that we will have some right to look on ourselves as ill-used gentlemen if we have not a few pleasant days in July and August, and I wish you to come down and enjoy them with us. Bring Sharp with you if possible, and if you care not to encounter the fatigue of a long land journey, the steamboat will bring you to Leith in sixty hours. Pray do think of this in the course of the season.

'If you do not think it too great a bore to go to the theatre—and God knows as now managed it is no small one—I want you, and any of our friends who love the art, to see an actor from Scotland, Mackay by name, who plays one single part (the Bailie in "Rob Roy") with unrivalled excellence. The truth is I never saw anything so much like truth upon the stage. I doubt the English will not understand what a very excellent representation it is of the Scottish peculiarities, because it wants the breadth of caricature usually expected in national portraits. I therefore wish you, and one or two of my friends, to see him as something very extraordinary. He is only to play for one night. He is otherwise a respectable comedian, though not often first class, except in that particular character, and, I am told, is a deserving sort of person.

'Allan is returned here, delighted with the reception his picture met with in London. He tells me he could have sold it repeatedly. Yesterday I hunted out for him an old gipsy woman whose figure and features I was much struck with as I passed her on the road. As I found the artist studying a sketch of the recovery of a child which had been stolen by gipsies, my old woman was quite a windfall, but as she was unconscious of her own charms it was no easy matter to trace her out. I succeeded, however, by some police interest.

'I am here on a visit of two days to Lord Chief Commissioner (once your William Adam), in company with our Lord Chief Baron (once your Sir Samuel Shepherd), which makes very good society. Always, my dear Rogers,

'Most truly yours,
'WALTER SCOTT.

'Blair Adam: 10 June (1821).

'Sophia bids me say she longs to repay you some well-remembered breakfast. She is now quite stout and busy with her little cottage, being precisely that where

'Lucy at the door shall sing
In russet gown and apron blue.'

'I have a black-eyed brunette besides—a sunburnt Scotch lass that longs to make your acquaintance. So pray look northward and bring Sharp if possible.'

Lord Holland to Samuel Rogers.

'July, 1821.

'Dear Rogers,—I hear with great pain that you have been seriously ill. I hope that it is one of those many reports invented, or at least augmented, by distance, but I cannot but be uneasy till we hear from you, especially as your neither coming here nor writing seems to confirm the rumour. The Court here affect to speak

---

[1] From Rogers's poem, 'A Wish,' beginning 'Mine be a cot beside the hill.' The lines are—
'And Lucy at her wheel shall sing
In russet gown and apron blue.'

of the great man they dreaded and persecuted, with tenderness and even admiration—L[ouis] XVIII. is no Cæsar, but—

'Cæsar would weep, the crocodile would weep,
To see his rival of the universe
Lie still and peaceful there.

'I need not tell you how gratified (even in her grief at the loss, or rather death of such a man) Lady H. was at his recollection of her.

'"L'Empereur Napoléon à Lady Holland : témoignage de satisfaction et d'estime," were the words, and remarkably well chosen. Write me word how you are.

'Excuse hurry, which you know the idleness of Paris always produces.

'My Lady's love.   'Yours,
                'VASSALL HOLLAND.'

In August Rogers was in Paris on his grand tour, and Moore writes—

'1821.

'August 1st.—Found Rogers was arrived. Drove about a little with Mrs. S., then called upon Rogers at four; his sister and niece with him; received me most cordially.

'August 2nd.—Called upon Rogers; Luttrell with him. Luttrell said that he has all his life had a love for domestic comforts though passing his time in such a different manner, "Like that King of Bohemia who had so unluckily a taste for navigation, though condemned to live in an inland town." Walked about the Tuileries Gardens for an hour and a half with Rogers : sarcastic and amusing as usual.

'August 3rd.—Rogers having proposed to come out to the *pavilion* to-day with his sister, I bustled away early with a pigeon pie and some other provisions for dinner. The Rogerses arrived before two o'clock, and went with me to Meudon and the Sèvres manufactory. Our dinner very lively and agreeable; Villamil and Lord John of the party. Rogers quite distressed at hearing from me that Lord Byron had just finished a tragedy on the story of Foscari.

'*August* 10*th.* — Breakfasted with Rogers. Went afterwards to the Louvre with him. Rogers spoke depreciatingly of Chantrey and Canova. Said Gerard's "Henry IVth" was "like a tin shop," which is true; a hard glitter about it. Explained to me what is called breadth of light by Correggio's picture of the "Nymph and Satyr."

'*August* 12*th.*—In talking to Rogers about my living in Paris, I said, "One would not enjoy even Paradise if one was obliged to live in it." "No," says he; "I dare say when Adam and Eve were turned out they were very happy."

'*August* 13*th.*—A dinner given by Lord John, at Roberts's, to the Rogerses, Luttrell, and me; gayer day than Saturday. Rogers's story of his having called a lady *une femme galante et généreuse* at Père la Chaise to-day; her anger and the laughter of her companion, who seemed as if she said, "It's all out; even strangers know it." Went to the Variétés in the evening. Rogers joined us, after a visit to Miss H. M. Williams, and gave us an amusing account of it; the set of French Blues assembled to hear a reading of the "Mémoires de Nelson," which R. was obliged to endure also; the dialogue with Miss W. on the stairs, &c., &c.

'*August* 15*th*.—Breakfasted with R.; read me his story of Foscari, which is told very strikingly. Joined the Rogerses at Tivoli. Rogers, speaking as we walked home of the sort of conscription of persons of all kinds that is put in force for the dinner of the Hollands, said, "There are two parties before whom everybody must appear—them and the police." Took leave of them: he starts for Switzerland to-morrow.'

Rogers went on to Switzerland with his sister Sarah and their niece Martha Rogers, where they stayed through September, paying a visit to his old friend J. P. Kemble at Lausanne. Mrs. Siddons and her daughter were there, and there he parted with his companions and went on alone to spend the winter in Italy. His sister and niece returned with Mrs. Siddons and her daughter by way of Paris to London, where she superintended the publication of the first part of 'Italy.' In a series of letters Rogers tells a good deal of the story of this interesting visit which had great results on his future.

Samuel Rogers to Sarah Rogers.

'Milan: 6 October, 1821.

'My dear Sarah,—When I left you, I travelled on into the night—what could I do better? but to my great joy it cleared up soon, and I flattered myself you would have a better drive than you thought of. The next day too, was fine, though the morning was wet, so I hope you

did pretty well—and found a letter to your mind from
Bellesite. You must now be well on your road to Paris,
and I hope your young lady—not a child by the way—
has proved useful, if not entertaining. As for me, I slept
the first night at Brieg, and the second at Domo; the
Simplon lost none of its credit with me, but I am destined never to get to Domo d'Ossola in daylight, for
something wrong in the carriage kept me at the Simplon
an hour, and as I had tired horses from Brieg, I
was later than we were before. The third day I breakfasted at Baveno—saw the islands in glorious weather,
and slept at Arona in the very room you slept in and we
passed the day in together. The next day I was waked
by a great bustle, and found a full market, and ten or
twelve large boats drawn up under the window. It was
a most amusing scene, the day beautiful, and I wished
much to stay in such a room, in such a place, but Como
was to be seen, the weather might change, so I went off
with great regret, and slept at Como after seeing an
opera and a dance, and next morning at six set off, embarking on the lake. In the night my windows had
given many signs of a great wind, but the morning was
bright as the night had been starry, and I was told it
was occasioned by snow falling in the mountains, and
was a sure sign of fair weather—a sign fulfilled; for
three finer days I never had than on the lake—I need
not say how I wished for you. It is a noble lake—but a
little too solemn for me—though the shores are peopled
with Milanese villas and palaces like Richmond Hill.
When you run under the shore the entertainment is endless. When you look up, or down, or across the lake you

are awed and saddened. It is a Swiss lake with an Italian margin. The view from our window at Arona is more joyous, more truly Italian than anything at Como —but *that* Sharp never saw. His station at Bellaggio is a very noble one—I call it his, though it is in all the books. I was rewarded for leaving Arona. The weather changed the instant I left Como—and to-day I met Agar Ellis, the only acquaintance I have seen, in a heavy rain on his way thither from Milan, where he had been loving the sunshine. He has a dismal prospect. I arrived here half an hour ago. All the inns are full, but I have got a tolerable room in the Imperiale, and mean to stay three or four days, and then go to Venice. The Beaumonts—Sir G., Lady, and Mr. Beaumont—passed through Baveno for Rome, as they described themselves in the book there, on the 21st Sept. So they could not have gone at all into Switzerland as we were told. You were afraid I should lose the vintage here, but it has not yet begun anywhere where I have passed; the autumn has been so cold and wet. Sharp's burnings, it seems, have done very little for it. But the vineyards are very beautiful, and the trellises particularly; the black grapes hanging, as we saw them, in clusters.

'Along the Lago Maggiore trellises are run out into the lake, ten or twelve yards over the water, and sometimes for a quarter of a mile together—a thing I don't remember. I must say I like the people, and admire the country and the women more than ever, and I think I might have persuaded you to have ventured as far as Milan but for Mrs. Siddons. At Baveno I was accosted by one of our Swiss drivers, who was conducting an English family from Neuchatel to Milan, and would have been delighted to have had you back again. Farewell, my dear Sarah. I shall write home from Venice and shall then trouble you with some more lines for the press. I like your idea of troubling Miss Mallet better and better the more I think of it, and if you still approve of it, pray do so, and beg her, if she does not object to it, to apply to Mr. Rees confidentially, not letting him or anybody else into the secret; that is, engaging him not to reveal the circumstance of her applying to him about it, at the same time concealing my name from him—proposing to print 500 and no more; the booksellers to share the profits with the author—contract not to extend beyond that edition; the property then to revert to the author. If you have changed your mind about Miss Mallet, proceed as before. If they object to those terms, then let them publish it entirely for the author and at his risk. I hope you have found Henry at Paris. Maltby must be gone. Pray give my love to Patty, our fellow-traveller, and everybody when you write home. I have been afraid to touch the music. I thought it would give me more sadness than pleasure. If you write at Paris on or before the 15th, pray write to Venice. If afterwards, and before the 21st, to Bologna. After that to Florence.

'I write a day after the limit you gave me, but hope it will not be too late. The figs are very good, but the peaches are Michaelmas ones, and I have taken an indifference to grapes. Lord Clare and Mr. Sneyd are at Venice. I hope you will fall in with the King, if he does not annoy you. He cannot take your horses. I have not yet taken a Courier and have gone on tolerably, murdering more Italian words than I did the whole of our journey. 5 *o'clock*.—I am just returned from a walk in the Cathedral—the only thing to be done this rainy day.. Your inkstand has been of great use to me, as will be your maps. I am going to the Opera to-night—a new one, so I fear good for little. Patty, I fear, I shall not see for ages, as she must [have] left you before I return. They will be very anxious to have her home again to hear all about it. I shall tell Sir G. B. when I see him how desirous you were to catch him on his way. I hope you will find Henry. I think it will do you all good. My love to him and the party now at Brighton, as I conjecture. I shall not pester you often with such long letters—though I mean to write often.'

Samuel Rogers to Sarah Rogers.

'Venice: 15 October, 1821.

' My dear Sarah,—I wrote you a long letter to Paris, which, I hope, you received. It was from Milan, where I arrived on the 6th, and stayed till the 10th, during excessive rain. There I fell in with three we saw at Paris—Ellis, Sneyd, and Lord Clare. I dined with them at their hotel, and they with me at mine. There, too, I hired a Courier—a man young and intelligent, and, I think, gentle, though a Roman. He has a high character from Scarlett's brother, whose service he lived in eleven months. He is now laid up with a lame knee, but is getting better. I left Milan and found beautiful weather all the way to this place, sleeping in our old rooms at Desenzano; but all the inns are so brushed up and painted

you would not know them. I admire Italy more than
ever, and wonder how anybody should talk of anything
else. I came here yesterday and found the Beaumonts.
I have passed all to-day with them and shall to-morrow,
as they go the next. I have sent to the post, and, alas,
there was no letter any more than at Milan, but will
hope all is well. I shall stay here, I think, five or six
days, and then proceed to Florence, where I hope I shall
find a letter. I have been very unlucky; as to the
vintage, it had not begun on the lake, and was over all
the way to Venice. I have very comfortable lodgings in
the Gran Britannia on the Great Canal, and the boatmen
are at this moment making a great noise under my
window. The Beaumonts have delightful ones on the
sea opposite St. Giorgio's Church. They were very sorry
to miss you. He has some sketches, but they are none
of them such as I like, memorandums like yours. He
has a broken shin, but contrives to float about in his
gondola; I believe we are the only English here. You
will here have the alterations and additions I threatened
you with in my last; I have written over each the title
or number they refer to, and hope you will find the places
out easily. Pray substitute the new passages *instead of
the old*. The chapter I have given no title to I have
called *Italy*, and have added to it eleven new lines. The
notes you will insert in their places at the end. In my
last I said I liked much the idea of Miss Mallet, if she
would be good enough to undertake it, and if you still
approve of it; but not unless you do. I hope you are
now at Paris with Henry, but shall write home, and the
letter will keep very well till you get it. I am very well,

and have nothing the matter with me but gnats. Here are beccaficos innumerable, but I have met with none so good as a lark. I came here on Sunday afternoon, and went to church to hear the young ladies play on the fiddle and blow flutes and trumpets. It lasted half an hour, and was very well. You see them very indistinctly. Hoppner, the Consul, is in Switzerland with his wife's relations. Pray, when you go to St. James's Place, search in the drawer of the table that stands in the middle of my bed-room, and I think you will find a thin blue copy-book in a blue cover, as blue as the inside of a band-box. It contains "The Brides of Venice." If you find it, print it in its place. If not, it must be left out altogether, as I have forgot it, and have in vain tried to recall it. Among the chapters is one entitled "A Retrospect." Pray entitle it "The Alps" instead. I have ventured to send some lines on Mont Blanc for a *note*. If you don't think them tolerable, don't let them be printed. Which do you like best, the sixth line, those or this—

'Only less bright, less glorious than himself.

'My love to all. Ever yours,

'S. R.

'Pray find fault through the whole work.

'I.

'the mirror of all beauty.

[*Note.*—There is no describing in words, but the following lines were written on the spot, and may serve, perhaps, to recall to some of my readers what they have seen in this enchanting country—

I love to watch in silence till the sun
Sets; and Mont Blanc, arrayed in crimson and gold,

Flings his broad shadow half across the Lake ;
That shadow, though it comes through pathless tracts
Of Ether, and o'er Alp and desert drear,
Only less glorious than Mont Blanc himself.
But while we gaze, 'tis gone ! And now he shines
Like burnished silver ; all below, the Night's—

Such moments are most precious, yet there are
Others, that follow them, to me still more so ;
When once again he changes, once again
Clothing himself in grandeur all his own ;
When, like a ghost, shadowless, colourless,
He melts away into the Heaven of Heavens ;
Himself alone revealed, all lesser things
As though they were not !]

' II.

' But the Bise blew cold ;
And, bidden to a spare but cheerful meal,
I sate among the holy brotherhood
At their long board. The fare, indeed, was such
As is prescribed on days of abstinence,
But might have pleased a nicer taste than mine,
And through the floor came up ; an ancient matron,
Serving unseen below ; while from the roof
(The roof, the floor, the walls of native fir)
A lamp hung flickering, such as loves to fling
Its partial light on Apostolic heads,
And sheds a grace on all. Theirs Time as yet
Had changed not. Some were almost in the prime ;
Nor was a brow o'ercast. Seen as I saw them,
Ranged round their hearthstone in a leisure hour,
They were a simple and a merry race,
Mingling small games of chance with social converse,
And gathering news of all who came that way,
As of some other world.

'*Italy.*

(This to be the title to this chapter.)

'Am I in Italy? Is this the Mincius? &c.

down to "and self-congratulation." Then what follows is to be in a new paragraph.

> 'O Italy! how beautiful thou art!
> Yet I could weep—for thou art lying, alas,
> Low in the dust; and they who come, admire thee
> As we admire the beautiful in death.
> Thine was a dangerous gift, the gift of Beauty;
> Would thou hadst less, or wert as once thou wast,
> Inspiring awe in those who now enslave thee!
> —But why despair? Twice hast thou lived already;
> Twice shone among the nations of the world,
> As the sun shines among the lesser lights
> Of heaven; and shalt again. . . .'

From Venice Rogers wrote to Lord Byron, whom he had not seen for five years and a half, proposing to visit him. Byron answered in a letter from Ravenna, which Moore publishes, saying that he had taken a house in Pisa for the winter, to which all his 'chattels, furniture, horses, carriages, and live stock' were already removed, and whither he was preparing to follow. 'If you will go on with me to Pisa,' said Byron, 'I can lodge you for as long as you like (they write that the house, the Palazzo Lomfranchi, is spacious—it is on the Arno), and I have four carriages and as many saddle-horses (such as they are in these parts), with all other conveniences, at your command, as also their owner. If you could do this, we may, at least, cross the Apennines together, or, if you are going by another road, we shall meet at Bologna,

I hope.' This proposal was acted on. They met at Bologna, travelled over the Apennines together, and at Florence visited the gallery in company. There the English crowd annoyed Byron. 'I told Rogers,' he writes, ' that I felt like being in the watch-house! I left him to make his obeisances to some of his acquaintances, and strolled on alone, the only four minutes I could snatch for any feeling for the works around me. I do not mean to apply this to a *tête-à-tête* scrutiny with Rogers, who has an excellent taste and deep feeling for the arts (indeed, much more of both than I can possess, for of the former I have not much), but to the crowd of jostling starers and travelling talkers around me.'

Byron remained but one day in Florence; Rogers refused to go on then to visit him at Pisa, having set his face to go to Rome. From Florence, where he stayed a week, and afterwards from Rome, he wrote the two following letters.

Samuel Rogers to Sarah Rogers.

'Florence: Sunday, 11 November, 1821.

' My dear Sarah,—I wrote you a long letter from Milan, and a large budget of verse and prose from Venice. At Milan I slept four nights, at Venice seven, and passed much of my time with Sir G. Beaumont at Venice, overtaking him for a day at Bologna and for an hour only here. At Bologna I waited a day for Lord Byron and crossed the Apennines with him. Our party consisted of a dog, a cat, a hawk, an old gondolier from Venice, and other sundries. His " Foscari " is already printed, and will, I fear, get the start of us. I hope you passed some time, and very agreeably at Paris. Perhaps you are not returned home yet, for I am quite in the dark, having heard nothing since we parted at the inn door that dismal morning. I begin now to be a little fidgety, but console myself with thinking all is well. Hoppner, I find, was sorry to miss me at Venice, as I was to miss him— I wished much to see the boy who lay stretched on the hearth at N. G. There is no end to the English on their road to Rome. I am at the little inn *vis-à-vis* Sneyder's—now belonging to him—for that leviathan swallows up everything, and is said to be worth half a million. I have three windows at top, and the sun is upon me before ten o'clock. I am always up at seven, and out by eight, for the weather, though very cold, is sunny. Snow is on all the hills—but the sunsets are beautiful, the hills over the Cascine of a bright rose colour. I have been here just a fortnight—and had only one rainy day. Just now, however, I have a wretched cold, having committed a great folly in going with Miss Fanshawe in an open carriage to see Galileo's house. From my windows I look over to Sneyder's, as you know —and every morning see English carriages with mules or post-horses at the door for Rome. Lord Byron is gone to live at Pisa. He spent only one day here. I wish you had seen him set off, every window of the inn was open to see him. My dinner comes over the bridge to me, and is cold enough. To-day I mean to omit it.

'The Beaumonts were very impatient to get to Rome. Sir G. to his old haunts at Tivoli and Albano. Lady Westmoreland is at Civita Vecchia just now. I expect a sad change in my quarters at Rome. Our old house,

Casa Joubert, at least Lord Holland's part of it, is now an hotel. Several have offered to hire for me, and Sneyd writes me word (I gave him a sort of commission) that he has secured for me one in Via Babuino between Piazza d'Espagna and del Popolo, as you know—a sad fall from ours—and at twenty louis a month! However, he has done better than Dr. Holland, for I see by the drawing he sends me there are two fire-places. Here is nobody I know but the Dysons and Miss Fanshawe. The Ponsonbys and Bessboroughs are just arrived, but I have seen only Lord B. The boy we saw at Mornay died at Parma; "I suppose you have heard of the accident we have had?" Lord Bessborough said to me on the bridge yesterday—I could not conceive he alluded to it. Lady Ellenborough, five daughters and a son, passed through to Rome yesterday. It was but last May she returned to England. The ortolan season is over, and no orange blossoms, no violets are about in the streets, only a pink carnation and china roses. The figs are gone. I have twenty in a basket here on the table—one of the old baskets—but they are tasteless and frost-bitten, and the grapes begin to shrivel.

'Florence is to me as beautiful as ever; the Tribune and the Pitti as glorious; but somehow or other I should not be sorry to find myself home again among you, and am sorry the Easter falls twelve days later than it did when we were here. How my winter will turn out I don't know; but hitherto I have lived almost entirely to myself. Yesterday I engaged our old laquais de place (till then I had none); he accosted me on the bridge (my walk) and asked after you, so I took him directly, though to-day I fear I have not much for him to do. The instant I can I shall set out, I hope in three or four days, so henceforth pray write always to me at the Poste Restante at Rome. I received a visit from our old friend the poet, with his book. Lord Byron amused himself with writing a sonnet for him, in which he makes him describe himself as a bore; whether he will shew it about I don't know. You will here receive three more things. On second thoughts I think something more is wanting (considering the material) to give it any importance, so pray add them at the end, printing the notes in their place among the rest—all together numerically—and not broken by the heads of this chapter or that. The printer to use a figure or a letter of reference as he pleases. The notes to be *en masse* at the end, lumped together. I have been sadly perplexed by information, true and false. Till my second visit to Padua I could not learn the truth about Ezzelino's tower. You will here receive the lines about it as they are to stand. The opening of "Venice," too, must be changed, or I should be found out. You will here receive a new one to as far as "by many a dome," omitting all before. I have also been obliged to alter about Masaccio and the sons of Cosmo, as you will see, having found out the portraits with much trouble in another house, and finding no tombstone of Masaccio in the chapel, though he lies thereabouts. You must be heartily sick of your commission by this time. Pray don't send me these three new ones unless you are much perplexed about them indeed, which I hope you will not [be], or think the new lines so bad as to want alteration. When I return the sheets of the others they will help you much with these, and sending them would, I fear, cause a great delay of two months at least.

'Only think—poor Lady Bessborough died this morning at the "Pelican"—Sneyders could not take her in—Lord B. mentioned her being ill and unable to see me yesterday, but he looked very cheerful and I thought nothing of it. She arrived only on Friday, travelling all night, ill, from Bologna ('twas from an inflammation in the bowels) and to-day is Sunday. After she was given over, she wrote three letters to her three children in England and took the Sacrament with great composure.

'I think the Tuscans the least handsome people I have seen. They walk every Sunday afternoon under my window, as thick as they used to do in the Green Park—and I can hardly meet with anything pretty. The Boboli Gardens I lounge in constantly when they are open—Thursdays and Sundays. The moonlight nights here are divine. From my window at this moment the river, the bridges, and the houses are as bright as day—even the heights and villas over the town are visible. At Bologna I saw a lizard in the sun, such as we never saw—seven or eight inches long and very like the diamond beetle! The mosquito is still about; but he does not bite me to signify. Nobody I know has been to Vallombrosa. The view from your window which you took is just as it was, the garden on this side next the bridge just as you left it. What memories some people have! When I went to the banker's yesterday he called me by my name. I hope you have found "The Brides of Venice." If not, I think I must have locked it up in the secrétaire in the dressing-room, the key (a gold one, a patent) is, I believe, lying in one of the drawers, hid. I dare say Jemima could find it. Pray tell her to tell Andrews to hang the Guercino and the Tintoret as he has hung the Charles V. and the Titian, opposite to them on irons that come out. I take it for granted that the pictures are come back from the Institution in Pall Mall. The Titian is, I believe, gone to the Royal Academy; at least, they wrote to borrow it, but it was to return in January. I hope you met Maltby at Paris. I hope, what is more to the purpose, that Patty and her children are all well. Pray give my love to all. I shall direct this to Henry.

'Ever yours,
'S. R.

'For the future I shall write little and often, and pray do you write often. If you knew how lonely I feel, I am sure you would. I met Boddington's lacquais (at Rome), acting as courier to Sir Henry Lushington and Lady A'Court, yesterday. He saluted me with the familiarity of an old friend, and I him.

'I hope all your pictures are hung and to your mind. I have seen nothing like your Bassano and think of it very often. Has Philips done nothing about Webb's picture, the Callcott. Do get Henry to speak to P., a word or two would shame him out of it.

'I hope the watch deserves its high character, and that Ariel sings as well as ever in his prison. My sylphs are pretty well. . . . I was very sorry to hear of Miss Agar's death; but I expect a great many to slip out of life in my absence. May none of them be friends.'

Samuel Rogers to Sarah Rogers.

'Rome: 25 Nov., 1821.

' My dear Sarah,—Your kind letter of 2nd November came to-day, and did me a great deal of good. I am glad to find Mrs. S[iddons] and the voiturier turned out so well, though not Miss S.; a journey lets out strange things. I left Florence on 18th (the day we did), slept at Sienna the first night, Radicofani the second, and Viterbo the third, arriving at Rome about 2 o'clock on Wednesday last. I had fine weather all the way; the inns in the papal country are no better than before, not a jot. Indeed, I suffered much more than before, expecting, perhaps, something better and having no novelty to keep me up.

' I had no fears, though to please Francesco, the courier, I took guards twice as we drew near Rome. I wish you could have seen me setting off before daybreak from the market-place of Viterbo with six white horses to the carriage, and two shining helmets drawn up in form, while I got in to the great admiration of a full market. I had my journal, so I looked out for St. Peter's at the fifteenth stone, and drove in directly to my lodging in the Babuino. Walking in the Piazza di Spagna I found Sir G. Beaumont, and many of my mornings have been spent with him. I like my rooms very well, though they have no sun, no orange garden (Canova says he lodged in it once in an attic, so it is classic ground); they are fitted up, like any at Paris, with carpets and ormolu. Rome has made an amazing jump in that respect, so powerful is English money, and (only think) an opera every night, and very good, they say. I was only once there for half an hour; it is a sad way off, and a strange thing, for they give a comedy instead of a dance, and not after the opera, but first an act of one, then of the other, and so on; so that the English are obliged to gulp what they don't understand, much to their annoyance. I have had nothing but enquiries about you from Lady Westmoreland, Canova, the Torlonias, the Dodwells, &c. I have dined out three times, with Lady W., the Beaumonts, and Barings. Canova I thought I should never see. I called every day on him and he on me. At last we met. He called yesterday morning at eleven, with his brother the Abbé, and gave me such a salute as I have not had since I was at Bellesita. At Lady W.'s, in the evening, came the Dodwells—Mrs. D. was quite cordial and very pretty. They never miss the Corso, and their barouche is indeed a very smart one. The Torlonias give a ball next Wednesday, and are sorry you cannot be there. I need not say I am. The only thing that has surprised me since I came is, alas! the little sensation everything produces in me. I went into St. Peters, the Pantheon, the Coliseum, as if I had been in them the day before. Is it that the impression was so deep it has not changed, or is it that I am grown colder? Perhaps a little of both. Six years in a young person would obliterate a great deal—impressions are so lively and so numerous. Not so now with me.

'To-day I ventured out on a white horse with a long tail; a lady's, they say. I received your letter in the Forum, the courier brought it me. I dismounted and went into the Coliseum, and sat down there to read it.

Mem.—I had not been there before. I won't say which gave me most pleasure. I have not met a funeral, but I saw one at a distance the other night from the Beaumonts' window in the Piazza di Spagna, just as we were going to dinner. It crossed the place with many lights, and was said to be that of a most beautiful young woman by those who saw it. The woods on the Lake of Bolsena are sadly cut down, as we were told. The Vatican and the Capitol are both thrown open now to the world on Thursday and Sunday, and at the Vatican there is now a fine collection of oil paintings. I have had a carriage twice for the day, the price is about ten shillings, my horse six shillings, so I think I shall indulge most in the first. My courier is a very good cook, and performs for me when I dine at home, though he will not undertake for more than myself.

'I have not seen Thorwaldsen. The Abbé Taylor is a great loss.[1] Nobody supplies his place. Next Sunday is the function in the Sistine and Pauline chapels, which we attended on 27th November; but whether I shall get in I don't know. The Pope walks every fine day between two high walls in a cross road near the Albani Villa, and the other day I met him there. He is almost double, so weak in his body, but his countenance is very little altered. The courier's wife has applied at Milan for your letter, but without success. One to another Mr. Rogers there was brought to me, perhaps yours went to him and he did not return it to the Post Office, as I did his. Perhaps it would be as well to add the Christian name, and to write

[1] The Abbé Taylor was an Irishman who was appointed by the Pope to present English visitors.

Samuel R., Esq., Gentilhomme Anglais. I have written to Bologna to-day. None had arrived when we left it on the 29th of Oct. I will not fail to get the bronze of Duke Lorenzo, if there is one. I have been to Ignaccio's, and have bought an earring or two, but they are now much dearer than before.

'The days are here very mild, but I wear my great coat, though my cold is almost gone. The Corso is really very gay in the afternoon, and I think better of it than I did. I have looked down our narrow street, which looks deplorable, and mean to visit the house. Mrs. Millingen I don't mean to call upon. Dodwell says she does nothing but say M. has deserted her, and begs and borrows money wherever she can. I should like to see what Cornelia is like. Dodwell sometimes meets Mrs. M., and she grins in his face. The Pope allows her a pension. You surprise me about Moore, though Ellis had written to Lord Clare that Lord Lansdowne had advanced him the money, 1000*l.*, and that all was settled. I am very glad to hear it; but I am surprised to hear that he continues in town. My notion was, and his too, that he was to pass two or three nights in disguise in St. James's Place on his way to Ireland. I hear he has been in Dublin. Surely, if he could go to Woburn he might have had the grace to pay you and Henry a visit, but *that* does not surprise me. So Sutton has been again to Paris. I had no idea he had any thoughts of it. Did you find him and Maltby there? I never pass a bookseller's shop here but I think of M. I am rejoiced that your pictures hang to your mind. Sir G. Beaumont, in going through the galleries, often mentions the Bassano.

We sometimes see something of his almost as good, not quite.

'What a long list of deaths. Young Best's is, indeed, a sad event. I have been looking out for them as I came along. Such a loss might hasten some people and retard others. I have bought some rubbishing pictures, three at Venice, two at Bologna, one at Florence, and have sent them to Molini in Paternoster Row. Pray open them and criticise them. I have insured them for 100*l*. Really the Italians are a strange people, but I have now no fear of them, and could walk about alone at night as in the day, which I would not have done before. At night, here and at Florence, as they walk by under my windows, they sing, when alone, to themselves, and as loud as they can—and *that* very ill—when together and in a number, in parts, and still I think very ill. The Arch of Constantine has tumbled down in the Forum and they are putting it up again. The flocks of goats I met in the Apennines were most beautiful, as white as driven snow. Hundreds cross the Arno every day in Florence, and some say that they go to suckle the *enfans trouvés* in the Foundling Hospital, and that every goat knows her child. There was a reading-room in Florence, and one is here, where the "Times" and "Chronicle" are taken in, but I would go to neither, I wish to think of things here.

'Sir George Beaumont saw the "Coronation" at Drury Lane, and says it is much the finest thing he ever saw. Have you seen it? Madame Arponi, the Austrian Minister's wife here, is very gracious to the English; she is very strict to the Austrians, but admits us *all*, and is at home every Monday. They say her Palace is a very splendid one, but I thought I would defer my appearance and stay at home and talk to you. I sent you another long letter and large budget from Florence, directing it to Henry. I hope it arrived. It contained three more parts: "Ginevra," "Florence," and "Don Garzia." I am glad you have found the "Brides." Many, many thanks to you for your great kindness and patience under such an affliction. You will now taste some of the miseries of an author, with none of his vanity to support you under it. I am reading "Corinne" again, and with new pleasure, and get on with Sismondi tolerably well. Inclosed you will receive another, "Arqua." Pray insert it after "St. Mark's Place." I was at Florence in the Chapel on the day of the Morti; the day, I believe, after All Souls' day. At Florence I went every evening (almost) to the opera, paying a franc and a half. The last day I dined with the Mintos, who are arrived there. . . . Lady Minto is a very agreeable and pretty woman, daughter of Brydone, the traveller, and granddaughter of Robertson. They are coming on here. Ward and Fazakerly are at Nice. Lord Derby's daughter, Lady M. Stanley, is going to marry Lord Wilton, so we shall lose her smiles at the concert.'

Samuel Rogers to Sarah Rogers.

'Rome: 6 Dec., 1821.

'My dear Sarah,—You have done it admirably. I wish the printer had done half as well. Pray see he begins his new paragraphs at the top of a page thus—in page eight—

'Day glimmered and I went, a gentle breeze
　Ruffling the waters of the Leman Lake;

the second line standing out before the first in the margin. How otherwise could it be known as a new paragraph? ... Formerly all new paragraphs began so, as you will see by turning to any books of poems—see Crowe. Perhaps it is not worth while to alter the rest. Pray, too, see that he makes the paper no bigger, or the page, than Crowe or "Human Life." He seems to print fifteen lines, and Crowe, I believe, prints fourteen; at all events, don't let it be larger than "Human Life." Your criticism is excellent, I wish you gave me more.

'I hope you have received a letter from Florence, and another from Rome inclosing "Arqua," "Ginevra," "Florence," "Don Garzia." If that from Florence has failed, pray go to press with the inclosed and no more, and whenever you are in any doubt pray consult your own judgment and I shall be satisfied. The paper is so thin that I much fear the marks on one side will pass for marks on the other, but I shall trust to your judgment, and pray don't send me the additional sheets, if you feel pretty sure about them. If you don't like "Arqua," leave it out. If you send me the new sheets, pray correct them to the full, as two or three days make little or no difference. But perhaps you have done it and sent them before this arrives. If you find "Foscari" forthcoming immediately, don't wait for the new sheets, though they may be printed, but let it be published in its present size directly. But, I suppose, Moore knows pretty well about them.

'I came here a fortnight ago, and wrote you a long

account of Rome. Last Sunday was the ceremony in the Capella Sistina. The Pope did not perform at high mass, but as soon as it was over, two Cardinals went out and brought him in; he carried the Host under the Canopy into the Capella Paulina, but nobody went in there while he knelt but Lady Abercorn, and she by accident. The man was in the basket snuffing the lights as before. Somehow or other the whole struck me much less than formerly; and the singing particularly. But what I saw last Monday far exceeded my expectations. [To] Frascati, Sir G. Beaumont and I went together, and there, mounting donkeys, rode to Tusculum and Grotta Ferrata, through galleries or avenues of ilex and cypress along those hills, catching the most delightful views of Rome, and the Campagna, and the villas above and below us. It was sunny and clear (we have often a July without three such days) and too hot, though it was the 3rd of December. It was a day I shall never forget, and to be equalled only by the afternoons I spent with you at Albano and Mola. I am very sorry indeed to hear of Mrs. W.'s death, it must make a great gap at Amersham. Your visit will be a great comfort to them. I think I must say something about Lord Byron, but I don't know how. Pray let the following be the note, and pray decide for me which of the two conclusions you like best. It is unnecessary for me to see it again.'

He then gives, as a note to the lines—

> Down which the grizzly head of old Falieri
> Rolled from the block,

the 'something about Lord Byron'—

'"Of him and his conspiracy I had given a brief

account; but he is now universally known through a writer, whose poetical talents command as much the admiration of other countries as of his own."'

He adds two other forms of expression, and says—

'Here are three readings, and pray choose for me. I think you will choose the last, I don't care which; and pray spell Falieri's name as Lord Byron spells it, with an *i* or an *o*, I forget which. In the same manner I am puzzled about Jackimo. There is no J in the Italian, but the English would not pronounce it right with an I, and are much perplexed in reading Shakespeare. I incline to the old Venetian spelling, Giacomo, so pray, if you approve of it, alter it back again to that.

'I am glad Moore came to see you for *his* sake. . . .

'Last night your old friend Mme. Massena gave a grand concert, and in one of the rooms the Discobulus was seen. Very few English were there; I was not, having never called, and perhaps she has forgot my name. The Princess Borghese is here, and has her evenings, but I have not seen her. For three or four days I have kept very quiet, in consequence of an unlucky fall with my donkey at Frascati, but am quite well again. Since your dispatch the day before yesterday, I have seen not a face but Lady Westmoreland's, who called and sat an hour last night over my fire to the great interruption of business. I hope I have left nothing that will perplex you, having read everything over and over again till I cannot see. Adieu, my dear Sarah. Pray forgive so much trouble, and believe me to be,

'Ever yours, S. R.

'At Frascati, just under the hill, I saw a beautiful group, which was well worthy of your pencil—two shepherd boys with their pipes playing before an image of the Virgin in a niche in a vineyard wall, and a cluster of smiling children of all ages round them.'

These letters show the great confidence Rogers reposed in his sister Sarah's judgment. As the poem was to be published anonymously he could not consult his friends about lines, phrases, and words as he had consulted Richard Sharp, and sometimes Moore, about his other works, and he therefore took counsel with the sister who shared his secret. I have omitted from these letters many of the alternative passages and expressions which he leaves to her choice, but enough remain to show the important part she took in preparing the volume as well as in seeing it through the press. It was, in fact, carefully edited by Sarah Rogers.

After wintering at Rome Rogers set out homewards, taking Pisa by the way. Here he stayed with Byron, and the events took place which Medwin has described in his 'Conversations of Lord Byron' and his 'Life of Shelley.' In the former of these books Medwin reports some remarks of Lord Byron which are full of a spirit of satirical depreciation of Rogers, but the observations are made in response to far more hostile comments by his interlocutor. In his 'Life of Shelley' Medwin tells us that this conversation was between Byron and Shelley; and he adds, with the worst possible taste, that in that dialogue Byron throws off the mask, and shows his real opinion of the head and heart of 'the Beau, Bard, and

Banker,' whose dinners and coteries had begun to fade from his memory by time and distance, and the improbability of his ever again participating in them. The writer who could, in this inconsequent sentence, hint at so base a motive for Byron's professed appreciation of Rogers, must have had a constitutional incapacity for understanding honourable conduct or for estimating men.

Shelley knew Rogers but slightly. He had called at St. James's Place to ask Rogers to assist him in a generous scheme of his for helping Leigh Hunt, which Rogers at the time was unable to do. In the intercourse which he had with Shelley during his stay at Pisa, Rogers was pleased with him, and always spoke of him afterwards with respect. He used to say that in argument Byron treated him with great rudeness, replying by such discourteous phrases as 'Ah! that's very well for an atheist,' and that Shelley bore it with a quiet, gentle, and resigned manner, while firmly holding his own in argument. Rogers described in conversation his own experiences of Byron's manner. They quarrelled constantly, and Byron said all the cruel things he could think of to mortify his guest. Rogers bore them with composure, and on the next morning Byron would meet him with an effusive welcome, an air of making it up, which immediately made them friends again.

Medwin gives some very clever verses of Byron's on Rogers, which are as abusive as anything ever written. He tells us that this cruel satire, this piece of unmeasured personal invective—which, if we are to take it as Medwin takes it, seriously, was one of the most unmannerly attacks ever made by a host upon his guest—was placed under the cushion of the sofa on which Rogers sat in friendly intercourse with its author. Medwin fails to see that this practical joke reveals the true spirit of the whole performance. It was like the evening attacks on Rogers, which were atoned for by extra kindness in the morning—a piece of rollicking fun, a caricature meant to turn a moment's laugh against its object, and nobody would be more astonished than its author that it should ever be taken, even by dulness itself, for earnest. The lines were published in one of the magazines in which Rogers was made the constant butt of certain envious minds, but nobody took them seriously, and Byron never included them among his works. Rogers never resented them, never complained about them. He treated the attack as the joke it was. His own version of Byron's behaviour in the Pitti Palace at Florence illustrated Byron's manner. I have already given Byron's account of it with his acknowledgment of Rogers's 'excellent taste and deep feeling for the arts.' Yet, when Rogers had exclaimed, 'What a noble Andrea del Sarto!' Byron had answered with a mocking quotation from 'The Vicar of Wakefield.'—'Upon asking how he had been taught the art of a cognoscente so very suddenly, he assured me that nothing was more easy. The whole secret consisted in a strict adherence to two rules—the one always to observe the picture might have been better if the painter had taken more pains; and the other to praise the works of Pietro Perugino.' There can be no question which of these two views of Rogers's taste for art Byron really held, nor can there be any as to his true affection for Rogers himself, or his admiration

for his poetry. After Byron's death Rogers wrote the
lines which were added to the First Part of his 'Italy,'
under the heading 'Bologna.' It tells the story of their
meeting, and if Byron in that last intercourse treated
Rogers as Medwin says he did, this poem is a remarkable literary instance of the return of good for evil.

>   Much had passed
> Since last we parted; and those five short years—
> Much had they told! His clustering locks were turn'd
> Grey; nor did aught recall the Youth that swam
> From Sestos to Abydos.   Yet his voice,
> Still it was sweet; still from his eye the thought
> Flashed lightning-like, nor lingered on the way,
> Waiting for words.   Far, far into the night
> We sat conversing—no unwelcome hour
> The hour we met; and when Aurora rose,
> Rising, we climbed the rugged Apennine.
>   Well I remember how the golden sun
> Filled with its beams the unfathomable gulfs,
> As on we travelled, and along the ridge,
> Mid groves of cork and cistus and wild fig,
> His motley household came.—Not last nor least
> Battista, who upon the moonlight sea
> Of Venice had so ably, zealously
> Served, and at parting thrown his oar away
> To follow through the world; who without stain
> Had worn so long that honourable badge,
> The gondolier's, in a Patrician House,
> Arguing unlimited trust.   Not last nor least
> Thou, though declining in thy beauty and strength,
> Faithful Moretto, to the latest hour
> Guarding his chamber door, and now along
> The silent, sullen strand of Missolonghi
> Howling in grief.   He had just left that place
> Of old renown, once in the Adrian sea,

Ravenna; where from Dante's sacred tomb
He had so oft, as many a verse declares,
Drawn inspiration; where, at twilight time,
Through the pine forest wandering with loose rein,
Wandering and lost, he had so oft beheld
(What is not visible to a Poet's eye?)
The spectre knight, the hell-hounds and their prey;
The chase, the slaughter, and the festal mirth
Suddenly blasted. 'Twas a theme he loved,
But others claimed their turn; and many a tower,
Shattered, uprooted from its native rock,
Its strength the pride of some heroic age,
Appeared and vanished (many a sturdy steer
Yoked and unyoked), while, as in happier days,
He poured his spirit forth. The past forgot,
All was enjoyment. Not a cloud obscured
Present or future.
     He is now at rest,
And praise and blame fall on his ear alike,
Now dull in death. Yes, Byron, thou art gone;
Gone like a star that through the firmament
Shot and was lost, in its eccentric course
Dazzling, perplexing. Yet thy heart, methinks,
Was generous, noble—noble in its scorn
Of all things low or little; nothing there
Sordid or servile. If imagined wrongs
Pursued thee, urging thee sometimes to do
Things long regretted, oft, as many know,
None more than I, thy gratitude would build
On slight foundations; and if in thy life
Not happy, in thy death thou surely wert;
Thy wish accomplished; dying in the land
Where thy young mind had caught ethereal fire;
Dying in Greece, and in a cause so glorious.

 They in thy train—ah, little did they think,
As round we went, that they so soon should sit

Mourning beside thee, while a Nation mourned,
Changing her festal for her funeral song ;
That they so soon should hear the minute-gun,
As morning gleamed on what remained of thee,
Roll o'er the sea, the mountains, numbering
Thy years of joy and sorrow.
                              Thou art gone ;
And he who would assail thee in thy grave,
Oh ! let him pause ! For who among us all,
Tried as thou wert—even from thine earliest years,
When wandering yet unspoilt, a Highland boy—
Tried as thou wert, and with thy soul of flame ;
Pleasure, while yet the down was on thy cheek,
Uplifting, pressing, and to lips like thine,
Her charmed cup—ah, who among us all
Could say he had not erred as much and more ?

CHAPTER X.

1822-24

The First Part of ' Italy '—Moore and Rogers in Paris—Wordsworth on his Sister's Diary—Dorothy Wordsworth to Rogers—Wordsworth at Rogers's—J. P. Kemble's Death—Mrs. Siddons's Letter—Rogers and the Duke of Wellington—Uvedale Price—An English ' Ginevra '—Walter Scott's Remuneration—Southey's Letter—Rogers and Lord Grenville—Lord Grenville on Dante—Lord Ashburnham's letter—Moore, Wordsworth, and Rogers—Letter of Miss H. M. Williams—R. Sharp to Rogers—Lord Byron's Death—Rogers and Byron's Memoir—The Funeral—Rogers's Commonplace Book—Uvedale Price on Dropmore; on Queen Caroline's Oysters—Luttrell on a Greek Epigram—Letters of Sir J. Mackintosh and Uvedale Price.

WHILE Rogers was still in Italy his sister carried out her commission, and the First Part of ' Italy ' was published. It was a small duodecimo volume of 164 pages. The poem was in eighteen divisions and was little more than a mere rough sketch of the First Part of ' Italy ' as it was issued, in twenty-two sections, in the Illustrated edition, some years afterwards. The secret of the authorship was well kept by the few who knew it, of whom Moore was one. The publishers, Messrs. Longman & Co., who had no idea who was the writer of the poem, sent the manuscript to Moore, asking him to tell them whether it was worth publishing anonymously. ' Upon opening it,' says Moore, ' found to my surprise that it was Rogers's " Italy," which he has sent home thus privately to be published.' Among the precautions taken to prevent identification was that of leading the reader into Italy by the Great St. Bernard, whereas in both journeys he entered it over the Simplon. The poem was not his first attempt at blank verse. In the same volume with his 'Human Life' he had published, in 1819, the 'Lines written at Paestum,' which formed a sort of first sketch of the longer and more developed poem headed 'Paestum' in the ninteenth section of the second part of 'Italy.' I have already, in Chapter V., showed how the poem grew out of his Diary in Italy in 1814 and 1815. The spirit of that Diary is summed up in the lines—

> From my youth upward have I longed to tread
> This classic ground.—And am I here at last?
> Wandering at will through the long porticoes,
> And catching, as through some majestic grove,
> Now the blue ocean and now, chaos-like,
> Mountains and mountain gulfs, and, half-way up,
> Towns like the living rock from which they grew?
> A cloudy region, black and desolate,
> Where once a slave withstood a world in arms.

The 'Lines written at Paestum,' from which the above are taken, were much praised by his friends, but few of them seem to have suspected that 'Italy' was by the same writer, though Wordsworth did so, and told Rogers he was detected. The poem had been several years in hand. The lines beginning 'But the Bise blew cold,' quoted in the letter to his sister, were written in June 1816, and the rest at various times between the first Italian journey in 1814 and the second in 1821–22.

The poem had not the popularity of his previous efforts. It attracted but little notice, though one reviewer attributed it to Southey. It was some time before Rogers acknowledged it publicly, though the authorship was soon understood among his friends, and when he did so it added nothing to his fame.

On his return homewards in the early part of May he again visited Moore in his temporary exile in Paris. Moore, in his Diary, gives an account of the visits to various distinguished people they paid together during the four or five days Rogers remained in the French capital. At a dinner at Roberts's, 'at fifteen francs a head exclusive of wine '—of which Moore says, 'Poets did not dine so in the olden time '—he records that Rogers told him a good deal about Lord Byron, whom he saw both going and coming back, and who ' expressed to R. the same contempt for Shakespeare he has often expressed to me.' There is not a hint that Rogers had complained of Byron's treatment of him, but the significant statement that he ' treats his companion Shelley very cavalierly.'

The letter in which Wordsworth referred to ' Italy ' was on another subject of literary interest.

William Wordsworth to Samuel Rogers.

'Lowther Castle [16 Sept., 1822].

' My dear Rogers,—It gave me great pleasure to hear from our common friend, Sharp, that you had returned from the Continent in such excellent health, which I hope you will continue to enjoy in spite of our fogs, rains, east-winds, coal fires, and other clogs upon light spirits and free breathing. I have long wished to write to you on a little affair of my own, or, rather, of my sister's, and the facility of procuring a frank in this house has left my procrastinating habit without excuse. Some time ago you expressed (as perhaps you will remember) a wish that my sister would publish her recollections of her Scotch tour, and you interested yourself so far in the scheme as kindly to offer to assist in disposing of it to a publisher for her advantage. We know that your skill and experience in these matters are great, and she is now disposed to profit by them, provided you continue to think as favourably of the measure as heretofore. The fact is she was so much gratified by her tour in Switzerland, that she has a strong wish to add to her knowledge of that country, and to extend her ramble to some part of Italy. As her own little fortune is not sufficient to justify a step of this kind, she has no hope of revisiting those countries unless an adequate sum could be procured through the means of this MS. You are now fairly in possession of her motives; if you still think that the publication would do her no discredit and are of opinion that a respectable sum of money might be had for it, which she has no chance of effecting except through your exertion, she would be much obliged, as I also should be, if you would undertake to manage the bargain, and the MS. shall be sent you as soon as it is revised. She has further to beg that you would be so kind as to look it over and strike out what you think might be better omitted.

'I detected you in a small collection of poems entitled "Italy," which we all read with much pleasure.

"Venice" and "The Brides of Venice," that was the title, I think, please as much as any, some parts of the "Venice" are particularly fine. I had no fault to find, but rather too strong a leaning to the pithy and concise, and to some peculiarities of versification which occur perhaps too often.

'Where are the Beaumonts, and when do they come to England? We hear nothing of them.

'Lord and Lady Lonsdale are well, Lady Frederic is here, so is Lady Caroline; both well. Before I close this I will mention to Lady F. that I am writing to you. My own family were well when I left them two days ago. Please remember me kindly to your sister, and believe me, my dear Rogers,
'Faithfully yours,
'WM. WORDSWORTH.

'P.S. Lady F. says, if Holland House were but where Brougham Hall is, we should see more of Mr. Rogers. She adds that we have really some sunshine in this country and now and then a gentle day like those of Italy. Adieu.'

In November Moore was again in London, and makes the usual record of visits to Rogers and with Rogers. He records one *bon mot* of Rogers's told him by Shee. On somebody remarking that Payne Knight had got very deaf, ' 'Tis from want of practice,' said Rogers—Payne Knight being a very bad listener. The sequel of Wordsworth's request about his sister's Diary is contained in two letters from her. Both are in reply to letters from Rogers.

Dorothy Wordsworth to Samuel Rogers.

'Rydal Mount: Jan. 3rd, 1823.

'My dear Sir,—As you have no doubt heard, by a message sent from my brother through Mr. Sharp, I happened to be in Scotland when your letter arrived, where (having intended to be absent from home only a fortnight) I was detained seven weeks by an illness of my fellow traveller. Having not had it in my power to thank you immediately for your great kindness to me, and your ready attention to my brother's request, I was unwilling after my return to write for that purpose merely, many circumstances occurring to prevent me from coming to a decision upon the matter in which you are inclined to take so friendly an interest. The most important of these was a protracted and dangerous sickness of my nephew William, which began the day after my arrival at home, and engrossed the care and attention of the whole house. He is now recovered, but his looks continue to show that his frame is far from being restored to its natural strength.

'I cannot but be flattered by your thinking so well of my Journal as to recommend (indirectly at least) that I should not part with all power over it till its fortune has been tried. You will not be surprised, however, that I am not so hopeful, and that I am apprehensive that after having encountered the unpleasantness of coming before the public I might not be assisted in attaining my object. I have, then, to ask whether a middle course be not possible, that is, whether your favourable opinion, confirmed perhaps by some other good judges, might not induce a bookseller to give a certain sum for the right to publish a given number of copies. In fact, I find it next to impossible to make up my mind to sacrifice my privacy for a certainty *less* than two hundred pounds—a sum which would effectually aid me in accomplishing the ramble I so much, and I hope not unwisely, wish for. If a bargain could be made on terms of this sort, your expectation of further profits (which expectation I would willingly share) need not be parted with, and I should have the further gratification of acting according to your advice.

' I have nothing further to say, for it is superfluous to trouble you with my scruples and the fears which I have that a work of such slight pretensions will be wholly overlooked in this writing and publishing (especially *tour*-writing and *tour*-publishing) age; and when factions and parties, literary and political, are so busy in endeavouring to stifle all attempts to interest, however pure from any taint of the world, and however humble in their claims.

' My brother begs me to say that it gratified him to hear you were pleased with his late publications. In the " Memorials " he himself likes best the " Stanzas upon Einsiedeln," the " Three Cottage Girls," and, above all, the "Eclipse upon the Lake of Lugano "; and in the " Sketches " the succession of those on the Reformation, and those towards the conclusion of the third part. Mr. Sharp liked best the poem on " Enterprise," which surprised my brother a good deal.

' We hope to see you in summer; you will be truly welcome, and we should be heartily glad to see your sister as your companion, to whom we all beg to be most kindly remembered.

'If you knew how much it has cost me to settle the affair of this proposed publication in my mind, as far as I have now done, I am sure you would deem me sufficiently excused for having so long delayed answering your most obliging letter. I have still to add, that if there be a prospect that any bookseller will undertake the publication, I will immediately prepare a corrected copy to be sent to you, and I shall trust to your kindness for taking the trouble to look over it and to mark whatever passages you may think too trivial for publication, or in any other respect much amiss.

'My brother and sister join with me in every good wish to you for the coming year, and many more.

'Believe me, dear Sir, yours gratefully and with sincere esteem,

'DOROTHY WORDSWORTH.'

It is evident from this letter that Rogers had advised the publication of the Journal, and was ready to negotiate with a publisher for its issue. The scruples and apprehensions of which Miss Wordsworth speaks in the next letter seem to have stopped it. The Journal afterwards appeared in pieces, and considerable extracts from it were given in the 'Life of Wordsworth' by his nephew the late Bishop of Lincoln. The whole diary was not published till 1874.

Dorothy Wordsworth to Samuel Rogers.

.' 17th February, 1823.

'My dear Sir,—I cannot deny myself the pleasure of thanking you for your last very kind letter as Miss Hutchinson is going directly to London, and, through her, you will receive this. At present I shall do no more than assure you that I am fully sensible of the value of your friendly attention to the matter on which I have troubled you, as I hope that my brother and sister will soon have the pleasure of meeting you in London, and he will explain to you all my scruples and apprehensions. They will leave home to-morrow with Miss Hutchinson and (parting with her at Derby) will turn aside to Coleorton, where they intend spending about three weeks with our kind friends Sir George and Lady Beaumont, and will then, if nothing intervene to frustrate their present scheme, proceed to London. Their visit will be a short one, but I hope they will have time to see all their friends.

'My brother is glad that you came upon the stone to the memory of Aloys Reding in such an interesting way. He and Mrs. W., without any previous notice, met with it at the moment of sunset, as described at the close of those stanzas. I was rambling in another part of the wood and unluckily missed it. I was delighted with your and your sister's reception at that pleasant house in the Vale of Schwyz, which I well remember. Mr. Monkhouse and I, going on foot to Brennen from Schwyz, were struck with the appearance of the house, and inquired to whom it belonged—were told, to a family of the name of Reding, but could not make out whether it had been the residence and birth-place of Aloys Reding or not.

'The passage in Oldham is a curious discovery.

'You say nothing of coming northward this summer. I hope my brother and sister may tempt you to think about it. I am left at home with my niece and her brother William, now quite well.

'Pray make my very kind remembrances to Miss Rogers. You must not leave her behind when you come again to the lakes.

'Do, my dear sir, excuse this hasty scrawl. We are in the bustle of preparation for the long journey—a great event in this house!

'Believe me to be, with great respect,
'Yours very sincerely,
'DOROTHY WORDSWORTH.'

This visit of Wordsworth and his wife and sister-in-law to London is spoken of in Moore's Diary, Crabb Robinson's Diary, and Lamb's Letters. Moore met the party at Rogers's, and his account of it is interesting though rather full of himself.

'*April 1st*, 1823.—Walked, for the first time since I came to town, to Rogers's. Very agreeable. In talking of the "Angels," said the subject was an unlucky one. When I mentioned Lord Lansdowne's opinion that it was better than "Lalla Rookh," said he would not rank it so high as the "Veiled Prophet" for execution, nor the "Fire-worshippers" for story and interest, but would place it rather on the level of "Paradise and the Peri." Asked me to dine with him, which I did—company: Wordsworth and his wife and sister-in-law, Cary (the translator of Dante), Hallam, and Sharp. Some discussion about Racine and Voltaire, in which I startled, or rather shocked, them by saying that, though there could be no doubt of the superior taste and workmanship of Racine, yet that Voltaire's tragedies *interested* me the most of the two. Another electrifying assertion of mine was that I would much rather see " Othello " and " Romeo and Juliet " as Italian operas and played by *Pasta*, than the original of Shakespeare as acted on the London stage. Wordsworth told of some acquaintance of his, who, being told among other things to go and see the " Chapeau de Paille " at Antwerp, said, on his return, " I saw all the other things you mentioned, but as for the straw hat manufactory, I could not make it out." Sharp mentioned a curious instance of Walter Scott's indifference to pictures: when he met him at the Louvre, not willing to spare two or three minutes for a walk to the bottom of the gallery when it was the first and last opportunity he was likely to have of seeing the "Transfiguration," &c., &c. In speaking of music and the difference there is between the poetical and musical ear, Wordsworth said that he was totally devoid of the latter, and for a long time could not distinguish one tune from another. Rogers thus described Lord Holland's feeling for the Arts, " Painting gives him no pleasure, and Music absolute pain."

'Wordsworth's excessive praise of "Christabel," joined in by Cary, far beyond my comprehension. The whole day dull enough.'

Moore gives an account of a dinner at Mr. Monkhouse's, on Wordsworth's invitation, at which Coleridge, Charles Lamb, and Rogers were present. He speaks of Lamb as ' a clever fellow certainly, but full of villainous and abortive puns,' and records that ' Coleridge told some tolerable things.' Crabb Robinson, who was present, says that besides the five bards were no one but Mrs. Wordsworth, Miss Hutchinson, Mary Lamb, and Mrs. Gilman and himself at the bottom of the table. 'Coleridge alone,' says Crabb Robinson, 'displayed any of his peculiar talent. I have not for years seen him in such excellent health and with so fine a flow of spirits. His discourse was addressed chiefly to Wordsworth, on points of metaphysical criticism. Rogers occasionally interposing a remark. The only one of the poets who seemed not to enjoy himself was Moore.'[1] Lamb gives an account of the day in a letter to Bernard Barton, in which he says, ' I dined in Parnassus with Wordsworth, Coleridge, Rogers, and Tom Moore—half the poetry of England constellated in Gloucester Place. It was a delightful evening. Coleridge was in his finest vein of talk—had all the talk.'

A day or two later Moore records a breakfast at Rogers's to meet Lamb, and on the 10th of April a distinguished party at Rogers's—Sydney Smith, Luttrell, Payne Knight, Lord Aberdeen, Abercrombie, Lord Clifden, &c. Moore says he had hitherto held out against Smith, 'but this day he fairly conquered me.' 'What Rogers says of Smith very true,' adds Moore, ' that, whenever the conversation is getting dull, he throws in some touch which makes it rebound and rise again as light as ever.' Another day Moore meets Barry Cornwall (Mr. Procter) at Rogers's house, ' a gentle, amiable-mannered person in very ill health, which has delayed his marriage with a person he

---

[1] *Diary, &c., of H. Crabb Robinson*, vol. ii., p. 246.

has long been in love with; she too, an invalid; and somebody the other day described the two lovers supping together at nine o'clock on water gruel.' It is curious to read this remark now that Mrs. Procter has lately died, sixty-five years after it was put on record. Moore's Diary goes on through May and June. There is a hitch in the publication of his 'Fables,' and Rogers is consulted. He gives five pounds towards the Greek subscription, in which Rogers was interesting himself. He meets Constable of Edinburgh at breakfast at Rogers's, and notes that in talking of Walter Scott and ' the Author of Waverley' the great publisher ' continually forgot himself, and made them the same person.' Another day Rogers shows him Gray's poems in his actual handwriting, and the original manuscript of a sermon of Sterne's. Three times in ten days he meets Kenny at Rogers's at breakfast. Rogers tells stories of Foote, one of which Moore records. A canting sort of lady asked him, 'Pray, Mr. Foote, do you go to Church?' 'No, madam,' replied Foote. 'Not that I see any harm in it.'

At the end of February John Philip Kemble died in Switzerland, whither he had retired. He had just reached his sixty-sixth year, being about a year and a half younger than his celebrated sister, Mrs. Siddons. Rogers had always admired him, and used to say that he had never missed going to see Macbeth when Kemble and Mrs. Siddons played Macbeth and Lady Macbeth. He used to repeat the *mot*, that the way to wealth would be to buy John Kemble at other people's valuation and sell him at his own. When Kemble was living at Lausanne he was jealous of Mont Blanc, and was vexed to hear

people asking ' How does Mont Blanc look this morning ? '
He was most amusing when he had drunk plenty of wine,
but Rogers always regarded him as an over-estimated
person. Rogers was present at the dinner given to
Kemble when he quitted the stage, and Mrs. Siddons—
a far greater performer, as Rogers maintained—alluding
to the small attention her own retirement had attracted,
said to him, ' Perhaps in the next world women will be
more valued than they are in this.' He wrote to her on
her brother's death, and she replied as follows.

Mrs. Siddons to Samuel Rogers.

' Friday [9 May, 1823].

' A thousand thanks, my dear Mr. Rogers, for your kind
and friendly note. The sympathy of the good and wise
(after those heavenly consolations which are mercifully
accorded to our prayers) is the most efficacious, as it is
the sweetest medicine of our sorrows. I know not why,
but I did fancy I was almost forgotten by you, and it
grieved me; for, alas! death and change have left *me*
also almost a bankrupt.

' This last, and I think heaviest of my many afflicting
visitations, I have felt, and long shall feel, very severely.
Sickness and sorrow have pursued me almost ever since
we met, and but for the tender unremitting cares of my
darling inestimable child, and excellent friend, I should
probably not have lived to meet with you again. I was
scarcely recovered from an illness which confined me to
my bed for three whole months, when this last sad blow
was struck. But it is no less irrational than blameable
to cherish an unavailing sorrow, and I have at length

aroused myself to the effort of seeing my friends again, and I hope to meet you at Sir George Beaumont's (I believe it is) on Monday; in the meantime present my kind compliments to your sister, and believe me,

'Your obliged and affectionate,

'S. SIDDONS.

'I generally take my airing at two, and cannot endure the chance of missing you again, therefore do not give yourself the trouble of calling, for I hope soon to be able to arrange something better than a morning call. There! I have lost the pleasure of seeing you again. How vexatious, but if you are good enough to call any day before two it shall not happen.'

On the day before this letter was dated, Rogers had a remarkable conversation with the Duke of Wellington at Lady Shelley's in Berkeley Square. It is to be found in the 'Recollections' (p. 218), and I am surprised that it has not attracted more general notice. Speaking of Napoleon, the Duke said that he was sure Moscow was burnt down by the irregularity of Napoleon's own soldiers, and that the pamphlet to this effect, published by the Governor of Moscow, states what he (the Duke of Wellington) was persuaded was the truth.

One of the best letter writers of his time thus acknowledged a copy of 'Italy':—

Uvedale Price to Samuel Rogers.

'Foxley: May 25th, 1823.

'My dear Sir,—I have to thank you for a most acceptable present in every respect; it tells me in the pleasantest manner that you have not forgotten me, and the reading of it has afforded me no common degree of pleasure. This work of yours has given me two longings: the one to revisit that enchanting country of which you have drawn so many varied and striking pictures; the other to induce you to revisit this place, where you have left a very pleasing remembrance of the short time you passed amongst us. As to the first, I believe I should view Italy even with increased delight after more than fifty years' absence. I was then a very young, though a very eager observer; I am now a very old one, and hardly less eager, but age and infirmities, were there no other obstacles, forbid any hope of so long a journey. The second, that of seeing you here, I will not despair of, and of being able to talk to you *vivâ voce* about many things in your poems, and thence of many others connected with them in your mind, and which I should delight to hear. I also wish to have my revenge and to shew you (*anch' io son pittore*) a number of pictures I have been producing since you saw the place, working with the materials of nature; they are, as you may remember, most abundant; and I have endeavoured to form with them such compositions, from the foreground to the most distant objects, as would satisfy the eye of a judicious painter. I have had the satisfaction of seeing more than one excellent artist, and one of them—Lord Aylesford—extremely averse to have anything pointed out to him as a good subject for a drawing, take his stand exactly where I wished, and where I had secretly conducted him, and draw the composition as if he had discovered it himself, *tale quale* and *con amore*. This picture-making (you well know the delight of it in poetry) is a most amusing and interesting operation; it is, however, a very nice one, and the varied frame of each composition, itself an essential part, is to be studied almost to a twig. You remember, I dare say, a fanciful but ingenious idea, I forget whose, that in every block of marble a beautiful statue lay concealed, and that you had only to clear away the rubbish. It is the same, *mutatis mutandis*, in this place, and in every place of a similar kind; innumerable pictures are concealed, and I am endeavouring *poco a poco* to clear away what, after due deliberation, I judge to be rubbish. You have lately been viewing all that is most excellent in real and painted landscapes, and must come here and look at my operations and see whether I have followed the principles of the great masters of composition. All this, I am afraid, will not appear very seducing; but I know you love drawings of the old masters, and have yourself some very good specimens. I particularly remember one of Giorgione that I envied you. Now I have books full of the old masters which I believe you have scarcely looked into, and though I have no Giorgione I have a Titian or two, and many drawings well worth your notice.

'I must now ask you a question or two by letter, *en attendant mieux*. Is the story of Jorasse, his fall into the barathrum, the dreadful canopy of ice, the river that ran under it, his plunge into the deep water, and his rising into Paradise—all true? A more striking one never was invented, and the *dénouement* is the most sudden and most delightfully surprising of all *dénouements*. You have done it justice, and that is saying everything. I pointed it out the other day to a friend of mine of great taste and sensibility, and he was as much delighted with it as I was.

'Now a word or two about the ancient larch. I wish I had been with you, for I never saw an ancient larch and long very much to see one, and particularly on one account. The larches I have, some of them nearly ninety feet high, are mere infants compared with yours, for they were all planted by my father and are probably about my age, if so old. Several of them have roots above ground of a size and character that seem to belong to trees of at least twice their age, as you shall see when you come here, for come you must. Now I want to know whether you happened to notice the roots of your ancient larch, "majestic though in ruins." I am afraid you were occupied with the human figure sitting near it, and scarcely observed them. You love a little anecdote, and I will tell you one of Sir Joshua. He mentioned to me his having once gone down the Wye from Monmouth to Chepstow. I asked him whether he was not very much struck with the inside of Tintern Abbey at the opening of the door. "I believe," he said, "it is very striking, but I was so taken up with the groups of begging figures round the door, and their look of want and wretchedness, that I could not take my eyes from them." The fact is, that he did not care very much about landscape of any kind in nature, and had only a high relish for it in the works of the greatest masters, particularly in the backgrounds of Titian.

'Among other numerous longings, you have given me a very strong one for a sight of the Orsini Palace, its noble gardens, terrace above terrace, and of the Domenichino, so interesting a subject by such a painter. I did not stop at Modena, shame upon me, and never heard of this Ginevra; but the main part of her story I remember hearing from my mother when I was quite a child, and it made a deep and lasting impression on me. You may perhaps be curious to hear it in its simple English dress, and I believe I can tell it you very much as I had it from my mother. A number of young girls, she said, were playing at hide-and-seek in an old rambling mansion; one of them, a very lovely and beautiful girl and very eager in the sport, could never be found by her companions during the game, and after it was over was still missing. Weeks passed and still no tidings of her, when one of the family going into a lumber-room in a remote part of the house smelt a terrible stench, which seemed to come from a chest that was locked. It was burst open, when the putrid remains of the poor girl appeared, and the spring-lock told the horrible story. The same catastrophe may certainly have happened in England, and the name of the person and the place have been forgotten, but it seems more probable that the whole was taken from Ginevra, though the circumstances are altered. In any case, I was highly pleased to read my nursery story so impressively told, and with so many circumstances that give it both dignity and interest and what mine wants, " a local habitation and a name." In mine, however, to which I have an early attachment, the play of hide-and-seek seems more naturally to account for an unfrequented part of the house, and a hiding-place being sought after, and there is something peculiarly terrible and affecting in the idea of the discoverer, the father or mother, or perhaps the lover of the miserable victim, being led by the alarming stench to the fatal chest, and seeing, when it was forced open, the corpse of what they so loved, got green in death and festering in her tomb, and while all her loveliness was fresh in their memory. I never can think without shuddering of the moment

> 'When the spring-lock that lay in ambush there
> Fastened her down for ever,

of the unavailing screams and struggles, the lingering agonies, and so near those she loved, so near assistance —*si forte pedem, si forte tulissent.*

'You have been equally happy in your gay and your gloomy pictures. As to the first, I have no lakes to shew you, no passage boats with peasant girls, fruits and flowers gliding by, nor trellises and corridors, vintages in their hey-day, barks sailing up and down, all pleasure, life and motion on land and water; but as to your dark tints, I have ancient yews that will match the lonely chapel of St. Bernard, or the gloomy silence of St. Bruno. Your ancient larch is probably a child to my yews, some of which must remember the Conquest, and one or two the Heptarchy. Rembrandt would delight in them, and give full effect to their black massy trunks and spreading branches; but I should beg Claude's assistance for the aerial tint of a distant mountain that I have let in, and that appears in one or two instances, under the solemn canopy. I long to shew you what relief and value they give to each other. I should have thanked you sooner for all the pleasure you have given me, but the foul fiend Dyspepsia, who never quite leaves me, has lately been unusually harassing, and as you well know, when the stomach, *Magister artis, ingenique largitor*, is out of order, the head is good for nothing.

'Believe me, my dear Sir,

'Ever most truly yours,

'U. PRICE.'

'When will the Second Part come out? Another longing.'

Crabb Robinson records an evening he spent in the middle of June at the house of Miss Catharine Sharpe, the step-daughter of Rogers's sister Maria, a sketch of whose noble life I have already given. Rogers and the Flaxmans were there, and Daniel Rogers from Wassall. Crabb Robinson describes the latter as having 'the appearance of being a superior man, which S. Sharpe reports him to be. Rogers,' he adds, 'who knows all the gossip of literature, says that on the best authority he can affirm that Walter Scott has received 100,000*l.* honorarium for his poems and other works, including the Scotch novels. Walter Scott is Rogers's friend, but Rogers did not oppose Flaxman's remark that his works have in no respect tended to improve the moral condition of mankind.'

Among Rogers's correspondence this summer are letters from Lord St. Helens, who speaks of himself and Rogers as devotees of Gray, and says that 'a tracing from the curious portrait of Etough' is the best production of Mason's pencil he has seen, and proves 'that its real *forte*, as may perhaps also be said of that of his pen, was in the way of satire and caricature.' Certain references in the following letter give it value.

Robert Southey to Samuel Rogers.

'Keswick: 21 Sept., 1823.

' Dear Sir,—Having been asked for a letter of introduction to you, I somewhat hastily promised it, presuming upon your kindness to excuse a liberty which at this moment I feel that I have no right to take. Mr. Carne came to me with a letter from Wordsworth, De Quincey having found him at Professor Wilson's and taken him to Rydal. He has travelled in the East, has visited Lady Hester Stanhope, passed ten days in captivity with the Arabs in the Desert, and seen something of the horrors which are going on in Greece, and as he likes better to tell his adventures than to set them forth in a book, his conversation is very interesting. It will remind you perhaps of poor Kemble by making you ready to exclaim, "O my *a-ches*!" but his stories are not the worse for the want of aspirates, nor his pronunciation the better for being Ionic, as well as Stafford or Lancashire.

' Should you be in town during the winter, I hope to have the pleasure of seeing you and receiving your forgiveness for this intrusion. Believe me, my dear Sir, yours with sincere respect,

' ROBERT SOUTHEY.'

Rogers was at this time visiting Lord Grenville at Dropmore; and more than five pages of his 'Recollections' (177, 178, 179, 180, 181 and part of 182) consist of notes of Lord Grenville's talk during this visit. Lord Grenville was four years older than Rogers. He had been Prime Minister in 1806 and 1807, but was not now in office; and though only sixty-four, regarded himself as a statesman retired from business. There are the materials of history in the talk of such men when, like Lord Grenville, they tell of what they have seen and done, and their listener has the accurate and retentive memory of Samuel Rogers. Lord Grenville was one of the men for whom he felt, and always expressed, an affectionate admiration. Writing the notes of his next visit, in July 1825, Rogers describes him as sitting summer and winter on the same sofa, his favourite books on the shelf just over his head. One of these was Roger Ascham, whose works were close to his hand. Another was Milton, who was always within reach. Lord Bathurst left them one day as they were walking in the garden. He was Secretary of State, and Lord Grenville was out of office. 'Lord Bathurst is gone to his business,' said Rogers. 'I would rather he was there than I,' replied Lord Grenville, 'if I was to live my life over again I should do very differently.' 'We sat down to rest in the Pinery seat,' says Rogers, 'inscribed with the Virgilian motto "Pulcherrima pinus in hortis," and the clock of the stables struck twelve.' 'That voice will be heard,' said Lord Grenville, 'long after I am in my grave and forgotten;' and Rogers adds affectionately to his record, 'Not forgotten. S. R.' It was this sympathy with the great men whose words he has reported to posterity, this capacity for admiration, which has made Rogers's 'Recollections' pleasant and instructive reading to the statesmen, the historians, and the thinkers of two generations.

In the succeeding chapter there will be found other proofs of the confidence with which Lord Grenville treated Rogers. One sign of this confidence, in addition to those recorded in the 'Recollections,' is found in Moore's Diary.

In the autumn Rogers was at Bowood, and Moore records that he produced some English verses of Lord Grenville's, to the surprise of all the party (which included Lord Aberdeen, Lord John Russell and Abercromby), 'who seemed to agree that he was one of the least poetical men they could point out. The verses were a paraphrastic translation of the lines at the beginning of the "Inferno," "O degli altri poeti onore e lume," and very spiritedly done.' I find the lines in Rogers's Commonplace Book.

From Dante, by Lord Grenville.

> Thou art that Virgil, thou that fountain head
> Whence the rich stream of eloquence has spread
>   From age to age its pure and ample tide;
> And by the zeal and love I ever bore
> For thee, thy volumes, and thy sacred lore,
> Glory and light of those famed bards of yore,
>   Through all my studious course be Thou my guide.

Moore continues that he walked out with Lord John Russell and Rogers, and a few days later saw Rogers and Lord Aberdeen off to Longleat. The autumns were usually spent either abroad or in a long round of these visits to country houses.

A letter illustrates his relations with another eminent person who had sent him a New Year's gift, and to whom Rogers had consequently addressed a letter of thanks and social gossip.

Lord Ashburnham to Samuel Rogers.

'Ashburnham: Jan. 21st, 1824.

'My dear Rogers,—As many thanks to you for encouraging me to flatter myself that the memento which I lately ventured to obtrude upon you was not unacceptable.

'I wish that I could have had that opportunity, which you mention, of congratulating Knight. He is more to be congratulated than any other man, on any acquisition, of any sort; being gifted with such extraordinary powers of enjoyment, both intellectual and sensual; from Homer to a haunch of venison; from a drawing of Claude's to a dish of coffee; from Venus de' Medici to Venus de' Meretrici.

'But what I have most to congratulate him, and all his friends too, is on the accomplishment of my prediction. When I saw him in the beginning of November, full of blue pills and blue (not to say black) devils, I told him that he would, should, and must be himself again. And so he nearly was before I left town; at least he was then more than anyone else.

'I thank you for telling me what Angostini's pictures are really sold for. If I could get for mine what they are worth, I am sure that I ought not to keep them—with such a collection (that I cannot part with) of children. To all of them, great and little, I have remembered you according to your injunctions, as well as to Lady Asburnham. They all charge me to express their acknowledgments.

'Your treasured tale, and legendary lore, are among *their* Pleasures of Memory. Believe me to be,

'Most truly and sincerely yours,

'ASHBURNHAM.

'Rubens arrived safe. I know not where to put him. You must assist at a consultation in the spring.

'I wish you had had our present January weather when you were here last July.'

Moore's Diary for 1824 is fuller of Rogers than ever. The fourth volume, which reaches from September 1822 to October 1825, appropriately contains an admirable engraving of Sir Thomas Lawrence's portrait of Rogers. Whenever Moore went to London he spent much time at his house, and met him continually at the houses of other people. On the 29th of February he finds Luttrell, Lord John Russell, Mrs. Graham, Miss Rogers, and Lady Davy, at Rogers's dinner table. A day or two later he and Rogers call on Lord Essex and Lady Jersey; the latter asks them to her house to a party to celebrate her birthday, and says that, 'Brougham has bargained for a broiled bone for supper.' Rogers, however, prefers the 'Antient Music' concert to Lady Jersey's party, and so Moore goes home to dine with him and to work in the evening. Next day Rogers pleases Moore by reporting Luttrell's opinion that if anybody can make such a subject as 'Captain Rock' lively, Moore will. Rogers was just as fond of reporting pleasant things to his friends as he was of saying sharp things. There is more of him in Moore's Diary than in any other book, and he is constantly presented there as saying what gave Moore pleasure and doing acts of generous kindness to him and others. But Moore's Diary is too long to read, and Rogers is buried in it rather than enshrined. Wordsworth was in London this spring, and Moore finds him in Rogers's company at Miss White's. He meets him also at dinner at Hallam's. Hallam was then principally known as one of the Edinburgh Reviewers. His 'View of the State of Europe during the Middle Ages' had been published several years, and he was now writing his 'Constitutional History.' At this period the Athenæum Club was founded: Davy, Faraday, Chantrey, Scott, Lawrence, Heber, and Moore being among its founders, and Rogers one of its earliest members.

Two letters of this period from old friends give interesting glimpses of people and places.

Helen Maria Williams to Samuel Rogers.

'My dear Sir,—You have probably forgotten the handwriting of this letter, and even the remembrance of the signature must be almost lost in the lapse of time—yet, I venture in quality of our long, long acquaintance, to introduce to your notice a very amiable foreigner who goes to pass a few weeks in London, and who has claims to your attentions of far more value than my recommendation. M. Van S. Gouvensvert is one of the most distinguished men of letters of Holland, has translated Homer into Dutch verse, and is the author of many elegant poetical compositions confined to his own country only because they are written in that unknown language, Dutch. He wishes to know what is best worth knowing in England, and I therefore address him to the author of the "Pleasures of Memory." The kindness you may show M. Van S. Gouvensvert will, like other good actions, bring its own reward, for you will, I am sure, be much pleased with his conversation and manners.

'I last summer talked of you, a subject never indifferent to me, with Sir James Mackintosh, whom I saw here *en passant*. He told me a trait of your conduct towards a brother poet, that made me weep.

'I lost not long since the last surviving member of my own family, Mrs. Purvis Williams, the most virtuous character I ever met with, if virtue consists, as I believe it does, in living only for others. She had always been to me a second mother. She was old, but I see no reason in that circumstance for regretting the objects of our affection less; we had passed life together, and had remembrances that were our own. I should now be quite alone in the world if my nephews did not still give interest to my life. I have passed some time in Holland with the eldest, who is a Protestant minister at Amsterdam,[1] and has acquired very great celebrity as a preacher. He is certainly one of the first of the present day on the Continent. He is married, and surrounded by a little smiling race, who enter the world as gaily as if there was nothing to do in it but to be happy. My youngest nephew is deeply versed in the sciences, and has already obtained distinguished reputation in France as a writer. For myself, I am among the number of past things, but I can

[1] This was Athanase Coquerel the elder, the leader of the French Unitarians, the popular preacher of the Oratoire; representative of Paris after the Revolution of 1848, who proposed in the Assembly the abolition of the punishment of death.

still hold my pen, and am scribbling a little sketch which will perhaps have some interest. I hope you still employ your elegant and happy leisure in courting the beautiful moral muse to whom you owe so many partial favours, and whom it would be ungrateful indeed were you to neglect. Pardon, my dear Sir, this long letter, and believe me, with the highest esteem,

'Your faithful friend,

'H. M. WILLIAMS.'

'Amsterdam: April 24th, 1825.

'Do you ever see the venerable Mrs. Barbauld? If so, I should wish to be recalled to her remembrance.

Richard Sharp to Samuel Rogers.

'Rome: 21 April, 1824.

Lured by thy verse, behold once more
Thy friend fair Italy explore.
And tho' by suffering taught I shun
Her unrelenting summer sun,
Yet now I woo its beams to cheer
The gloom of an expiring year;
Where, 'mid the ruins round her spread
Rome proudly lifts her mitred head
Once circled by th' imperial crown
To which the conquer'd world bow'd down.
 Feeble, though reverend in decay,
She claims not now her ancient sway,
But begs a homage, freely paid,
Less to the living than the dead,
Whose honoured tombs now mouldering round
Have power to consecrate the ground,
And though a thousand Domes arise,
More sees the Memory than the eyes.

Yet here, the work of modern hands,
In state the noblest temple stands
That to his great Creator's praise
The piety of man could raise;
Here, too, as breathing nature warm,
Dwells many a bright angelic form,
Hewn from the rock by matchless skill,
Once Gods, and almost worshipped still.
And here the pencil's magic hues
Along the walls their spells diffuse,
Calling saints, heroes from the grave
Again to teach, again to save.

The Eternal City as I trace
The Present to the Past gives place,
The spirits of the dead appear
And sounds divine transport my ear.
I listen, heedless of the throng,
To Tully's speech or Maro's song,
Or at the storied arch I view,
Gaze at the Triumph winding through,
Or mark the horse and horseman leap
Fearlessly down the yawning steep,
Or him who singly dares oppose
(Striding the bridge) a host of foes;
Now shuddering, the stern Consul see
His rebel sons to death decree,
Or in the Senate hail the blow
That lays the Great Usurper low,
But who, on thrones and robed in state,
Sit silently and smile at Fate,
The conscript sires. Though fierce and rude,
The conqueror is himself subdued,
Drops his red spear and bends the knee,
Esteeming each a Deity.

Oh! how in latter life it cheers
To triumph o'er the power of years!

Calm'd, not exhausted, to perceive
That we can feel, admire, believe
E'en to the last, as in our prime,
Spite of the malice of old Time;
Not more our joy than pride to know
That the chill'd blood again can glow,
That fancy still has wings to soar
As high as she was wont before,
And Hope still listens to her song
As erst, when credulous and young;
That there are vales where smiling spring
Is lovelier than the poets sing,
And Nature's bright realities
Transcend what painting can devise,
Where May can trust, in field or bow'r,
Her blossoms to the morning hour,
Nor dreads the venomous East should breathe
To blight the flow'rets in her wreath,
And scarcely swells a bud in vain
Of blushing fruit or golden grain.

 Alas, fair land, that thy rich dower
Should be the prize of lawless Power!
Yielded to Vandal, Moor, or Gaul,
Or bigot sloth, far worse than all.
Oh, grief! that blessings too profuse
Should change to curses by th' abuse
That virtue, freedom, still must fly
For shelter to a frozen sky.
Like gold, all good requires alloy,
And man must suffer to enjoy.
Once thy possessors, great in arms,
Defended and preserved thy charms,
Well taught (alas, in times gone by!)
Bravely to conquer or to die.
Then the rude Hun rude welcome found
And with his blood manured the ground,

Though now, his haughty banner waves
High o'er his humbled fathers' graves.
  Now must thy sons thy fate regret,
The present bear, the past forget,
Blush when they hear their fathers' fame,
And hide in smiles their grief and shame.
Not long—soon shall the smouldering fire
Explode in thunder or expire,
Oh, not the last!—in vain they dare
(The crown'd conspirators) to share
The world between them as their prey,
Willing to own their sovereign sway.
As soon shall they forbid the sun
His daily course thro' Heav'n to run,
Arrest the ocean tides, or bind
The pinions of the wandering wind.
  But let this pass, here still we find
Much to console the cultur'd mind;
Art, Science, Letters still survive
The Liberty that bade them thrive,
And many a poet of high name
Upholds his country's ancient fame.
Thy last great theme: well chosen by thee
The bard inspired by Memory!
And greatly shall thy lasting lay
Her hospitality o'erpay,
Long long the rival to remain
Ev'n of her noblest native strain.

'Genoa: 12 May, 1824.

'My dear Friend,—I have detained these newly born natives of Italy some weeks in the hope of their improving, but I find them incorrigible. They stammer sadly, and when they speak plainly they often talk nonsense. I now send them to you chiefly because I do not wish to appear to want respect for the country that you have adopted. Indeed, what could I hope to say, on a subject which you have attended to, that has escaped your observation, who have a sharper sight than I pretend to have?

'I verified, on this visit, the Venetian story which I told you in 1821, and saw every evening the lamp and the torches in St. Mark's Place. On the lake of Como I heard of a recent tragedy well known to the inhabitants of its shores.

'An old lady and her daughter Rosalia lived at Domaso in narrow circumstances. The latter was very young and very beautiful, the glory of the lake. At a sort of half fair, half religious fête, Vincenzo, a young man of Menagio, saw her, fell in love with her, watched her all day at a distance, and at length was fortunate enough to become known to her by saving her from a wild heifer that pursued her. Intimacy and mutual love followed, but Vincenzo's father was rich and refused his consent. The young man fell dangerously ill on being thwarted in his affection, and wrote to her, as he thought on his death bed, to pray for a last interview; the mother allowed her to go, but would accompany her, and being fearful of the water, they took a lad for a sort of guide along the narrow path. In one place it ascends a rocky precipice called *Sasso rancio* where in 1799, some years before, a company of Russian foot soldiers fell into the water and were drowned. The mother being feeble leaned on the boy, but suddenly hearing a shriek looked round and saw Rosalia sink for ever into the lake. Vincenzo after a severe struggle for life recovered, but became unsettled in his mind. The first thought that occurred to him was to fly to the *Sasso rancio* and to throw himself down the rock where Rosalia had fallen. It, however, struck him that as she was innocent and would go to heaven, he should never see her more, as his wickedness in self-murder would consign him to another place. He led for a few months, among the mountains, a rambling life, when he was found dead, having been killed by a bear. Take this as a specimen of my " Tour on the Continent," in four quartos, which in proper time you will have the advantage of reading. The principal chapters will be on the Rhine, Heidelberg, Baden (pretty Baden), the Black Forest (this will be full of dangers and escapes), the Lake of the Four Cantons, the Pass of the Brunig, the Oberland of Bern (this will contain many interesting recollections of a visit paid to it in 1821 along with a great living poet), Vevay, Dumont, Chamouni, St. Gervais, the Simplon, Como, Milan, Venice, Bologna, Florence, Rome, Naples, Paestum, Lucca, Genoa, Mont Cenis, and the Chartreuse. France must be a separate publication, though, as I was asleep while I crossed it, I must poach for materials in the travels of Lady Morgan and Lord Blantyre. Do speak to Murray in time. I only ask ten thousand pounds for the copyright.

' We were hardly five months at Rome, in excellent apartments once tenanted by Miss Berrys, and basked in the sun almost the whole winter. It was troublesome to get out of the way of invitations, for Rome was a sort of Brighton in that respect; Lord Kinnaird, Lord Dudley, the late Duchess of Devonshire, and Lady Mary Durham almost kept open house, so did many others. Lord and Lady Normanby and Lord and Lady Belfast acted private plays every week, and great was the canvassing to procure tickets. Fazakerley was my daily companion, and I saw a good deal of Morrit and of Lord and Lady Compton. Much going out in the afternoon and a walk twice a day on the Pincian Hill filled up my time very amusingly; that is, the time I could spare from the statues, pictures, studios, &c. &c. At Naples I had equal resources, especially in an old acquaintance, Mr. Hamilton's, house and in Lord Ponsonby. The latter has taken great pains with himself, and is the most improved man that I know. I always liked his manners, but now he is full of sense and information. Adversity is an excellent schoolmaster.

My sister's health and spirits had induced her to beg, or rather to make it a sort of condition, not to visit, and Maria is not come out, but her time was fully occupied by sights, music, and masters. The latter came daily, and I got a young Italian lady, known to Fazakerley, to go about with us in the morning and to dine with us, &c., that she might acquire facility in speaking Italian. However, much as I liked every thing, I must own, to speak out, that I greatly prefer home to travelling (except for short tours), and my own country to the Continent. What compensation is there for the absence of friends? None; not even the Alps and the Vatican. What society is there abroad to be compared, for instance, to Holland House or to the little dinners in St. James's Place, or to be mentioned when the conversation of London is thought of? What is the Pincian to our little strollings from your window in the Green Park?

> Ecquid erat tanti Romam vidisse sepultam,
> Ut te tam dulci possem caruisse sodale![1]

[1] *Silvarum Liber*, 'Epitaphium Damonis,' lines 115 and 118

'I dislike quotation, but these lines are Milton's, and they so exactly express what I felt that I could not resist the temptation of using them. He laments in them his absence from Charles Deodatus, his friend, and Rome is his instance.

'I am obliged to count over my riches of this kind that are left, having lost so much in the little year of my absence. Our warm-hearted friend Lord Erskine was so young at his age that I somehow considered him as immortal. Payne Knight too! Ricardo! but I thank God still nearer friends are left. I send this by a private courier either to Paris or to London, and I hope to take you by the hand about June 10. So do not trouble yourself to write. You have, I hope, been well, happy and diligent during my absence.

'Ever yours most affectionately,

'R. SHARP.

'Pray mention my remembrances to Miss Rogers.'

The death of Lord Erskine (which took place on the 17th of November, 1823), of Payne Knight, and of Ricardo, to which Richard Sharp refers, were not the only literary losses of the time. On the 14th of May Moore was calling at Colburn's library when the shopman told him of the death of Lord Byron, the news of which had just arrived in London. After verifying it at the *Morning Chronicle* office and writing a note to Murray about the Memoirs, he went off to Rogers and found that the intelligence had not reached him, and he records that in the same way Rogers had called nineteen years before and found him uninformed of the death of Nelson.

Moore's one anxiety was the Memoirs, which he had sold to Murray, and had half arranged to redeem. His first impulse was to seek Rogers's advice. Rogers advised him to wait for some movement by Murray, and meanwhile to ask Brougham's opinion on the whole subject. Lord Russell omits the long account Moore gave in his Diary of the negotiations which resulted in the burning of the Byron manuscript, a proceeding of which Rogers always consistently expressed his disapproval. He was quite sure that Byron never thought the manuscript would meet with such a fate. He had glanced it through, and had not seen the gross things in it, which Lord John Russell, who had read it nearly all, says were confined to three or four pages. Rogers recollected one story Lord Byron had told in it. On his wedding night, starting suddenly out of his first sleep, he saw that a taper which was burning in the room was throwing a ruddy light through the crimson curtains. He woke up with a start, exclaiming in a voice loud enough to wake his sleeping wife, "Good God, I am surely in hell." Lord Russell assures the world that it is no loser by the burning of these Memoirs, but Rogers thought it unjustifiable, and said that Moore did not consult him about it, but went to Luttrell, who did not care, and who at once consented to the sacrifice. Moore paid Murray back with interest the 2,000 guineas he had advanced for the manuscript, and there was a great desire to compensate Moore for his loss. Moore, however, refused the money, and when he had done so called to tell Rogers of his resolution. He found Rogers and his sister equally inclined, with his other friends, to consider the refusal as altogether too romantic a sacrifice. 'Recapitulated my reasons,' says Moore, 'much more strongly than I could ever put them to paper. Saw they were both touched by them, though Rogers would not allow it; owned that he would not receive the money in such a case, but said that my having a wife and children made all the difference possible in the views he ought to take of it.' Moore adds, with a feeling which does him lasting honour: 'This avowal was, however, enough for me. More mean things have been done in this world (as I told him) under the shelter of "wife and children" than under any other pretext that worldly-mindedness can resort to. He said at last, smiling at me, "Well, your life may be a good poem, but it is a d——d bad matter of fact!"'

The business did not end there. In July the funeral took place, and Moore came up to it, and persuaded Rogers to go with him to the ceremony. 'Our coachful,' says Moore, 'consisted of Rogers, Campbell, Colonel Stanhope, Orlando (the Greek Deputy), and myself.' After the funeral Moore and Rogers walked in the park, and Rogers not only advised him not to make any communication to Byron's family about materials for his Life, but said, 'I entreat of you to take no step of this kind till I release you. I have particular reasons for it.' Moore thought he knew that the mystery related to some plan for settling the 2,000*l.* on little Tom.

Moore records during this visit to London that one evening he looked, with Rogers, over his 'Commonplace Book,' and found some highly curious accounts of his conversations with Fox, Grattan, and the Duke of Wellington. These are the 'Recollections,' published after his death, to which I have often referred. He quotes from Rogers the statement that Sheridan had twice told him that every sentence in 'The Stranger' as it is acted was written by him. In August Rogers was at Bowood, where Dumont and the Hollands were staying. Moore was, of course, full of Sheridan. Rogers mentioned that Sheridan's father had said of him, 'Talk of the merit of Dick's comedy, there's nothing in it. He had but to dip the pencil in his own heart and he'd find there the characters of both Joseph and Charles.' Rogers quoted Lord Chatham's saying, on a motion which nobody seconded, 'My lords, I stand alone; my lords, I stand, like our first parent, naked but not ashamed.' Another day Rogers quoted Chatham's saying when commenting on a speech of the King's, written by Mr. Fox (afterwards Lord Holland) and the Duke of Newcastle, 'Here rolls the Rhone, black, turbid and rapid, while here steals the Saône, whispering with flowers on its banks.' Another day Rogers walked home with Moore to his cottage. 'Looked over Bessy's books, kissed the children, and was very amiable.'

There are further glimpses of interesting people in one of Uvedale Price's amusing letters.

Uvedale Price to Samuel Rogers.

'Foxley: July 26, 1824.

'Dear Rogers,— . . . We were detained at Cashiobury two days longer than we intended. . . . With me these were by no means idle days; I was most busily employed on a part of the place that is known, and that perhaps you may know, by the name of the Horse-shoe

Dell: it is a little amphitheatre, a hollow, nearly flat in the middle, and surrounded on every side by gently rising ground. Many years ago cedars of Lebanon, red cedars, laurels, laburnums, cockspur thorns, &c.—these last the largest and the most picturesque I have ever seen—were planted there, and most judiciously (for it can hardly have been mere accident) placed on the top and the sides of the swelling ground, the bottom being left unplanted; in short, exactly as I could have wished such ground to be planted. Many of the trees, however, though by no means crowded, had from their luxuriant growth begun to injure one another, and the arena, which had so properly been left unplanted, was choked up with chance seedlings, chiefly ash, which concealed the varied form of the banks, and would soon have concealed even the trees upon them. Lord Essex gave me *carte blanche*, and though in the midst of the hay, gave me several workmen. I began by clearing the *arena*; and, after cutting out a quantity of dead boughs from the beautiful plants they disfigured, cautiously gave room to the principal trees, and those of the best forms, by pruning the others from them. I then made some paths and openings where none appear to have ever been made, so as to enter this little *sanctum* in the best directions. I wish you had been with me: I should have liked to show you the *status ante* and *post bellum*, and I think you would have been amused in seeing the progress of the work; it is, however, only *sbozzato*, for I had only two days, those very hot, and I not very stout, though "very eager." My principal operator in pruning, &c. was a common labourer, but sufficiently intelligent, and who took to it all very kindly: his name is John Elliman, and if you should happen to light upon him at your next trip to Cashiobury, he will be a much better cicerone than the Bostanghi Pacha, *Dominusve terræ fastidiosus*: but this quite between ourselves. It must be owned that I am not a little unconscionable, first to try your patience with a long account of all I have been doing and then to propose your looking it all over with such a cicerone! but we are mighty fond of our own little performances in every way. So ends the history of the last days at Cashiobury.

'Postera lux oritur multo gratissima,

for I never passed a pleasanter day in all respects than that at Dropmore. I delight in Lord Grenville, so we do all, and in his creation; and wish I had happened to see the spot before he began the work, and while the ale-house was standing. This was my case in regard to London. I left it with Swallow Street, &c., in all their dirt and meanness: Waterloo Bridge and all the grand openings from Carlton House to the Regent's Park were made during my ten years' rustication; and the impression was, I am sure, in proportion. I never heard of any one who regretted Swallow Street, and of one only who was angry at anything Lord Grenville had done at Dropmore; that one, as Peploe told me yesterday, was our late Dean of Hereford, Dr. Gretton. It seems that Lord Grenville had been sacrilegious enough to pull down a house where he had kept a school, and he talked of it with as much indignation as an ancient Greek would have done if the Academy where Plato taught had been destroyed. This Dean of ours—begging Lord Ashburnham's pardon, who has been his pupil—was the arrantest pedagogue that ever wielded a rod; his head, face, wig, and his whole person seemed cut out of wood, and, as some one said, there was syntax in every line of his countenance.

'To return from this digression, we got to Dropmore in time enough for a short walk before dinner, which, instead of that absurd fashionable hour of seven, which cuts off the most delightful part of the whole day, was at five, and after coffee, the weather being exactly what one could wish it, set out on our walk. To me, who am not less fond of highly ornamented than of wild picturesque scenery, the whole garden was extremely interesting, and my pleasure was enhanced (many a time have I found it otherwise) by looking it over with the proprietors. Lady Grenville seems as fond of everything as her lord, and from the observations she occasionally made appeared to me to have very just feeling and discrimination. There is an amusing contrast in their manners: his remarkably placid and calm, though far from cold; hers as strikingly eager. I have seldom seen any rockwork in gardens that had not rather a trifling paltry appearance: that of Lord Grenville's is on a scale which alone would preserve it from such epithets; and he has managed to give it—the blocks themselves being large and massy—a sort of architectural grandeur, and when the various plants and creepers begin to shoot luxuriantly as they promise to do, the effect will be excellent. He has, I think, been no less successful in a no less difficult and risky operation with other materials—that of placing large bodies of trees, many of them singularly bent, so as to form arches at various directions at the foot [of] an artificial mound he has raised so as to command a view of the distant country; and on the edge of the mound by way of foreground to the distance (I don't know what has possessed me to describe to you what you know better than I do) he has placed large stumps and roots of trees. I had heard of all this, and thought it rather a hazardous undertaking: and the whole at present, being but just done and not quite finished, has, of course, a crude appearance, but it is so well designed that I have no doubt of the effect when the plants and climbers begin to answer the purpose for which they were intended, that of a disguise and an ornament. Methinks I hear you crying out in a lamentable tone, *Ohe! jam satis est!* and in truth, I am rather ashamed of having given you, and for the second time in the same letter, such a *plat de mon métier*, but I was so full of what I had been doing and seeing, that I must have burst if I had not given it vent; and you are the victim. Nothing could be more flattering than the wish both Lord and Lady Grenville expressed that we would prolong our stay. We were well inclined to do so, had it been possible, for the style of living is remarkably easy, and everything, without any parade, full of comfort; we shall have no scruple in accepting their invitation for another year, when I hope you will meet us, and share and add to our enjoyments.

'After this one day at Dropmore, but, in Homer's language, πάντων ἄξιον ἦμαρ, we went to St. Anne's with the full intention of going from thence to Asburnham, although the two additional days at Cashiobury had thrown us very late; when I, in my turn, was disabled from travelling by the most disabling of all complaints

... and thus, after all the suspense in which we had been keeping Lord and Lady Ashburnham, after their extreme kindness and indulgence, we were most reluctantly obliged to give up entirely what we had so much set our hearts upon. His answer in some degree comforted us: they could have received us on the day we proposed, and have allowed us to stay the whole of the next, but must have sent us away on the following one. The whole day would have been another ἄξιον ἦμαρ, and well worth the journey, yet after all, however amiable, we must have been very troublesome guests at the eve of such a departure. Four quiet days at St. Anne's restored me a good deal; but as my complaint and also my daughter's were not unlikely to return, we thought it both safest and best to give up our intended tour, and get to Foxley *pian piano* by easy journeys; and here we are, feeling the delights and comforts of home, and looking forward with great pleasure to the time when you and your sister will arrive. We depend on your promise, and shall be grievously disappointed if anything should prevent your coming. I am busily employed with my two squirrels, well provided with high ladders and various cutting implements, in retouching my pictures, and clearing away the random foliage, as Mason calls it, that begins to disturb my compositions, and hide some of the distances; and all *à votre intention*; so you must have a black heart if you fail me. With our best regards to you and Miss Rogers, and wishing you a pleasant journey into Herefordshire, believe me,

'Most truly yours,
'U. Price.'

The same admirable letter writer writes again later in the same year.

Uvedale Price to Samuel Rogers.

'Foxley: Oct. 6, 1824.

'You are a very pretty fellow indeed to talk of breaking your heart if we do not come to town next year, when you are breaking ours, and your promise into the bargain, by not coming to us this; then, you throw out hopes of your coming another time, and talk of *next* year to a man of seventy-seven and upwards, and with one foot—but I won't tell lies; neither of mine is in the grave, nor, I really believe, very near it, and I hope to have many a pleasant walk and talk with you, though not here.'

He then fills several sheets with an elaborate discussion of the Latin and Greek pronunciation, and proceeds—

'I remember hearing that Queen Caroline, the wife of George II., when she first came to England, being very fond of oysters and having heard the fame of ours, desired to have some; the finest and freshest Colchester were procured; she would hardly touch them. Pyefleet were tried; she kicked at them, and declared that English oysters were good for nothing. One of her attendants guessed how the case stood, and luckily found out some refuse oysters, all but stinking, and brought them to her. "Ay," she cried, "these are the right sort; these have the true flavour of ours in Germany," and devoured the whole dish. Such, whether in an oyster or in higher matters, is the omnipotence of habit, and I am persuaded that if the change I have supposed in the execution of music were to be made, and to be continued (like our change in ancient recitation) for some centuries, and that then a few musicians, convinced of its absurdity, and wishing to bring about a reform, were, after practising in private, to execute a piece of music *according to time*, they would be hissed out of the orchestra, because their new mode, like the fresh oysters, had not the accustomed flavour; *noto contingit odore*, is the main point, to whatever sense we may address ourselves. I shall make no further excuses for the length of this discussion, if you happen to take an interest in it, a few pages are nothing, if you do not, a single page is a volume; *mais parlons d'autres choses.*

'And so, by your own frank confession, you showed my letter to Lord and Lady Grenville, and to a breach of promise added a breach of confidence. *Ah! double traître.* As, however, they were pleased with the manner in which I spoke of them, I cannot be angry, and I must say that I have great reliance on your tact, and am sure you would never show anything at all likely to hurt the feelings of either party. I certainly did leave Dropmore with a very strong and most favourable impression of everything there, in every way, and I wrote to you under that impression, just as it had remained in my mind. I regret not having known them earlier in life. I have lost a great deal, and I now feel truly anxious about him. I really believe I should have had the very great pleasure of seeing them both at Foxley this year, if he had not thought it necessary or, at least, prudent, to keep a stricter regimen than he well could from home, and to be within reach of his medical adviser; next year, I have some hopes, and if they should come who knows who might like to meet them? Whoever they may be, and however ill they may have behaved themselves, they shall be most kindly received.

'I wish I could have met you and the grand chorus of Bards at Bowood; it would have been a lucky moment, for though I so much like both Lord and Lady Lansdowne, and am so curious to see the place again after a very long interval, that I should have wished for nothing more, yet such a party I must own would have enhanced the pleasure. The only time I ever saw Bowood was with Knight, just forty years ago, for it was just before he published his " Landscape " and I my " Essay." Lord Lansdowne, I remember, used to look at us with some surprise when we were making very bold remarks on all that we saw. " He does not know," said Knight to me, " that we are great doctors." Not long afterwards we laid our respective claims before the public. This visit of ours was at the early part of the French Revolution; we found at Bowood the Duchesse de Levis and her mother; the next day Talleyrand arrived while we were at dinner. I was very much struck with the look he cast round the company, as he slowly walked in—it had the appearance of sullen haughtiness with a sort of suspicious examination. The day after in came the Duc de Levis, with a very different *allure*; a more ill-looking, mean-looking fellow I never saw, and so his handsome wife seemed to think by her manner of receiving him. So much for old times and the company I *did* meet at Bowood, now for those I unluckily did *not*. Bowles, as you know, I am well acquainted with, but not as a flute-player, and on that, as well as on every other account, I should have been very glad to have met him, and have heard him perform his water-music and do the honours of his water-party. A Greek poet is very severe on flute-players; he allows that the gods have given them a mind, but that out it flies with the first puff of their breath. . . .

'Crabbe, I once saw and that's all. I might have been acquainted with him, for Sir Joshua invited me to dinner, and told me I should meet Crabbe and Johnson. I had some engagement, probably (for I was then, as Ste. Fox used to say of himself, a young man of wit and pleasure about town) at some fine house to meet fine gentlemen and ladies : whatever it was, I was blockhead enough not to break it, and I have never forgiven myself. The dinner I went to and the company there I have never thought of from that time to this ; the dinner I did not go to I never should have forgotten, and if I had gone should now be recollecting every circumstance with pleasure and satisfaction, instead of crying, Oh, fool! fool! fool! I am, as you know, a great admirer of Crabbe; so were Charles Fox and Fitzpatrick. The first poem of his I ever saw (I believe his first work) was "The Library": Charles brought it to Foxley soon after it came out and read a good deal of it to us, Hare being one of the audience. I particularly remember his reading the part where Crabbe has described "the ancient worthies of romance," and has given in about twenty lines the essence of knight-errantry. When Fox came to

'And shadowy forms with staring eyes stalk round,

Hare cried out (you remember his figure and eyes), "That's meant for me."

'Moore I do not even know by sight. I could wish to be as well acquainted with him as I am with many of his works, for by what I have been told I shall not like him less than I do them; if I should be in town next year you must bring us together. His "Life of Sheridan" I shall send for the moment it is out, both on account of the writer and the subject. At one time I saw a good deal of Sheridan: he and his first wife passed some time here, and he is an instance that a taste for poetry and for scenery are not always united. Had this house been in the midst of Hounslow Heath, he could not have taken less interest in all around it. His delight was in shooting all day, and every day, and my gamekeeper said that of all the gentlemen he had ever been out with he never knew so bad a shot. This sorry performer "dans la guerre aux oiseaux" was, as all can bear witness,

'Dans les combats d'esprit savant maître d'escrime.

As Hare was with us there was some excellent sparring between those doughty knights, and the more amusing from their play being—as you well know who knew them both—very different. You must have known the first Mrs. Sheridan and have often heard her in private, though you have the misfortune—I wish I could share it with you—of not being old enough to have heard much of her in public. Hers was truly "a voice as of the cherub choir," and she was always ready to sing without any pressing. She sang here a great deal, to my infinite delight. But what had a peculiar charm was that she used to take my daughter, then a child, on her lap and sing a number of childish songs, with such a playfulness of manner and such a sweetness of look and voice as was quite enchanting. "Tempo passato, perchè non ritorni?" This I may say without meaning any offence to *il tempo presente*, for in spite of certain drawbacks that time *will* produce, and "of all that must accompany old age," I still have from various pursuits, and the interest I continue to take in them, and through the kindness and indulgence of my friends and of those who are most near and dear to me, many enjoyments suited to my time of life, in some degree even belonging to it,

> ' And from the dregs of life sometimes receive
> What the first sprightly runnings could not give.

One of the pleasures and privileges of old age is garrulity, and in that I have indulged myself to the top of my bent.

' With all our best regards and wishes *rancune tenante*, believe me, most truly yours,

'U. PRICE.'

Rogers was again at Dropmore in the late autumn, and here is a hint of further plans of pleasure—

Henry Luttrell to Samuel Rogers.

' My dear Rogers,—Lord and Lady Cowper will be—what shall I say, since you like neither the word "delighted" nor any of its synonyms?—they will feel just what you wish them to feel, neither more nor less, on your appearance at Panshanger on Saturday next. In brief, you will be most welcome, and they desire me to say so.

'We had here yesterday Lord and Lady Tankerville, Lords Lansdowne and Dudley, and William Ponsonby. Lord and Lady Gower came over to-day from their father's lately purchased villa in the neighbourhood. And so on I conclude, with a fresh infusion daily from town at the dinner hour, some sleepers and some returners, after the manner of villas. I shall remain here till Friday, and on Saturday without fail go to Panshanger.

'I thought I would finish my translation of the Greek epigram we talked of yesterday with reference to a certain gentleman. Here is the original, as well as I can recall what has not occurred to me since my boyhood. I wish you well through my Hellenic pothooks—

> Μῦν Ἀσκληπιάδης ὁ φιλάργυρος εἶδεν ἐν οἴκῳ,
>   Καὶ, " Τί θέλεις ἄρ', ἔφη, φίλτατε μῦ, παρ' ἐμοί ; "
> Ἡδὺ δ' ὁ μῦς γελάσας, " Μηδὲν, φίλε, φησὶ, φοβήθῃς,
>   Οὐχὶ τροφῆς παρά σοι χρῄζομεν, ἀλλὰ μονῆς."

'The following is as close a *fit* as I can make of it in English—

> 'Cries ——, in his closet once spying a mouse,
> "Pray what business have *you*, little friend, in my house?"
> Says the mouse with a smile to the lover of hoarding,
> "Don't be frightened, 'tis lodging I look for, not boarding."

To which might be added in the way of retort *courteous*

> 'Since that's all, replies ——, 'twould be hard to deny you,
> You may lodge how you can, but to board I defy you.

'Perhaps you will write me a line to say if it is *done and done* between us for Saturday. In that case you may direct here.

'Ever truly yours,
'HENRY LUTTRELL.

'Should you mention me in the house, pray offer my best compliments to Lord and Lady Grenville.

'Roehampton: Monday, Nov. 8, 1824.'

Rogers was not back in London till the middle of December, when Moore was there consulting him about undertaking to write Byron's Life. He in his turn showed Moore some of the prose essays which he had written to insert in 'Italy.' Of one of these now headed 'National Prejudices,' Moore reports Mackintosh's praise, and says he feels it 'would do one good to study such writing, if not as a model, yet as a chastener and simplifier of style, it being the very reverse of ambition or ornament.' Mackintosh wrote.

Sir James Mackintosh to Samuel Rogers.

'Cadogan Place: Thursday, 9 Dec. 1824.

'My dear Rogers,—I admire your beautiful little essay so truly that I don't know how to criticise it. I assure you sincerely that in my opinion Hume could not have improved the thoughts nor Addison amended the language. It is such a jewel that I am anxious to know where you are to place it.

'Ever yours,
'J. MACKINTOSH.

'Your last sentence but one reminds me of the famous sentence of St. Augustine on Toleration, and is as good.'[1]

Two letters—one on business, the other of pleasant talk—from the admirable letter writer already quoted, fitly close the year 1824.

Uvedale Price to Samuel Rogers.

'Foxley: Dec. 8th, 1824.

'You will very much oblige me by giving me your opinion and advice on what I am going to mention. In the sheets I am preparing for the press there are a number of Greek and Latin quotations, with some new marks over the syllables, and others employed in an unusual manner, it therefore is of consequence to me that my printer should be accurate and intelligent. Valpy had been often mentioned to me as such; and Knight, whose "Carmina Homerica" he printed, spoke highly of him, and from these accounts, without having any acquaintance with him myself, I intended to make use of his press. Valpy, by some means, had heard of my having written remarks on parts of Knight's Homer, and he wrote to me requesting that if I meant them for the public I would allow him to insert them in his "Critical Journal." I had written such remarks and had sent them to Knight, with whom I had a correspondence on the subject, but had no thoughts of making them public, as

---

[1] The sentence is: 'Who, did he but reflect by what slow gradations, often by how many strange concurrences, we are led astray, with how much reluctance, how much agony, how many efforts to escape, how many self-accusations, how many sighs, how many tears—who, did he but reflect for a moment, would have a heart to cast a stone?'—*Italy*, pt. 2, v.

I told Valpy; but told him at the same time that I had a work on hand which, when finished, it was my intention to send to his press; and not long afterwards, having sent a sort of epitome of the work to Lord Aberdeen, I desired him to send it to Valpy, which he did, and thus stands the case between us. I have never heard his merits as a printer called in question, but I have lately been told that he is *en mauvaise odeur* with some of the most eminent scholars—Bloomfield was particularly mentioned—who are strongly in opposition to him and ill-disposed to whatever comes from his press, and though I do not wish to curry favour with these great men, I should be sorry to have them prepossessed against my performance. What occasioned this enmity I never heard, but I have heard that Valpy has a certain mixture of presumption and affectation, which, if such be the case, may very naturally give offence and disgust; and, I must own, I did not much like the manner and style of the letters I received from him. The point upon which I particularly wish for your opinion is, how far you think I am engaged to Valpy; and whether, supposing the circumstances seemed strongly to require it, I might make my excuses to him and employ another printer. Mawman, you know, was my last *publisher*; I should suppose he is not particularly used to print books of a learned kind, and that he would not much care who was the printer provided he had the publication. I have great confidence in your advice and opinion; but am afraid I have very much indisposed you from giving me any assistance on the subject in question, by having harassed you upon it so unmercifully in my last letter.

I hope you will forgive me, and as it was my first fault of the kind, so I faithfully promise it shall be the last. If it should have been the chief cause of your silence I have been well punished.

'Believe me, with all our best regards,
'Ever most truly your
'U. Price.'

Uvedale Price to Samuel Rogers.

'Foxley: Dec. 26, 1824.

'You are always a long time in answering; but always make ample amends for the delay, and I am almost afraid of saying how much pleasure I received from your last letter, for fear you should think delay a necessary ingredient and be confirmed in your bad habit. As for confidence, you contrive to make it—according to the most hackneyed of quotations—"more honoured in the breach than the observance"; this is the second breach, and I hardly know by which of the two I have been most honoured. I began to repent having sent you such a long dissertation on accent, quantity, &c., but am now quite cock-a-hoop.

'. . . It gives me great pleasure to hear that at your last visit to Dropmore you found Lord Grenville in good spirits. They so generally rise and fall with good and bad health that I hope his is gradually and steadily improving. I am not a little pleased to find that he was occupied with my last letter on the subject that so much occupies me, as you know to your cost; in one of his which I had received not long before, he had expressed his doubts on various points, and I thought the best way of answering was by a sort of epitome, stating my leading positions and arguments, but, as I told him, without meaning to draw him into any further correspondence. This was very discreetly and properly said, but, I must own, not without a secret longing for its continuation.

'The account you give of Lord Ashburnham is very pleasing and satisfactory. He always writes gaily and very agreeably; his frame of mind is naturally a cheerful one, and, as far as I have observed, he is not at all apt to see things *en noir*; but he left England with great reluctance under depressing circumstances and with the care of a large family and suite during a long journey. This must have been a weight on his spirits; it is now removed, and he can fully enjoy those interesting objects for which he has that keen relish and true feeling which is so often affected. I remember when I was at Florence (I dare say Lord Fitzwilliam would remember it, though it is not very far from sixty years since we were there) a young handsome French colonel, *Français jusqu'à la moelle des os*, arriving in his regimentals from Corsica. He did us English the honour of noticing us, and one day, when several of us were together in the Tribune, he advanced towards us with a true French air: "Messieurs," said he, "je suis en extase! des bustes, des tableaux, des statues!" he never looked at any of them for two minutes together, or at anything but himself in the glass.

'Lord Aberdeen's journey must be a very melancholy one; and with little hope, I should fear, of his daughter's recovery. The consumptive taint from the first Lady Aberdeen seems to have been uncommonly deep and virulent. I shall never forget my having seen, some twenty or thirty years ago, a number of children coming out of a house in Grosvenor Square. I was so struck with their beauty that, when they had passed by me, I went up to the Porter, who, with the door half open, was following them with his eyes, and asked him whose children they were. "Lord Aberdeen's," he answered, "and there is not a finer family in all Britain." I soon afterwards became acquainted with Lord Aberdeen, and soon very intimate; was continually at the Priory and saw these beautiful and amiable children growing up in all their loveliness, but mixed with the colour of youth and beauty was that of disease, with the "terrific glory" of Homer's Sirius—

Λαμπρότατος μὲν ὅδ' ἐστὶ, κακὸν δέ τε σῆμα τέτυκται,
Καί τε φέρει πολλὸν πυρετὸν δειλοῖσι βροτοῖσιν.

'This πυρετός, this inward feverish heat, slowly undermined their constitutions; they dropped off one after another, and of all that sportive group of cherubs that I had gazed at with such delight in their infancy, not one remains.

'This is a melancholy subject, and I must go to another: poor Lady Oxford. I had heard with great concern of her dangerous illness, but hoped she might get through it, and was much, very much grieved to hear that it had ended fatally. I had, as you know, lived a great deal with her from the time she came into this country, immediately after her marriage, but for some years past, since she went abroad, had scarcely had any correspondence or intercourse with her, till I met her in town last spring. I then saw her twice, and both times she seemed so overjoyed to see an old friend, and expressed her joy so naturally and cordially, that I felt no less overjoyed at seeing her after so long an absence. She talked, with great satisfaction, of our meeting for a longer time this next spring, little thinking of an eternal separation. There could not, in all respects, be a more ill-matched pair than herself and Lord Oxford, or a stronger instance of the cruel sports of Venus, or, rather, of Hymen—

'cui placet impares
Formas atque animos sub juga ahenea
Sævo mittere cum joco.

'It has been said that she was, in some measure, forced into the match; had she been united to a man whom she had loved, esteemed, and respected, she herself might have been generally respected and esteemed as well as loved; but in her situation, to keep clear of all misconduct required a strong mind or a cold heart; perhaps both, and she had neither. Her failings were in no small degree the effect of circumstances; her amiable qualities all her own. There was something about her in spite of her errors remarkably attaching, and that something was not merely her beauty; "kindness has resistless charms," and she was full of affectionate kindness to those she loved whether as friends or as lovers. As a friend, I always found her the same; never at all changeful or capricious; as I am not a very rigid moralist and am extremely open to kindness,

'I could have better spared a better woman.

'Sir Thomas Lawrence's discourse I have not seen,

but shall send for it immediately. As you have a *protégé* in the same line, by your account a very interesting person, and with every sort of claim to your protection and best offices, I shall never say a word more to you of mine, who, instead of having six children, is still a bachelor.

'With all our best regards, believe me ever most truly yours,

'U. PRICE.

'A few words in the cover about Valpy. As you do not give any direct opinion respecting the degree in which I am engaged to him, I conclude that you judge the case to be a doubtful one. Such, too, is my opinion ; so I think it both safest and best to decide in his favour. This I am the more inclined to do from having lately heard some circumstances which shew that he is not likely to take any slight or disappointment with the gentlest patience, and he would, perhaps, be a not less formidable enemy than Bloomfield, and much more sure to become one. Were I completely disengaged I should, from your report, prefer Mr. Taylor. As the matter stands, I must try and manage Valpy as well as I can. Your method is to return upon your printer sheet after sheet, at his own cost, not yours, till justice is done you—all very natural if he commits mistakes; but I should understand from your account, that if he sends you a proof sheet correctly printed from your MS., and that you should have any of what you call your whims and fancies and should make alterations in it, he is obliged to make them on a fresh proof ; and that if in that again you should make more, he is to go on *da capo* till you are satisfied, and write the decisive word *Press*; and all this without any charge for the extra labour. Is this, or whatever may be agreed upon, merely verbal, or is anything put down in writing? I have always found a proof sheet a great suggester of alterations, and the man who printed my first essay told me that Burke— whose printer he had been—used to say that he could never judge at all of his own works while they were in manuscript. Valpy, I should think, would not readily agree to the conditions your printer seems to have agreed to, nor to any out of his usual routine; and I should make a bad fight. When Mawman reprinted my "Essays," he shared in the expenses and the profits, employing his own printer. If he should have no objection to doing the same, and to employing Valpy, *he* would have to deal with him in all that concerns the charges, and would have an interest in keeping him within due bounds. I am afraid, however, he would have very little regard for my whims and fancies, and would think it quite proper that those who have them should pay for them. I am not a little puzzled with all these pros and cons.

'Trebati,
Quid faciam præscribe.'

CHAPTER XI.

1825-1827.

Rogers's Bank—Retirement of Henry Rogers—Samuel Sharpe a Partner—Letters from Wordsworth—Rogers's Advice to Wordsworth—Wordsworth and his Publishers—Moore at Rogers's—Uvedale Price—The University of London—Brougham—Rogers's Parties—Sir Thomas Lawrence and Lord Dudley—Sydney Smith at Rogers's—Lord Grenville's Inkstand—Letter from Lord Holland—Rogers with Wordsworth and Sir George Beaumont—Sir G. Beaumont's Last Letter—Moore and Rogers—Wordsworth and Rogers—Rogers in two New Characters—Appeal to Lord Lansdowne to join the Junction Ministry—Tom Grenville—Mackenzie's Appeal for R. Pollok—Rogers at Bowood—Letter from Wordsworth—Rogers at Strathfieldsaye.

THERE is very little trace through his letters and correspondence of Rogers's relation to the bank in Clement's Lane. He was, however, during all these years the chief owner of the business, and was in constant communication with his partners. Henry Rogers was the working head of the bank, and his admirable qualities as a man, as well as his energy and capacity in business, had relieved his elder brother of all anxiety. In the beginning of 1824, Henry Rogers retired from the banking firm, and his place was filled by his nephew Samuel Sharpe. He was the second son of Rogers's sister Maria Sharpe, of whose death in 1806 I have already spoken, to whom Rogers wrote some lines of tender recollection in his 'Human Life.' There are in his letters to his sister frequent references to this family of nephews and nieces, in whom they felt a very constant interest. Samuel Sharpe had been nine years in the bank, and had deservedly gained the complete confidence of his uncles. Like his uncle Sam he had gone to be a clerk in the bank at sixteen, had shown the utmost diligence in business, and now, at five and twenty, had been made a partner. The period was one of great stress and difficulty. The panic of 1825 must have severely tried even the Rogers's bank, and it was a period of severe anxiety to the young nephew on whom so large a responsibility had been placed. Samuel Sharpe's caution and thoroughness were fully appreciated by his uncles, and there is no trace in Rogers's papers of any change made by the panic in his usual mode of spending his time. His business faculty and experience were always at the call of his friends. There is scarcely any well-known contemporary for whom he did not undertake such commissions as Wordsworth gives in the following letters.

William Wordsworth to Samuel Rogers.

'My dear Rogers,—I take the liberty of enclosing a letter which I have just received from Messrs. Longman, which be so kind as to peruse : it was in reply to one of mine, wishing to know whether they could not make it answer for them to publish my poems on terms somewhat more advantageous to me than hitherto. What those terms were you learn from the letter, and I need scarcely add that after the first expense of printing and advertising was paid out of an edition, the annual expense of advertising consumed, in a great measure, the residue of profit to be divided between author and publisher. So that, as I frankly told them, it was not worth my while to undergo the trouble of carrying my works through the press unless an arrangement more favourable could be made.

'The question, then, is, whether there be in the trade more liberality, more enterprise, or more skill in managing the sale of works charactered and circumstanced as mine are, than have fallen to the lot of Messrs. Longman & Co. Of this you are infinitely a better judge than myself; I therefore apply to you for advice and assistance before I make a new engagement with any one, observing, by the by, to you, that I have no *positive* ground for complaint against my present publishers.

'Would you be so kind as to try for me wherever you think it most likely to effect a favourable bargain. I am aware that I am proposing a very disagreeable office, but it is not more than I would readily do for you if I had the same advantage of experience, influence, and judgment over you in these matters that you have over me. The letter shows that if Messrs. L. and I part, it is amicably. I must add that they have an interest in the "Ecclesiastical Sketches" and the "Memorials of a Tour," and which must be given up before I could incorporate them, according to my wish, into a new edition, which I think would contain besides, four or five hundred lines of verses which have not yet seen the light. I have no objection to any publisher whom you might approve.

'Where were you last summer? Mrs. W., my daughter,

and I spent three weeks in a delightful ramble through North Wales, and saw something of S. W., particularly the course of the Wye above Hereford nearly to its source.

'I saw Southey the other day; he was well, and busy as usual, and as his late letter shows, not quite so charitably disposed to Don Juan deceased as you evidently are, if I may judge by a tribute to his memory bearing your name, which I accidently met with in a newspaper; but *you* were the Don's particular friend, an equal indulgence, therefore, could not be expected from the Laureate, who, I will not say was his particular enemy, but who had certainly no friendship for him. Medwin makes a despicable figure as the salesman of so much trash. I do not believe there is a man living, from a shoeblack at the corner of your street up to the Archbishop of Canterbury or the Lord Chancellor, of whose conversation so much worthless matter could be reported, with so little deserving to be remembered, as the result of an equal number of miscellaneous opportunities. Is this the fault of Lord B. or his Boswell? The truth is, I fear, that it may be pretty equally divided between them.

'My amanuensis, Mrs. W., says that it is not handsome in me to speak thus of your friend—no more it is, if he were your friend *mortuus* in every sense of the word, but his spirit walks abroad, to do some good I hope, but a plaguy deal of mischief.

'I was much shocked when I heard of his death, news which reached me in the cloisters of that college to which he belonged.

'Where and how is Sharp, and what does he report

of Italy? Last autumn I saw Uvedale Price, our common friend (so I presume to call him, though really only having a slight acquaintance with him), striding up the steep sides of his wood-crowned hills, with his hacker, *i.e.* his silvan hanger, slung from his shoulder, like Robin Hood's bow. He is seventy-seven years of age and truly a wonder both for body and mind; especially do I feel him to be so when I recollect the deranged state of his digestive organs twelve years ago. I dined with him about that time at your table and elsewhere.

'Poor Mr. Monkhouse, you will be sorry to hear, is wintering in Devonshire, driven thither by a disease of the lungs, which leaves his friends little hope of his recovery. He is one of my most valued friends, and should he sink under this complaint, one of the strongest of my inducements, and the most important of my facilities, for visiting London and prolonging my stay there will be removed.

'Remember us all most kindly to your sister, and believe me, with all our united regards, my dear Rogers, most faithfully yours,

'WM. WORDSWORTH.

'Rydal Mount: 21 January, 1825.

'Pray send me Longman's letter back at your convenience.'

Among Rogers's business qualities, that of promptly answering letters does not seem to have been included. Wordsworth writes again.

William Wordsworth to Samuel Rogers.

'Rydal Mount : 19 Feb. (1825).

' My dear Rogers,—I wrote at least six weeks ago, enclosing a letter I had received from Longman, &c., and being unwilling to put you to the expense of double postage upon my own business, I enclosed it to Lord Lowther for the twopenny post-office. Not having had your answer, I am afraid his servant has not attended properly to it.

' The letter was to beg your assistance in the republication of my poems with some bookseller either more liberal, more adventurous, or more skilful in pushing off unfashionable books than Messrs. Longman. I have been accustomed to publish with them, they facing all risks and halving the profits. This is a wretched way for books of some established credit, but of slow, though regular sale. For the expense of advertising eats away (as conducted by Longman) all the profit which would otherwise accrue after the cost of printing, &c., has been discharged. L. declines publishing on other terms, but says that an edition both of the poems and the "Excursion" is called for, and if not by them, ought immediately to be published by *some* one. I have no [other] fault to find with Messrs. L. & Co. than is implied above ; if we part, it is on good terms, as his letter expressed, and I should not wish for a change without the hope of a better bargain.

' Now, you may think that I ought to undertake this disagreeable business myself, and so I should think, if I had not so kind a friend who has fifty times the talent for this sort of work which I possess, and who, besides, could say a hundred handsome things, which, egotist as I am described to be, and as in *verse* I am *willing* to be thought, I could not say of myself.

'I have additional short pieces to the amount of five or six hundred lines, which would not bear separate publication, yet might be advantageously interspersed with the four volumes of Miscellaneous Poems. These ought to be considered in the bargain, as there are many periodical publications that would pay me handsomely for them. But I never publish through those channels. The "Continental Memorials" and "Ecclesiastical Sketches" would also be added.

'It has sometimes struck me the matter of my Miscellaneous Poems might be [so] arranged (if thought advisable) as to be sold in separate volumes. One volume we will say of local poetry, to consist of the "River Duddon," the Scotch Poems with additions, the Continental pieces, and others. A volume of sonnets, perhaps, &c. I throw this out merely as a hint, being persuaded that many are deterred by the expense of purchasing the whole, who would be glad of a part. Yet I am aware there might be strong objections to this.

'Pray let me have an answer at your earliest convenience.

'My friend Mr. Robinson tells us he had the pleasure of seeing your sister not long ago *well*. Give our best remembrances to her, and accept them yourself, and let us know how you are and have been, where and how Sharp is, and what he reports of Italy and Italian scenery.

'Poor Monkhouse is removed from Devonshire to

Clifton, dying, it should seem, as slowly as ever any one did in such a complaint.

'Mrs. W. and I had a delightful ramble last summer through North and part of South Wales. I had not seen N. W. for more than thirty years. The scenery is much finer than my memory represented. I wish you had been with us.

'Ever faithfully yours,
'WM. WORDSWORTH.'

The tenor of Rogers's answer can only be gathered from what Wordsworth says in his next letter. Crabb Robinson, however, tells a story which probably gives in a distorted shape an idea of the kind of advice Rogers gave Wordsworth in the matter. He speaks of being one evening (on the 20th of May, 1826) at Miss Sharpe's, who was then living in New Ormond Street, at a small and agreeable party of the Flaxmans and the Aikins. Samuel Rogers came in and spoke with great respect of Wordsworth's poems, but with regret at his obstinate adherence to his peculiarities. Crabb Robinson says that there was at that time a 'current anecdote that Rogers once said to Wordsworth, "If you would let me edit your poems, and give me leave to omit some half dozen and make a few trifling alterations, I would engage that you should be as popular a poet as any living." Wordsworth's answer is said to have been, "I am much obliged to you, Mr. Rogers; I am a poor man, but I had rather remain as I am."' The story is not literally true, because Wordsworth would not have so addressed Rogers. But it probably represents pretty fairly the advice which Rogers gave, and the reception it got from Wordsworth. In writing to Rogers himself, however, Wordsworth adopts a different tone.

William Wordsworth to Samuel Rogers.

'Rydal Mount: 23 March [1825].

'My dear Friend,—I am obliged by your kindness in taking so much trouble about my poems, and more especially so by the tone in which you met Mr. Murray when he was disposed to put on the airs of a patron. I do not look for much advantage either to Mr. M. or to any other bookseller with whom I may treat, and for still less to myself, but I assure you that I would a thousand times rather that not a verse of mine should ever enter the press again, than allow any of them to say that I was to the amount of the strength of a hair dependent upon their countenance, consideration, patronage, or by whatever term they may dignify their ostentation or selfish vanity. You recollect Dr. Johnson's short method of settling precedence at Dilly's, "No, Sir, authors above booksellers."

'I ought to apologise for being so late in my reply, and, indeed, I scarcely feel justified in troubling even so kind a friend about an affair in which I am myself so indifferent as far as inclination goes. As long as any portion of the public seems inclined to call for my poems, it is my duty to gratify that inclination, and if there be the prospect of pecuniary gain, though small, it does not become me to despise it, otherwise I should not face the disagreeable sensations, and injurious, and for the most part unprofitable labours in which the preparing for a new edition always entangles me; the older I grow, the more irksome does this task become, for many reasons which you as a painstaking author will easily divine, and with which you can readily sympathise. But to the point.

'' I have seen Southey lately. He tells me that Murray can sell more copies of any book that will sell at all than Longman—but it does not follow from that that in the end an author will profit more, because Murray sells books considerably lower to the trade, and advertises even more expensively than Longman, though that seems scarcely possible. Southey's "Book of the Church" cost 100*l*. advertising first edition. This is not equal to my little tract of the Lakes, the first edition, for which *I* got 9*l*. 8*s*. 2*d*., was charged 27*l*. 2*s*. 3*d*. advertising. The second edition is already charged to me 30*l*. 7*s*. 2*d*., the immense profits are yet to come. Thus my throat is cut, and if we bargain with M. we must have some protection from this deadly weapon. I have little to say; the books are before the public, only there will be to be added to the Miscellaneous vols. about 60 pages of new matter, and 200, viz., the "Memorials" and "Ecclesiastical Sketches," not yet incorporated with them, and the "Ex." ["Excursion"] to be printed uniform with them in one volume. I mean to divide the poems into five vols., in this way.

' 1st Vol., as at present, to consist of "Childhood and Early Youth," "Juvenile Pieces," and "Poems of the Affections," withdrawing from it the "Blind Highland Boy" (to be added to the "Scotch Poems"), and "Ruth and Laodamia," "Her Eyes are wild," &c., to be added to those of the "Imagination."

'2nd Vol. to consist of the "Fancy and Imagination," as now, the "Scotch Poems" to be subducted, and their place supplied as above with the "Ode to Enterprise," and others.

'3rd Vol. "Local Poems"—"The River Duddon," "Scotch Poems," with some new ones, "The Continental Memorials," and "Miscellaneous Poems," selected out of the four vols., with some additions. Those on the naming of places and the "Waggoner."

'4th Vol. To consist of "Sonnets, Political and Ecclesiastical," meaning the Sketches and Miscellaneous, with the "Thanksgiving" and the other political odes.

'5th Vol. "White Doe," "Poems of Sentiment and Reflection," "Elegies and Epitaphs," "Final Ode," &c.

'6th Vol. "The Excursion."

'Now these vols., I conjecture, will run about 340 pages each, and the "Excursion" 450. Of the Miscellaneous, two vols., viz., the local poetry and the sonnets, might perhaps be sold separately to advantage. The others cannot be divided without much injury to their effect upon any reflecting mind.

'As to your considerate proposal of making a selection of the most admired or the most popular, even were there not insuperable objections to it in my own feelings, I should be utterly at a loss how to proceed in that selection. Therefore I must abide by the above arrangement, and throw the management of the business upon your friendship.

'I shall not be in town this year, nor can I foresee,

since the loss of Mr. Monkhouse, when I shall revisit London; the place does not suit me on account of the irritability of my eyes. I must look for you and other friends here. Pray come down this summer. I could let you have a quiet room, this house having lately been added to in a small way. Mr. M. is not only a loss to his friends and kindred but to society at large, as in all his dealings and transactions he was a man of perfect integrity and the most refined honour; he was not bright or entertaining, but so gentle and gracious, and so much interested in most of what ought to interest a pure mind, that his company was highly prized by all who knew him intimately. You say nothing of your sister, nothing of Sharp, but you Londoners have so many notes and letters to write that this must be excused. I often read your "Italy," which I like much, though there are quaintnesses and abruptnesses which I think might be softened down, and in the versification I would suggest that with so many trochaic terminations to the lines, the final pauses in the middle of the verse should be more frequently on firm syllables on that account. With best remembrances from all,

'Ever your obliged Friend,
'WM. WORDSWORTH.

'Pray read what part [you like] of the above to Mr. Murray; you will then hear what he has to say, and I leave it to you to proceed accordingly.'

Rogers carried out these suggestions and brought the negotiation with Murray almost to a conclusion. It broke down, nevertheless, and the following letters from Wordsworth show the reason why.

William Wordsworth to Samuel Rogers.

'My dear Rogers,—Pray forward the enclosed to Murray when you have looked it over. Copying from your letter, as you will observe, I have confined myself to the words "responsible for the *loss*," without using the word expense: ultimate loss I believe there will be none, but there will be a heavy expense, which the sale of the books, if M. does not push, and the leading reviews and periodicals should not take a fit of praising, may be some years in discharging. When am I to become answerable for this? This question I did not like to put directly to M., for it was suggesting a demand sooner than he might otherwise have been disposed to make it; and the new bargain will not eventually be advantageous to me, if I am to advance money and to be long out of it.

'Many thanks for your kindness on this occasion. I have been slow to reply, not from being insensible of your services, but from the extreme dislike which I have ever had to publication, as it is then that the faults of my writings, to use a conversational expression of your own applied to beauties, "shine out." How came I by this expression? Sir George Beaumont can tell.

'You are as mute as a mouse about coming here, and everything else, except a brief remembrance from your brother and sister. I forgive you. A man so prompt in deeds may be sparing in words.

'God bless you, and long. May you be healthy and happy in your delightful habitation, which is distinctly before my eyes.

'Ever faithfully yours,
'WM. WORDSWORTH.

'Yesterday I had the honor of receiving a book dedicated to my dear self by a lady, a fair one I hope, but I have never seen her or heard of her before. She is clever. Adieu.'

William Wordsworth to Samuel Rogers.

'Lowther Castle : 15 August.

'My dear Rogers,—Month after month elapses and I receive no answer from the grand Murray. I will not pay him the compliment to say I am offended at this; but really it is so unpromising for my comfort in carrying six vols. through the press, and also for the question of ultimate profit, that I have determined not to proceed in the arrangement; and now write to thank you for your kind exertions which have proved so fruitless. I have sent off a letter to Murray telling him that I have given up the arrangement with him; and shall look out elsewhere. I am persuaded that he is too great a personage for any one but a court, an aristocratic, or most fashionable author to deal with. You will recollect the time that elapsed before you could bring him to terms—for the pains you then took I again thank you. And believe [me], my dear Rogers,

'Faithfully your obliged friend,
'WM. WORDSWORTH.

'If I succeed in another quarter I will let you know. Everybody is well here.'

He was driven back to Longmans, who, in 1827, published an edition of his poetical works in five volumes, which contained 'the whole of the Author's published poems, for the first time collected in a uniform edition.'

There is less than usual about Rogers in Moore's Diary this year. Moore was very busy and was not much in London. He records several breakfasts at Rogers's in June, at one of which Sydney Smith and his family were present with Luttrell, Lord John Russell, and Richard Sharp. 'Highly amusing,' is Moore's remark. One of the stories told was that of a man named Forth, who, during the French war, informed Mr. Pitt that two persons from the north of Europe were on their way to England to assassinate him. They were tracked, seized at Brussels, and put in prison. There they lay for years, and at last it was found that they were creditors of Forth, who were coming to arrest him for debt, and that he had invented the plot to assassinate Pitt in order to get rid of them. On another day he 'went to Rogers's; looked over the notes he has had from Sheridan'; but either missed, was not shown, or passed over the one which, as I have pointed out, throws light on Sheridan's pecuniary resources. Rogers was at Lord Grenville's in July, but Moore records several merry meetings with him in London in August and September.

Wordsworth's description of the quaint figure Uvedale Price presented in his seventy-seventh year adds to the interest of his letters.

Uvedale Price to Samuel Rogers.

'3 July, 1825.

'This letter will not be objurgatory: we are all (that is, our *trio*) delighted at the near prospect of seeing you and your sister, and look forward to it with the greatest pleasure. We did hope, indeed, that you would have made us a longer visit than you talk of: three or four days will pass like three or four minutes: they did so when you were here last, but left a very pleasing remembrance, and a frequent wish for their renewal.

'This second Correggio from Spain I shall hope to see next spring, and—which always so much enhances the pleasure—with you, and under your guidance. What you say of the exquisite tenderness of the tints and the expression gives me a very favourable idea of it, as being according to my notions more truly characteristic of Correggio than splendour. The sum given for it is a large one; but not more than a *mezzo bajocco* compared with what the Duke of Wellington's prize cost the nation: "Ce n'est qu'une nuit de Paris," said the grand Condé when sacrificing a few regiments. "Ce n'est qu'une heure de guerre," say I; and for my own part wish we had less glory, more fine pictures, and more money to buy them.

'I do most earnestly hope that the sun will not be less brilliant during the short time you will be with us than he was ten years ago when you saw such a brilliant assemblage of ancient *donne e cavalieri* in what we call *the* valley *par excellence*. I dare say you will see them again, or, perhaps, a new set; for you poets have the enviable faculty of conjuring up whatever is most delightful to the mind's eye.

'Lady Beaumont wrote me word of the intended wedding, and of the great satisfaction it gave to her and Sir George. I once saw Mrs. Beaumont, when she, her mother, Sir George, and myself went together to the museum. All her beauty, as you say, must be her mind; of which last, however, I could not judge, as she was very modest and silent; she has a look of intelligence, and by all accounts she is an excellent person. If Mr. Beaumont fell in love, it could not have been by looking at her in the usual way, but with his mind's eye; and a very good way of looking at one's *future*.

'As you mention the 15th or 18th, or thereabouts, I will frankly tell you that the 18th will suit us best, and hope nothing will prevent us from having the pleasure of receiving you on that day.

'You are not to imagine that this pink note-paper is my own, or of my own choosing; my daughter brought it to me, and insisted upon my making use of it in my letter to you. With all our best regards to you and your sister, believe me,

'Most truly yours,
'U. Price.

'I am sorry this note-paper will make you pay for a double letter; I thought my son would have been in town, but have this moment heard of his being at Tunbridge.'

One of the most important movements in which Rogers interested himself at this period was that for the establishment of the University of London. He had an hereditary interest in unsectarian education. His father had taken an active and prominent part in the establishment of the college at Hackney, of which he became chairman, and where his youngest son, Henry Rogers, was educated. Dr. Price and Dr. Priestley, Dr. Kippis, the learned editor of the 'Biographia Britannica,' and the Rev. Gilbert Wakefield, who were all connected with Hackney College, were not only Samuel Rogers's early friends, but were apostrophised by him in the First Part of 'The Pleasures of Memory'—

> Guides of my life, instructors of my youth,
> Who first unveiled the hallowed form of truth;
> Whose every word enlightened and endeared,
> In age beloved, in poverty revered.

And again in the Second Part—

> The friends of reason and the guides of youth,
> Whose language breathed the eloquence of truth;
> Whose life, beyond preceptive wisdom, taught,
> The great in conduct and the pure in thought.

The project was Campbell's, who broached it at a dinner at Brougham's, where it was well received. Hume, Mill, Brougham, and John Smith took it up warmly, but Irving and his friends almost wrecked the scheme by their determination to have a theological faculty. Campbell succeeded in convincing them that the University should be, in his own words, 'without religious rivalship,' and it was eventually resolved to found it by the issue of shares of a hundred pounds each. Campbell retired from active participation in the business arrangements, but he regarded the successful establishment of the University as the only important event in his life. Brougham's active share in the work has somewhat eclipsed Campbell's, to whom, however, the honour of first starting the scheme belongs. Two letters from Brougham to Rogers show how far it had advanced in the summer of 1825. The deed of settlement was not completed till the succeeding February; the foundation stone of the College in Gower Street was laid by the Duke of Sussex on the 30th of April, 1827; the building was opened by Professor Bell on the 1st of October, 1828; but the charters were not obtained till 1836, when the college took the name of University College, and the existing University of London was established. Every step in this process was carefully watched and aided by Rogers and his friends.

Henry Brougham to Samuel Rogers.

'Penrith, Brougham: 5 August, 1825.

'My dear Rogers,—I sent you at length the large paper copy of my Discourse the day I left town, viz., Friday last, so pray give directions not to have it thrown among your rubbish, as it deserves.

'Also tell me how many shares of the London University stock you will have. It pays six per cent.—for we only call for sixty-six pounds a share, and pay four per cent. on a nominal hundred. So, in the market, we should be overrun with jobbers, and defeated in the vote at every turn. We are therefore anxious to get as many good men and true as we can to hold the shares, and already we have eleven hundred shares so disposed of.

Proxies vote. The Monasters (Oxford and Cambridge) are howling, and the Bishop of Chester preaching already. This is enough.

Direct your commands to me here. Yours ever,

'H. BROUGHAM.'

Henry Brougham to Samuel Rogers.

'London: 20 August, 1825.

'My dear R.,—I have chosen the number two for you—although not that in which gods delight—but as I have taken one myself, and Lord Fitzwilliam five, and Lord Lansdowne as many, I thought you would be better to excel me in glory—besides, you may transfer one to your brother, or any other trusty friend, if you don't like to keep both. It is a great matter to keep them in good hands. I rejoice to say we have now fifteen hundred so placed, and are going to begin.

'Do you know anything of the architects of the day (I mean excepting always Bernasconi, whom I know you to be very intimate with). We shall of course advertise for plans. But the first-rate men will probably keep aloof from such a competition, and it would be as well to sound them a little, although in our situation the advertisement will be necessary. 'Yours ever,

'H. BROUGHAM.'

Moore, who was in London in September, and found Rogers at home, makes the curious remark on dining at the Athenæum with Rogers, that it was 'the first time he ever dined at a club.' Every reader of my 'Early Life of S. Rogers' knows that his Diary in earlier days contains some instances at least of his dining at clubs.

The remark, however, throws much light on Rogers's habits. Much as he loved society, he was not a great frequenter of clubs, and, much as he visited, he was never a 'diner out.' His name is met constantly as forming one of some party of choice spirits, the meeting of whom some one or other of them has put on record; but his preference was to entertain his friends at his own house. He did this, however, in no promiscuous spirit. The company at his table was carefully chosen, and men and women who met there rarely found themselves antipathetically mixed. The table was not too large for the conversation to be general; the company was not numerous enough to break up into groups. When the host spoke his guests listened. His good things were not for his next neighbour only, but for all. So with his chief guests. They had the whole company for audience. Sharp's acute observations, Mackintosh's wonderful talk, Wordsworth's monologue, Sydney Smith's irrepressible fun, were not confined to their next neighbours, but were for the whole group. People went away, therefore, not merely remarking what agreeable people sat by them at dinner, but what a pleasant party it was. Rogers once wrote as an epigram :—

>When at Sir William's board you sit,
>His claret flows, but not his wit.
>There but half a meal we find:
>Stuffed in body, starved in mind.

And he carefully avoided providing for his guests in this sense but half a meal. The intellectual entertainment was as much cared for as the other part of the food.

In those days men made conversation, as Uvedale

Price made letter-writing, a fine art. They read for it, prepared it. I have read of one eminent talker, that he kept a kind of ledger account of his stories and witticisms, and entered down the times and places at which he used them, and the names of the company present to hear them, so avoiding the repetition which is the weakness of story-tellers. Many men sketched out their dinner-table talk or their evening conversation as they might sketch out a speech, and learned it, as Ward did his speeches, by heart. Rogers, however, had another resource. He had the whole volume of his 'Recollections' in manuscript in his Commonplace Book, and conversation was often enlivened by his bringing it out, as Moore says he did in 1825. Some of the men whose observations he had thus recorded—like Talleyrand and the Duke of Wellington—were still alive; others had only lately left the world, and their memories were fresh. Rogers tells us that his 'Recollections of Fox' ' were read by his nephew with tears in his eyes.' These, and the other 'Recollections,' were heard with ever-increasing interest as the years rolled on, and Rogers himself became to a new generation a venerable and dignified relic of a reverend past. His choice of visitors was almost as large as the London Society of his day, the most distinguished men of the time were glad to meet at his table, the less known felt honoured by an invitation, and everybody knew that a morning or an evening at Rogers's house was sure to bring them into contact with people whom it was a pleasure and a profit to meet.

There are plenty of proofs in these volumes and in the 'Early Life' that Rogers did not spend his whole time and fortune in entertaining and being entertained. He was always being appealed to for counsel, for business assistance, for pecuniary help. One night, towards Christmas, 1825, he found at his door his friend Sir Thomas Lawrence in a state of alarming agitation.[1] He had come to implore him to save the President of the Royal Academy from disgrace. Unless a few thousand pounds could be raised in twenty-four hours he could not be saved. He had good security to offer—drawings he would give in pledge or sell, as might be required. This was beyond Rogers's means of help, and he had to tell him he would see next morning what could be done. Next morning early he went to Lord Dudley, told him the story, and urged him to advance to Lawrence the sum required. Lord Dudley consented, and went off with Rogers to Sir Thomas Lawrence's house to see his pictures. There was some difficulty in settling what pictures Lord Dudley should have, and Rogers seems to have gone away before the negotiation was completed. Lawrence wanted him to have a Rembrandt, while Lord Dudley's fancy was for a Raphael. He writes on the same day.

Lord Dudley to Samuel Rogers.

'Park Lane: Friday morning.

'My dear Rogers,—

'Fugit improbus et me
Sub cultro linquit.

I am sorry you did not stay, as it might have saved some embarrassment by enabling us to settle *everything*

[1] See *Crabb Robinson's Diary*, vol. ii., p. 525.

at once, which we agreed was very desirable. The case, I found, was too urgent to admit of delay. I therefore engaged to finish what is required before dinner-time to-day. He also expressed a wish that the transaction should not be talked of just yet; and to that I, of course, readily consented. But the difficulty about the Raphael still remains. This is unluckily, but naturally, the object I most desire to possess, and which he is most unwilling to part with. You will, I am sure, recollect that in our first conversation in this room, even before I had seen it, I spoke of it as my greatest inducement, except that of rendering a service to Sir T. L., to entertain the proposal made to me. Besides, the arrangement cannot be easily made without it. The Rembrandt I must absolutely decline taking. It's merit is of a sort which my ignorance of art prevents me from perceiving, and the price of it, though not too high for so great a work, is vastly beyond what I can think of giving for a single picture. But if I bar the Rembrandt, and he also bars the Raphael, the remainder of the pictures will fall too far short of the value to which we ought at least to approximate. All this makes a difficulty, out [of] which I shall not be able to extricate myself without your friendly aid and mediation. I should be really sorry to insist upon a condition that should be painful to Sir T. L., and yet you will, I am sure, feel that it is rather hard upon me to take a picture that I want knowledge and taste to admire, particularly as the very nature of the case cuts me off from all those advantages of consultation and consideration and botheration that generally precede transactions of this kind. Pray think of this matter and tell me what you think when I see you.

'Your's ever truly,
'D.'

The matter was eventually arranged. The Raphael was to be his at a price of more than a thousand guineas, and a further large sum was to be advanced. Meanwhile Lord Dudley left London, and the completion of the transaction was left to Rogers, who reported to Lord Dudley what he had done. Lord Dudley answered.

Lord Dudley to Samuel Rogers.

'Bowood: Christmas Day, 1825.

'Quite right—your note will serve as a memorandum to which, however, as the transaction is not very complicated, and as the parties understand each other, it is not likely that we shall be obliged to have recourse.

'He desires secrecy, and so do I. Pray, therefore, say nothing about the matter to anybody. If he thinks that his sending the picture immediately will set people talking, and that any advantage on that side is to be gained by delay, I shall be quite willing to wait till a more convenient season. However, I had rather you would use your own discretion in what you say to him on this point.

'My horse fell with me yesterday, and I narrowly escaped breaking my neck. However, I pursued my journey, and in the evening began to study Crambo with tolerable success.

'We have the Abercrombys here, and the Ords, and

Macdon*ald*, and Macdo*nell*, and Miss Fox, and yesterday we had Pamela, who is delightful, more so (if possible) than her husband, Sir G. C.

'Ever truly yours,

'D.'

Crabb Robinson says that Lord Dudley was no loser by the transaction. He was not, so as far as the purchase of the picture was concerned; but the further loan was never repaid. Rogers himself frequently helped Sir Thomas Lawrence in his money difficulties. A promise to pay 'Samuel Rogers or his order,' 260*l.* on the 25th of this present month, written on an old-fashioned five-shilling bill-stamp and dated the 11th of January, 1829, is still among Rogers's papers. He never asked for the money, and it was never paid. A year later Sir Thomas Lawrence was lying dead.

Moore's Diary for 1826 is, as usual, greatly occupied with Rogers. Moore was in London in May and met at Rogers's, Lord John Russell, Milman and his very handsome wife, Brougham, Sydney Smith, Sir George Beaumont, and other celebrities of the time. Rogers was trying to make up Moore's quarrel with Murray, and consenting to go with him to Murray's house, when Moore should offer Murray his hand and have done with it. Moore met Murray by accident and they made up the quarrel; the next day he dined at Rogers's with Lord John Russell, Lord Lansdowne, Brougham, Barnes, Kenny, and Sharp, and on the next day to that Rogers introduced him to Danby, the painter, at Lord Stafford's gallery, where Moore says he was '*ciceronied* very agreeably round the room by Rogers, upon whose taste I have more dependence than on that of any of the connoisseurs who are about.' On the 27th of May he records a breakfast at Rogers's with Sydney Smith and three others. Smith, he says, 'full of comicality and fancy, kept us all in roars of laughter. In talking of the stories about dram-drinkers catching fire, Sydney Smith pursued the idea in every possible shape. The inconvenience of a man coming too near the candle when he was speaking. "Sir, your observation has caught fire." Then he imagined a preacher breaking into a blaze in the pulpit, the engines called to put him out, no water to be had, the man at the works being a Unitarian or an Atheist. He remarked of some one, "He has no command over his understanding, which is always getting between his legs and tripping him up."' These recollections of Sydney Smith's talk at Rogers's may be supplemented by one or two of Rogers's own. Speaking of a well-known lawyer who had a great liking for *pâtés de foie gras*, Sydney Smith said of him that his idea of heaven was that of eating *pâtés de foie gras* to the sound of trumpets. His physician advised him to take a walk upon an empty stomach, and Smith asked, 'Upon whose.'

Rogers was again at Dropmore in the early summer. Lord Grenville had given him, as a memento of their friendship, an inkstand, modelled in silver after that of Petrarch, which is preserved in his house at Arqua.[1] The inkstand bore an inscription on the rim, 'Samueli

---

[1] Petrarch's inkstand is described by Rogers in his Italian Diary See *ante*, p. 177.

Rogers, hoc amicitiæ pignus, W. W. B. G. MDCCCXXVI.';
and there were engraved upon it some Latin verses of
Lord Grenville's—

I.

Quod gratum tibi sit, poeta suavis,
Adsum, ΜΝΗΜΟΣΥΝΟΝ sodalis illa
   Non indigna tuâ putantis arma
   Dextrâ, qualibus utier solebat
Doctam mille iterans modis querelam
   Ipse, deliciæ tuæ tuæque
   Ingens Italiæ decus, Petrarca.

II.

Dulce tuum ingenium hinc seros mansura per annos
   Castalii spargat lumina pura Chori;
Defluat hoc de fonte probæ facundia Musæ
   Virtutum interpres fida animique tui;
Ut simili in longum studio sapiensque bonusque
   Vitam hominis laudent, carmina vatis ament.

III.

Amice, temporis fugâ
Franguntur hæc, et corruunt
   Ceræ, tabellæ, imagines,
   Ductumque cœlatumque opus;
Solum artis est tuæ viros,
Utcunque morti debitos,
   Famæ perenni tradere.

Lord Holland writes—

Lord Holland to Samuel Rogers.

'Brighton: 30 May (1826).

'Dear Rogers,—It happens in small as in mighty matters that an endeavour to do too much prevents one often from doing anything. I had not been here five days before I conceived the project of writing you, not a letter, but a dissertation—a book; the consequence has been that I have appeared ungrateful for your kind letter to Lady H., and unmindful of your wish to hear of her health—but I have nearly completed my long undertaking, and shall have my letter *from Brighton* ready to deliver to you with my own hands at Holland House next week. You will, I think, find Lady H. improved in looks, health, and spirits, though she is far from well to-day. Brighton affords no topics for correspondence. Poor Lord Banbury or General Knollys seems broken-hearted at the unjust decision of the House of Lords, and embarrasses his acquaintance as much as a heathen god to know by what name to address him. I am so tired of writing long reasonings on the Test Act and condolences on the loss of the Catholic question, that I must waive all parliamentary topics.[1] Could I see my way through Continental events, I should not dislike that subject, but I am at a loss to understand the history, motive, and probable effect of this Congress at Prague. I long for peace so much that I hardly dare believe my own judgment when it represents it to me as probable or possible—and yet—but I will not speculate on so large a subject. We have heard *of*, not *from*, Charles, nor does it appear that he had heard from us on the 16th of April last.

'Yours,

'VASSALL HOLLAND.'

[1] The Lords had thrown out the Catholic Bill on the 18th of May by a majority of 48 in a House of 308. (*Martineau*, vol. i., p. 392.)

Two letters to his sister are full of glimpses of interesting people whom he met in a journey to the Lakes in September.

Samuel Rogers to Sarah Rogers.

'Lowwood Inn: 12 Sept., 1826.

'My dear Sarah,—We arrived here on Friday at four o'clock, and were very glad to look upon the old lake again. Sir George's passion are the Langdale Pikes, and he is sketching them from morning till night. He uses white chalk upon a blue paper, and strongly recommends it to you for catching the momentary lights in the sky. I believe you have hitherto confined yourself to terrestrial objects. We set out on Tuesday and breakfasted at Derby, and saw Kedleston and slept at Matlock old Bath, as we had done so often before. At Derby I called upon Lucy,[1] and was shown up instantly by the maid into a large room looking to the garden and the river. She was sitting alone, and not a little surprised at the sight of me. She is very thin, and so much altered that I am not sure I should have known her at once elsewhere, but she is the same amiable, kind creature she ever was, and discovered at least half as much pleasure as she did once at Highbury, when she made one jump of it downstairs to meet her father. Her reception quite affected me. At Matlock we took a long walk till sunset, and returned an hour after the dinner hour, much, I believe, to the disappointment of the company, who had waited

[1] Lucy Rogers, daughter of Daniel and niece of Samuel, married Mr. Bingham of Derby.

half an hour for us—a company, however, not very
numerous, six in number, one of them a sister-in-law
of Sir Wm. Gell. At Sir George's desire we dined alone
and saw nothing of them. Next morning we saw Haddon
Hall with great delight and breakfasted at the Chatsworth Inn—when a heavy rain came on and lasted all
day. Chatsworth is really little worth seeing, though
full of Canova.

'Abercromby was there and I saw him for five
minutes. At Sheffield I wished to call upon Mont-
gomery, but the rain prevented me. We slept at
Barnsley (the inns in these manufacturing towns are
most uncomfortable). Next day it cleared up and we
had a sight of Gordale Scar, sleeping at Settle. The
next day we sat down, as I said, at Lowwood Inn,
and despatched a note to Wordsworth, who came next
morning to breakfast and spent the day with us. Next
day (Sunday) we returned the visit, and went to Rydal
Church (a new and very pretty one built by Lady
Fleming), and dined with them; at night came a mob to
tea—young men with letters of introduction, ladies on
short visits to neighbours—and the rooms were crowded.
Dora, the daughter, is much improved and not now ill-
looking. Miss Hutchinson much softer and more agreeable. The dinner very good and all very neat. The
place still more beautiful than I remembered it to be,
but they have notice to quit and have bought a field to
build in, a measure that disturbs Sir George mightily,
but may never take place. Sir G. is very amiable—
perhaps a little too talkative—for he talks for ever and [is]
more helpless than Miss Fox! Sharp was here a week,'

and a week at Ambleside. He saw but little of Wordsworth, who was electioneering. Miss Kinnaird, the waiter says, sang from morning till night to a small pianoforte that belongs to the house. Wordsworth has much to do. A wedding dinner at Grasmere yesterday; a christening, where he stands sponsor, at Ulverstone next Friday. Sir G. is gone for the day to him now, and has left me behind in another bilious fit, but it is a slight one. On Thursday we go to Keswick for four or five days, and then to Lowther for a week or so, and then I mean to fly home. This house is kept by Scotch people, and is very dirty. Their book for the season is tolerably full of names, but of hardly any I ever heard of. The quality perhaps go to Ambleside, if they come at all. . . . The Ws. lament your absence very much and make many enquiries after you. I fear they will not be soon in London again. We have written for a private lodging if we can get one at Keswick.

'Wordsworth is to come to us next Monday, and will go with us to Lowther, I believe, but we have not yet offered ourselves. There has been no regatta here this summer, but a very gay one last week at Keswick. Quincey, the opium-eater, lives in the house where we first found Wordsworth and dines with him to-day. W. keeps a pony-chaise, and I fear is as much eaten up as Dan—and even more—for all bring letters to him. In Grasmere Churchyard is the inscription I sent you once—

> 'Six months to six years added he remained
> Upon this sinful earth, by sin unstained.
> O blessed Lord, whose mercy then removed
> A child, whom every eye that looked on loved,

> Support us, teach us calmly to resign
> What we possessed and now is wholly thine.

He died in 1812. There is also another on a little girl who died six months before, four years old, being only the words, "Suffer little children," &c. They lie side by side. Farewell, my dear Sarah; give my love to Henry. I long much to return and would set off to-morrow but for Sir George. I hope to receive a line from you to-morrow, and will wait and keep this to acknowledge it.

'Yours very affectionately,

'S. R.

'Your letter is come, many thanks for it. Poor Caroline, I hope she will soon be well. As for you I don't like your prudence, much as I may commend it, for it shows how much you have suffered. My bile is almost gone, and here I sit by the fireside, Sir George at the window sketching the effects of a shower. We have had no right to complain altogether, but I believe scenery has lost much of its power with me. Not so with Sir George, who is always going to the window and looking earnestly out as if he saw somebody he knew, though it is only a cloud or a gleam of light on the water. *I* have had the sphinx, too—at Ampthill in the flower garden below, two or three times before breakfast. I watched it for twenty minutes at a time, and the ladies saw it while I was at Oakley. So its flight must have been a long one. Becky must have been a great comfort to you, but don't you keep Patty, now all are gone to the sea? You don't say she is gone. I wish Henry much pleasure on his journey. I wish myself back again and count the days, but Sir George is so happy, I have not the heart to turn. He desires to be remembered kindly to you both. Rubens, and Guido, and Claude, and Poussin, and Haydon, and Lawrence, are so much in my ears all day that I dream of them. My next direction is Post Office, Keswick, but we shall be gone in a week and I will let you know where we move next. We have excellent scalded codlins here, and so we have had all along—a luxury you know we had in Wales last year. We have not once been on the water, nor shall we.

'*Keswick, September* 15.—We came here on Thursday and drank tea with the Southeys in a company of sixteen people; among others, William Taylor of Norwich. Southey dined with us to-day and left us at six to entertain a party at home. What a bustle these poets live in! To-morrow we drink tea with him, and on Monday dine with him and Wordsworth, who comes here. Our mornings are taken up in laking, or, rather, mountaineering. The weather so far very fine. Pray direct to me on or before the 26th under cover to the Earl of Lonsdale, Lowther Castle, Penrith.'

Samuel Rogers to Sarah Rogers.

'Keswick: 26 Sept., 1826.

' My dear Sarah,—You will be surprised to hear that I am still here, but Sir George cannot stir, though he is wringing his hands all day long at the improvement of roads and bridges. Wordsworth came last Tuesday and, though he lives at Southey's, he rides out with us every day, and almost every evening we are all together. On Tuesday, W., Sir George, and I go to Ulleswater, and on Friday to Lowther, where Southey joins us for a day or two. We shall stay till the seventh or eighth of October, and then Sir George goes to Mulgrave. Almost all the way is homeward, and I shall most likely avail myself of his carriage as far as I can. He wants me to go to Mulgrave, which, I believe, is very beautiful, on the Scarborough coast. If I do I must go to Castle Howard, if but for a day or two. I wish much to come back to town, but I can't be in two places, and have decided nothing. It was Mr. Wm. Taylor we had at Southey's. We have since been at three crowded evenings there (they have entertained seventy-five people in the last fortnight) and once have dined at General Peachy's on the island. So we are not idle. I forget whether you know that Rothermirkus Grant is so ruined as to be going out to India as a counsel, where the ground is almost entirely pre-occupied. His son has behaved so nobly, sacrificing himself to his father and the creditors, that they have entrusted him with the whole management of the estate. This I had from Mackintosh—a sad prospect for them. We have had delightful weather, and Sir G. is every instant crying out, "This alone is enough to repay us for all our labours," but the country is certainly beautiful, and fascinates as much as ever. We have been to Buttermere and Watendlath, and most of the places. Last week Filler went up Skiddaw, a great effort for him. Mrs. Opie is said to be at Ambleside, and there appear to be as many lakers as ever. Our horses are very good and safe. I wish you were upon one of them. Have you met with a house to your mind yet. I fear not. Perhaps this will find you at the sea—but if not, I shall be very glad to be with you there by and by. We rise at seven, walk from eight to half-past nine, ride out from eleven till four, dine, and walk again till dusk—exercise enough perhaps to wear us out—but I am never out of bed at eleven at night. I wish much I had met with Sutton, and hope he was pleased. The Attorney-General has been here, and Wordsworth learnt a long history of the Wakefields from him. How does your new maid wear? I hope, when you call, you find Ellwood content, and going on well in St. James's Place. Next week are the Carlisle races, which, among other reasons, delays our visit to Lowther. The children here are innumerable and all shod with wood or iron, and as they are always clattering along under the window, they put one in mind of the French children in the villages, formerly. I will write again from Lowther, where I hope to receive a letter from you. My love to Henry. I hope Caroline is well again, and George still mending.

'Yours ever most affectionately,

'S. R.

'Mrs. Opie is living at Grasmere on a visit to Mr. Barber, who drives her about in an open carriage.'

Sir George Beaumont to Samuel Rogers.

'My dear Rogers,—It was some comfort to me in my disappointment to find it was not caused by violent illness on your part; indeed I had the satisfaction to find it was very slight indeed, and hardly deserved the name; moreover, the reception I met with from my noble host and hostess was so gratifying that it must have been a great evil indeed which could have been felt at all. I hope you are now quite well.

'You thank me for my kindness, and, as I am a very Frenchman at interpreting things in my own favour, I am in great hopes, that is as much as to say our journey has been a pleasant one, to which I can fairly add, that to *me* it has been delightful and profitable also.

'My good fortune did not quit me with you, for in my journey from Mulgrave, about two miles on the other side of Malton, I had an escape little short of a miracle. The postilion's horse stumbled, and in saving himself he gave a jerk to the rein by which he held the other horse, broke it, and the horse, who was blind, swerved towards a precipice which was guarded by a strong rail—the rail gave way, and both wheels went down the bank so far that I can form no idea how the carriage preserved its balance. My man with great activity leaped from behind, and held the carriage with all his strength, afraid to open the door lest, during the time, wanting his assistance, it would certainly upset; with difficulty I opened it myself, and it was so much on one side it was hardly possible to get out. Providentially, however, I escaped, and was very glad to find myself on terra firma. Observe my good fortune: had the horse not been blind his situation must have made him restless, and the least motion on his part would have precipitated me into the ditch, which was eight or nine feet deep at least, so that the carriage, followed by both the horses, would have been dashed on its top with inexpressible violence against the bottom, and I cannot form an idea how I could have escaped a fractured skull. Then came the difficulty of extricating the carriage, which took up an hour at least; six or seven lusty honest Yorkshiremen heartily set to work, and with the assistance of a lot of Quakers who were passing, and lent their heads on the occasion with great effect, it was recovered without much damage. I was so much pleased by the zeal of the Quakers that I forgive Mrs. Opie her whim and am almost inclined to applaud her. I must add, I find I was saved by a stone which was left (of an old bridge) in the bank and caught the carriage; had it been only the soft bank I had been gone! I hope I have piety enough not to attribute all this to mere chance. It made me too late to see the Marys to advantage, but I was in full time for dinner.

'I am afraid I have given you a puzzling account of this accident, but I was led into it somehow or other, and I hope you will forgive me.

'I know you will not be sorry to hear of the pleasure you have given my poor old friend and his family by your visit to Mulgrave. To-morrow I set off for Coleorton, where I hope to remain some months in perfect quiet.

'The post is just going out.

'Most truly yours,

'G. H. BEAUMONT.

'Castle Howard: 18 Oct., 1826.'

The last letter from Sir G. H. Beaumont to Rogers followed in the next month; and in February, 1827, he died.

Sir George Beaumont to Samuel Rogers.

'Coleorton Hall: 13 Nov., 1826.

'My dear Rogers,—By the time, or perhaps before, you receive this, Lord Hastings's library will be in the hands of Mr. Robins for sale. This was privately communicated to me, and as I thought there might be some things in it which you might wish to possess, I thought it not amiss to give you this hint in case you might choose to negotiate before the sale.

'I confess your observation upon parapets seems at first sight a "palpable hit, egad," but you mistake. I am no enemy to reasonable parapets, but I do not like to see a bridge overloaded; the guards, for instance, of the Simplon are not more than half a yard in height, and I never heard them complained of as insufficient—indeed, when a horse is alarmed nothing can protect you, and I rather think a moderate fence better than a very high one, because the animal can see his danger. Now, I hope I have parried this severe thrust, but whatever sentence you may pass upon me I shall not cease to do justice to your quick philanthropy, and should I survive you, which is not very likely, it shall not be my fault if you are not placed side by side with Howard (not him of Corby, though a very humane man) in the cathedral-church of St. Paul's. In the meantime I recommend for safety Westminster Bridge in preference to Waterloo.

'I have just received Ottley's catalogue, which I like very much on the whole. I hope you approve of it. The N. Poussin is well done, although I cannot agree with him in supposing the trees are intended for evergreen oaks, they are far more like the chestnut; but, in fact, his general practice is only to make the grand distinctions and not enter into the detail of ashes, elms, &c., which I, who am passionately fond of the heroic style of landscape, cannot but approve; to have given the beautiful variety of Claude would have been inconsistent with his plan, it would be like introducing silks and satins into the cartoons. I think he might have said a little more of the Rubens; he should, for instance, have introduced the *fowler* and his *dog*, both glowing with congenial instinct, and as animals much upon a par. Have you Bowles's poem? I wish you would show it to him. Am I giving you too much trouble in requesting you to talk with him on the subject? It would save him the trouble of a letter. Only assure him I am highly pleased with his work on the whole. I could almost wish he had said nothing derogatory of Rembrandt. Fuseli adored him, and thought the sublimity of his light and shadow made ample amends for his occasional vulgarities, the unlucky prejudices of his country. On the whole I have heard him say: Rembrandt's genius was equal to any, and that by his magic power he could make a dunghill "subloim." We expect Mrs. Siddons to-day!! and Lord and Lady Lonsdale in the course of the week. Now, if you were man enough to join the party, how I should admire you. Lady B. is flattered by your remembrance, and I must thank you again and again for our delightful tour.

'But I am afraid I have bored you so much with

this long letter you will never forgive me. Come and set my mind at ease.

'Ever truly yours,
'G. H. BEAUMONT.

'Do you know anything of Charles Mills, the editor of the travels of Ducas. We have been much entertained by the book, although it would have been more agreeable, I think, if he had given it more of the tone of the times. Excuse repetitions, &c. I write in haste.'

Moore had been in London again in October, and once more had recourse to Rogers for business help and counsel. He records meeting Rogers at Walter Scott's, when Rogers told the story of a tipsy man who had been rolled in currant jelly and then in feathers, and who, catching sight of himself in a glass, exclaimed, 'A bird, by Jove!' Rogers went with him to Murray, Moore walking about outside till Rogers had seen him first. On another day Rogers tells him some flattering things he had heard about the 'Life of Sheridan,' administering with the pleasant draught a little wholesome criticism on Moore's mode of telling some of the stories in the volumes. Later in the month Rogers was at Bowood, and Moore records his kind appreciation of the beauty of his 'Bessy.' Moore was busy with 'The Epicurean,' and the story was talked over with his friend. Early next year he was in London again, and the business with Murray occupied much of their attention. He tells in his Diary one or two of Rogers's stories. Lord Erskine said of a man who left a quarter of a million,

that it was a fine sum to begin the other world with—
an observation Rogers often quoted. Fuseli, standing
with his back to Rogers's fire on a cold day, remarked,
with his peculiar accent, 'Hell fire kept within bounds
is no bad thing.' Moore records Rogers's story told him
by the Duke of Wellington, that when Bonaparte's
escape from Elba was told to the persons assembled in
Congress they all burst out laughing. The Duke had
sent a special despatch to the Emperor with the news,
and the bearer of it afterwards remarked, 'What could
there possibly have been in that despatch, for the moment
the Emperor read it he burst out a-laughing.' After
Cintra, the Duke of Wellington said to Rogers's early
friend, Sir John Moore, 'There is now only you and me
left, and if you are appointed chief I will serve under you.'
Of Waterloo the Duke said to Rogers, 'It was a battle
of giants.'

In the next two letters Rogers appears in entirely
new and widely different characters.

*

Wordsworth to Samuel Rogers.

'Rydal Mount: 10 March, 1827.

'My dear Rogers,—I am going to address you in
character of Churchwarden of Little St. Clement's, East
Cheap: how came *you* by this odd distinction?

'My friend Mr. Johnson is minister of that church,
and having heard that certain pictures, and a fund for
the purchase of pictures, exist at the disposal of the
British Institution for the decoration of churches, he

has got a notion that, through your influence, one might be procured for his own church, and has begged me to intercede with you for that purpose. I have therefore readily complied with his request, though I should fear he may be too sanguine in his expectations.

'And now, my dear friend, let me condole with you on the loss we have sustained in the death of Sir George Beaumont. He has left a gap in private society that will not be filled up, and the public is not without important reasons to honour his memory and lament his loss. Nearly five and twenty years have I known him intimately, and neither myself nor my family ever received a cold or unkind look from him. With what tender interest do I think of the happy hours we three spent together last summer.

> 'I prized every hour that went by
> Beyond all that had pleased me before;
> And now they are passed and I sigh,
> And I grieve that I prized them no more.

'The printing of my poems is going on pretty rapidly.

'Ever, with kindest regards from all here,

'Most faithfully yours,

'W. W.

'Dora is improved in health, but the severe weather confines her to her room.'

Moore records that on the 22nd of April he met the Duke of Devonshire at Bowood. The Duke had come to persuade Lord Lansdowne to join Canning's administration as Irish Secretary. Two days later, after the

Duke of Devonshire had gone back to London, Lord Lansdowne said to Moore that he had that morning received a letter from a person he would little suspect as offering counsel on such a subject, 'one,' added Lord Lansdowne, 'more likely to counsel you than me.' It was this letter from Rogers at Dropmore.

Samuel Rogers to Lord Lansdowne.

'Dropmore: 20 April, 1827.

'My dear Lord Lansdowne,—I am just now under the roof of an old retired Statesman, whose sentiments all men, however they may differ from him, must listen to with respect; and perhaps at a crisis like the present you will not be sorry to hear what has fallen from him on the subject.

'When I mentioned, on my arrival here last night, the rumour in town that it had been proposed to form a Cabinet, the majority of which should be Catholic—the Home Secretary to be a Catholic, and the Irish Secretary a Catholic—and that the Home Secretaryship had been offered to you,—

'He said in reply, I have the highest opinion of Lord Lansdowne, and I can never believe that he would refuse such an offer under such circumstances if he was fully aware of what he refused. A Lord Lieutenant is little more than a mere pageant; with the Home Secretary, as I know well, rests, and I may say entirely, the government of Ireland; for with him rests the due execution of the law, now almost a dead letter to the Catholic. The Lord Lieutenant has only to further the orders he receives from the Home Office, little more, and if the Irish Secretary throws no obstacle in the way, everything that can be desired may in time be brought about. Whether the Lord Lieutenant is Catholic or Protestant is comparatively speaking of little or no importance. A Protestant Lord Lieutenant is perhaps the least thing the King can ask for. He thinks he is asking for much, while he is asking for little or nothing; and why refuse him? He must have his pride and his feelings like other men, and why not let him down gently?

'I wish I could give you all he said on the subject; but I believe I have given you the purport. By some men it may be thought that he once threw away such an opportunity as this himself, and now and then (is it not possible?) he may think so in his solitary hours. Perhaps I am mistaken, but the suspicion crossed my mind while he was speaking. There was a melancholy, a sadness, a something so like regret in the tone of his voice, that I was affected not a little by it. I write not unknown to him, and when I told him of my intention this morning he replied, "You are welcome to repeat all I have said. I am the last man to obtrude my opinion on anybody, but *he* would be welcome to it at all times. Whatever he does he will do for the best; but this I must say" (and it was with some agitation he said it, a thing now unusual to him), "whoever rejects such an offer is, in my opinion, guilty of *a great dereliction of public duty*. He may make motions and speeches for another twenty years to come, but he will never repair his loss. What a benefit, among others, to prevent the return of such people, exclusively, to power. They must now wonder at their folly; but still more must they wonder to find folly as great as their own. I hope and trust that Lord Lansdowne will not listen to such counsels. It is inconceivable what good may be done and what evil prevented. Such an opportunity can never occur twice to one man. A wedge, as you say, has a broad end and a sharp end. Who in his sober senses would think of driving it in at the broad end?"

'Pray forgive me, my dear Lord Lansdowne, for troubling you with so long a letter at such a time; and yet why should I make any excuse for it? I have now known you for many a year, and I am very sure you will receive it in good part, and as a testimony of the esteem and regard with which I am always yours,

'SAMUEL ROGERS.

'Mr. Grenville was present and went along with him in every syllable. A man who, like Lord Grenville, has filled so many high offices of the State, and who has himself discharged the duties of Home Secretary and Irish Secretary, must be supposed to know the degree and extent of the influence belonging to each. On that part of the subject he spoke with great confidence. He has once, I believe, if not twice, refused office under circumstances not very unlike the present, and may here be said to have given the result of his experience while in public life and of his meditation since he has left it.'

The effect of this letter was to decide Lord Lansdowne to join the Junction Government. 'If you find me gone,' he said to Moore when he told him of the receipt of this letter, 'you may conclude all is settled.' Next morning he was gone. He accepted the Home Secretaryship and discharged its duties with universal approval.

The Mr. Grenville whom Rogers mentions in the postscript was Mr. Thomas Grenville, an elder brother of Lord Grenville. He was usually spoken of as Tom Grenville. Uvedale Price, writing to Rogers on July 27th, 1827, says of him:—

'I always liked Tom Grenville, as he was familiarly called, and like him much better now, both outwardly and inwardly; his unpowdered head, to my mind, suits the character of his countenance more than powdered curls; as to the interior, in addition to the general quickness and pleasantness of his conversation, I found, during our walk together at Dropmore, that he was an eager observer on my particular line, and to a part of it that has so much employed my thoughts—to composition; and he pointed out several trees, bushy thorns, &c., which appeared to him to interfere with it; and I, of course, approved of his notions, as they exactly coincided with mine. There are few persons that I should be so glad to see here, and I will not despair of a visit. I nearly despair of a second from Lord and Lady Grenville; the first, and I fear the last, as ill-luck would have it, was to the place only.'

A melancholy interest attaches to a letter from the 'Man of Feeling' appealing to Rogers for assistance to the author of 'The Course of Time'—a book immensely popular forty or fifty years ago, of which Professor Wilson truly said that, 'though not a poem,' it 'overflows with Poetry.'

Henry Mackenzie to Samuel Rogers.

'Heriot Row, Edinburgh : 8 August, 1827.

'My dear Sir,—I hope I am not, as a satirist said a good many years ago of an obnoxious monster, "the most impudent man alive"; but certainly this is one of the most impudent letters I ever wrote. Without, however, troubling you with a long preface, I will state the fact. There is a poem lately published, written by a young man of the name of Pollok, a dissenting clergyman here, which I really think in point of genius and poetical power a very wonderful one. It is called 'The Course of Time,' and contains, among many passages liable to criticism, others, moral and descriptive, of infinite genius and merit, if I, whom age only entitles to speak of such things, may be trusted. Knowing the author a little, and more from other impartial persons, I believe him to be as amiable as a man as he is ingenious as a poet. But alas! young as he is, he has the seeds of disease and death in his frame, which make his life very uncertain and likely to be short. A journey, and short residence, to a warmer climate, his benevolent physician, whom he has interested in the strongest manner, thinks the only chance he has for life or health; but, alas! like most poets, the expense of such an emigration is beyond his means. To supply these, a subscription has been set afoot here, and there are great hopes that 100*l.* or 150*l.* may thereby be raised for his journey and other expenses. Now for my impudence—it is to lay your beneficence under the tax of two or three guineas to this subscription, to which the Muses, so much the friends of poor Pollok, have excited patrons. Mr. Rogers is one of their greatest favourites, and I may use their names in behalf of one of their youngest sons. Mr. Cadell's correspondent here, Mr. Blackwood, has taken a kind concern in Pollok, and any subscriptions which literary persons in London may contribute, may be paid in to him. If you can take that liberty with any poets who can afford it, you may use my name as certifying the merits of the man, and, though with more diffidence, of the poem. Again asking pardon for this letter, and wishing, at all events, to have the pleasure of hearing from you,

'I remain, my dear Sir, with the most sincere regard, your most faithful and obedient servant,

'H. MACKENZIE.'

Poor Pollok did not benefit much by the generosity of literary friends. He came to winter in the South, but died at Shirley Common, near Southampton, on the 17th of September.

Meanwhile Wordsworth's new edition of his poems came out, and Rogers having acknowledged its receipt, Wordsworth replied.

Wordsworth to Samuel Rogers.

'Rydal Mount: 20th September [1827].

'My dear Rogers,—Some time ago I heard from you in acknowledgment of the receipt of my last edition. Its contents you appear to esteem in a way which cannot but be highly flattering to me. I am now writing to consult you about a small matter of *virtu* in which I am inclined to incur a little expense. An advertisement has been forwarded to me of the prints of the Stafford Gallery, at one third of the original price. Are they well executed, and are they likely to be good or at least fair impressions and not refuse? The advertisement says that the public is secured against inferior impressions by the limited number. Do you know if this be true? or could you procure me a copy fairly culled? or, lastly, would it be at all an eligible purchase for one of my slender means, who is a passionate lover of the Art? If you think so, have the goodness to select me one; we have no works of Art near us, and must therefore be content with shadows.

'My wife and daughter are flown into Hampshire, where they will remain till the first swallow returns, for the sake of a dryer climate, which my daughter's health requires. I hope your journey to Italy will be deferred for one year, it would admit the *possibility* at least of my meeting you there. What a treat! How goes on your poem? The papers spoke of a new edition being intended, with numerous engravings, which, if executed under your presiding taste, cannot but be invaluable. I was at Lowther a week lately. I *missed* you and dear Sir George by the side of that beautiful stream. The weather was exquisite, and one solitary ramble through the Elysian fields and onwards I shall never forget. Could you believe that a flock of geese, tame geese, could on land make an interesting appearance? Yet that day so they did, reposing themselves under an umbrageous oak; thirty at least, all carefully shaded from the bright and over-warm sunshine, and forming groups that Rubens would have delighted in; with attitudes as various and action still more so than cattle enjoying like comfort.

'My sister, sons, and Miss Hutchinson are here; all unite in kindest regards. I wish you would join us for a week or two.

'Ever faithfully yours,

'W. WORDSWORTH.'

The postscript is by another hand.

'The Stafford Gallery complete in four volumes, folios, half bound, uncut, 12*l.* 12*s.* 0*d.*, published at 35*l.* 14*s.* 0*d.*, sold by samuel Leigh, 18 Strand.

'My brother has desired me to copy the above from the advertisement, and, with pen in hand and the blank page before me, I cannot help saying a word of friendly and affectionate remembrance to yourself and sister. The season is so far advanced that I fear there is no chance of your being moved hither by my brother's hint of the pleasure it would give us to see you; yet I will add, if you do come, you must bring Miss Rogers along with you, or I should not be half satisfied. My brother, I see, says nothing of his intention of visiting Mrs. W. at Coleorton, nor of a still larger scheme that he has of visiting London. I was very sorry not to see you at Coleorton, the last week of my enjoyment of dear Sir George Beaumont's society.

'Adieu, dear Sir; believe me yours truly,

'W. WORDSWORTH.'

In the autumn there was the usual company at Bowood, and Moore tells us almost as much about Rogers, who was there, as about himself. One or two of Rogers's stories Moore misreports. According to Rogers's Commonplace Book, it was of the House of Lords, and not of the House of Commons as Moore says, that Lord Maynard, returning from a visit to the Continent, asked, 'Is that going on still?' It was Madame de Staël who asked Talleyrand whether he would save her or another lady if both were in danger of drowning, and to whom Talleyrand replied, 'Vous savez nager, je crois.' Moore was then busy with Lord Byron's life, and there was much talk with Rogers about it, but most of the stories he records I have already given on other authority. Among other stories is Rogers's statement that Byron was nine months at Pisa without seeing the belfry or the baptistery; and that Canova had told him he was in love at five years old.

A couple of letters finish up the year.

Wordsworth to Samuel Rogers.

'Coleorton Hall [1st December, 1827].

'My dear Rogers,—Ten days ago Mrs. W. (she from the neighbourhood of Hereford, and I from the North) met at this place, which we quit Saturday, 8th of next month, going together into Herefordshire, where Mrs. W. will remain with her daughter till the warm and dry weather of spring returns. Thus is our little family broken up by the troublesome indisposition of my daughter, an affection of the throat, which returns along with a cough on rainy and damp days.

'Lady Beaumont was not well a few days after our arrival here, but she is now in good health and as little altered in appearance as could have been expected. She employs herself much in the concerns of this place, and has great resources in reading and religious meditation. You will be aware how much Mrs. W. and I miss Sir George in this house and in the grounds about. There is a little picture on the easel in his painting room as it was left on his seizure there with a fainting fit, the commencement of his fatal illness, which lasted no more than eight days. Lady B. begs that you will be quite easy on the subject of your not answering her letter, as she did not look for a reply, being in general as averse to letter-writing as you are. It seems that it was a consolation to her under her suffering to write to Sir George's friends. I sincerely believe that she did so without wishing for, or thinking about, any notice of her effusion. She took up the pen from impulse, and it was a relief to her.

'I am pleased to hear that the Stafford Gallery is thought a bargain, but I will not trouble you any more on the subject. Before I had heard from you I mentioned to Mr. Page, whom I think you saw at Lowther, that I had named this subject to you, and he engaged to knock at your door to learn whether you were at home or in England. I thought you might be gone to Italy. Whether he found you or not, he obligingly offered to inspect the prints himself, and report to me accordingly. I have not yet heard from him; at all events let the purchase be suspended at present. I know, and have often admired, the Rubens Lord Stafford has given to the British Gallery; it would be worthy of you to follow his example and enrich the same repository, either during your lifetime or by bequest, with some choice work of art, for the public benefit, and thus to connect your name, already distinguished in one of the fine arts, with another of the sisterhood. Think of this, and by so doing, and in fulfilling the prophecy I often made to Sir George when he was talking of giving his pictures to the nation, that his example would be followed by many others, and that thus, in course of time, a noble gallery would be produced.

'Italy, alas! is to me an *ignis fatuus*; every year the hope dances before me only to obstruct my sight of something else that I might attain. Were there no other obstacle, I could not think of leaving England for so long a time till I had disposed of my younger son, who, as I have just learned from him, is bent upon being a beggar either in the honourable character and profession of a soldier or of a farmer. Could you suggest to me anything better for this infatuated youth—any situation in a counting-house or a public office? He dislikes the thought of the University because he sees nothing afterwards open to him but the Church, which he does not think himself fit for, or that he ever can be made so. Excuse this weary epistle, and believe me ever, with true affection,

'Yours,

'W. Wordsworth.'

Samuel Rogers to Sarah Rogers.

'Strathfieldsaye [December, 1827].

'My dear Sarah,—The weather was so severe as we came that Rees travelled the greater part in the carriage. But we have been out every day. On Tuesday there was a large party to see Anderden's pictures. It seems he lives about five miles off, and I had no great fancy to go; but the Duke said they were excellent, and as he seemed to wish it, I went. On Wednesday some of us went to Sir John Cope's and we were rewarded. The gallery, unfurnished, is 130 feet long, and the house, as Lady Holland said, is much larger than Holland House. The passages and staircases are endless, and the views from the windows very extensive. We dine punctually at seven and breakfast at ten. On Tuesday the Duke sent for the Raivier family (the Tyrolese), and for the two last evenings they have sung (yesterday while we dined). To-day, I believe, the Duke is gone a-hunting. The church is in the park, and his nephew, Mr. Wellesley, is Rector. The commissioners wished the Duke to decide in favour of Sir John Cope's, then on sale; but he was deterred by the expense of repairing it. His architect told him that the roof must be taken off and that then the walls would come down—reason enough against the purchase if well founded. On Saturday I shall go to Dropmore and return to town early on Monday. Every day at dinner there has been the addition of some neighbours, and,

456 ROGERS AND HIS CONTEMPORARIES

among others, Sir Claudius Hunter. Yesterday some came in the evening.

'Yours ever,
'S. ROGERS.

'Of the society I will say nothing at present: some I like better than before, and some less. Silchester is within six miles of us, but the Roman Camp at Sandwich contents me.'

PRINTED BY
SPOTTISWOODE AND CO., NEW-STREET SQUARE
LONDON

www.ingramcontent.com/pod-product-compliance
Lightning Source LLC
Chambersburg PA
CBHW022056300426
44117CB00007B/480